First published 2023
by Routledge
4 Park Square, Milton Park, Abingdon, Oxon OX14 4RN

and by Routledge
605 Third Avenue, New York, NY 10158

Routledge is an imprint of the Taylor & Francis Group, an informa business

© 2023 selection and editorial matter, Róisín Ryan-Flood, Isabel Crowhurst and Laurie James-Hawkins; individual chapters, the contributors

The right of Róisín Ryan-Flood, Isabel Crowhurst and Laurie James-Hawkins to be identified as the authors of the editorial material, and of the authors for their individual chapters, has been asserted in accordance with sections 77 and 78 of the Copyright, Designs and Patents Act 1988.

All rights reserved. No part of this book may be reprinted or reproduced or utilised in any form or by any electronic, mechanical, or other means, now known or hereafter invented, including photocopying and recording, or in any information storage or retrieval system, without permission in writing from the publishers.

Trademark notice: Product or corporate names may be trademarks or registered trademarks, and are used only for identification and explanation without intent to infringe.

British Library Cataloguing-in-Publication Data
A catalogue record for this book is available from the British Library

Library of Congress Cataloging-in-Publication Data
Names: Ryan-Flood, Róisín, editor. | Crowhurst, Isabel, editor. | James-Hawkins, Laurie, editor.
Title: Difficult conversations : a feminist dialogue / edited by Róisín Ryan-Flood, Isabel Crowhurst, Laurie James-Hawkins.
Description: Abingdon, Oxon ; New York, NY : Routledge, 2023. | Series: Transformations | Includes bibliographical references and index.
Identifiers: LCCN 2022047616 (print) | LCCN 2022047617 (ebook) | ISBN 9780367542603 (hardback) | ISBN 9780367542627 (paperback) | ISBN 9781003088417 (ebook)
Subjects: LCSH: Feminist theory. | Feminism.
Classification: LCC HQ1190 .D573 2023 (print) | LCC HQ1190 (ebook) | DDC 305.4201—dc23/eng/20221027
LC record available at https://lccn.loc.gov/2022047616
LC ebook record available at https://lccn.loc.gov/2022047617

ISBN: 978-0-367-54260-3 (hbk)
ISBN: 978-0-367-54262-7 (pbk)
ISBN: 978-1-003-08841-7 (ebk)

DOI: 10.4324/9781003088417

Typeset in Times New Roman
by Apex CoVantage, LLC

Difficult Conversations
A Feminist Dialogue

**Edited by Róisín Ryan-Flood,
Isabel Crowhurst and
Laurie James-Hawkins**

LONDON AND NEW YORK

Difficult Conversations

This book explores 'difficult conversations' in feminist theory as an integral part of social and theoretical transformations.

Focusing on intersectionality within feminist theory, the book critically addresses questions of power and difference as a central feminist concern. It presents ethical, political, social, and emotional dilemmas while negotiating difficult conversations, particularly in terms of sexuality, class, 'race', ethnicity and cross-identification between the researcher and researched. Topics covered include challenging cultural relativism; queer marginalisation; research and affect; and feminism and the digital realm.

This book is aimed primarily at students, lecturers and researchers interested in epistemology, research methodology, gender, identity, and social theory. The interdisciplinary nature of the book is aimed at reaching the broadest possible audience, including those engaged with feminist theory, anthropology, social policy, sociology, psychology and geography.

Róisín Ryan-Flood is Professor of Sociology and Director of the Centre for Intimate and Sexual Citizenship (CISC) at the University of Essex. Her research interests include gender, sexuality, kinship, digital intimacies and feminist epistemology. She is the author of *Lesbian Motherhood: Gender, Sexuality and Citizenship* (2009), and co-editor of *Secrecy and Silence in the Research Process* (2010), *Transnationalising Reproduction: Third Party Conception in a Globalised World* (2018), and *Queering Methodology: Lessons and Dilemmas from Lesbian Lives* (2022). She is also co-editor of the journal *Sexualities: Studies in Culture and Society*.

Isabel Crowhurst is Reader in Sociology at the University of Essex. Her work explores the construction of social norms around sexual practices and intimate lives. Her recent books include *The Tenacity of Couple Norm* (with Sasha Roseneil, Tone Hellesund, Ana Cristina Santos and Mariya Stoilova), and *Third Sector Organizations in Sex Work and Prostitution* (with Susan Dewey and Chimaraoke Izugbara).

Laurie James-Hawkins is Senior Lecturer in Sociology and Deputy Director of the Centre for Intimate and Sexual Citizenship (CISC) at the University of Essex. She is a sociologist of health and gender, and her research interests include reproductive health, contraception, abortion, gender and sexuality among emerging adults. She has published widely on these topics. In recent years Dr. James-Hawkins has been studying sexual consent among university student populations.

Transformations
Series Editors
Dr Laura Clancy
Lancaster University, UK
Dr Rachael Eastham
Lancaster University, UK
Dr Patricia Prieto-Blanco
Lancaster University, UK

Feminist Cultural Studies of Science and Technology
Maureen McNeil

Arab, Muslim, Woman: Voice and Vision in Postcolonial Literature and Film
Lindsey Moore

Secrecy and Silence in the Research Process: Feminist Reflections
Róisín Ryan-Flood and Rosalind Gill

Working with Affect in Feminist Readings: Disturbing Differences
Marianne Liljeström and Susanna Paasonen

Feminism, Culture and Embodied Practice: The Rhetoric's of Comparison
Carolyn Pedwell

Gender, Sexuality and Reproduction in Evolutionary Narratives
Venla Oikkonen

Feminism's Queer Temporalities
Sam McBean

Irish Feminist Futures
Claire Bracken

Power, Knowledge and Feminist Scholarship
An Ethnography of Academia
Maria do Mar Pereira

Difficult Conversations
A Feminist Dialogue
Edited by Róisín Ryan-Flood, Isabel Crowhurst and Laurie James-Hawkins

Contents

List of Illustrations viii
List of Contributors ix
Foreword xiii
Acknowledgements xvii

Introduction 1
RÓISÍN RYAN-FLOOD; ISABEL CROWHURST
AND LAURIE JAMES-HAWKINS

SECTION 1
Difficult knowledge 9

1 **The gender wars and difficult conversations about trans: an interview with Meg-John Barker** 11
   MEG-JOHN BARKER AND RÓISÍN RYAN-FLOOD

2 **Facing uneasiness in feminist research: the case of female genital cutting** 27
   KATHY DAVIS

3 **Feminism and race in academia: an interview with Sandya Hewamanne** 39
   SANDYA HEWAMANNE AND RÓISÍN RYAN-FLOOD

4 **But you're not defending sugar, are you?** 50
   KAREN THROSBY

SECTION 2
Gender, power and intimacy 61

5 Difficult research effects/affects: an intersectional-discursive-material-affective look at racialised sexualisation in public advertising 63
JESSICA RINGROSE AND KAITLYN REGEHR

6 Calling out and piling on: deliberation and difficult conversations in feminist digital social spaces 90
AKANE KANAI

7 Interviewing with intimacy: negotiating vulnerability and trust in difficult conversations 102
RIKKE AMUNDSEN

8 Co-existing with uncomfortable reflexivity: feminist fieldwork abroad during the pandemic 113
XINTONG JIA

SECTION 3
Gender, sexuality and embodiment 131

9 Sexing in the cities: sex, desire, and sexual health of black township women who love women 133
PHOEBE KISUBI MBASALAKI

10 Researching sex: gender, taboos and revealing the intimate 144
LAURIE JAMES-HAWKINS

11 Building a community of trust: participatory applied theatre workshop techniques for difficult conversations on consent 159
NATASHA RICHARDS-CRISP

12 Women's experiences of marital rape in Turkey: ethics, voice and difficult conversations 172
GULCIMEN KARAKECI

SECTION 4
Bounded knowledge 189

13 Lost for words: difficult conversations about ethics,
    reflexivity and research governance 191
    SOPHIE HALES, PAUL GALBALLY AND MELISSA TYLER

14 Gender studies, academic purity and political relevance 206
    SABINE GRENZ

15 The feminist classroom in a neoliberal university 218
    AWINO OKECH

16 Focus groups and the 'insider researcher'; difficult
    conversations and intersectional complexities 231
    CLARE BOWEN

17 Queering the academy 243
    RÓISÍN RYAN-FLOOD

    Index 254

Illustrations

5.1	Are you beach body ready advert (girls' collaging exercise)	64
5.2	Participant talking about adverts including 'punish yourself buff' in the prompt binder	67
5.3	Disembodied Legs Treatwell Advert	68
5.4	Boohoo advert of a woman in tassel crop top and bikini bottoms with glitter on her butt cheeks	69
5.5	Boohoo. Man advert of man in jacket and trousers standing beside a Rolls Royce	70
5.6	Boohoo advert of woman in tassel bodysuit and thigh high boots	71
5.7	American Apparel Advert of woman in flesh coloured underwear and thigh high socks	75
5.8	Sierra on the bus with her walking supports and recording device	77
5.9	Sierra engaging with the prompt book	80
5.10	Boohoo She.The.Don advert	83
5.11	Pretty Little Things advert next to Orphan's in Need	85

Contributors

Rikke Amundsen is Lecturer in Digital Innovation Management Education in the Department of Digital Humanities at King's College London. Rikke's research is concerned with the digital mediation of intimacy, risk and trust, which is something that she explores in relation to intimate digital practices, like the creating and exchange of private sexual images and texts. Among Rikke's most recent publications is an article called "Hetero-sexting as mediated intimacy work: 'Putting something on the line'" (2022). In this article, Rikke looks closer at adult women's negotiations of risk and trust as they exchange private sexual images with men.

Meg-John Barker is an independent scholar/writer and associate member of the University of Brighton Centre for Transforming Sexuality and Gender. Research Interests: Gender, Sex/Sexuality, Relationships, Trauma/Mental Health. Recent Publications: Gender: A Graphic Guide (2019), Non-Binary Lives (2020), Sexuality: A Graphic Guide (2021), Hell Yeah Self-Care (2021), How To Understand Your Sexuality (2022)

Clare Bowen is a third-year PhD researcher studying at City University of London. Her PhD is entitled "Scapegoating, Survival and Self-Actualisation: Representations of single mothers in TV dramedies and the lived experiences of single mothers". This topic has been investigated via the use of 'text-in-action' research, combining focus group 'watch parties' with follow-up interviews and in-depth textual analysis.

Kathy Davis is a Senior Research Fellow in the Sociology Department at the VU University in the Netherlands. Her research interests include sociology of the body, intersectionality, travelling theory and transnational practices, biography as methodology and critical and creative strategies for academic writing. She is the author of many books, including *Reshaping the Female Body, Dubious Equalities and Embodied Differences, The Making of Our Bodies, Ourselves: How Feminism Travels Across Borders* and *Dancing Tango: Passionate Encounters in a Globalizing World*. She has recently edited *Silences, Neglected Feelings, and Blind-spots in Research Practice with Janice Irvine* and is currently editing a Handbook on Intersectionality Studies with Helma Lutz.

x *Contributors*

Paul Galbally is Senior Lecturer in Counselling and Psychotherapy at the University of East London. He recently completed his Doctorate in Applied Psychology at the University of Essex. His research interests include the sociology of family, separation and conflictual relationships.

Sabine Grenz, Assistant Professor Dr., is a tenure track professor for interdisciplinary Gender Studies at the University of Vienna. Before, she was professor for Gender Studies at the University of Vienna (2017–2020) and for Diversity Research at the University of Göttingen (2015–2017). Since 2014, she holds the honorary position as associate professor at Humboldt University. In Vienna, she also serves as head of the Gender Research Office. Her current research interests include feminism and post-secularity as well as feminist epistemologies and methodologies. Previously, she was concerned with masculinity and (hetero-)sexuality in sex work, femininity constructions during the Second World War and gender equality in higher education.

Sophie Hales is a Lecturer in Organization Studies and a co-director of the Centre for Work, Organization and Society at the University of Essex. Her research on embodied experiences of sexualized labour has been published in edited collections, and in journals including *Organization* and *Organization Studies*.

Sandya Hewamanne is Professor of Sociology at the University of Essex. She is the author of *Stitching Identities in a Free Trade Zone: Gender and Politics in Sri Lanka* (University of Pennsylvania Press, 2008), *Sri Lanka's Global Factory Workers: (Un)Disciplined Desires and Sexual Struggles in a Post-Colonial Society* (Routledge, 2016) and *Re-stitching Identities in Rural Sri Lanka: Neoliberalism, Gender and Politics of Contentment* (University of Pennsylvania Press, 2020). She has published numerous journal articles on labour and human rights, gender and economic anthropology. She is the Founder and Director of IMPACT-Global Work, a non-profit promoting positive policy outcomes for global workers.

Xintong Jia is a PhD candidate in Sociology at City University of London. Xintong's PhD project examines reality dating shows to explore female subjectivity and the changing gender relations in contemporary China, shifts in the way that intimacy is practised, and the dynamics of (post)feminism. Her research interests intersect media and gender, popular culture, feminism in post-socialist China, and qualitative research methods. Xintong's chapter 'Victoria's Secret goes to China: Femvertising and the failed promise of empowerment' appears in the edited volume *The Cultural Politics of Femvertising* (2022).

Akane Kanai is a Senior Research Fellow in the School of Media, Film and Journalism at Monash University, Australia. Her interconnected research interests explore identity in digital culture, feminism, cultures of femininity, and the gendered and racialised politics of emotion and relationality. She is currently undertaking an Australian Research Council research fellowship investigating the everyday impacts of online feminism for young feminists. Her book,

Gender and Relatability in Digital Culture: Managing Affect, Intimacy and Value, was published in 2019.

Gulcimen Karakeci is a Lecturer in Criminology at the University of East London. Dr Karakeci's research interests include domestic abuse, gender inequalities, feminist criminology, and youth crime. She has a background in quantitative and qualitative research. Her publications include "Islam and Support for Gender Inequality among Women in Turkey: Comparing Attitudes across Institutional Contexts" (2018).

Phoebe Kisubi Mbasalaki is a Lecturer in Sociology at the University of Essex. Prior to that, she was a post-doctoral research fellow on the GlobalGRACE project (www.globalgrace.net) housed at the African Gender Institute (AGI) and the Centre for Theatre, Dance and Performance Studies (CTDPS) – University of Cape Town as well as the NGO – Sex Workers Advocacy and Educational Task Force (SWEAT). She was also a lecturer on the gender studies program at the AGI – University of Cape Town. Her research interests are in critical race, gender, class, sexuality, creative activism, public health as well as decolonial thought and praxis.

Awino Okech is a Reader (Associate Professor) in Political Sociology at SOAS, University of London, where she teaches in the Department of Politics and International Studies. As a feminist scholar activist, Awino's teaching and research interests lie in the nexus between gender, sexuality, security and nation-state making projects as they occur in conflict and post-conflict societies. Awino's recent publications include Movement Building Responses to COVID-19: Lessons from the JASS Mobilisation Fund (2021), Feminist Digital Counterpublics: Challenging Femicide in Kenya and South Africa (2021), African Feminist Epistemic Communities and Decoloniality (2020) and Gender, Protests and Political Change in Africa (2020).

Kaitlyn Regehr is Associate Professor of Digital Humanities. Her research is focused on the cultural impacts of social media and other new technology, especially on the experiences of young people. Regehr's work has informed policy on gender and diversity in advertising for the Mayor of London and legislation on cyber flashing and image-based abuse in youth relationship cultures. She has also researched the online indoctrination of young people and the digital "INCEL" community and has provided consultation to the Metropolitan Police and Education Scotland on these themes. Current research includes the AHRC-funded *"Understanding the Cel: Vulnerability, Violence and In(ter)vention"*.

Natasha Richards-Crisp is an AHRC-funded doctoral student at the University of Essex, United Kingdom. Her research interests include applied theatre, Relationships and Sex Education (RSE), and feminism. She is the Director of Running At Walls, a company that provides creative education for personal exploration. She is the author of *Sexting can be sexy . . . if it's consensual: challenging victim-blaming and heteronormativity in sext education* (2021).

Jessica Ringrose is Professor of Sociology of Gender and Education at IOE, UCL's Faculty of Education and Society, where she co-directs the UCL Centre for Sociology of Education and Equity. She is an internationally recognized expert on gender and sexual equity. She has worked with a wide range of stakeholders to shape policy and practice. Her current research explores young people's experiences of technologically facilitated sexual and gender-based violence and how to reduce and prevent online harm through educational interventions. Her latest public report (2021) with the Association of School and College Leaders is Understanding and Combatting Youth Experiences of Image-Based Sexual Harassment and Abuse.

Karen Throsby is Professor of Gender Studies at the University of Leeds. Her research focuses on the intersections of gender, technology, health and the body and she has published research on reproductive technologies, the surgical management of fatness, ultra-endurance sport, and most recently, food and consumption. She is the author of *Immersion: Marathon Swimming, Embodiment and Identity* (2016) and her most recent book, *Sugar Rush: Science, Obesity and the Social Life of Sugar*, will be published in 2022.

Melissa Tyler is Professor of Work and Organization Studies at the University of Essex and a co-director of the Centre for Work, Organization and Society. Her recent books include *Soho at Work: Pleasure and Place in Contemporary London* (Cambridge University Press, 2020) and *Judith Butler and Organization Theory* (Routledge, 2019). Melissa is currently working on a collaborative project on the impact of COVID-19 on self-employed live performers in the UK.

Foreword

It has long been clear that meaningful social change to address inequalities is forged from numerous difficult conversations. Shifts in thinking about and legislation on gender, racialisation and sexuality, for example, have all required discussions of difference and social justice across social divisions. Resistance to the status quo is central to producing shifts in power relations. In retrospect, responses to difficult conversations might appear linear and straightforward. Addressing issues that matter, however, is accompanied by difficult, protracted processes that require affective investment often seen in expressions of pain, anger, incomprehension and implacable opposition until a particular argument gains sufficient traction for power relations to shift.

A key but often unaddressed question concerns the reasons that such conversations are both difficult and crucial. Yet, there are many examples from within feminisms where difficult conversations have been central to social change. For example, some of the most difficult conversations have been those forced onto feminist agendas by black, African American and British African Caribbean feminists. Why? One major reason was that white feminists, making crucial claims to social change for gender equality in the 1960s, 70s and 80s, generally treated the category 'woman' as unitary and a source of solidarity. Yet, black women (as well as lesbians, working-class women and those with disabilities) were frequently implicitly omitted or othered in demands for change (Amos et al., 1984; Hull et al., 1982). Reproductive issues were a case in point. The crucial campaign for access to contraception and abortion on demand (threatened anew by 2022 changes to US abortion laws) ignored the fact that black women's motherhood had never been valorised in the way white (middle-class) women's childbearing has been (Solinger, 2020). As a result, black women have frequently been subjected to unwanted sterilisations without consultation, disapproval of their pregnancies and offered unsolicited abortions (Davis, 2019; Ross and Solinger, 2017). For black feminists, reproductive justice could not be achieved while black women continued to be implicitly omitted from the category 'woman'. Such omissions were already highlighted in 1851 by the black enslaved woman, Sojourner Truth, at an Ohio women's convention (Brah and Phoenix, 2004), and led Kimberlé Crenshaw (1989) to coin the term 'intersectionality'.

From black feminists' perspectives, there was clearly so much at stake that it was an issue that demanded to be raised, but that many white feminists were not convinced should be addressed in campaigns for reproductive rights. This was particularly the case since campaigns for reproductive justice required a shift in understanding of power relations that many white feminists found unpalatable. The differential positioning of black and white feminists, experienced as oppositional, meant that black women were only heard if they made their case forcefully and collaboratively. Some white feminists did not recognise the defensiveness and difficult emotions that this raised for them or why black women were both angry and hurt by this defensiveness and histories of reproductive injustice. Instead, they reinforced stereotypes that black women are aggressive and to be feared. This goes some way in explaining why the conversations that resulted when the arguments could no longer be ignored were difficult (although some white women always supported the campaigns). The potential identity threat that comes from the incommensurate narratives that have to be faced in difficult conversations seems a recipe for disaster, rather than social justice. The importance of these issues means, however, that they are dynamic. Black women's continued campaigning in organisations such as the Organisation of Women of African and Asian Descent and the Combahee Women's Collective produced a groundswell of recognition that began to shift understandings.

The 21st century marks a period where climate change, Covid-19, Black Lives Matter, #MeToo, debates on sex/gender identities and wars have all generated often-heated debate about inequalities, identities and social justice. It has increasingly been recognised that difficult conversations are part of everyday relationships and include power differentials. One of the conclusions from the Harvard Negotiation Project is that conversations become difficult because of fear about the degree of harm (to self and others) that may be caused (Stone, Patton and Heen, 1999). Levine et al. (2020) suggest that this is due to the tendency to focus on fears of short-term harm rather than the potential for long-term benefits. According to Stone et al. (1999), all difficult conversations involve contestations about what happened or should happen, the feelings they evoke and the identity issues they raise.

In that context, *Difficult Conversations: A Feminist Dialogue* is timely in illuminating the breadth of feminist issues and range of scholars who produce and/or require conversations that are uncomfortable because they highlight divisions that many people would rather not face. It engages with issues that generate as much heat as light, including genital cutting, trans and the 'gender wars', neoliberal universities, feminist research and digital communications. It grapples with an inherent tension for feminisms, particularly in the academy, between political activism and theoretical framing of difficult conversations.

The chapters show that difficult conversations are essential to new knowledge production and are indeed an inherent part of research on topics such as marital rape, mediated intimacy, sexual desire, sex and sexuality, raising ethical issues of consent, gendered and racialised power relations and reflexivity. Indeed, attempts to research such issues can be hampered by gatekeepers aiming to protect participants by refusing difficult conversations (Chapter 12). Various chapters show how the institutionalisation of gender studies is both threatening (in neoliberal contexts marked by histories of misogyny) and promising, allowing resistance and the creation of 'brave spaces' for difficult conversations that have the potential to be transformative (Chapters 14 and 15). Chapter 17 vividly illuminates how anonymously defacing a poster (which some might consider a trivial action) can be violently exclusionary, have physical impact, produce overwhelming emotions, and potentially silence. The fact that Roisin Ryan-Flood used a threatening and painful episode to initiate conversations and that colleagues were shocked into having conversations about queering the academy and acting in solidarity made an important difference.

Chapters 2 and 3 are presented as interviews and model ways of staging conversations on difficult topics (trans and the gender wars and feminism and race in the academy). Both illuminate a key issue highlighted in this volume, that issues that matter can often be dangerous to broach, whether in talk or writing. Yet, the conversations they engender are simultaneously difficult and productive because they pose fundamental issues for social justice and ontological and epistemological construction. They illuminate intersectionality and recognition of plurality that disrupts homogenizing, normative tendencies which implicitly exclude less powerful groups from constructions of the normative and indeed from humanity itself. Equally, they show the possibilities for change that can be produced by opening and sustaining such conversations if the conversations enable coming together across socially constructed boundaries in strategic alliances.

Three further key messages that run through most of the chapters are: first, the importance of the affective to conversations that matter. Rather than avoiding difficult emotions such as pain and anger, therefore, focusing on the emotion can help to make sense of debates (Hickey-Moody, 2013; Kofoed and Ringrose, 2012; St Pierre, 1997). As argued in Chapter 1, uneasiness itself can be methodologically productive, constituting a resource for understanding contradictions and disentangling difficulties. Similarly successful research, as in focus groups, requires emotion work on the part of the researcher (Chapter 16). A second key message is that institutions, structures and economics are central to the power relations that hinder and facilitate difficult conversations and systemic shifts. The psychosocial is therefore central to (productive) difficult conversations. A third key message is that mundane, quotidian issues can be simultaneously conversationally easy and difficult. A case in point is the discussion of sugar (Chapter 4). As explored in Chapter 6, disagreements have their own dynamics and it is important not only to broach difficult conversations, but to stay with disagreements, something that Donna Haraway (2016) advocates in thinking about anthropogenic climate change. Complexities such as these require that all of us have to be prepared to engage in 'pedagogies of discomfort' (Zembylas, 2018) and to deal with the uncomfortable reflexivity resulting from self-positioning (Chapter 7).

This book provides an antidote to the fatigue that can arise from issues like dealing with recognition of the recurrent violence of racism (Winters, 2020) or transphobia (Malatino, 2022). Yet the fact that authors from different generations in different institutional spaces and geographical places grapple with difficult conversations is galvanising while showing the difficulties to be faced. They suggest strategies for change towards social justice through collaborative action for building communities of trust and engaging with intersectional differences. Yet, they leave open the space for recognising that sometimes resistance through complaint or acting in ways that others define as 'feminist killjoys' are equally important strategies (Ahmed, 2019, 2021) for making difficult conversations hearable when our attempts at dialogue are refused.

By Ann Phoenix

References

Ahmed, S (2019) Living a feminist life. *Contemporary Political Theory* 18(2): 125–128.

Ahmed, S (2021) *Complaint!* Durham: Duke University Press.

Amos, V., Lewis, G., Mama, A, et al. (1984) Many voices, one chant: black feminist perspectives. *Feminist Review* 17(Special Issue).

Brah, A. and Phoenix, A (2004) Ain't I A woman? Revisiting intersectionality. *Journal of International Women's Studies* 5(3): 75–86.

Crenshaw, K. (1989) Demarginalizing the intersection of race and sex. *University of Chicago Legal Forum*, 1: 139–152.

Davis, D-A (2019) Reproductive injustice. In *Reproductive Injustice*. New York: New York University Press.

Haraway, D (2016) Staying With the Trouble: Making kin with the Chthulucene. Duke University Press.

Hickey-Moody, A (2013) Affect as method: Feelings, aesthetics and affective pedagogy. *Deleuze and Research Methodologies*: 79–95.

Hull, G.T., Bell-Scott, P. and Smith, B (1982) *All the Women Are White, All the Blacks are Men, but Some of us are Brave: Black Women's Studies*. Boston: Kitchen Table Women of Color Press.

Kofoed, J. and Ringrose, J (2012) Travelling and sticky affects: Exploring teens and sexualized cyberbullying through a Butlerian-Deleuzian-Guattarian lens. *Discourse: Studies in the Cultural Politics of Education* 33(1): 5–20.

Levine, E., Roberts, A. and Cohen, T. (2020) Dirricult Conversations: Navigating the tension between honesty and benevolence. *Current Opinion in Psychology*, 31, 38–53.

Malatino, H (2022) *Side Affects: On Being Trans and Feeling Bad*. Minnesota: University of Minnesota Press.

Ross, L. and Solinger, R (2017) *Reproductive Justice: An Introduction*. California: University of California Press.

Solinger, R (2020) Race and "Value". In *The State of Families: Law, Policy, and the Meanings of Relationships*. Routledge: Taylor & Francis.

St. Pierre, E.A (1997) Methodology in the fold and the irruption of transgressive data. *International Journal of Qualitative Studies in Education* 10(2): 175–189.

Winters, M-F (2020) *Black Fatigue: How Racism Erodes the Mind, Body, and Spirit*. Oakland: Berrett-Koehler Publishers.

Zembylas, M (2018) Affect, race, and white discomfort in schooling: Decolonial strategies for 'pedagogies of discomfort'. *Ethics and Education* 13(1): 86–104.

Acknowledgements

A project such as this is made possible through the collaboration of co-editors, contributors, publishers and more. We would like to thank the Department of Sociology at the University of Essex, which provided support for the preparation of the manuscript. Agnes Skamballis did wonders making the final manuscript ready for submission.

Róisín would like to thank her son, Daniel, who brings so much light and laughter to daily life and whose patience enables her to complete projects such as this. She would also like to thank the following friends who have been sounding boards for many difficult conversations over the years and unfailingly generous with their support, wisdom and insight: Christina Bodin, Kellie Burns, Rosalind Gill, Tamara Herath, Giovanni Porfido, Julie Shanahan and Embla Säfmark,

Isabel would like to thank Tone Hellesund, Sasha Roseneil, Ana Cristina Santos and Mariya Stoilova for having been and continuing to be a precious source of feminist inspiration and friendship.

Laurie would like to thank her husband, Brian, and children, Emily and Mira, who are the lights of her life. Their support means the world to her, and she wouldn't be who she is today without them. She would also like to thank her father, Larry, who always has her back, and her dear friend Cara Booker, who is always there when she needs someone.

Introduction

Róisín Ryan-Flood; Isabel Crowhurst and Laurie James-Hawkins

In spring 2019, Professor Ann Phoenix gave a presentation at a conference in London. During her compelling talk, she spoke of how difficult conversations can be the positive impetus for growth and change. We were struck by this fascinating notion, of how rather than simply being something to dread or view negatively, difficult conversations were not only necessary but an intrinsic part of positive change. We recognised the value of this in relation to feminist theory and practice, where difficult discussions have always led to important shifts in feminist thinking and mobilisations. For example, critiques of Western and white privilege by scholars and activists from the Global South and black and minority ethnic feminists have been and continue to be a vital part of promoting greater equality, inclusivity and complexity in feminist thought. It seems to us that difficult conversations have always been a crucial part of pivotal shifts in feminism. We are also conscious of the many difficult conversations that are currently taking place in contemporary feminism: for example, in relation to trans rights during what can be described as a period of both greater visibility and also increased attacks on trans identities. Difficult conversations are also taking place against feminism by those who see it as a threat, whether in the context of attacks on gender studies by governments or against reproductive rights. Yet even when those conversations are profoundly frustrating, it seems to us that dialogue remains an important part of addressing and challenging inequalities.

We took this notion of difficult conversations as the positive impetus for change as the starting point for a symposium that was hosted by the Centre for Intimate and Sexual Citizenship (CISC) at the University of Essex. This day-long event was the basis for this resulting edited volume. We are delighted to build on Ann Phoenix's work to bring together scholarly contributions from that day, as well as some new solicited chapters in this book. Professor Phoenix also provides the foreword for this volume, for which we are thrilled and grateful. The chapters in this book highlight some of the challenging moments when difficult conversations occur. They explore these moments across a range of contexts and issues – methodology, epistemology, identity, politics, rights, citizenship, intimacy and ethics, for example. The broad range of topics explored in this volume testifies to how difficult conversations remain not only an important and necessary aspect of feminist work, but are intrinsic to how feminist thought emerges, changes and

DOI: 10.4324/9781003088417-1

transforms. In the following section, we will look at some of the ways in which difficult conversations have led to changes in feminist theory and practice.

Difficult conversations, feminist theory and practice

Kimberlè Crenshaw (1991) coined the term 'intersectionality', and this is now a key concept in both feminist theory and practice. It is now taken as axiomatic that we all inhabit multiple identities that may inhabit different spaces of privilege or vulnerability in what Patricia Hill-Collins (1990) refers to as the 'matrix of domination'. Rather than isolate identities, a critical engagement with intersectionality requires that we take complexity as a starting point and address multiplicity in relation to wider social formations of power. This important contribution challenged the white, middle-class centredness and epistemic narrowness of much Western feminism and required an active engagement with racial and class privilege, anti-racist social movements and incorporating the experiences and perspectives of working-class and Black and ethnic minority women.

Chandra Talpade Mohanty (1984) challenged the ethnocentrism of much Western feminism in her classic article 'Under Western Eyes: Feminism and Colonial Discourses' and how it was situated in global power dynamics in relation to race and colonialism. Similarly, Hazel Carby (1996) demanded recognition of the ways in which white women occupied a privileged position in relation to race. Myra Marx Ferree (1980) shed light on the underestimation of working-class feminism and its impact on the fight for equal pay and in improving women's working conditions. Rawwida Baksh and Wendy Harcourt (2015) note the complexity of feminist transnational movements and the importance of awareness of their global impact. Very much entwined with these significant contributions which, with many others, have had a lasting impact on feminist theory is the powerful feminist activism and political work of social movements, collectives and alliances across the globe that have pushed feminism as a political and intellectual project to consider other dimensions of difference and how the category of 'woman' is inherently a multiplicity of identities. This diversity includes many differences, including across sexuality, class and (dis)ability. We cannot possibly do justice to the thriving landscape of feminist activism that has intersectionality at the core of its mobilisation, claims and demands globally. However, here we include some examples, both old and more recent, and others still are presented and discussed in the contributions of this collection. Formed in 1974 and active until 1980, the US-based Combahee River Collective explicitly strove to challenge singular notions and experiences of womanhood and claimed to be "actively committed to struggling against racial, sexual, heterosexual and class oppression, and [to] see our particular task the development of integrated analysis and practices based upon the fact that the major systems of oppression are interlocking" (1977). In Guatemala, Sector de Mujeres is an example of indigenous feminism, a network of feminist organisations active since the 1990s with a strong emphasis on indigenous and peasant women's rights, territory and environmental rights (www.sectordemujeres.org.gt).

And as a final example, we cite the cross-issue activism of the European Sex Worker Alliance which has been campaigning for an intersectional perspective on sex workers' rights that needs stronger alliances and convergence with the feminist movement, as emphatically expressed in the title of a recent position paper *Feminism needs sex workers, sex workers need feminism: towards a sex-worker inclusive women's rights movement* (ESWA, 2016).

Adopting an intersectional approach can present challenges on both practical and theoretical levels. But it is nonetheless one of the most significant ways in which contemporary feminism has continued to grow and evolve. It came about because feminists were willing to bravely speak out and address the ways in which feminism did not include them and hold wider feminism to account. This involved both speaking out and addressing social formations of power within feminism, as well as active listening and a willingness to learn and grow on the part of those whose views or practices were challenged. This is never an easy process, and it continues to be ongoing.

Feminist theory and practice have also transformed the field of epistemology and methodology, providing important critiques of how traditional positivist and scientific approaches were inherently bound up with a model of objectivity and scientific rationality that was based on an androcentric model (Oakley, 1981; Stanley and Wise, 1983; FINRRAGE, 2016). This critique of positivism (and the accompanying exclusion and pathologisation of women's voices) highlighted how epistemology and ontology are inherently political. The post-structuralist claim that all knowledge is partial and situated enabled the reflexive approaches that created a greater transparency and rigour in the research process. Feminists challenged the exclusion of women's voices and stories from both research and the political sphere and highlighted how the normative values ascribed to knowledge masked patriarchy. Ann Phoenix (2010), for example, explores how examining intertextuality reveals further complex power relations between the researcher and researched. Thus, the research process and data analysis are not neutral fields, but rather constituted through relationships of power, vulnerability, privilege and meaning, as further reflected upon in the chapters in this book.

The practice of difficult conversations

An etymological investigation of the word conversation reveals its roots in the Latin verb *conversari*, literally: to turn towards – as opposed to against – and broadly meaning: keeping company with, denoting some degree of familiarity and/or intimacy. To converse, in other words, means to con-verge, to come together by way of establishing an intellectual and/or emotional contact between invested parties. This contact might be difficult to achieve, it might even be painful, but it is not meant to be an assault, nor should it be intentionally hurtful, violent or forcefully extractive. To converse therefore entails making a commitment to listen, being listened to, and to being open to change. For this to happen, conversations require dedicated time and work, not just to find a point of con-vergence with others but also to reflect on one's own positionality, including epistemic privilege, and to work through the discomfort that this might bring. In a blog discussing the

BLM movement, Ann Phoenix, Afiya Amesu, Issy Naylor and Kafi Zafar powerfully state that change *"will only come through ongoing commitments to speak and to listen across differences"*[1].

As obvious as it might sound, difficult conversations are indeed difficult. While the focus of this book is on the generative potential of difficult conversations and on their impetus for positive change, many of our contributors do not shy away from detailing how they struggled to make sense of complex encounters and exchanges as productive forces. We read about how addressing sensitive topics entails navigating tensions and conflicts that can incapacitate productive dialogue, especially when the underlying intention of an exchange is not to converse/con-verge but for one view to prevail over another. In this volume, Akane Kanai captures this dynamic when discussing the 'pile-on' as a practice that, she writes, "demonstrates that the *one* position must be reached" and any other is wrong, and either vilified or silenced. In these contexts, not saying anything or leaving the space of engagement become the safest options. Withdrawal and silencing, however, come at a price. Not only do incomplete exchanges, misunderstandings, misrepresentations and exclusions generate hurt that linger for a long time, but they also inhibit exchange and dialogue and the learning and change that can come with them. In other instances, difficult conversations are prevented through institutional interventions aimed at avoiding the discomfort or even the reputational issues that might come with confronting difficult issues. Again, drawing on Ann Phoenix's and colleagues' previously mentioned reflections, it takes courage and reengagement with pain to tell difficult stories that might be painful to listen to, but this is essential work to move beyond silences and exclusions and drive forward real change.

As this volume aims to show, difficult conversations are often about challenging normative power relations and social and/or epistemological exclusions. This means confronting power, including among those who may not see themselves as practising exclusionary practices. Speaking up and speaking out is a difficult endeavour. The power to listen and effect change is in itself a privileged position. Yet it lends itself to important solidarities and social and epistemological transformations. With chapters highlighting the complex ways in which this takes place in different fields, circumstances and settings, we wish to emphasise both the challenges and the transformative potential of conversations. Our commitment to advancing feminist knowledge is also reflected in the inclusion of scholars at different career stages (early, mid-career and senior) who experience the world through different intersectional perspectives. It is our hope that this volume will contribute to wider discussions that may provoke difficult conversations but also promote dialogue and positive shifts in complex debates.

Organisation of the book

The book is divided into four sections: 'Difficult Knowledge'; 'Gender, Power and Intimacy'; 'Gender, Sexuality and Embodiment' and 'Bounded Knowledge'. In the first section, authors explore the challenges that arise when we engage in difficult conversations in order to gather 'difficult knowledge'. The next chapter, by Meg-John Barker and Róisín Ryan-Flood, takes the form of an interview and explores the ways in which difficult conversations in academia often surround issues that evoke strong feelings, the antithesis to the 'ideal' in academia that is firmly rooted in rational and analytical thinking. This discussion explores the current 'gender wars' and trans rights. The authors challenge the reader to engage in these difficult conversations and to get to know our subjects as human beings first and members of particular social groups second. The second chapter, by Kathy Davis, examines the ways in which researching difficult topics can make scholars themselves uneasy. In this, she challenges researchers to use the emotions such research produces to inform and enrich the research process. Róisín Ryan-Flood also interviews Sandya Hewamanne in the third chapter about her experiences as a female minority scholar within academia. Hewamanne emphasises the importance of intersectionality and the need to accurately represent the voices, traumas and lived experiences of minority and disadvantaged populations. In the final chapter in this section, Karen Throsby interrogates the moral values we associate with food and the ways in which this can perpetuate gendered, raced and classed inequalities. She examines emotions such as shame, guilt, pride and pleasure that we often link to food and the social meanings that we attach to food as a marker of being 'good' or 'bad'.

Part Two of the book considers the difficult conversations that arise when we study 'power, gender and intimacy'. Contributors consider the ways in which power is linked to both how we enact gender and the intimate relationships in which we engage. Jessica Ringrose and Kaitlyn Regehr examine advertising and body-shaming, especially among women. They use an intersectional approach to examine the ways in which advertising power and visual images can be used to shame women and maintain existing gendered power relations. Akane Kanai explores how digital culture and social media has impacted the feminist movement and broader feminist debates. She suggests that while digital culture can expand the reach of the movement, it also can dilute the power of the movement and limit the depth with which women engage in feminist debate. Rikke Amundsen's chapter explores how power and gender relations can impact negotiations of trust and connection in the context of a research interview. She outlines some of the ethical issues that arise in researching intimate topics and how power within the research process itself can impact how interviews are negotiated. The final chapter in this section, by Xintong Jia, addresses reflexivity, trust and power in relationships between the researcher and the researched in the context of conducting research during the COVID-19 pandemic. As she explains, conversations should be interactive, communicative and dialogic, demanding a degree of uncomfortable reflexivity.

The third section in the book addresses 'gender, sexuality and embodiment'. These chapters highlight the difficulty faced in researching intimate topics and the embodied self. Phoebe Kisubi Mbasalaki addresses the association of sex with the discourse of disease in gender and sexuality studies, and how it silences investigations into sexual pleasure, especially in the context of same-sex relationships and Black women. She uses decolonial feminist approaches to suggest that this perspective removes the lens of heteronormativity from the research topic and allows more in-depth investigation of the lived experiences of her participants. The next chapter, by Laurie James-Hawkins, addresses the ways in which research on sex and sexual behaviour creates a tension between the needs of the researcher and the needs of the researched. She suggests that though these conversations can be difficult, they are necessary to move the field forward and to represent the lived experiences of the women who are willing to spend their time sharing their most intimate stories. Natasha Richards-Crisp' chapter interrogates the ways in which the current relationship and sex education program in the UK silences the experiences of LGBTQI+ youth. She suggests that building a community of trust provides the potential for engaging in these conversations with young people, drawing on participatory applied theatre workshop techniques. In the final chapter in this section, Gulcimen Karakeci elaborates on researcher dilemmas when forbidden by her gatekeepers to collect experiences of sexual violence in her research on domestic abuse and women's shelters in Turkey. She had to navigate this issue when her participants nonetheless shared their stories of marital rape. As a researcher, she chose to give voice to their otherwise institutionally silenced experiences.

Part Four explores 'bounded knowledge', or the ways in which we must navigate institutions and the boundaries they impose on us in our efforts to generate new knowledge. A chapter by Sophie Hales, Paul Galbally and Melissa Tyler examines ethics and reflexivity in research governance and the granting of institutional ethical approval. Their illuminating analysis suggests that institutional requirements can sometimes function to reinforce gendered inequalities in academia. The next chapter, by Sabine Grenz, addresses how the development of women, feminist and gender studies within academia has been met with institutional scepticism in some places, as it is considered 'too political' and thus not 'proper' knowledge. She notes that ideas about who can and should be an academic are shaped by both masculinity and whiteness and that the field of women and gender studies produces difficult conversations by challenging these deeply held institutional assumptions. Awino Okech's chapter explores feminist classrooms as safe spaces within the neoliberal university. She suggests that these spaces offer a place where difficult conversations can become transformative conversations addressing institutional limitations and marginalisation. In the next chapter, Clare Bowen examines how using focus groups in social research may unwittingly serve to silence the voices of the less powerful and the marginalised. Her chapter proposes developing an insider researcher position, which reflexively allows for more diverse voices to be included. Finally, Róisín Ryan-Flood explores 'queering the academy' through the lived experience of being an out LGBTQ member of staff in higher education. She uses autoethnography to consider the implications of equality, diversity and inclusion practices. Together, the chapters in this volume outline important examples of difficult conversations and the dilemmas, difficulties and opportunities that they entailed. We hope that you will find them as thought-provoking as we do.

Note

1 https://blogs.ucl.ac.uk/ioe/2020/09/22/when-black-lives-matter-all-lives-will-matter/

References

Baksh, R. and Harcourt, W (2015) *The Oxford Handbook of Transnational Feminist Movements*. Oxford: Oxford Handbooks.

Carby, H.V (1996) White woman listen! Black feminism and the boundaries. *Black British Cultural Studies: A Reader* 61.

Collins, P.H (1990) Black feminist thought in the matrix of domination. *Black Feminist thought: Knowledge, Consciousness, and the Politics of Empowerment* 138: 221–238.

Combahee River Collective (1977) *Combahee River collective statement*. Available from: https://americanstudies.yale.edu/sites/default/files/files/Keyword%20Coalition_Readings.pdf (accessed 25th August 2022).

Crenshaw, K (1991) Mapping the Margins: Intersectionality, identity politics, and violence against women of color. *Stanford Law Review* 43(6).

Expert System with Application (2016) *Feminist needs sex workers, sex workers need feminism: Towards a sex-worker inclusive women's rights movement*. Available from: www.eswalliance.org/feminism_needs_sex_workers_sex_workers_need_feminism_for_a_sex_worker_inclusive_women_s_rights_movement (accessed 25th August 2022).

FINRRAGE (Feminist International Network of Resistance to Reproductive and Genetic Engineering) (2016) *FINRRAGE*. Available from: www.finrrage.org/ (accessed 25th August 2020)

Marx Ferree, M (1980) Working class feminism: A consideration of the consequences of employment. *The Sociological Quarterly* 21(2): 173–184

Mohanty, C.T (1984) Under western eyes: Feminist scholarship and colonial discourses. *Boundary* 2: 333–358.

Oakley, A (1981) Interviewing women: A contradiction in terms? In H. Roberts (ed.) *Doing Feminist Research*. London: Routledge.

Phoenix, A (2010) Suppressing intertextual understandings: Negotiating interviews and analysis. In R. Ryan-Flood. and R. Gill (eds.) *Secrecy and Silence in the Research Process*. London: Routledge (pp. 177–192).

Stanley, L. and Wise, S (1983) *Breaking out again: Feminist Consciousness and Feminist Research*. London: Routledge & Kegan Paul.

Section 1
Difficult knowledge

1 The gender wars and difficult conversations about trans

An interview with Meg-John Barker

Meg-John Barker and Róisín Ryan-Flood

Róisín Ryan-Flood: Firstly, thank you, Meg-John, for participating in this book about difficult conversations and feminist dialogues! As you know, we've struggled to find somebody to write a chapter for this book about 'the gender wars', as they've been called, despite this being perhaps the most obvious difficult conversation happening within feminism at the moment. Indeed, you yourself declined to write the chapter the first time we approached you. Can you say why you think it's such a difficult conversation right now that people are reluctant to go near it?

Meg-John Barker: Sure. I think a big part of the answer lies in feeling. We're frequently called upon – in academic and media discussions about this subject – to engage in intellectual, rational debate: to put our feelings aside. Perhaps there's even more pressure to do this given that women and queer people – like many marginalised groups – are often dismissed by connecting us with emotions and the body, rather than rationality and the mind – which is still regarded as the proper mode for scholarly and public discourse.

But this topic, for all of us engaged with it, brings up intense, painful feelings. This is the case with many of the polarised debates happening around us right now: climate crisis, Covid vaccinations, Brexit, etc. They touch into deep, old emotions, connected as they are with fundamental themes of life and death, safety and danger, belonging and exclusion, who gets included in the category of human and who does not. They're also an agonising illustration of how capitalism and white supremacy rely on divided populations in order to thrive, frequently fanning the flames of culture wars to scapegoat, to pit groups against each other and/or to detract attention from the actions of the political elite, regardless of the impact this has.

We may steer clear of engaging at all to avoid these feelings. We may engage in intellectualised versions of the conversation to avoid these feelings. We may shunt all the blame for what's happening onto the other in the conversation to avoid

DOI: 10.4324/9781003088417-3

these feelings. When I declined to produce a chapter the first time around, it was partly because I didn't want to spend any more time going towards these feelings.

Last year, I was interviewed for a project about the gender wars in feminism. The researcher told me that most of the people she'd interviewed – whatever their position – had expressed deeply painful feelings, particularly fear. Several cried during the interviews. I certainly felt my own body clench as I spoke with her, becoming tense and tight, to avoid going into such challenging feelings talking about this vulnerable topic with a relative stranger. I also found myself struggling and stuttering over ideas I know so well, having thought and written about them for years. Being asked for my responses to various arguments put me on the defensive, fogging my thinking and rendering me far less articulate than I'd like to be.

So, part of the reason I didn't want to go near this is because I might struggle to do it justice. It's such an urgent topic, taking such a huge toll, that I desperately want to contribute something helpful, and certainly not something that might inflame things in any way. I'm also aware that I haven't read as much as I might about what's currently going on and the key perspectives involved. Again, this is because of not wanting to evoke any more tough feelings during a time of pandemic and personal trauma, when daily life often feels like enough of a challenge.

However, on receiving the second request to contribute something, I realised that I could take a different approach than attempting to park my feelings and write something intellectually coherent and compelling. This approach is informed by the reading and practice I've been doing towards my new graphic guide on mental health, and involves going (slowly and carefully) towards the feelings, insisting on including them rather than avoiding or eradicating them. Indeed, this approach questions the whole mind/body split model that even imagines we could ever do such a thing.

I'm wondering whether trying to sever from our feelings in these conversations has been part of the problem. I'm reflecting on something Kenneth Gergen once wrote about approaches which enable conversations across intractable group conflicts. The facilitators encouraged people to get to know each other as humans first – talking about everything in their life except for the issue. They then asked people to share their experiences rather than their views or opinions: what had happened to make this so important to them, and how they felt about that. Finally, they got everyone to talk about their areas of uncertainty, to move away from the binary of one singular fixed view versus another.

I want to experiment here in foregrounding feelings in my answers, rather than attempting to muster persuasive arguments, or synthesise other people's theories and research in the hope of convincing through impressive names and statistics.

Róisín: **When you talk about the painful feelings this conversation can bring up – or which people endeavour to avoid – what kind of thing do you mean?**

Meg-John: Some main ones would be terror, rage, grief, shame, yearning and despair. To me they have a fundamental existential quality, tapping into some of the deepest needs and wounds, hopes and fears involved with being human. For many of us, they also relate to our earliest experiences of abandonment and/or annihilation, as well as to our ongoing experiences of marginalisation and oppression, violence and silence.

Here are a few of the feelings that came up when I tuned in to myself and talked with others about this chapter. I believe most of them apply regardless of how we're positioned in the conversation (e.g. as firmly on one 'side' or another, as disengaged, or as trying to hold a nuanced position):

- Loneliness at feeling an outcast, unwelcome, rejected from community or culture, as if we're no longer part of humanity or never have been.
- Yearning for simple ways of dividing those who are safe from those who are dangerous, so that we can finally find secure relationships and communities, having experienced the opposite so many times in our lives.
- Terror that we'll suddenly be exposed, judged, attacked or ostracised.
- Loss over so many seemingly irreparable rips and rifts in our communities. Sadness when close relationships can't survive in the face of such difference.
- Anger at not being seen or heard. Fury that we're speaking these important – dangerous – truths in a world that acts like we're crazy and deluded, and seems keen to silence us.
- Grief and/or rage that we live in such violent, unjust, unsustainable societies, where our needs are pitted against each other and hierarchised. Longing for something different.
- Envy at other – often younger – people who seemingly have options and freedoms that weren't available to us, or are being cared for in areas where we've been harmed.
- Horror that we might be hurting others in similar ways to the ways we've been hurt ourselves. Shame that we – who have always identified strongly with helping others – might actually be harming them, or contributing to individual and/or collective suffering.
- Despair as all our energy goes into this conversation instead of into the other places – both personal and political – where it's so desperately needed right now.
- Hopelessness around how we might intervene in any way which might be useful, rather than further escalating the situation.
- Powerlessness at the ways in which wider society – and institutions within it – act in ways which exacerbate the conflict, misrepresent those involved and seem to care nothing for the toll this takes.

Another key feeling I've heard from many friends is a sense of being ripped apart inside. So many of us have long histories in both feminist and queer communities, have strong identifications and/or experiences with both womanhood and transness or otherwise embody that which has become so polarised within us. It's incredibly hard to see these things being pulled apart and pitted against each other, and we may experience this as a kind of internal tearing or severing.

All this is not to say that we feel all these feelings explicitly each time we engage in these conversations. But perhaps the times when we don't feel them are more concerning than the times when we do. For me that's certainly the case. It's when I'm defended and covered over, that these feelings are more likely to leak – or lash – out during an encounter in ways that hurt me or others, and certainly confuse and cloud my thinking, taking me towards overly simple binaries of us versus them, blame out or shame in.

Róisín: **One of the main tasks you've set yourself – as a writer – is to make understandings of gender (and of sexuality, relationships and mental health) available in accessible ways to the general public, for example through graphic guides (e.g. Barker and Scheele, 2019) and (anti) self-help books (e.g. Iantaffi and Barker, 2017). What understanding of gender do you present? And how does that relate to this difficult conversation?**

Meg-John: Here's my attempt at an inclusive understanding of gender – which I try to convey in my work – drawing on what I've learnt from gender theorists and researchers across various disciplines, as well as activists, creatives and practitioners:

We all grow up steeped in what it means to be a man and a woman in our culture, so the dominant forms of masculinity and femininity are readily available to us all. We're constantly swimming in them like a fish in water. We learn from very early on that we must embrace and embody one set of things, and reject and repress the other – if we're to be afforded safety, dignity and belonging in the world. Therefore, we must learn both very well indeed. Intrinsically linked to this, at the same time we learn what's deemed attractive about both masculinity and femininity, and to embrace our attraction for one, and reject it for the other.

For whatever reason – likely a complex combination of the body we're born in, our early experiences and the wider cultural messages in the time and place we grow up, people have very different experiences of this embracing/rejecting process.

- For some of us, it feels relatively comfortable and congruent. It may leave us with some sense of loss and lack, but we can live our lives this way.
- For others, there's a deep sense of wrongness about it, but we are able – through resisting the messages and consciously shifting the relationships and communities we engage with – to reshape the categories of man or woman, and what's encompassed under them, in a way we feel able to inhabit.
- For others, there's a sense – often from very early on – of intense incongruence and discomfort involved in embracing/rejecting in the expected way – to the point that life simply isn't livable that way, and this is hugely relieved if there's support available to inhabit the other position in the world and/or in our bodies.

- For others, neither of the available options feels possible as a fit – even significantly reshaped – and inhabiting a place of both, between or beyond is the most congruent and comfortable way of navigating this.
- For others, the best path for us through this terrain is unclear and there may be movements in several of these directions before any kind of settling – if that ever happens.

One thing I've learnt from mental health survivor movements is how necessary it is to hold all lived experiences of distress as valid. For example, some have a biomedical understanding of our struggles, others a psychological or relational one, others sociopolitical, others spiritual and many a combination of two or more of these. This impacts both the meaning we make of our experiences and the paths we follow in relation to them. It's complex work to hold all of these stories, especially in the places where they seem to contradict each other: for example, when it comes to questions of whether psychiatric diagnosis and treatment is helpful and/or harmful.

I wonder whether it might be possible to shift conversations around gender in ways which value all the above listed experiences as equally valid. It's so tempting to impose our experience and understanding of something as personal and political as gender or mental health on everyone in an attempt to validate ourselves, or to find some sense of safety. Instead, we might all recognise that others can hold vastly different experiences and understandings to us and benefit from hearing these.

In my work on gender, my aim is always to illuminate culturally dominant understandings, and how these limit all of us whether we fit, or are marginalised, or invisible, within it. Thus the problem is reframed as the limited system, rather than any specific group which we might position ourselves inside or outside, for or against. There's a sense of how we're interconnected – rather than divided – by the impact of gender trauma.

Róisín: **Can you explain what you mean by gender trauma? Is a trauma-lens helpful for addressing this conversation?**

Meg-John: My co-author Alex Iantaffi has written a wonderful book called *Gender Trauma* which deals with this in depth. I think it's about recognising that we carry so much historical, cultural, intergenerational and developmental trauma into these conversations. We also inevitably engage from the survival strategies that we've learnt as a result of this trauma, which have the potential to retraumatise ourselves and others.

In all areas of life, I believe it's important to become as aware as possible of where we carry trauma and how it impacts our relating. In this area, specifically, we might usefully inform ourselves around:

- *Historical trauma:* How the current dominant understanding of gender came into being, and how it is implicated in the violence and injustice that forms a key part of our cultural and personal ancestry, such as the subjugation of women and working-class people, the colonising – and sometimes genocide – of indigenous people with different gender-related systems, the ways young men are expected/forced to fight and die for nations and the pathologising of those with non-normative gender expressions or experiences.

- *Cultural trauma:* What the dominant cultural understanding of gender is, how it operates and how it affects us; for example, the impact of toxic forms of masculinity on women and others, and on men themselves (whether or not they fit within these).
- *Intergenerational trauma:* How we pass on normative gender – explicitly and or implicitly – down the generations; for example, in messages about what boys and girls should or shouldn't do, and attempts to force babies' bodies – and developing children – to conform to social expectations of heterosexual masculinity and femininity.
- *Developmental trauma:* The traumatising impact on our developing bodyminds of not being held and heard in our feelings. This is deeply gendered in terms of the ways caregivers and others respond to children's emotional expression. When adults are unable to tolerate emotional states in children, either ignoring them or implicitly/explicitly punishing them, these feelings – and the experiences that elicited them – remain unprocessed and linger in our bodyminds. We construct defences to avoid feeling/expressing them in future, but may well become dissociated and/or dysregulated when current situations inevitably elicit them again.

The current gender wars may well – consciously or not – connect us with our own early experiences of violence and silence. For example, many of us engaged in these conversations experienced or expressed gender in non-normative ways as children and were policed and punished for this in our families, education systems, healthcare systems, etc. Most of us are culturally marginalised in one or more ways, so have ongoing lived experience of being dismissed and/or perceived as some kind of threat by others. We may well have internalised some of these messages about our supposed delusion or dangerousness or constructed strong defences against such accusations.

If we're unaware of the trauma we carry it will continue to haunt these conversations as we act outwards towards others, and inwards towards ourselves, based on it. For example, those of us who learnt to survive with more fight-based strategies may well attack others, blame them for our distress or attempt to control people and impose our views on them. Those of us with flight-based strategies may engage in ways that overstretch us and burn us out, struggling to see the ways in which fast, busy, urgent engagement prevents us from tuning into ourselves and others. Those of us with freeze-based strategies may become too frightened to continue engaging at all, potentially losing important work, relationships and community as we withdraw to protect ourselves. Those of us with fawn-based strategies may attempt to placate everyone or internalise these conversations as yet more evidence of our own shamefulness or unworthiness.

While it's helpful to be informed about trauma and the way it operates, and about the different forms of trauma that exist around gender in particular, trauma-sensitivity is far more about embodied practices than it is about increasing knowledge. We need to learn how to notice when we're becoming dissociated or dysregulated, and how to tolerate intense emotions rather than repressing them or acting them out. This is long, slow, challenging work, and requires relationships and systems of support.

One of my major concerns is how little understanding our communities and institutions have of trauma, and how little support we therefore have to engage in affective and embodied practices as a major part of our activism or study in these areas. Again, this applies to difficult conversations beyond this one, of course.

Róisín: **Can you say a bit more about your own personal experiences of being caught up in the gender wars, and the impact that's had on you?**

Meg-John: Right now, I'm sitting with the toll it's taken in terms of mental health. My close community has seen three deaths due to suicide by trans and/or non-binary people in the past six months. Ruth Pearce has written eloquently on what it's like to be an activist-academic working in an area where you're losing friends and colleagues in this way with appalling regularity. I believe that the heightened background level of trauma of these gender wars – interwoven with the stress and isolation of the pandemic – has a big part to play in why increasing numbers of us are being pushed over the edge.

In 2017, I wrote a post labelling the trans conversation as a 'moral panic', having noted that the number of negative media pieces about trans had gone from around one per month at the start of that year to one per day by the end (Barker, 2017). Trans as a big news story has continued since then. It's now into its fifth year, seemingly undaunted by the other, rather major, things going on right now. The impact of seeing your community – and these conversations – (mis)represented in the media day after day, week after week, has a grinding, wearing effect. There's also a related stress of having to handle the opinions of others based on these representations, and never quite knowing where a new contact may be coming from.

I left academia myself in 2019, but my previous institution – and one of the ones that I'm currently closest to – have both been hubs in the media reporting about trans. Had I been working at either place I would have had to go off sick, or even leave, because – as one of the most senior trans academics present – it would have been impossible for me not to be drawn into these conversations – internally and publicly. I'm not sure that my own mental health would have survived such an experience, as I'm well aware from previous times how re/traumatising media scrutiny can be (Cardoso, 2021).

I had my own brush with media reporting of the gender wars in 2018. A resource I'd written the previous year about gender, sexual and relationship diversity (GSRD) was suddenly the subject of social, and then mainstream, media discussion. The headlines said that the therapy body who'd commissioned the resource was a 'dinosaur' as it included out-of-date stereotypes about women. Hopefully, anybody familiar with my work will know unlikely that is!

After many papers repeated this story, one journalist actually read the original document and realised that something strange was going on. They found that the original source was a Mumsnet post criticising a cherry-picked quote from the document, which outlined common stereotypes of femininity. The suggestion was that the document was saying that women *were* like this, rather than that these were culturally dominant messages which take a huge toll on many women's mental health. Once the conversation migrated to Twitter, people quoted the Mumsnet comments rather than the resource itself, and once it hit mainstream media, journalists quoted the tweets.

The story deemed newsworthy in the gender wars is that of a fight between trans people who are anti-women, and feminists who are anti-trans. So, the story of the GSRD resource was contorted to fit this narrative. Bridgette Rickett has suggested that the story media generally tells about feminism is that of infighting: one set of overly emotional women attacking another. As with reporting around so many groups – such as migrants or people on benefits – this story leaves systems and structures of power unchallenged and unchanged by scapegoating those who are most marginalised as the cause of societal problems.

If this is how distorted my own story became, how about everything else we read about trans – or indeed about anything? It's unsurprising, perhaps, that when I train practitioners about gender, many believe that it's common practice for children to receive hormones and surgeries, that the rate of trans women assaulting cis women is high or that a large proportion of trans people regret medical interventions – none of which has any basis in reality.

My experiences also brought home the toll of having yourself – or your group – presented in ways that are so incongruent with how you experience yourself. Seeing yourself depicted in unrecognisable ways by powerful others is literally crazy-making, as you wonder whether that image is more legitimate than the one you have of yourself. The documentary *Disclosure* does a great job at exploring the toll this takes on a collective level, when a marginalised group is only represented in specific stereotypical ways.

I've learnt – from both my experiences of media reporting, and from accompanying friends through their own – that institutions rarely stand by individuals under these circumstances. The risk to their own reputations is deemed so great that they're more likely to focus on damage limitation. So, we have this traumatising situation whereby neither media nor institutions are operating from an ethics of care – considering the impact on those of us caught up in these moments – but rather from a focus on maximising whatever sells products, and minimising whatever risks selling products.

I think we need to be very cautious around whatever we read in mainstream or social media about this conversation, whoever is being represented. It also saddens me that it often feels too risky for us to have the kinds of complex, nuanced conversations about gender that are commonplace in my feminist and trans communities more publicly, because we know how they're likely to be contorted to fit the set of binary oppositions media prefers, such as pro/anti trans, good/bad feminist, nature/nurture, etc.

Róisín: **You've written about the value of a non-binary approach to far more than gender. How does such an approach relate to these – often very polarised – debates?**

Meg-John: In *Life Isn't Binary*, Alex and I reflected on how non-binary understandings of sexuality and gender might expand to encompass bodies, relationships, feelings and more. We explored the risks in how mainstream media frames everything as a debate, suggesting two, and only two, equally valid positions. The common notion of 'media balance', as giving equal room to someone who disputes any given position, is well worth questioning; for example, when climate scientists are presented alongside celebrities who deny the reality of climate change.

Debate framing also suggests a level playing field rather than acknowledging the power gradients involved in how groups are positioned or what's at stake for them. As Sara Ahmed (2021) puts it:

> There cannot be a dialogue when some at the table are in effect or intent arguing for the elimination of others at the table. When you have "dialogue or debate" with those who wish to eliminate you from the conversation (because they do not recognise what is necessary for your survival or because they don't even think your existence is possible), then "dialogue and debate" becomes another technique of elimination. A refusal to have some dialogues and some debates can thus be a key tactic for survival.

Some years back, I was involved in feminist activist-academic events aimed at communicating across divides around sexualization. In an attempt to disrupt binary debate framing, I suggested that we first check whether we're talking about one thing, or clustering many things under the term 'sexualization', which confuses the issue because we might find ourselves in very different positions in relation to each of them. Secondly, rather than asking whether any option for engaging with key issues was good or bad (either/or), I suggested we might ask what each might open up and close down (both/and).

Applying this to the conversation around trans, we might usefully tease apart the different elements in the conversation rather than lumping them together under 'trans' as something people could ever position themselves in relation to, in 'pro' or 'anti' positions.

For example, common issues that come up in the gender wars include how best to:

- Support young people to reach comfortable and congruent places in relation to their genders and sexualities, without pressure to follow any particular pathway.
- Prevent violence, and support survivors of violence, acknowledging the heavily gendered ways in which this plays out, and maintaining everyone's safety in both public and private spaces.
- Understand the ways in which sex/gender operates in our bodyminds, embedded within particular cultures and relational systems.
- Address cultural misogyny, and increase the agency of women and girls.
- Enable everyone who wants to have sex to experience it in ways which are consensual rather than coercive.

Under each of these categories, we could explore the range of options that exist, and what each option might open up and close down for everyone involved. We could attend carefully to how we might address each issue to maximise the safety, belonging and dignity of all, rather than putting the needs of one group in opposition to those of another. We could creatively engage by trying things out, acknowledging that no response will be perfect and being prepared to learn from our mistakes. Needless to say, the prevailing climate does not make such an approach easy!

I think it's helpful to decentre trans, as I've done in this list above, expanding out to encompass everyone for whom each issue is relevant. For example, when it comes to questions about gender affirmative treatment, instead of asking whether trans people should or shouldn't receive it, I think it'd more helpful to recognise that many people would benefit from it at some point in their lives, and to aim towards providing gender affirmative healthcare for everyone, whatever kinds of gender-related transitions they're going through (e.g. adolescence, parenthood, menopause and other periods of significant hormonal shift, the 'feminising'/'masculinising' impact of various medical treatments and surgeries, retirement, etc.).

Returning to feeling, when I have these conversations, I'm trying to notice what results in a sense of embodied contraction or expansion. It's often helpful simply to name that contraction is happening, and to wonder about this. It can mean that I'm being drawn into binary thinking and a desire for simple either/or answers. It can then be helpful to get curious about what might enable expanding out towards a more spacious perspective, whether that's by taking a break, shifting the conversation from the content to the process of *how* we're discussing it for a while, naming our feelings and refocusing on our experiences or some other way of bringing in some space or expansion.

Róisín: **Speaking of binaries, I am often struck by how contemporary anti-trans perspectives focus almost exclusively on the figure of the trans woman, while trans masculinities are often ignored. What are your thoughts?**

Meg-John: Many suggestions have been put forward for this. For example, some people have related it to the fact that femininity is mercilessly policed and punished – on all genders – in our misogynist culture in ways that masculinity isn't. Any sign of femininity (e.g. painted nails) on somebody read as a man is cause for comment, while those read as women can express all kinds of masculinity with very little reaction from others.

Other people have suggested that many of us have been deeply wounded *in* our femininity – both personally and culturally – which can make it very hard to understand anybody moving *towards* femininity. It can also result in us projecting these wounded attachments we have with womanhood onto the 'figure of the trans woman', because these attachments are, perhaps, too painful to address in ourselves.

Certainly, trans women are put in some horrendous double binds by the ways in which this focus on them manifests. For example, trans women are treated very much *as* women in relation to the disproportionate levels of sexual, intimate partner, and other forms of violence that they experience. However, they are often excluded *from* the category of woman when it comes to this being recognised or supported in any way. Trans women are told that they mustn't transition as a young person, but if they wait and transition later on, they're told they can't possibly be women because they were 'socialised male'.

It's also worth questioning whether it's true that the focus is predominantly on trans women, or whether it's more a matter of a different focus, with trans feminine people often being portrayed as agentic perpetrators of violence, and trans masculine people often been infantilised and portrayed as victims and lacking agency – which is also deeply problematic. It can be helpful, too, to recognise the long history of other groups of women being positioned outside of femininity – as aggressive rather than passive and as (potential) perpetrator rather than victim, including Black women, working-class women, sex workers and lesbians.

None of this is about denying the relationship between violence and dominant forms of masculinity, or the devastating impact that this has in all kinds of ways. However, it is important to recognise that trans people do not have equivalent socialisation experiences to cisgender people, and to reiterate that there is no basis to the claim that trans women are more violent than cisgender women. In fact, they are disproportionately the *victims* of violence, particularly trans women of colour.

Going back to my previous point, I think that the urgent need – in relation to gendered violence – is to stop bringing up children in binary ways which disable/punish some emotional states and behaviours while enabling/enforcing others along gender lines. This agenda would seem to be an excellent fit for also bringing up kids in ways that embrace gender diversity, sexual diversity, and other forms of bodymind diversity, as well as holding and hearing all children's emotional states and thus – hopefully – decreasing current levels of developmental trauma.

For those of us who weren't fortunate enough to be brought up in such a way, I think it behooves us all to reflect deeply on our (gendered) relationship with anger, and indeed all emotions. Particularly, it's vital to recognise how we can enact anger in violent ways when we repress it and/or react from it, rather than welcoming it and responding to it wisely. Locating anger and violence purely out there in others – of whatever group – is a dangerous strategy indeed.

Róisín: **What do you think about how academic institutions and communities should handle this conversation?**

Meg-John: As with so many of the difficult conversations of the moment, the tendency seems to be to focus on specific individuals and whether or not they should be removed or cancelled. My concern with this approach is that removing individuals gives the impression of action while often leaving wider systems unchanged.

In academia, we need much broader conversations about the histories – in so many of our disciplines – of studying and theorising 'the Other', whoever they are, in ways that don't include their own voices, needs, or perspectives, and which treat 'them' as a problem that requires explanation, or as exotic and fascinating in their difference to our accepted norm.

Just as the treatment of trans in the media points to much larger concerns about journalistic ethics and the role of media in scapegoating vulnerable groups and maintaining the status quo, trans debates in academia point to the need for much wider-ranging conversations about the ethics of how we engage in research and theorising, teaching and management. We need to interrogate the colonialist histories of normal/abnormal divisions in our disciplines, and the practices which make academic worlds so much more accessible to some than to others, as well as the privileging of intellect over emotion that I mentioned at the start. H Howitt's video about their journey in researching trans sex, *How We Fuck and Unfuck The World*, and Kit Heyam's historical book *Before We Were Trans* illuminate these issues further, and include some great suggestions on how we might do things differently.

Personally, I'd love to see anybody who wants to speak, write or intervene about a group outside their own lived experience start by listening carefully to the diverse voices within that group, and exploring their own relationship to the axes of oppression that impact that group. If we're in any doubt as to whether we can engage with this topic in helpful ways, then it would be wise to refrain and 'do no harm' until we feel on more solid ground in terms of our understanding, compassion and emotional capacity in this area.

Róisín: **How would you like to see the conversation about trans change?**
Meg-John: There's something vital about learning from history here, including how various marginalised groups – and their related movements for justice – have been constructed in popular culture and academic study. Julia Serano's book *Excluded* does an excellent job of examining how the representation of trans people mirrors representations of other groups over time, and pulling out common features in how such representations operate.

I've been struck particularly by resonances between the trans moral panic, and the moral panic around gay men in the 1980s, including concerns about children being 'exposed' to messages of sexual diversity, a marginalised group being represented as both deluded in terms of their identity/experience and as dangerous perpetrators, and now the impact of cultural shaming in the context of a pandemic.

Many trans activists and academics have pointed out that the time, energy and resources given to the gender wars take away from more urgent and pressing issues, such as rates of violence against trans people, access to trans-inclusive healthcare with reasonable waiting times, and the high rates of homelessness, suicide and distress in trans communities due to the backdrop of moral panic and commonplace experiences of bullying, family rejection, discrimination and/or being treated as unintelligible. It's very hard to get anyone other than specifically LGBTQ+ journalists to treat such issues as newsworthy.

Judith Butler's recent work is also important in revealing the wider sociopolitical context in which this difficult conversation is happening, particularly in relation to global backlashes against the rights of both women and LGBT+ people.

Róisín: **What might we learn from this conversation to inform all difficult conversations?**
Meg-John: I would love to see everyone engaging with emotions and lived experience, rather than endeavouring to detach intellectual/political debate from feeling, and taking positions on groups without being informed by connection with the actual humans involved and what they're going through. Doing our individual and collective work around trauma seems essential to this.

My main suggestion for practitioners who want to work across gender diversity is that they engage in deep self-reflection on their own experience of gender and how this impacts their lives and practice. Many intersectional feminists have argued that we need to explore deeply our positioning across all axes of injustice – including global and climate injustice – and how that operates in us. They also suggest that we need to learn how to be with our experiences – and capacities – as both victims/survivors and as abusers/oppressors. Much harm comes from believing that we're only capable of being victim or rescuer, not perpetrator or bystander, and from clinging tight to this belief, defending against any suggestion to the contrary. Beth Berila's work usefully brings together various embodied practices and contemplative pedagogies for enabling people to process the challenging feelings such explorations inevitably bring up.

We might explore the temptation – within ourselves and our communities – to focus our energy on fighting a 'near enemy' who we can see and name, rather than on addressing wider interlinked systems of oppression, understandable though this is when such desperately painful feelings are present, and when we long to feel some kind of empowerment when operating from such a disempowered place.

We might also think carefully about the tactics we use to address these issues, informed by Audre Lorde's famous line that 'the master's tools will never dismantle the master's house'. Can we find ways to oppose abuse and oppression – towards anyone – which do not perpetuate abuse or oppression? Can we move towards shame-competent and trauma-sensitive engagement, recognising that policing and punishing people may well harm them and/or make them – and others – more defended and rigid, less likely or able to engage wisely and compassionately?

Having written this, I'm also painfully aware of how hard it is to convey feelings in the way I wanted to in writing. I still feel like I'm stumbling and stammering to do so as I was in that interview last year. Perhaps – to *get* it on a visceral level – we need to hear the exhaustion in our voices as we talk around this territory for the hundredth time, to witness the tears during the silent vigils on trans day of remembrance, to observe the moments of breakdown and terror which we generally keep to ourselves, and which feel so dangerous to share in this climate. I'm deeply grateful to trans creatives like Travis Alabanza and CN Lester, who've managed to convey these kinds of feelings through their art and performance.

Róisín: **Finally, where can people go if they want to find out more about all this?**
Meg-John: I'd recommend the following, several of which I've mentioned in this chapter, as well as other work by the people mentioned in this list:
Meg-John: Much gratitude to H Howitt, Helen Spandler and Ellis Johnson for our ongoing conversations on these subjects which continue to inform my thinking greatly.

Bibliograhy

Alabanza, T (2022) *None of the Above: Reflections on Life Beyond the Binary*. London: Canongate.

Ahmed, S (2021) Gender Critical = Gender Conservative. *Feminist Killjoys*, 31st October 2021.
Barker, M-J (2017) A trans review of 2017: the year of transgender moral panic. *The Conversation*, 27th December 2017.
Barker, M-J (2017) *BACP Good Practice in Action Fact Sheet 095: Gender, sexual, and relationship diversity (GSRD)*. London: British Association of Counselling & Psychotherapy.
Barker, M. J. and Iantaffi, A (2019) *Life Isn't Binary: On being both, beyond, and in-between*. London: Jessica Kingsley Publishers.
Barker, M-J. and Scheele, J (2019) *Gender: A graphic guide*. London: Icon Books.
Berila, B (2015) *Integrating Mindfulness into Anti-oppression Pedagogy: Social justice in higher education*. London: Routledge.
Butler, J (2021) Why is the idea of 'gender' provoking backlash the world over? *The Guardian*, 23rd October 2021.
Cardoso, D (2021) Interview with Meg-John Barker. *Sexualities* 24(8): 1081–1099.
Choudrey, S (2022) *Supporting Trans People of Colour: How to make your practice inclusive*. London: Jessica Kingsley Publishers.
Faye, S (2021) *The Transgender Issue*. London: Penguin.
Feder, S. and Scholder, A (2020) *Disclosure: Trans lives on screen*. Available from: netflix.com/title/81284247.
Gergen, K (2015) *An Invitation to Social Constructionism*. London: Sage.
Gill-Peterson, J (2018) *Histories of the Transgender Child*. Minneapolis, MN: University Of Minnesota Press.
Heyam, K (2022) *Before We Were Trans*. London: Hachette.
Howitt, H (2022) *How We Fuck and Unfuck The World: Intimacy as method in trans sex research*. Available from www.youtube.com/watch?v=gfEBhfhePdk.
Iantaffi, A (2020) *Gender Trauma: Healing cultural, social, and historical gendered trauma*. London: Jessica Kingsley Publishers.
Iantaffi, A. and Barker, M-J (2017) *How to Understand Your Gender: A practical guide for exploring who you are*. London: Jessica Kingsley.
Lester, C. N (2017) *Trans Like Me: A journey for all of us*. London: Hachette.
Lorde, A (2018) *The Master's Tools Will Never Dismantle the Master's House*. London: Penguin.
Mackey, F (2021) *Attacking Stonewall for defending trans rights is a slippery slope*. The Guardian, 20th December 2021.
Pearce, R (2020) *A methodology for the marginalised: Surviving oppression and traumatic fieldwork in the neoliberal academy*. Sociology 54(4): 806–824.
Rickett, B. Craig, G. and Thompson, L. O (2013) *'Bad wigs and bed wetters': Constructions of gender and class in trans-popular discourse*. Psychology of Women's Section, British Psychological Society Annual Conference. Windsor, UK.
Roche, J (2019) *Trans power: Own your gender*. London: Jessica Kingsley Publishers.
Serano, J (2013) *Excluded: Making feminist and queer movements more inclusive*. New York, NY: Seal Press.

Spandler, H (2022) *Beyond the TERF wars*. Asylum: the radical mental health magazine. Winter 2022.29:1: 4–5.

Stryker, S. and McCarthy Blackston, D (Eds) (2022) *The Transgender Studies Reader Remix*. London: Routledge.

Vincent, B., Erikainen, S. and Pearce, R (Eds) (2020) *TERF Wars: Feminism and the fight for transgender futures*. London: Sage.

2 Facing uneasiness in feminist research

The case of female genital cutting[1]

Kathy Davis

Introduction

Female genital cutting[2] arouses a range of strong feelings – from the vicarious 'ouch' at the imagined pain of the actual practice, to feeling uncomfortable that women engage in practices that are harmful or demeaning, to worries about the role of culture in genital cutting. When I told my colleagues and friends that I was writing about the subject of female genital cutting, their invariable reaction was to gasp, look horrified, and add a disbelieving 'Oh?!' It was as though no one in her right mind would willingly want to immerse herself in a subject like that. The mere mention of female genital cutting – whether it is labiaplasty, circumcision, hymen reconstruction, or trans-surgery – seems to evoke an involuntary, 'gut-level' reflex of shock and – in some cases – even revulsion.

In this chapter, I want to take a closer look at some of the uneasiness that arises around the subject of female genital cutting. Drawing on a specific debate among feminists about female genital circumcision of African women, I will explore some of the ways embodied, affective responses to the practice are ignored, silenced, or censured. I will analyze how the denial of uncomfortable emotions stands in the way of a critical feminist response to genital cutting, obstructing the difficult conversations that are necessary for understanding what is at stake in the practice. In conclusion, I will argue that feminist scholars might use discomfort as a resource for critical inquiry.

A feminist debate

In 2004, the well-known journal *Feminist Theory* initiated a debate around the subject of African female circumcision. Several feminist scholars were invited to respond to an article written by Wairimũ Ngaruiya Njambi in which she criticized Western feminist anti-FGM discourse (Female Genital Mutilation) on female circumcision in Africa. Using her own experiences as a circumcised woman and as a US-based scholar who is well-versed in feminist theory, she problematized the way African women were represented in feminist discourse about female circumcision. She concluded that Western feminists would do well to listen to what African women have to say about female circumcision before assuming they know what is best for them.

DOI: 10.4324/9781003088417-4

The editors of the journal invited several feminist scholars, myself included, to respond to the article, indicating, somewhat vaguely, that it was an article that perhaps should not stand alone and that it would be good to have some responses in place before publishing it. Reading the article, I immediately realized that the journal's hesitation had nothing to do with the (academic) quality of the article (which was excellent), but rather that it was too controversial to be published on its own. What was controversial about it was, however, not mentioned, let alone further explained.

In my response, I did what the other commentators did as well – namely, to applaud Njambi for her critique of how poorly informed Western feminists have been about the differences in the practice of genital cutting. We heartily agreed with her assessment that anti-FGM discourse often reproduces colonialist stereotypes of 'savage' or 'barbaric' societies in need of a civilizing mission from the Western world. We also confirmed her critique that assumptions of normalcy that relegate the circumcised body to the abnormal and pathological were, indeed, arrogant and Eurocentric. And finally, we were in absolute consensus that feminists in the West needed to listen to the voices of women who engage in genital cutting, to take a self-critical look at their own histories of colonialism and racism, and to treat female circumcision as a cultural body practice, not inherently different nor more reprehensible than other cultural practices aimed at shaping femininity through the alteration of the body.

Despite all this unabashed consensus, our responses displayed unmistakable traces of uneasiness. For example, one commentator noted that while she was 'moved' by the combination of personal narrative and historical contextualization in Njambi's article, she found herself searching for something she 'couldn't quite find' and engaging in an 'obsessive re-reading of the article' (Casteñeda, 2004: 311, 314). She explained that she, too, was critical of Western feminist anti-FGM discourse, but at the same time, she felt the need to open some space for less-than-positive experiences of women who have been cut, as well as for the local activists who might be opposed to the practice. Another commentator explained that while she agreed with Njambi's critique of Western anti-FGM discourse, she also found herself saying, 'YES, BUT ...' (Henry-Waring, 2004: 318). She explained that her 'gut response' made it hard to view some practices of genital cutting as acceptable. At the same time, however, she worried that this could be due to her position as an outsider who was perhaps just importing her own beliefs (319). She ended with a somewhat lame call for 'dialogue'. And last but not least, my own response, which – to my surprise and dismay, now that I look back on it – entirely avoided my emotional response to Njambi's account. I adopted a comfortable meta-position in which I framed both the presence and absence of feminist outrage about female genital cutting as a political problem. I argued that the absence of an emotional response would indicate a lack of compassion or a denial of the suffering of others, representing the self-serving inability to imagine (or feel with) the plight of those regarded as 'Other', which is endemic to the Western world (see, for example, Cohen, 2001). A transnational feminist politics of engagement – one which would be both sympathetic (not guilty of cultural relativism and indifference), but also critically reflexive (and, therefore, not culturally imperialistic) – was what was needed. In short, I talked about the emotional responses of others without saying anything about my own.

While the other two commentators at least gave some indication of their discomfort and hesitation, my response was strangely disembodied and devoid of any personal uneasiness about the subject of genital cutting. Moreover, we were all quick to shelter behind our enthusiastically shared critique of anti-FGM discourse. All of us, in different ways, seemed to find it easier to adopt a critical stance toward Western feminist debates on female genital cutting than to explore our own embodied reactions to a narrative that presented female circumcision as a positive and beneficial experience. We made no mention of any uneasiness we might have felt at Njambi's insistence that she had not been coerced into circumcision and, indeed, had to threaten to run away from home before her Catholic parents relented and allowed her to be circumcised (Njambi, 2004: 294). Nor did we comment on her contention that circumcision should be viewed as a decision, albeit one which is taken within the 'realm of cultural possibility' (283).[3] Looking back on the debate, I would argue now that all of us, despite our support for Njambi's critique, also had reason to feel some discomfort about her account. It is to this discomfort that I will now turn.

The 'Ew! Factor'

In the prize-winning book *Genital Cutting and Transnational Sisterhood*, which she edited with Stanlie James, Claire Robertson takes a critical look at the reactions of shock and revulsion among Western women toward female genital cutting and the indignation and anger they provoked among women in Africa and the Middle East (James and Robertson, 2002). She calls these reactions to genital cutting the 'Ew! Factor'. Ew! is the sound of disgust often made by Western audiences when the subject of female genital cutting is raised (Robertson, 2002: 54). It expresses the imagined pain of the cut, the horror at the gaping wound, and the disgust at the flow of blood.[4] It is a spontaneous manifestation of an unease that cannot be suppressed. Bubbling up from below the surface of their political commitments to anti-racist, anti-colonial politics, Western audiences can't seem to help but say 'Ew!'

In retrospect, I would argue that the avoidance and ambivalence within our responses as commentators to Njambi's article are an illustration of what Robertson meant by the 'Ew! Factor' in Western feminist debates about female genital cutting. The embodied emotions which female genital cutting – along with a host of other practices which women engage in that are painful and harmful yet are fervently desired, disturbing, and yet passionately defended – can evoke, is pushed under the table as irrelevant to the more important business of criticizing the discourses and practices of colonialist, racist, and Eurocentric Western feminism. In this way, these emotions become peripheral to feminist engagement with female genital cutting and are not subjected in their own right to further analysis and critique.

This disconnect between emotions and feminist critique is not inevitable. In fact, feminist scholarship has often explored the essential role of feelings in feminist knowledge production and political activism (Gorton, 2007; Tyler, 2008; Pedwell and Whitehead, 2012). Feminist scholarship has always been concerned with the ways that emotions shape feminist politics. Initially, it was assumed that feminism (politics and theory) were inevitably 'suffused with feelings, passions, and emotions' (Gorton, 2007: 333). Many feminist scholars have tried to find ways to bring together the analysis of emotion, feeling, and affect with the more conventional forms of discursive (ideological) critique that have been the hallmark of feminist scholarship.

Initially, feminist scholars tended to focus on feelings that were positive for feminism. For example, Alison Jaggar (1989) argued that 'outlaw emotions,' which were incompatible with dominant perceptions and values, were essential for feminism. Thus, anger at sexual harassment was positive because it could provide a valuable motor for feminist protest (Jaggar, 1989: 160). In a similar vein, care, often associated with undervalued tasks like housework and childcare, was redefined as a basis for feminist ethics (Tronto, 1994; Held, 2006), while the feeling of love, so long integral to women's subservient position *vis-à-vis* men, was taken up as a useful resource for feminist epistemology and politics (Rose, 1994). In recent years, however, feminist scholars have been less inclined to look for positive 'feminist' emotions and have instead turned their attention to the ways positive emotions get distorted and can even disrupt feminist politics.

In what follows, I will take a closer look at some of the ways feminist scholars have proposed to understand affective discomfort. I will apply this work to the debate mentioned earlier in which the unease about female circumcision was avoided. My intention is not to criticize the participants in this debate, all of whom were clearly trying to engage in a critical, reflexive, and constructive discussion about a difficult subject. However, I will show how the avoidance of an explicit analysis of the uncomfortable emotions the subject of genital cutting evokes was a missed opportunity for a dialogue that could have provided space for differences, contradictions, and the inevitable messiness in the meanings of bodily practices which are both harmful and fervently desired.

Politics and feelings

The philosopher Sara Ahmed has played a key role in theorizing the importance of emotion for feminist (and queer) politics. She has always been skeptical that positive feelings such as love, care, and sympathy are necessarily empowering for feminism (2004, 2008, 2010). The moral outrage that many Western feminists have expressed at the practice of female genital cutting and their desire to express solidarity with its victims is an example of what could be called a 'good feminist feeling.' Ahmed (2008) is, however, distrustful of such feelings in general, and favours acknowledging the – for some of us – uncomfortable realities of others' lives. As she puts it, we all should be thinking more about how injuries stay alive rather than assuming that good feelings will simply make them disappear (Ahmed, 2004: 16). This means attending to the ugly, non-cathartic feelings and states that evoke irritation, anxiety, or avoidance. In her opinion, we need to embrace feelings of discomfort not only because they indicate a lack of ease with available heteronormative and ethnocentric scripts, but also because they signal 'excitement in the face of the uncertainty of where the discomfort may take us' (Ahmed, 2004: 155).

In her pivotal book *The Cultural Politics of Emotion* (2004), she shows how 'bad' or unpleasant emotions like shame, disgust, hate, and fear circulate in the public sphere where they become attached or 'stick' to particular bodies or objects, thereby shaping interactions between bodies. Disgust (or what I have been referring to as an ingredient of the 'Ew!' factor) is a good example of such a 'sticky' emotion. Something which is disgusting both attracts and repels. It attracts because we can't stop ourselves from looking at it. We find ourselves constantly coming back to the very things that repel us and, indeed, the enormous attention paid to FGM by Western feminists attests to this attraction. As a subject, it fascinates to such a degree that it has become attached to representations of the oppressed 'Third World woman.' (Gunning, 1991; James and Robertson, 2005; Pedwell, 2007). Disgust not only attracts us to an object; at the same time, it pulls us away and it does so in a way that may feel completely involuntary and outside our conscious control. The spontaneous 'Ew!' which follows the mention of female genital cutting is an example of such a reaction. It is almost as if our bodies are thinking for us, on behalf of us. According to Ahmed, it is precisely this disgust that prevents us from getting close to what has already been designated as a 'bad' thing (Ahmed, 2004: 99). (Think about the nervous skittishness which we as commentators displayed toward Njambi's narrative of her own circumcision. We circled around her narrative, unable to let it go, and yet the closer we came, the more our bodies seemed to pull us back into the comforts of a more discursive feminist critique.)

In short, Ahmed's theory of emotions provides a valuable theoretical framework for approaching the relationship between emotions and feminist politics. She makes a strong case that emotions should not be avoided just because they make us feel uncomfortable. On the contrary, 'bad feelings' are precisely the ones that feminists should be embracing. Unfortunately, Ahmed does not provide much practical help in how to put her theoretical insights into the cultural politics of emotions into practice. We are left with the problem of how actually to analyze feelings as embodied, lived experiences.

Analyzing gut-level responses

The feminist theorist Iris Marion Young (1990) provides a promising starting point for including embodied or 'gut-level' emotions in feminist analysis.[5] She used phenomenology to explore typically feminine bodily experiences like throwing a ball or breastfeeding or pregnancy to understand how discourses of gender and bodily experiences are mutually constitutive. In an essay on what she called the 'aesthetic scaling of bodies,' she daringly explored the gut-level feelings which accompany reactions of aversion, disgust, nervousness, or stereotyping in encounters with bodies perceived as different (Young, 1990: 134). The essay is daring because Young showed that a commitment to social justice and equality does not make the gut-level feelings related to sexism, racism, ageism, homophobia, and Eurocentrism go away. Rather than disappearing in the face of progressive politics, they go underground, where they dwell in habitual and unconscious fears and aversions that define politics in ways of which we are not aware (124). Thus, Young shows how it is possible for white Western feminists to decry the ills of cultural imperialism and the stigmatization of black bodies in all sincerity and yet feel uncomfortable and threatened when confronted with differences in bodies and cultural bodily practices. Since such feelings are often perceived by the subject herself as undesirable and even shameful, they are subject to suppression in order to prevent cognitive dissonance with cherished feminist identities and political ideals.

Drawing upon Kristeva's notion of abjection, Young argues that feelings become threatening when something is experienced as close enough to constitute a menace. It has to be 'just on the other side of the border . . . too close for comfort' (Young, 1990: 144). The very mention of female genital cutting can evoke such 'border anxiety'. For example, border anxiety can occur when a person imagines what it might feel like to be cut or how her circumcised body would look or what a circumcision would mean for her sexual practices. At the same time, a person may distance herself from female circumcision by labeling it a product of a (barbaric) culture and pushing the circumcised woman away as someone who is comfortingly 'other'.[6] The 'Ew!' represents a gut-level feeling which is structured by abjection, a spontaneous utterance slips out, escaping rational control. I would argue that, for example, Njambi's positioning of herself as a happily circumcised woman AND as an active, sexual feminist subject made us as commentators uncomfortable and even a little nervous. Our cognitive desire to be respectful of her experiences and take her reasons seriously collided with our gut-level feelings of anxiety and confusion, and maybe even a hint of disgust at the practice itself.

According to Young, such feelings need to be brought out into the open. Just because gut-level feelings are habitual or semi-conscious does not make them innocent or unproblematic. In fact, gut-level feelings can wreak havoc with our discursively held convictions and lead to abuses of power, whether we wish this or not. An example of such havoc was provided by Njambi herself in her reply to the comments on her article. She described an earlier occasion where she presented a similar paper in a feminist graduate student conference and was asked by the chair to withdraw her presentation because it offered far too positive a view of female circumcision. She writes: 'I felt sad, silenced, and lonely in the midst of other presenters who appeared to me to be so lucky for choosing uncontroversial topics' (Njambi, 2004a: 325). Here she expresses the problematic effects that denial and gestures of silencing have on those who (courageously) attempt to open up discussions about differences in bodily experiences and practices. Although Njambi complimented us as commentators in the *Feminist Theory* discussion for being so 'open to dialogue,' she also added that none of us had addressed what she considered to be her 'main point': namely, differences in women's bodies, bodily experiences and sexualities, and the assumption that circumcision is always harmful (Njambi, 2004a: 326–327). In that sense, our openness to her critique of anti-FGM discourse and our refusal to acknowledge our discomfort concerning her circumcision may well have been experienced by her as the kind of denial or silencing of experience which can – as Young points out – make a member of a marginalized or oppressed group 'feel slightly crazy' (1990: 134).

In conclusion, Iris Young takes the exploration of emotions and politics a step further, by showing how to think about the relationship between gut-level feelings – feelings that are unintended, habitual, and unconscious – and consciously held discursive political convictions. We cannot always prevent unconscious reactions, habits, and stereotypes from cropping up, but we can take responsibility for them after the fact, explore the ways they sustain and enact power inequalities, and submit them to reflection and analysis (Young, 1990: 150–51). Ultimately, however, Young wants to change those gut-level feelings that are sabotaging progressive feminist, anti-racist politics. She seems to suggest that getting our gut-level feelings out into the open and taking responsibility for them will inevitably lead to change. But how easy is it to change feelings?

Changing 'ugly feelings'

Clare Robinson's (2002) solution to Western feminist debates about genital circumcision among African women is to 'get beyond the 'Ew! Factor.' She has criticized the anti-FGM debate for what she calls the Rs: reducing all of Africa to one uncivilized place, reducing African women to their genitals, reducing Africans to victims or perpetrators, and reducing all genital cutting to infibulation. In her view, getting beyond these reductions would require: contextualizing the practices of genital cutting in different places with different histories, seeing African women as more than their genitals (i.e. they can be cut and still be happy/strong/productive, etc.), listening to their voices rather than subsuming them under the categories of victim or perpetrator, and finding out more about the actual practices (i.e. some are more damaging than others; all circumcision does not necessarily entail infibulation). In her view, a good feminist critique of female genital cutting would involve becoming informed about the history, context, and nature of the practice, deconstructing one's own stereotypes about the women who engage in it, and being more modest about what one can say about it.

There is nothing wrong with this as far as it goes. Indeed, much of recent Western feminist scholarship on female genital cutting would agree wholeheartedly with this critique (Gunning, 1991; Meyers, 2000; Weil Davis, 2002; see also, Pedwell, 2007). However, while Robertson believes that reactions of disgust, incredulity, and curiosity are a hindrance to feminist critique, she does not have much to say about how one can actually 'get beyond' them.

Sianne Ngai (2005) is instructive here. She argues that feminists need to pay more attention to the 'ugly feelings' and their negative consequences for feminism. In her view, feminism has too often used its ideals to shame and exclude other women who fall short of or do not subscribe to them. Women are forced to embody particular ideals if they are to pass into feminism. This universalistic tendency among Western feminists has been problematized by the critics of anti-FGM discourse, who have argued that the ideals of bodily integrity, autonomy, and the norm of the 'natural' body have been used to inspire outrage among Western women against the practice of female genital cutting among African women. As Njambi's article nicely shows, these are precisely the ideals that have squelched possibilities for dialogues with African women concerning genital cutting as – under some conditions – a desirable and beneficial practice. These ideals have also left circumcised African women feeling demeaned, excluded, and 'othered' by Western critics of genital cutting.

As we saw in the debate about Njambi's article, strong emotions do not necessarily disappear with the right kind of information and a shared critical analysis. All the commentators were aware of the differences and degrees in female genital cutting and each one agreed wholeheartedly with Njambi's critique of Western feminist anti-FGM discourse. Yet did we really 'get beyond' the 'Ew! factor'? I would argue that we did not. Instead, we skirted the discomfort the article evoked, waffled about our feelings, and eagerly placed ourselves on the firmer ground of discursive feminist critique.

How might the debate on the pages of *Feminist Theory* have been different if we had owned up to and tried to analyze our own 'ugly feelings' and discomfort rather than retreating to the more familiar discursive level of feminist politics? What if we, the commentators, had explored our restlessness, our uneasiness, and our desire to say 'yes, BUT . . .' in more detail? We might have been less worried or apologetic about our feelings and instead treated them as a valuable resource, something to be taken seriously in their own right. And – in my own case as the commentator who was least forthcoming about her own feelings – I might have questioned why I felt compelled to take a meta-position in the debate about female genital cutting, a position which allowed me to separate myself both from Western feminists with their arrogant meddling into the affairs of African women and from Njambi, who wanted 'us' just to 'back off.' Instead, I might have confronted the shame of being a Western feminist with all the historically-based complicities with racism and colonialism that that entails. Or I might have acknowledged the fear of having no role to play in this struggle, of being, as it were, caterwauled out of feminist political activism around female genital cutting. But, perhaps most important of all, I could have faced the anxiety provoked by the knowledge that some women really do embrace practices that I find upsetting yet that make perfect sense to them, given the circumstances of their lives. It is to this particular anxiety – one which evokes a kind of *déjà vu* in retrospect – to which I will now turn.

Contradictory practices and feminist balancing acts

Many years ago I wrote a study about (Western) women's involvement with cosmetic surgery (Davis, 1995). This was well before the advent of Western forms of female genital cutting such as labiaplasty and vaginal 'rejuvenation' surgery, yet the operations that women I interviewed undertook 'in the name of beauty' seemed plenty problematic to me at the time. I was critical of cosmetic surgery as a particularly pernicious expression of feminine beauty culture, reproducing patriarchal ideologies of feminine inferiority and the Western obsession with the makeability of the body. I saw, as did many feminists at the time, cosmetic surgery as a way – literally – to 'cut women down to size.' At the same time, however, I could not get around the fact that many women fervently desired cosmetic surgery and defended it as their best option under the circumstances. While many feminist scholars at the time regarded such women as duped victims who had been lulled into surgery by false media promises, sexist male partners, and knife-hungry surgeons, I found these explanations unsatisfactory because they robbed the recipients of cosmetic surgery of any agency. I therefore opted for an approach to women's involvement in cosmetic surgery that:

> balanced on the razor's edge of a feminist critique of cosmetic surgery along with the discourses of feminine inferiority which sustain it and an equally feminist desire to treat women who have cosmetic surgery as agents who negotiate their bodies and their lives within the social and cultural constraints in which they live.
> (Davis, 1995: 5; Davis, 2003: 14–15)

What would such a 'balancing act' mean in the case of my discomfort with female genital cutting as Njambi describes it, and my desire to criticize the arrogant colonialist overtones of Western feminist discourse that refuses to acknowledge differences in bodies and bodily practices?

For one thing, it would mean a willingness to explore the deep-seated unease, apprehension, and ambivalence that female genital cutting evokes. This discomfort provides an opportunity for trying to make sense of why and under what circumstances women and girls become circumcised. While many girls are too young to be in a position to freely decide to undergo circumcision, some women, as was the case with Njambi, appear to willingly and actively choose to have it. It is relatively easy to take a uniformly critical stance against female genital cutting in cases where minors are involved and there can be no question of informed consent. More difficult and much more disconcerting for me, however, is trying to understand how and why a woman might desire genital cutting as something positive and beneficial. And yet, this is precisely what I need to be able to understand if I want to engage with the practice of female genital cutting and the viewpoints that sustain it. It is my contention that the exploration of my own discomfort here might allow me to rethink some of my own views about what a 'normal' body is – something Njambi missed in the critical comments on her article. Why do I find certain practices (female genital cutting) less acceptable than other, equally but differently, harmful ones (breast augmentations, tattoos, navel piercings and, for that matter, male circumcision)? In what ways do my own cultural obsessions (with autonomy and 'natural-ness') shape my perceptions about bodies and bodily practices? Perhaps, as Njambi suggests, there is no one 'normal' body and certainly no 'natural body,' but only a multitude of variations in bodily practices. But most importantly, I could use discomfort to keep the discussion open rather than close it down through the 'politics of the correct line.' Drawing upon the philosopher Paul Ricoeur's et al. (1999: 12) ethics of conflict, I might become wary of consensus, find danger in assumptions of shared identity and identical histories, and regard living in conflict as a desirable form of practical wisdom, making a debate about female genital cutting an opportunity to engage in 'reasonable disagreement.' In practice, this would have meant that we as commentators would not have been so eager embrace the critique of Western feminism and anti-FGM discourse at the expense of what we were unsure about or did not agree with. We might have asked Njambi to reflect on her assumptions and to think critically about some of the missing pieces in her position. In other words, we would have actively looked for the ways we differ and, in so doing, remained in dialogue with one another.

In defense of uneasiness in feminist research

Using a specific feminist debate on female genital cutting, I have explored some of the ways feminist scholars deal with (or refrain from dealing with) their feelings of uneasiness and discomfort. In order to do this, I drew upon the work of several feminist thinkers (Ahmed, Young, Ngai) on emotions as well as my own earlier research on cosmetic surgery to think about what was left out, avoided, or silenced in this debate. I have tried to show how, despite our best attempts to engage in a critical, reflexive, and open discussion about female genital cutting, we missed an opportunity for a dialogue that might have provided space for difficult but necessary conversations about differences, contradictions, and the inevitable messiness of bodily practices which are both harmful and fervently desired.

I have argued for an approach to female genital cutting which does not dismiss the embodied 'ouch' that accompanies (Western) feminist reactions, but rather treats it as a resource. I have concentrated primarily on the unease and discomfort which is part of this response. Yet there is also a deep sense of despair that accompanies this discomfort – sympathy regarding the consequences many forms of genital cutting have for women's sexuality and health – as well as solidarity with the women who undergo the practice. While sympathy is not a sufficient precondition for an informed dialogue about genital cutting, neither is this feeling irrelevant. Nor do I agree that Western feminist outrage at female genital cutting among African women that has been so strongly criticized can be reduced to nothing more than the arrogant 'refusal to acknowledge differences.' An absence of outrage may also indicate a lack of compassion or a denial of the suffering of others and thereby represent the self-serving inability to imagine (or feel with) those regarded as 'Other.' The lack of compassion or sympathy that is already so endemic to the Western world also requires critique (see, for example, Cohen, 2001). As Sandra Bartky (2002) has convincingly argued, Western feminists not only need to acknowledge and appreciate the differences and divisions among women, but they also need to find ways to overcome self-interest, indifference to the plight of others, as well as despondency and inertia concerning possibilities for change. To do this, it is necessary to enter imaginatively into the worlds of others without 'stretching these Others on the Procrustean bed of . . . (one's) own experience' (Bartky, 2002: 83).

In conclusion, there can be no feminism without feelings. We need to integrate all kinds of feelings – disgust, anger, and shame, but also attraction, sympathy, and compassion – into our scholarship. Feelings should not be an obstacle, but rather an opportunity and resource for feminist scholarship that is critical, reflexive, and – above all – open to the messy contradictions of women's lives as well as feminist politics.

Notes

1 This chapter appeared in a slightly different version in *Body, Migration, Re/Constructive Surgeries. Making the Gendered Body in a Globalized World*, edited by Gabriele Griffin and Malin Jordan (London: Routledge, 2019).
2 I prefer female genital cutting to 'female genital mutilation,' which obscures the agency of women who participate in the practice. 'Genital surgery' medicalizes the practice, while 'circumcision' underplays risks, pain, and impairment (see Meyers, 2000).
3 Njambi describes her desire to be circumcised as 'just wanting to become a woman' with all the pleasures and privileges that go along with it. She admits, however, that if she were growing up today in Kenya, she might not have the same desire to be circumcised as she did in the 1960s and 1970s (Njambi, 2004: 297).
4 Yet these reactions hardly stand alone. They have been shaped by media images of innocent and unsuspecting African girls waiting to have their genitals ceremonially cut (http://sokodirectory.com/2016/06/where-female-genital-mutilation-still-reigns/, accessed 8 June 2016) or photographs of genital cutting replete with rusty razors, screaming victims, and traumatized survivors (https://answersafrica.com/top-10-reasons-why-female-genital-mutilation-in-africa-is-evil.html, accessed 20 November 2017). Such images make it difficult to imagine circumcision as something which might be regarded as a positive coming-of-age ritual, as Njambi argues.
5 Interestingly, Young's work on emotion predates not only Ahmed, but also the recent 'affective turn' in critical feminist theory. I have argued elsewhere that it is unfortunate that her phenomenological writing on gut-level emotions as well as the work of other early feminist theorists has not been taken up by more recent feminist theory on affect (Davis, 2017).
6 In contrast, the body modifications involving cutting or piercing the skin that many Western women engage in are made more acceptable by the familiar discourses of beauty, where women learn that beauty usually hurts. For a popular version of this discourse, see the song and video of 'Pretty Hurts,' recorded by the US singer Beyoncé, in which she criticizes women's willingness to endure physical and mental anguish in order to meet the norms of feminine beauty (www.youtube.com/watch?v=LXXQLa-5n5w). For more scholarly feminist critiques of women's involvement in the beauty system, see Wolf (1990), Davis (1995), Brand (2000), and Etcoff (2000).

References

Ahmed, S (2004) *The Cultural Politics of Emotion*. Edinburgh: Edinburgh University Press.
Ahmed, S (2008) The Politics of Good Feeling. *ACRAWSA-e Journal* 4(1): 1–18.
Ahmed, S (2010) Killing joy: Feminism and the history of happiness. *Signs* 35(3): 571–594.
Bartky, S (2002) *'Sympathy and Solidarity' and other Essays*. Lanham: Rowman & Littlefield.
Brand, P.Z (2000) *Beauty Matters*. Bloomington: Indiana University Press.

Casteñeda, C (2004) Entering the dialogue. *Feminist Theory* 5(3): 311–317.
Cohen, S (2001) *States of Denial: Knowing about Atrocities and Suffering*. Cambridge: Polity Press.
Davis, K (1995) *Reshaping the Female Body: The Dilemma of Cosmetic Surgery*. New York: Routledge.
Davis, K (2003) *Dubious Equalities and Embodied Differences: Cultural Studies on Cosmetic Surgery*. Lanham: Rowman & Littlefield.
Davis, K (2017) Passion. In J. C. Nash (ed.) *Gender: Love. Macmillan Interdisciplinary Handbooks*. Farmington Hills: Macmillan Reference USA (pp. 81–91).
Etcoff, N (2000) *The Survival of the Prettiest: The Science of Beauty*. New York: Anchor Books.
Gorton, K (2007) Theorizing emotion and affect: Feminist engagements. *Feminist Theory* 8(3): 333–348.
Gunning, I.R (1991) Arrogant perception, World-travelling and Multicultural feminism: The case of female genital surgeries. *Columbia Human Rights Law Review* 23: 189–248.
Held, V (2006) The Ethics of Care. New York: Oxford University Press.
Henry-Waring, M (2004) Commentary. *Feminist Theory* 5(3): 317–323.
James, S.M. and Robertson, C.C (2005) *Genital Cutting and Transnational Sisterhood: Disputing U.S. Polemics*. Urbana: University of Illinois Press.
Meyers, D.T (2000) Feminism and women's autonomy: The challenge of female genital cutting. *Metaphilosophy* 31(5): 469–491.
Ngai, S (2005) *Ugly Feelings*. Cambridge: Harvard University Press.
Njambi, W.N (2004a) Dualisms and female bodies in representations of african female circumcision. *Feminist Theory* 5(3): 281–303.
Njambi, W.N (2004b) A reply: A discourse in transition. *Feminist Theory* 5(3): 325–328.
Pedwell, C (2007) Theorising "African" female genital cutting and "Western" body modification: A critique of the continuum and analogue apoproaches. *Feminist Review* 86: 45–66.
Pedwell, C. and Anne, W (2012) 'Affecting feminism: Questions of feeling in feminist theory. *Feminist Theory*, 13(2): 115–129.
Ricoeur, Paul with Brian Cosgrave, Gayle Freyne, David Scott, Imelda McCarthy, Redmond O'Hanlon, Brian Garvey, John Cleary, Margaret Kelleher, Dermot Moran. and Maeve Cooke (1999) Imagination, Testimony and Trust: A Dialogue with Paul Ricoeur. In R. Kearney and M. Dooley (eds.) *Questioning Ethics: Contemporary Debates in Philosophy*. London: Routledge (pp. 12–17).
Robertson, C.C (2002) Getting Beyond the Ew! Factor: Rethinking U.S. Approaches to African Female Genital Cutting. In S. M. James and C. C. Robertson (eds.) *Genital Cutting and Transnational Sisterhood: Disputing U.S. Polemics*. Urbana: University of Illinois Press (pp. 54–86).
Rose, H (1994) *Love, Power and Knowledge: Toward a Feminist Transformation of the Sciences*. Cambridge: Polity Press.
Tronto, J (1994) Moral Boundaries: A Political Argument for an Ethic of Care. New York: Routledge.
Tyler, I (2008) Methodological fatigue and the politics of the affective turn, *Feminist Media Studies* 8(1): 85–90.
Weil, D.S (2002) Loose lips sink ships, *Feminist Studies* 28(1): 7–35.
Wolf, N (1990) *The Beauty Myth: How Images of Beauty Are Used Against Women*. London: Chatto & Windus.
Young, I.M (1990) *Justice and the Politics of Difference*. Princeton: Princeton University Press.

3 Feminism and race in academia
An interview with Sandya Hewamanne

Sandya Hewamanne and Róisín Ryan-Flood

Firstly, thank you, Sandya, for participating in this book about difficult conversations and feminist dialogues

Róisín: What would you describe as the key intellectual concerns that run throughout your work?

Sandya: Thank you, Róisín, for inviting me to be part of this fabulous edited volume.

In one sentence: 'Gendered labor and human rights in an increasingly neoliberalizing world.' The area focus is the Global South. But as an anthropologist, I connect to Global South Studies and South to North connections via Sri Lanka and South Asia. My specific anthropological field sites are firstly global assembly lines in Sri Lanka, and then more recently, Bangladesh and Vietnam. Ethnographic studies at these venues provide data for my feminist political economic take on global value chains and capitalist hierarchy.

Recently, I have started developing a methodology which combines social justice activism with intellectual concerns and am waiting eagerly for the pandemic-related difficulties to ease so I can test a new approach I call 'measured intervention.'

Róisín: How did you come to have an academic career?

Sandya: I am not sure whether to give the shorter standardized version or the longer, funnier version. Going by a hunch, I'll go with the latter. I had always been good in school, always felt I needed more challenging schoolwork. I did not have a role model in my orbit who could have guided my sense of curiosity and already well-developed critical thinking abilities. I knew I would be selected to the university (a very difficult opportunity only provided to about 10% of the students who take the qualifying exam) in whatever stream of study I chose. After that, a blank space. I was worried that if there was no plan, then I would be expected to get a job as a teacher and then get married and so on and so forth. So, I hatched a plan to escape being pressured to marry early. I think it was when I was in Grade 10, I saw a newspaper clipping on

DOI: 10.4324/9781003088417-5

someone who had received a Fulbright fellowship to study in the USA. I like the word 'Fulbright.' Teachers always referred to me as a 'bright' girl. I had deceived myself into thinking that this meant the fellowship is for people who are full of brightness, like me. From then on, my ambition had been to get this fellowship and do a Masters in the US, and doing so to escape early marriage and continue with my intellectual explorations. The rest is kind of known history.

Róisín: An important aspect of your work is intersectionality. What are your thoughts on intersectionality and feminist theory?

Sandya: I was introduced to old-fashioned Western hegemonic feminism at the University of Colombo, Sri Lanka, where I did my undergraduate studies. I fell hard for early feminist writings as well as French feminist writings; in the context, at that time such one-dimensional analysis of gender inequalities made enormous sense, and I was very happy to have an existing body of literature to frame my own thinking of social justice and equality.

I experientially understood intersectionality before reading Kimberly Crenshaw and others. The understanding came to me through the differences I felt with second-generation South and East Asian women I sought to find sisterhood with when I first arrived in the US. Although we all identified as women and looked somewhat alike (South Asians, at least), our different childhood experiences, citizenship rights and social cultural capital positioned us differently. I found more solidarity with men who have migrated recently for studies. It did not help to know that the second-generation Asians called people like us FOBs (Fresh Off the Boat). This understanding led to a critical analysis on hegemonic feminism as Western-centric and somewhat clueless. There are huge improvements brought about by critical feminist thinkers who have refuted the sisterhood myth. Gloria Anzaldua, Norma Alarcon, Sandra Cisneros and the Chicana feminist movement have been very influential in bringing the awareness of differences among women and commonalities with men belonging to racial and sexual minorities and people with disabilities. Chela Sandoval and her theorization of US Third World Feminism opened many eyes to the fractions and power relations among differently positioned women. Chandra Mohanty and Kamala Visweswaran's writings build on these thoughts to show how in every society, women are positioned differently, making different groups of women join hands with men of their social class or ethnic minority group against other women.

I think it is crucial for feminist theory to embrace intersectionality and make it an integral part of analysis. It is important to not look for feminist homes; instead, to look for strategic collaborative opportunities with different groups of women.

Róisín: During your time at the University of Essex, you have co-founded the staff race equality forum. How did this come about?

Sandya: This came about through the sheer loneliness I felt for five years at Essex. Coming from a very liberal environment of a prestigious private university in the US, where institutional racial discrimination had been acknowledged and discussed often, I was flabbergasted by the non-acknowledgement of very clear (at least to me and the very few non-white academics) institutional racism. The university forged ahead as if racism was something that happened in the past and happens in the US. Not here, no way. To compensate, the university focused rather on amending gender disparities (as it should), forgetting that gender does not exist alone. Absence of intersectional perception was deafening.

When I joined, I was the only self-identified person of color in the Sociology department. Pretty soon, I became a victim of workplace bullying. There was no support system in place departmentally or university-wide that took race and ethnicity into account. It was in fact impossible for the university or individual departments to provide that support, as the all-important acknowledgement that racism exists and that it adversely affects the very few academic staff members of minority (BAME for lack of a better moniker) backgrounds had not happened.

The few discussions I had with other such academics showed how clueless the HR professionals were in handling complaints of racial bias and discrimination, and how they continued with highly problematic practices, such as appointing a single white male academic to investigate a complaint by a female BAME staff member, etc.

I co-founded the forum (with Hannah Gibson) to bring together self-identified BAME staff members (both academic and professional services) to not only support each other in difficult moments but to create a collective political voice fighting for anti-racist policies and practices, to help the university strategize the best ways to promote an anti-racist university. The staff forum was co-founded about six months before the infamous George Floyd murder in the US and the worldwide Black Lives Matter protests. This led to a self-reflection at the university level and an acknowledgement that institutional racism exists, resulting in a 'listening' phase (which allowed students, staff and alumni to report experiences of racial discrimination). A working group to tackle racism and to propose action toward an anti-racist university was formulated (Tackling Racism Working Group – TRWG). The BAME staff forum had been strongly represented in this group, and individual members contributed to the action plan for an anti-racist university that was formulated via weekly meetings. The forum members actively pushed for an external report on racism and had been involved with several other working groups in association with decolonizing the curriculum and Race Equality Charter, etc.

Although founded informally, within a year the forum became the official voice of BAME staff and we have regular meetings with the Vice Provost for education and EDI manager/staff, contributing to strategic action toward institutionalizing fair and equal policies and practices. I consider co-founding this forum as the biggest achievement of my academic career. This is one tangible moment that demonstrates the power of citizen action – if your specific experiences, challenges and difficulties are not recognized, then make those visible via collective organizing. There is strength in collective voice. Sooner or later, it becomes too noisy to ignore (still, thanks, Black Lives Matter!)

Róisín: What are your thoughts on being a POC within contemporary UK academia?

Sandya: Although it should be otherwise, UK academia for the most part reflects the attitudes of the wider society in which it is embedded. Since UK society seems to feel that because it abolished slave trade long before the US, it has a moral one-up on North America (never mind the long colonization of Asia and Africa), and that fair and equal laws alone lead to fair and equal opportunities; a reflection of that in academia makes POC within isolated, invisible and voiceless.

The shock that I described earlier in fact resulted from the very clear recognition that racism exists and that it is embedded in institutional structures that prevailed in US universities (at least in the social sciences) and the absence of such self-understanding within UK academia (at least as experienced at Essex prior to mid-2020). Again, my thoughts of how the University of Essex operated prior to BLM protests in 2020 is somewhat representative of how UK academia operated. It was great that self-searching and acknowledgement of institutional racism within the universities happened (despite the infamous Sewell report, which declared that no institutional racism exists in the UK). However, the proposed actions are slow to move ahead. Bureaucracy has changed only slightly. There is much to work toward in fostering an anti-racist university. The need for collective organizing among Black, Asian and Minority Ethnic academics, and the support of White allies are greater than ever, because this is the time to fight against complicity. Fight against token recognition of discrimination, crude understanding of diversity as numbers and narratives of equal opportunities to all, when the playing field is already historically skewed toward one group.

I strongly believe that the few POC have a big role to play in changing these circumstances for the future. During most of the voluntary work the BAME academic staff did with TRWG and other groups, a frequent complaint was how the existing BAME staff members are called upon to do an enormous amount of voluntary work in rectifying past wrongs done by other groups. We all felt that exhaustion, mostly because there were not enough BAME academics to share the burdens (I don't think I need to provide the glaringly low numbers of academics of BAME backgrounds here). Thus, I feel that we are the generation to take that burden and forge ahead in working toward meaningful diversification of UK academia. It is unfair that we have to do this voluntarily, for no personal gain, but that is the burden of the few who have made it despite barriers. This is at a very minor scale; but the march at Selma by MLK and civil rights activists comes to mind; someone needs to face the fire so that others can walk safely.

I also feel that our white colleagues have responsibilities too. Now I feel more comfortable in publicly talking about racial discrimination. But still, it is much more heard when discrimination is pointed out by white colleagues. Not to drown out other voices, but to be more vocal and to come up with creative, innovative ways to support initiatives for race equality and promote anti-racist university culture.

Róisín: There are notably few women professors of color in HE in the UK today. What steps do you think can be undertaken to change this?

Sandya: Just because the murder of George Floyd and BLM protests awakened academia to self-reflection and remedial action, qualified professionals of BAME backgrounds are not going to magically appear. Years of non-acknowledgement and the absence of specific positive affirmative action has seen to it that students from BAME backgrounds are doing less well in school, and entering universities in fewer numbers and dropping out in much larger numbers than others. People from BAME backgrounds ending up with poor housing, falling through cracks in welfare, health services, lack of transport facilities and care support had seen to it that fewer people of BAME backgrounds are going back to school later in life. Even the brightest who somehow managed to get into post-graduate programs find it difficult to get jobs in academia due to long-held prejudices. Even when they succeed, they are subjected to institutional racism resulting in such individuals not receiving the same support to thrive and succeed as others at the same level. Even among BAME academics, the situation is more difficult for women due to prejudices as well as almost non-existent support for carers.

Thus, to change this situation, changes ought to be undertaken at several levels, starting with political economic changes that would provide everyone with an equal chance to sustain a livelihood, which will allow families to better feed their kids and provide safe, healthy housing. This will automatically improve school performance. But school cultures, curriculum and extra-curricular activities all need to go through some carefully planned changes to include children from all ethnic groups and to provide fair and dignified grounds to succeed in their chosen fields. Validation and celebrating their diverse cultural backgrounds and life experiences starting from kindergarten is a must – mostly because it will mold non-BAME students' mindsets, allowing them to accept difference and appreciate diverse ways of being.

Some sort of an affirmative action where promising students of color are encouraged and supported to succeed at exams to enter grammar schools seems imperative. Financial support systems for them (especially if from working-class backgrounds) to attend clubs, camps, foreign tours and cultural activities that ultimately enhance their curiosity and critical thinking will lead to more academically oriented students who set their goals high. Of course, this leads to the beginning of the problem again – there are very few role models for them to find inspiration from. Perhaps this is a way for feminists to be involved – by doing public outreach activities with schoolchildren. This doesn't have to only be feminists of color; our white allies can develop workshops focusing on brilliant Black, Asian and Minority ethnic scholars and their contributions. It could be as simple as showing a film like 'Hidden Figures' and encouraging discussion.

I think the biggest interventions need to be made at undergraduate level. Again, a carefully thought-out affirmative action program seems to be crucial to support intelligent students of color to complete. Such students with clear aptitude for academia should then be encouraged (not only in words, but via financial support) to enroll in Masters programs. Full-program PhD scholarships – in the mold of the recently instituted SeNss widening participation scholarship – for students of color, especially from Black and Minority ethnic backgrounds, will be the key to changing this shameful lack of women professors of color in UK academia. This is even more shameful when you look at the numbers for Black women professors. For instance, until October 2021, there was only one Black woman professor at the University of Essex.

Not only for women academics of color but for any man or woman who is a carer, there needs to be more comprehensive institutional support. Such support will help retain women academics of color.

Róisín: Your work is centrally concerned with gender and economic inequality, and you have done extensive fieldwork with marginalized and vulnerable groups. What do you see as the responsibilities of the researcher when doing research on and with vulnerable populations?

Sandya: To be very careful to not cause further harm. To remember that these people are entrusting their stories of suffering, agony and trauma, not just for you to meet your career goals. They may not utter these things in so many words; but they expect their stories to be told, and to ensure that as many people as possible will hear. In other words, make sure to take your data to policy makers, fight for changes, and agitate for positive policy outcomes. If there are organic struggles within to agitate for changes, support in any way you can – be it making tea for the protestors or carrying supplies. If there are no struggles forthcoming due to extreme forms of hegemonic oppression, devise creative ways to plant seeds of desire for positive changes. Usually this can be done through democratic dialogue and educational activities. It is important to not enforce changes that YOU see fit. Let the cry for change emerge as grassroots movements by helping in small ways, such as facilitating the community members to meet and talk, etc. For it is not up to the researcher to determine what is empowerment, happiness or improvement for a specific group of people.

For this end, it is important to not TELL their stories, but to let the story EMERGE via the voices of the people. Try not to overpower the experiential quality of a story with analysis. It is important not to treat vulnerable populations as pathetic victims. It is ethnocentric to consider people who have been made structurally vulnerable as weak or victims with no resistance or fighting spirit. We just have to look carefully, as their vulnerability had rendered them unable to resist in obvious, conventional ways. The creative ways they protest/resist are intertwined within the moments of oppression in their everyday lives. It is our responsibility to figure out such moments and validate these creative means and bring it to the mainstream.

Again, going back to activism: lobbying at the global stage is where such groups would need a researcher to support their cause. This may be a place where people, especially if they are based in the non-Western world, may not have any voice or means of entering. Your world language skills, technical know-how and any reputational weight you have accumulated over time would be of much importance, and every researcher who writes so passionately about a group's vulnerability has a moral responsibility to engage in efforts to reduce such vulnerability. Even if well-intentioned, many back down from such efforts due to the challenges of engaging sensitively and without harming people's dignity. Yet it is important to remember that it is our responsibility to take this difficult path. Otherwise, researchers end up being an additional part of the oppression and vulnerability of the said population.

Róisín: How have your thoughts on feminism developed over time in your work?

Sandya: As I have said in response to the question on intersectionality, my feminist journey started with a passionate internalization of Western hegemonic feminism. I wanted all Sri Lankan women to change and live just the same way as Western feminists. I remember reading a book about Sri Lankan rural women by a Scandinavian feminist (Carla Risseeuw) titled 'Fish Don't Talk about the Water.' In my intellectual immaturity, I failed to understand the neo-imperialist attitude toward women living in a wholly different context than the author. From my introduction to feminism till the start of my graduate studies in the US, I too believed that feminism means all women pursuing individual desires, dreams and pleasures irrespective of the families and communities they live with. In a way, I cannot blame the early Western feminists, as they wrote for/about Western middle-class women. It was up to us in more socio-centric societies to critically reimagine those concepts and expectations. And non-Western feminists in fact were already doing that, just that I was a bit late to get to those materials. Imagine how my eyes may have opened when I first read 'Under Western Eyes: Feminist Scholarship and Colonial Discourses' by Chandra T. Mohanty. This was just before I left for the US to start graduate school at the University of Texas at Austin.

Meeting and taking graduate courses with Kamala Visweswaran was the next lucky stroke. It was in these classes that I was introduced to feminists such as Gloria Anzaldua, Norma Alarcon, Chela Sandoval and Chicana feminism, and the US Third World feminism. It was Visweswaran's classes that introduced me to feminist postcolonial theory. Interestingly, I came to know of Sri Lanka's very own feminist theorist (who wrote 'White Woman's other Burden'), Kumari Jayawardena, through these classes. Interesting how my own undergraduate education focused on French feminists and not our own world-famous feminist theorist, right?

Visweswaran's own 'Fictions of Feminist Ethnography' was pivotal for me in both a theoretical and methodological sense. Her theorizing on feminist research tools has informed my own long-term ethnographic research. I credit that book and training under her for my against-the-grain reading of global assembly line workers' lives. Kamala's short chapter 'Sari stories' was also crucial in developing my own tools of intersectional analysis. Chela Sandoval's 'Methodology of the Oppressed' has also marked an important turning point in rejecting universal sisterhood and Feminism with a capital F, and embracing feminisms. Feminisms – locally grounded, contextual and organic means of understanding inequalities and fighting for social justice. For a transnational scholar from a non-Western country, like me, there cannot be any other choice.

As an economic anthropologist, my chosen analytical perspective is feminist political economy. For I believe the critique of capitalism and the quest for alternatives is an integrally feminist quest as it hinges on a desire for global social justice. History of the development of Feminist Anthropology also impacted the way I connected with feminism, especially to academic writing. I strongly believe that the standard writing practices are not suitable for writing about marginalized women from non-Western societies. Experimental writing that combined research participants' poetry, short stories, visuals, film clips and academic analysis brings the uneven lives in flux that we so often write about. In this sense, Zora Neale Hurston's 'Their Eyes Were Watching God' was influential for me. Although she was forced to write in novel format due to racism and strict writing standards of that time, her research and sensory experience-based fiction made perfect sense in the context of other writings on the same subject. It was social memory written as a composite of community life. I haven't had the courage to write like this yet, but soon I will, because I believe that writing in the standard style and structure of Western-centric, logo-centric academia does not do justice to the vivid, vibrant, resilient lives of marginalized people in the Global South.

Róisín: Much of your published work looks at questions of empowerment for women in the Global South. What are your thoughts on this as a feminist researcher?

Sandya: Again, along the lines of non-Western-centric theorizing, I take empowerment as context-specific. Empowerment not as one static goal that one can achieve and can be measurable. It is a journey from where you start and thus a process. I cannot emphasize enough the need for long-term, deeply immersive ethnographic studies in understanding contextual empowerment. It is a combination of empowering moments that lead to more decision-making and shaping their lives in a way that is beneficial and meaningful for them and their families. My own research had shown that for marginalized women in Sri Lanka (and Bangladesh), empowerment is not something that they would achieve just for themselves. Empowerment for them is something that makes them gain more say/control of their own lives as individuals and as members of families and communities. For many short-term researchers, the women's choice to refuse an individually empowering opportunity because it affects the dignity of other family members is perplexing. In the local context, however, where women would like to be part of families and communities, empowerment looks a bit different. Thus, they do have to shape their own views of what meaningful empowerment is. My 2020 book in fact conceptualized the particular ways the Sri Lankan former garment factory workers understand, seek and achieve empowerment as 'politics of contentment.'

Róisín: In your work, you often write about complex ethical scenarios. How do you view research ethics in relation to your work?

Sandya: I think ethics are very important, especially within the long-term immersive ethnographic research I do. First and foremost, I am bound by the American Anthropological Association's very open yet thorough code of ethics. It allows a lot of space for the researcher to make decisions guided by the main codes of ethics. Ethics applications to institutional review boards have been much more restrictive and problematic. These boards are understaffed and mostly run by reluctantly volunteering academics. Thus, they do not have the capacity to work with differing guidelines appropriate for different disciplines and sub-fields. The guidelines and requirements are normally for the most extreme situations, specifically applying to medical sciences. Unfortunately, such guidelines restrict social science research. While some checks and balances in place are crucial to prevent abuse of power and harm to the people, the generalized understanding of vulnerability cuts off access to interviewees with varied life experiences.

As an anthropologist who studies non-Western societies, I found existing UK IRB guidelines to be unusually restrictive (at least as far as my own institution goes). They seem to take all people in poorer countries as vulnerable, and certain groups as a whole are seen as victims. Not having built-in mechanisms to allow for researcher discretion – an increasing scale of allowance appropriate for the years of experience with a particular context and group – is sometimes debilitating. Specifically, for anthropologists who enjoy the discipline-specific privilege of getting to know people intimately before and during research, and who engage in affirming qualitative informed consent throughout the research, practices such as getting people to sign a formal letter of consent sound laughable.

I will end my response with an example from my doctoral research time – I stayed together with 60 global factory workers in a poorly ventilated, dilapidated line of boarding rooms for seven months before I asked permission from the boarding house owner to video-tape the boarding house compound. He refused, citing that he did not want the state of toilets and bathing facilities to be leaked to the health ministry. When I reported this to the boarding residents, who were gathered in anticipation of a video shoot, they got very upset and wanted me to continue with the video-taping as the boarding house belongs to them as well and that getting the state of affairs out into the public is one way I can thank them. I made a snap decision to go with their enthusiastic, rebellious request, even as ethical restrictions played in the back of my head. There ensued a really fun protest of a sort where workers helped me to video-tape the whole boarding compound in secret. They acted as lookouts for the owner or his friends and created fun moments by issuing false alarms. It was a happy memory from the fieldwork for me as well.

After I came back to the US, I thought deeply about what occurred and what I could do with the material. Turned out nothing much. Of course, I could not use the video for any publication purposes. But there was a loophole in that I could write about the whole experience of the video shoot as a self-reflective moment, which I did in my 2008 book. The whole incident leaves many questions to be answered: who really owns a space, the legal owner or its inhabitants? Does everyone in a social context deserve the same attention to meaningful consent and privacy? Isn't exposing forms of abuse, violence, neglect and oppression a part of an engaged scholar's role? Especially when that scholar is a feminist?

Róisín: How can UK academia become more inclusive?
Sandya: I am glad you used 'inclusive' instead of diversity. Right now, there seems to be a renewed interest in recruiting academics belonging to different groups. Whether this would lead to an inclusive UK academia remains to be seen. If the administration is going to wipe their hands and be happy at hiring members of diverse groups without meaningfully including the valuable perspectives and cultures that they bring to a department or university, then no real change is going to happen. Many practices in academia today are biased against non-white, working-class and international faculty. There is accent discrimination and expectation that all faculty adhere to one ideal mold that deprive our students of experiencing a comprehensively inclusive university. These expectations affect SAMT scores and in turn affect promotions of people belonging to BAME backgrounds. We have a dire need for female professors and senior management of BAME backgrounds. Out-of-date expectations of leadership qualities see to it that people from diverse backgrounds do not get departmental leadership positions, which then affects their ability to get promoted.

To be more inclusive: Be open to new ways of thinking, perspectives and working ethos. Let people forge their own leadership paths, thus allowing for role models to emerge (simply put: abandon the out-of-date leadership ideal of an 'old, white male'). Together with the earlier explained ways to make affirmative interventions from primary school to doctoral programs, such inclusivity will lead to more diversity.

Róisín: How can feminist academics make an impact beyond the ivory tower?
Sandya: This is interesting. I have always understood feminism to be not just theory but a body of knowledge that is so intricately intertwined with praxis. Feminist theory is one that needs to be connected to social justice activism in the broadest intersectional sense. Challenges of such activism and recorded mistakes aside, almost all feminist scholars seem to understand this at some level.

Work of feminists throughout the world have shown how feminist theories can initiate and augment protests for equal rights and positive policy changes. It is my experience that feminist theorists find it easier to engage with activist organizations than with policy makers. Having said that, there are some inspiring instances in which transnational feminist networks have been able to successfully liaise through local partner organizations to lobby policy makers into initiating positive policy outcomes supporting intersectional social justice. There are also instances of dedicated feminist scholars working tirelessly on pet issues bringing attention to hidden problems, formulating comprehensive solutions and promoting funds and solutions through local law-makers.

Challenges involved with particular forms of engagement depend on some of the points noted in the response to the question on researching in vulnerable communities and the question on empowerment. If university-educated feminist theorists – Western or non-Western – are going to connect with local organizations not as an equal partner but as a charity dispenser and the holder of the absolutely correct ideological framework, their interventions would potentially backfire. Case in point: early feminist interventions to stop female genital cutting, especially in African villages. These interventions can only succeed if the intellectual connect with the local organizations, initiatives and movements with an open and flexible mind set with the hope of learning from them at the same time as disseminating one's knowledge.

Róisín: What changes would you welcome from white feminist academics?

Sandya: Shifting perspective from hegemonic feminism to feminisms; the openness to different forms of perceiving and fighting for gender justice. Recognition of the need and value of organic strategizing and the pedagogy of the oppressed. Climbing down from the unconscious ethnocentric pedestal some of them stand on and deep reflect-out the desire to lead forms of social justice initiatives world over. Stop hijacking the leadership of organic movements built on the backs of ordinary people and grassroots activists. Learn by doing empirical research and dialogue with grassroots organizations, communities and policy makers. Work on supporting organic solutions that come out of these conversations.

It is not at all enough being non-racist. Feminism is not just a theory and an intellectual framing. It is a way of life. One cannot research and write about social justice and equality and not practice those ideals in their lives. For example, it is not enough to be non-racist. But a feminist needs to fight for the voiceless and the oppressed to build anti-racist institutional environments. One should do this by being allies of organic anti-racist movements led by people who experience racial discrimination in their daily lives. One must advocate for broad global economic justice or, in other words, alternatives to current global capitalist hierarchies so that context-specific ideological transformations will organically occur.

It is simply not enough to write papers/books and theorize. We need to be politically involved and active in social justice struggles. There are many contemporary feminists who are actively engaged with social and racial justice movements of their own countries. There are few who have tried their best to respectfully connect with initiatives and movements in the Global South and also organize and participate in transnational solidarity networks. Respectful and meaningful participation has to be continually negotiated. Western feminists can best engage with global social justice movements by embedding themselves in long-term research and activist work in local communities and developing a multitude of connections with local grassroots organizations, policy makers and local think tanks.

4 But you're not defending sugar, are you?

Karen Throsby

Sugar has increasingly supplanted fat as the dietary enemy *du jour*, and is the latest in the parade of food scares that marks the waxing and waning of consumption trends and the knowledge claims that underpin them (Levenstein, 2012). Hidden inside everyday processed foods and packed with 'empty' calories, sugar is seen as wreaking havoc on bodies, particularly those of children, disrupting metabolic functions, rotting teeth and laying down layers of fat which are seen as leading to expensive, productivity-damaging and life-shortening health problems. It is a crisis about which *something must be done* – an urgency articulated in national and international policy documents (PHE, 2015, WHO, 2015) and public health campaigns (Action on Sugar, 2014, Change for Life, 2017), as well as in the proliferating roster of TV and film documentaries and popular science and 'wellness' tracts advocating low-sugar/no-sugar lifestyles (Gillespie, 2008, Lustig, 2009, Lustig, 2014, Wilson, 2014, Taubes, 2017). The rapid proliferation of these texts signals the ease with which the anti-sugar conversation has gained purchase. This ease is facilitated by the dovetailing of anti-sugar with anti-obesity rhetoric and practices, which are driven by the same urgency to action (Boero, 2012, Saguy, 2013); to talk about sugar is always to talk about obesity, and the popularity of these responses speaks to the successful sedimentation of the 'wrongness' of sugar in the popular imagination, and the persistent demonisation of the fat body as something that always must be apologised for and subjected to management and control, especially for women (Murray, 2008).

For the last three years, I've been researching the contemporary social life of sugar[1] and in particular, its role in reviving a flagging 'war on obesity' which has consistently failed over the last two decades to achieve its own objectives of significant reductions in obesity rates. Informed by Fat Studies scholarship (Gard and Wright, 2005, Rothblum and Solovay, 2009, Tomrley and Kaloski Naylor, 2009, Farrell, 2011, Boero, 2012, Saguy, 2013), my research challenges the prevailing 'truths' of sugar, instead locating it in the wider social and cultural context of austerity and social inequalities within which the attack on sugar has come to make sense. I argue that rather than simply being a knowable and singular threat to health, sugar is a vector for social anxieties around deserving and undeserving citizenship, run through with gendered, raced and classed assumptions about what constitutes the 'good body' (Throsby, 2018a, Throsby, 2018b). As such, the aim

DOI: 10.4324/9781003088417-6

of my research is never to intervene in, proscribe or prescribe eating behaviours, but rather, to ask what 'work' sugar is performing in the social domain, what the singular focus on sugar obscures and what inequalities it facilitates.

The most common first response when I present the research is the alarmed question: "But you're not defending sugar, are you?" or, in another manifestation of the same impulse, "But it *is* bad for you, isn't it?" At the heart of these questions is the imperative for me to acknowledge the 'wrongness' of sugar; that however marked by the troubling social inequalities and problematic assumptions about fat bodies that I have discussed, sugar *is* unhealthy and its consumption must somehow be curtailed. But this is not what I want to say. Instead, my work begins from the premise that the categorical presumption of 'badness' actively forecloses other, more pressing, conversations that cannot proceed from the foundational assumption that sugar is the primary cause of expensive health and social problems. As such, the difficulty of the conversation lies in the refusal to allow the discussion to be derailed into the narrow pathways of the healthy/unhealthy food binary. While for the questioner, the conversation cannot proceed without the assurance that sugar is 'bad', for me, it cannot proceed without refusing that conversational foundation. As such, sugar's difficult conversation is a disagreement about *which* conversation to have, rather than about the un/healthful status of sugar itself.

In this chapter, I argue that these difficult conversations create new spaces to move beyond entrenched discussions of the goodness/badness of particular foods and styles of eating, and that the difficulty of those conversations serves as warning against simplistic exhortations to think or behave differently without attending to the complex personal investments that always accompany talk about food and bodies.

Good food/bad food

Sugar is habitually and normatively positioned on the negative side of the good/bad food binary. Products that once trumpeted their 'fat-free' credentials now rush to declare their no-sugar/low-sugar status, and there is a thriving market in books, goods and services aimed at weaning people off sugar (Throsby, 2018a). In 2014, as part of the launch of the campaigning group Action on Sugar, Professor Simon Capewell – a clinical epidemiologist at the University of Liverpool – was widely reported in the media for his description of sugar as "the new tobacco", further cementing its increasingly unassailable position in the pantheon of enemies to good health (Action on Sugar, 2014). Recent campaigns by Public Health England's *Change4Life* have invested heavily in the discourse of 'sugar as threat to health' and have explicitly mobilised fear to drive that message home. For example, a January 2019 campaign ad showed monstrous and angry-faced sugar cubes bursting out of boxes of cereal and other snacks and drinks, overwhelming the terrified children who are eventually saved by their mother arriving home from grocery shopping having made a series of 'smart swaps' which drive the rampaging cubes away (Change4Life, 2019).

Within this binary framing, the refusal to condemn sugar can only ever be cast as coming to its defence, hence the shocked concern that I might be defending sugar in my critical engagement with its social life. This draws the battle lines of sugar's difficult conversations, locking the discussion into a debate about whether or not it is healthy. In these moments, my refusal to join the chorus of voices denouncing sugar risks placing me in dangerous alignment with the forces of "Big Sugar", who staunchly position their products as part of a 'healthy' lifestyle governed by informed choice and the balancing of consumption with exercise and other practices commonly coded as healthy (Coca-Cola, 2015). Consequently, one of the challenges that I face in this project is finding ways to articulate my position without sounding like I am shilling for the food industry, and in particular, for "Big Soda", whose public demonisation even exceeds that of sugar itself (Nestle, 2015). This is part of sugar's difficult conversations – finding a language to express critique in a context where the terms of the debate are already firmly entrenched in ways that delimit that critique.

If I were to concede temporarily to the terms of the debate, I would argue that as much as any food can be categorised as 'good' or 'bad', sugar is not especially healthful, but that nutritionist approaches to food – that is, approaches that measure food entirely by its nutrient properties and perceived health effects (Scrinis, 2015) – cannot begin to capture food's social meanings and values. It misses the pleasures and sociality of cooking and eating, and in relation to sugar, it dismisses as dysfunctional the deliciousness of sweetness and its fond associations for many with love and care. If forced to engage with debates about the health status of sugar, I would argue that the demonisation of sugar as irretrievably health-damaging is contradicted by the fact that, apart from the most zealous of anti-sugar advocates, the moderate consumption of sugar is treated as legitimate. It is, however, important to note that this legitimacy is closely circumscribed by class, with middle-class 'treats' given approval that is not granted to foods associated with working-class consumption (Guthman, 2003, Guthman, 2007, Naccarato and LeBesco, 2012, Johnson and Baumann, 2015). And finally, I would argue that the case for the specific harms of sugar, particularly those relating to obesity, lacks a firm evidentiary foundation. There is considerable uncertainty about the impacts of specific eating practices on health and bodies and their interactions with other factors (Gard and Wright, 2005), and this is particularly true in the case of sugar, which is rarely consumed in isolation, but rather is always incorporated into other foods.

But the more interesting – and difficult – conversation is whether we should even be talking about sugar and health at all, and instead, to ask what other conversations the desire for consensus around the health-damaging properties of sugar might be distracting us from. The next section begins this search for these alternative conversations by looking at another very common response to my sugar research: confession.

Confessing sugar

The ubiquity of sugar as a familiar and appealing foodstuff, alongside its high profile as a 'problem' food, make it a research topic to which people relate both quickly and personally, and when they learn that I am researching the social life of sugar, I become a magnet for spontaneous confessions of a weakness for sugary foods, with people describing themselves as 'addicts', or laying claim to a hopeless 'sweet tooth'. Assuming that I am aligned with the attack on sugar and that my research aims at finding new (perhaps less discriminatory and shaming) ways to reduce sugar consumption, they apologise when eating sugary foods in front of me or make throwaway declarations of their intentions to eat less sugar tomorrow. This exemplifies sugar's easy conversations, with the familiar performances of guilt and shame flowing freely alongside the shared understanding of the delicious temptations of sugar.

Sugar does not have a monopoly on dietary confession, and sugar confessions are not unique, but rather, reflect its status as the latest in the catalogue of 'problem' foods whose consumption requires careful management and regulation (Levenstein, 2012). The guilt and shame associated with the consumption of foods coded as 'bad' has a long history and is a core feature not only of the weight management industry but also of the wider social context within which that burgeoning industry is made possible (Levenstein, 2003, Biltekoff, 2013). Dieters, for example, are urged to document their eating meticulously and minutely, publicly declaring slips which are forgiven through those acts of confession and declarations of (re)commitment to the process (Stinson, 2001, Heyes, 2006), and this attention to detail extends far beyond the specific site of the weight loss meeting into the everyday. For example, nutritionist ideologies encourage consumers to maximise health by attending scrupulously to the micronutrients that comprise their meals (Scrinis, 2015), and the recent proliferation of biosensing and self-tracking apps to monitor consumption and its impacts on the body extend, facilitate and intensify this monitoring, accounting and confessional imperative (Abril, 2016, Lupton, 2016). In the case of sugar, this minute accounting is reflected in contemporary demands to track the number of teaspoons or cubes we are consuming and to be 'sugar smart' by exercising meticulous economies, swapping out high-sugar items for low-sugar equivalents (Change for Life, 2017). Sugar slips have to be confessed and errant consumption corrected in order to construct the self as the deserving dietary citizen.

But as with 'fat talk' more generally (Nichter, 2000), being rendered the repository of those confessions in itself raises the prospect of a difficult conversation if I am unwilling to accept the role of confessor – a role which risks rendering me complicit in the circulation of guilt and shame that attaches so easily to food and bodies, but whose refusal may dismiss the very real concerns and struggles with food that people may be articulating through their confessions. Furthermore, in refusing the role of confessor and trying to avoid complicity with other people's body and food anxieties, I am also at risk of downplaying my own quietly rumbling, mundane insecurities around food and embodiment and of overstating the ease with which those insecurities can be cast off (Throsby and Gimlin, 2009).

The confessional response, then, is best understood not as a binary choice between complicity with, or repudiation of, embodied food anxieties, but rather as an opportunity to consider the complex and multiple ways in which those confessions constitute confrontations with sugar. Sugar confessions rest upon the shared understanding that sugar is 'bad' and that its consumption should be curtailed.

But they also expose our ambivalent relationship with sugar: it is desirable, even irresistible, even while being morally and physiologically threatening; we give it to those we love as treats but feel guilt and shame when we eat sugary foods and experience anger or disgust at the perceived (over-)consumption by others (and ourselves). This ambivalence plays a major role in sugar's difficult conversations; sugar can be eaten, enjoyed and regretted, but it can never be defended since restitution lies in renewed commitment to its repudiation. And yet, the inherent recognition of its pleasures (however delegitimised) and our affective attachments to sugar (however pathologised) opens up a space for thinking about sugar as always *more than* its nutritional content. And this 'more than' in turn opens up spaces for thinking about the social and cultural context of sugar and the conversations that are silenced in the rush to secure its place in the good/bad food binary.

Inequality matters, but . . . .

One of the primary effects of the accusatory question "But you're not defending sugar, are you?" is to sediment the foundations of the 'problem' of sugar as lying within sugar itself rather than the social and cultural context within which sugar has found its way so thoroughly into our food systems. The 'but' here speaks volumes, often reflecting agreement with my critical points about the ways in which individual sugar consumption is used to distract from the vast social inequalities that characterise food and eating, while clinging to the certainty that sugar is 'bad'. This puts the *how* of sugar reduction up for grabs without dislodging the imperative to *do something* about it.

This same discursive strategy of treating one aspect of the attack on sugar critically without letting go of its foundational claims is also a familiar feature of mainstream attempts to address the many harms that arise from the stigmatising of fatness. For example, Latner and Stunkard (2003) highlight the intensifying and damaging stigmatisation of fat children and argue that we need to work to actively reduce stigma, but always *alongside* ongoing efforts to treat obesity in children. And while Puhl and Brownell's work on bias, discrimination and obesity offers a comprehensive account of the multiple ways in which fat people are discriminated against because of their size and presumed moral failings, they still maintain the importance of enabling access to weight loss programmes for people who are fat. This is justified on the grounds that "[denying] obese people access to treatment may have medical consequences, but also denies people an opportunity to lose weight, which may itself reduce exposure to bias and discrimination" (2001: 795) – an extraordinary claim that places responsibility for managing bullying and discrimination on the victims rather than the victimisers and the social and commercial structures that facilitate those oppressions. Indeed, three years later, Brownell co-authored the popular text *Fat Fight*, which, while laying blame for the 'obesity crisis' at the door of the food industry (rather than the consuming individual), remains unambiguous in its calls for *something to be done* (Brownell and Horgen, 2004). Fatness may not be a matter of individual blame in these models, but the fat body remains unacceptable and the extent to which the problematisation of fatness itself is implicated in that stigmatisation is left unconsidered.

One effect of this failure to interrogate context is the erasure of the social inequalities that characterise our food consumption, choices and preferences. Campaigns that begin from the premise that we *all* eat too much sugar flatten out the classed nature of these programmes, obscuring the ways in which particular social groups become the targets of anti-sugar/anti-obesity campaigns alongside the 'bad' foods that they are presumed to eat (Evans et al., 2011). This is not to argue that social inequalities are absent from anti-sugar discourse. Indeed, social inequalities are commonly mobilised as *justifications* for the demonisation of sugar. For example, in March 2016 as debates around the sugar tax were raging in the UK, the Guardian cited Simon Capewell, in his role as vice-president of the UK's Faculty of Public Health, as saying:

> If you apply a sugary drinks tax across the board and everyone consumes 10% less, that produces a 1% reduction in disease overall. But in poorer areas that would be a three-times-bigger reduction compared with more affluent areas, because poorer people are two to three times more likely to get heart disease, diabetes, cancer or have a stroke.
>
> (Campbell, 2016)

These speculative figures position the targeting of the poor as a social and financial win-win, with interventions into poorer communities giving the biggest bang for their buck. Sugar here figures as both the cause of and solution to social and health inequalities, and the neat circularity of the argument quietly shifts responsibility for resolving inequalities onto those already most disadvantaged who will be nudged towards the 'right' food choices by the sugar tax.

Arguments in favour of interventions such as taxation in order to reduce sugar consumption rely on understandings of the 'crisis' of sugar (and by extension, obesity) as rooted in so-called obesogenic environments which limit our choices and expose us to endless temptation to eat foods commonly categorised as 'bad'. In particular, socially and economically deprived areas are singled out for their high prevalence of fast-food outlets, a paucity of accessible stores selling affordable fresh food, limited space for exercise and outdoor activity and threats to personal safety which lead people to favour driving over walking or cycling. The self-interested behaviours of 'Big Sugar' and the food industry loom large in anti-sugar and anti-obesity campaigns as the creators of these obesogenic environments, leading to efforts to place restrictions on advertising or to regulate access to sugary (and other 'junk') foods in public spaces such as schools and hospitals.

These food environment campaigns have a particular appeal to those committed to reducing inequalities, since they appear to offer a progressive alternative to stigmatisation and the individualising of blame. However, Kirkland argues that we should be sceptical towards seemingly benign commitments to the environmental argument since it "seems structural, but it ultimately redounds to a micropolitics of food choice dominated by elite norms of consumption and movement"

(2011: 464). Environmental accounts, she argues, presume subjects duped by capitalist forces into health-damaging consumption, while at the same time presuming self-determining individuals who will make the 'right' choices once the proper context for those choices has been created (2011: 467). This replicates the conviction that elites are thriving *because* of their lifestyles (2011: 480) and returns the focus of attention back onto individual choices under cover of the more palatable target of the obesogenic environment and the capitalist giants whose profits depend on it.

This sleight of hand, however well-intentioned, ignores the extensive evidence on the social determinants of health and the profound health impacts of social gradients (Wilkinson and Pickett, 2010, Marmot, 2015); as Guthman argues in her trenchant advocacy for food justice, "we cannot change the world one meal at a time", with meaningful change requiring different political rather than consumer choices (Guthman, 2011: 194). This unpalatable claim pushes back against the neoliberal logics of meritocracy, whose 'justice narratives' "recognise structural injustice but then offer to sell neoliberal meritocratic solutions to them" (Littler, 2018: 215). This pushing back displaces the easy conversations of informed dietary choices and just desserts with the more difficult conversations of middle-class complicity in the solidifying of social hierarchies of embodied consumption. Kirkland also warns that environmental accounts can be mobilised as a cover for other reforms that are directly against the interests of those who are already most disadvantaged. For example, she highlights the free market tying together of health care, insurance and rewarded statuses and behaviours that "keeps the focus on fat's costs and burdens to society and emphasises personal responsibility for one's body" (2011: 480). This is not to suggest that those endorsing environmental arguments are not acting out of genuine concern over health inequalities, but rather, that the privileging of fatness (or sugar) as *the* problem to be solved limits the terms of the debate and the solutions that can be imagined – for example, by focusing on facilitating 'better' choices rather than economic redistribution (2011: 481).

The recognition that there is genuine concern over health inequalities at work in the determined seeking of a consensus around sugar's 'badness' is an important contributor to sugar's difficult conversations. When I try to highlight what I understand as the harms of anti-sugar interventions and the conversations from which I think they distract attention, my interlocutor effectively stands accused of inflicting or endorsing that harm, however inadvertently. Similarly, to someone who is heavily invested at a personal level in the reduction of sugar from their diet, my argument can be experienced as devaluing the work they have put into that project and the feelings of empowerment that can come from exercising control over the body (Heyes, 2006). I am also aware of my own privilege here as a white, middle-class, middle-aged academic on whom the burdens of gendered bodily surveillance weigh less heavily than they do for many. Conversely, Kirkland notes how, in making her argument against environmental accounts, she has been accused of a racist and sexist refusal to help poor minorities (2011: 464), and that refusing to ground her arguments in the 'wrongness' of obesity (or, in my case, sugar) can be construed as wilful complicity in the degradation of the health of those already made vulnerable by poverty and discrimination. This echoes King's observation in her research on pink ribbon campaigns that raising critical questions about the foundational assumptions of those campaigns risks being cast as mean-spirited, or even as opposing the search for a cancer cure (2006: 79). The urgent question – "But you're not defending sugar, are you?" – follows a similar pattern, recasting the refusal to condemn sugar as complicity in the harms that sugar is presumed to inflict, particularly on its poorest and most disadvantaged consumers. Sugar's difficult conversations, therefore, always have the potential to wound sincerely held convictions about who we see ourselves to be and how we want to be seen in the world.

Conclusion

In spite of the ease of conversational flow about food, food conversations are saturated with difficulty. Sugar, as the most recently targeted food enemy, is no exception to this. While conversations premised on the shared understanding of sugar as 'bad' can flow with relative ease, the refusal to ground an understanding of sugar upon its 'badness' constitutes a major disruption to that flow that exposes the tensions already present but subsumed by that foundational consensus. Contemporary attacks on sugar raise important questions about food justice and health inequalities, while simultaneously speaking to individually-held (and socially endorsed) concerns about food, embodiment, responsibility and citizenship. These are bound up with the feelings of guilt, shame, pride and pleasure that characterise our complex relationships with all food, including sugar, and in which we are all to some degree implicated. Consequently, the difficult conversations triggered by the accusatory question "But you're not defending sugar, are you?" are never really about whether or not sugar is bad for you. Instead, the most difficult, and important, conversation to have about sugar is deciding which conversation to have.

Note

1 This project – "Sugar Rush: Science, Obesity and the Social Life of Sugar" – was supported by a Leverhulme Trust Research Fellowship in 2017–18 (Ref: RF-2017–382).

References

Abril, E (2016) Tracking myself: assessing the contribution of mobile technologies for self-trackers of weight, diet or exercise. *Journal of Health Communication* 21(6): 638–646.

Action on Sugar (2014) *Worldwide experts unite to reverse obesity epidemic by forming 'Action on Sugar'*. Available from: www.actiononsugar.org/news-centre/press-releases/2014/items/worldwide-experts-unite-to-reverse-obesity-epidemic-by-forming-action-on-sugar.html Published 9 January, 2014 (Accessed 12 March 2019).

Biltekoff, C (2013) *Eating Right In America: The Cultural Poltiics of Food and Health*. Durham: Duke University Press.

Boero, N (2012) *Killer Fat: Media, Medicine and Morals in the American "Obesity Epidemic"*. New Brunswick: Rutgers University Press

Brownell, K.D. and Horgen, K.B (2004) *Food Fight: The Inside Story of the Food Industry, America's Obesity Crisis and What We Can Do About It*. New York: McGraw-Hill.

Campbell, D (2016) 'Sugar tax: financially regressive but progressive for health?' *The Guardian*. Available from: www.theguardian.com/society/2016/mar/18/sugar-tax-financially-regressive-but-progressive-for-health Published 18 march, 2016 (Accessed 12 March 2019).

Change for Life (2017) *Sugar*. Available from: www.nhs.uk/change4life-beta/food-facts/sugar#PcuzmXCo5dPZZK2y.97 (Accessed 11 March 2019).

Change for Life (2019) *Smart swaps*. Available from: www.youtube.com/watch?v=PWE_UMno5P8 (Accessed on 11 March 2019).

Coca-Cola (2015) *Choice and Information: Delivering on our Commitments*. Britain: Coca-Cola Great.

Evans, B.R.C. and Hörschelmann, K (2011) Change4Life for your kid: Embodied collectives and public health pedagogy. *Sport, Education and Society* 16(3): 323–341.

Farrell, A (2011) *Fat Shame: Stigma and the Fat Body in American Culture*. New York: New York University Press.

Gard, M. and Wright, J (2005) *The Obesity Epidemic: Science, Morality and Ideology*. London: Routledge.

Gillespie, D (2008) *Sweet Poison: Why Sugar Makes Us Fat*. London: Penguin.

Guthman, J (2003) Fast food/organic food: Reflexive tastes and the making of 'yuppie chow'. *Social and Cultural Geography* 4(1): 45–58.

Guthman, J (2007) Commentary on teaching food: Why I am fed up with Michael Pollan et al. *Agriculture and Human Values* 24: 261–264.

Guthman, J (2011) *Weighing In: Obesity, Food Justice and the Limits of Capitalism*. Berkeley: University of California Press.

Heyes, C.J (2006) Foucault goes to weight watchers. *Hypatia* 21(2): 126–149.

Johnson, J. and Baumann, S (2015) *Foodies: Democracy and Distinction in the Gourmet Foodscape*. London: Routledge.

King, S (2006) *Pink Ribbons, Inc: Breast Cancer and the Politics of Philanthropy*. University of Minnesota Press, Minneapolis.

Kirkland, A (2011) The environmental account of obesity: A case for feminist skepticism. *Signs* 36(2): 463–485.

Latner, J.D. and A.J. Stunkard (2003) Getting worse: The stigmatization of obese children. *Obesity Research* 11(3): 452–456.

Levenstein, H (2003) *Paradox of Plenty: A Social History of Eating in Modern America*. Berkeley: University of California Press.

Levenstein, H (2012) *Fear of Food: A History of Why We Worry About What We Eat*. Chicago: University of Chicago Press.

Littler, J (2018) *Against Meritocracy: Culture, Power and Myths of Mobility*. London: Routledge.

Lupton, D (2016) *The Quantified Self*. Cambridge: Polity Press.

Lustig, R (2009) *Sugar: The bitter truth*. Available from: www.youtube.com/watch?v=dBnniua6-oM (Accessed 11 March 2019).

Lustig, R (2014) *Fat Chance: The Hidden Truth about Sugar, Obesity and Disease*. London: Fourth Estate.

Marmot, M (2015) *The Health Gap: The Challenge of an Unequal World*. London: Bloomsbury.

Murray, S (2008) *The 'Fat' Female Body*. New York: Routledge.

Naccarato, P. and LeBesco, K (2012) *Culinary Capital*. London: Berg.

Nestle, M (2015) *Soda Politics: Taking on Big Soda (and Winning)*. Oxford: Oxford University Press.

Nichter, M (2000) *Fat Talk: What Girl and Their Parents Say About Dieting*. Cambridge: Mass Harvard University Press.
Patrick, R (2017) *For Whose Benefit? The Everyday Realities of Welfare Reform*. Bristol: Policy Press.
Public Health England (2015) *Sugar Reduction: the Evidence for Action*. London: Public Health England.
Puhl, R and Brownell K.D (2001) Bias, discrimination and obesity. *Obesity Research* 9(12): 788–805.
Rothblum, E. and Solovay, S (Eds.) (2009) *The Fat Studies Reader*. New York: New York University Press.
Saguy, A.C (2013) *What's Wrong with Fat?* Oxford: Oxford University Press.
Scrinis, G (2015) *Nutritionism: The Science and Politics of Dietary Advice*. New York: Columbia University Press.
Stinson, K (2001) *Women and Dieting Culture: Inside a Commercial Weight Loss Group*. New Brunswick: Rutgers University Press.
Taubes, G (2017) *The Case against Sugar*. London: Portobello Books.
Throsby, K (2018a) Giving up sugar and the inequalities of abstinence. *Sociology of Health and Illness* 40(6): 954–968.
Throsby, K (2018b) Sweetening austerity. *Sugar Rush*. Available from: https://social-lifeofsugar.blogspot.com/2018/12/sweetening-austerity.html (Accessed 11 March, 2019).
Throsby, K. and Gimlin, D (2009) Critiquing thinness and wanting to be thin In R. Flood and R. Gill (eds.) *Secrecy and Silence in the Research Process: Feminist Reflections*. London: Routledge.
Tomrley, C. and Kaloski N.A (Eds.) (2009) *Fat Studies in the UK*. NewYork: Raw Nerve Books.
Wilkinson, R. and Pickett, K (2010) *The Spirit Level: Why Equality is Better for Everyone*. London: Penguin.
Wilson, S (2014) *I Quit Sugar: Your Complete 8-Week Detox Program and Cookbook*. Monument: Bluebird.
World Health Organization (2015) *Guideline: Sugars Intake for Adults and Children*. Geneva: World Health Organisation.

Section 2
Gender, power and intimacy

5 Difficult research effects/affects

An intersectional-discursive-material-affective look at racialised sexualisation in public advertising

Jessica Ringrose and Kaitlyn Regehr

Introduction: "#EachBody's Ready"?

In 2015, an advertisement for Protein World protein powder – depicting a blonde, white, thin woman in a yellow bikini – appeared on the Transport for London Network (TFL). The model's ribcage could be seen, a large gap between her thighs looked altered, and copy to either side of her slight body read: 'Are you beach body ready'?

70,000 people signed a petition on change.org, calling for the removal of the adverts (Boland, 2015), and more than 370 complaints were made to the Advertising Standards Authority, positioning the add as 'socially irresponsible' (Rodgers, 2018). Responding to the Protein World controversy, the mayor of London, Sadiq Khan, issued a public statement that he was banning body-shaming adverts (The Guardian, 2016) from TFL, saying:

> As the father of two teenage girls, I am extremely concerned about this kind of advertising which can demean people, particularly women, and make them ashamed of their bodies. It is high time it came to an end. Nobody should feel pressurised, while they travel on the tube or bus, into unrealistic expectations surrounding their bodies, and I want to send a clear message to the advertising industry about this.

Based on a deficit logic of idealised whiteness and thin-ness as the recipe for women's confident empowerment (Gill and Orgad, 2015), the advert reduces women's value to these elements of embodiment and challenges the viewer to live up to this standard of measurement. The idea that this type of advertising could make people feel 'ashamed' and the concept of 'body-shaming', which came out in the public outcry and the mayor's response, inserts an important new lexicon into the public sphere. Discursively derived from body positivity and fat activism frameworks (Murray, 2013), the 'body-shaming' critique is important in that it offers a window into thinking about the relational encounters with such advertising material and its supposed effects and affects and its possible social harms.

Following this controversy and the public's growing demand for accountable advertising, a TFL steering group and affiliates commissioned research into the public

DOI: 10.4324/9781003088417-8

Figure 5.1 Are you beach body ready advert (girls' collaging exercise)

perception of gender and media in greater London. Critically, as noted by TFL's commercial development director, Graeme Craig: "Advertising on our network is unlike TV, online, and print media. Our customers cannot simply switch off or turn a page if an advertisement offends or upsets them, and we have a duty to ensure the copy we carry reflects that unique environment" (Ibid). In the autumn of 2017, we were contacted by the PR firm Freuds to carry out this research. Eventually titled "The women we see: Diverse girls and women's experiences of gender and advertising in London's public spaces" (Ringrose and Regehr, 2018), the project grew to be a multimedia documentary-style study that involved commuting travelling interviews with women throughout London, two interactive 'craft back' art projects with schoolgirls, and a survey of 2000 Londoners responding to advertising content in the Transport For London (TFL) network. The research is part of a wider competition launched by City Hall and TFL, calling on creative agencies and brands to challenge gender stereotypes, increase diversity, and create more positive and inclusive campaigns directly responding to the recommendations in the research report. The winning campaign and runner-up won £500,000 worth of advertising space across the TFL network.

In this chapter, we explore some of the 'difficult conversations' that emerged in our travelling research interviews, focusing on two encounters with Black women. We show how the women grapple with advertisements of women's bodies, and how these are affectively experienced as shameful, unpleasant, and shocking, but also politically critiqued as sexualising, objectifying, racist, colonialist, and voyeuristic. We unpack how the travelling interview methodology enabled the cultivation of participant 'voice', but not in some easy mode that 'elides tensions' (Róisín, CFP). Rather, we demonstrate how a multimodal engagement with public representations of women, cultivated by moving through space and time and engaging with a series of prompts with our participants, enabled diverse and multiple pathways to exploration. Often lengthy and taking place in a range of locations, our process enabled us to work with discomfort, pauses, breaks (Ringrose, 2007), sometimes returning to an image or discussion point multiple times.

Drawing on affective-discursive psychosocial approaches (Wetherell, 2012) as well as the materiality of the encounters (Ringrose and Regehr, 2020), we felt our way through the travelling discussions. We also cultivated what we would call an intersectional feminist rapport (Ringrose, 2007) through strategies of affirming the participants' experiences of discomfort with sexualisation and racism, which offered spaces for them to share deeply personal and political feelings about advertising. Thus, we will argue that our intersectional lens, attentive to discursive, material, affective elements of our research encounters, enables us to showcase how participants not only negotiate but also sometimes resist sexist and racist advertising content in a variety of ways.

Designing travelling research encounters

The original research brief from the PR firm asked for a research project that could "look at the perception of women in media and investigate: 'In what way are women portrayed in media in comparison to men? What are the outstanding gender-based generalizations/sexism/stereotypes?'" It read further:

Our vision is:

- Using head-cam equipment, a representative from each of the 32 London boroughs captures video content of the media they see during their daily commute or routine

- The video content x 32 is analysed – a report summarising outstanding gender-based generalisations/sexism/stereotypes is created.

Whilst negotiating the research project parameters, we immediately expressed concern at the thought of sending women around London's public transport with cameras attached to their heads as some sort of conduit to their pure experience, a methodology that in a way does away with participant voice, replacing it with participant eyes or view upon the cityscape. We engaged in a discussion explaining how interviewing and working with participants to capture experiences would be not only ethically sound, but would yield better and more complex and more easily interpretable data for the researchers. Although the original camcorder idea was flawed, we saw that this emphasis on women travelling in space and place could lend itself to innovative multimedia research design. This directly led to the decision to create travelling interviews, where we would take film and record the journeys drawing upon both documentary film and mobile methodology approaches to understanding experiences in public spaces (McPhie and Clarke, 2018).

We used this methodology to construct journey-based qualitative interviews with diverse women as they travelled through London, eventually completing 16 research encounters; as some did not follow through, we found replacements, particularly when we saw the need to interview particular types of women, such as a recent mother and a self-identified lesbian.

We insisted that the research design move from a single axis perspective on gender or 'sexism' conceived in a narrow way with a referent back to an implied universal woman (Mohanty, 1989), to consider diverse girls' and women's complex intersecting identities and the ways this shaped their experiences of advertising in highly complex ways that had not yet been understood in a 'super diverse city like London (Mintchev and Moore, 2017).

We were fortunate that the budget allowed for a specialist qualitative recruitment company to comb London marketing databases to create a sample that could ensure diversity based not only on postcode region, but also age, race, religion, physical ability, sexuality, number of children, socioeconomic status, as well as trans identity (although we were not able to meet with the trans participant due to scheduling conflicts). Final selection of participants occurred during an initial phone call interview conducted to gather information about the women's relationship to public space in London. We wanted to know how they used the city – what frequent journeys they took within it, and then based on this information, the participant and researcher together would determine an encounter that was indicative of their common use of London and therefore their day-to-day encounters with public advertising.

These encounters employed narrative inquiry as a methodological approach: a performative and generative method that places emphasis on stories, narratives, or descriptions of a series of events (Pinnegar and Daynes, 2007). This dialogue was recorded through film ethnography and digital storytelling methodologies including voice, image, and film recording practices. Since we were not sure what

Figure 5.2 Participant talking about adverts including 'punish yourself buff' in the prompt binder

type of advertising would be encountered on the journeys, we also brought key advertisements we had located running in the TFL just prior to undertaking the interviews. We came to call this our "binder full of women", given the images included literally captured 'the women we see' on public transport during that period. These included any advertisements where women were visible, including

Figure 5.3 Disembodied Legs Treatwell Advert

themes of fitness/slimming/exercise, clothing, furniture, travel, insurance, banking investment, food, etc.

Although it is beyond the scope of this chapter, we conducted a feminist discourse analysis of the major discursive relations of gendered power articulated in the adverts (Lazar, 2006). One category, such as the Gymbox advert shown, as well as the investment advert for Nutmeg, featured a trend toward perfect and muscular, 'strong', empowered femininity (see Khors and Gill, 2021). We included any images where women's bodies were being used to sell the adverts, but we also provided contrasts to show how this differed for men and women in the same brand:

In addition, we included advertising content identified as explicitly sexist, such as one for mobile spa treatments that featured a middle Eastern-appearing bearded man's head (first advert), with the caption

> Out late with the guys till 4am again . . . ?!
> Keep her sweet with a spa mani/pedi at home
> #SAVEYOURSELF

Finally, we included several advertisements that were not in the current TFL content which have been seen as positive examples of inclusion, such as Dove Real

Difficult research effects/affects 69

Figure 5.4 Boohoo advert of a woman in tassel crop top and bikini bottoms with glitter on her butt cheeks.

Beauty with multiple sizes, shapes, and colours of women's bodies, as well as an advertisement of an elderly woman and a prosthetic leg, as there was minimal content of older women and NO disabled women in the London adverts collected at the time of our study.

Our research team comprised Jessica, Kaitlyn, and two research assistants, Shiva Zarabadi, who undertook the fieldwork with us, and Emilie Lawrence, who worked on the advertisement sample and analysis. In each travelling encounter, we first explored advertisements in real space and time on our journeys, and

70 *Jessica Ringrose and Kaitlyn Regehr*

Figure 5.5 Boohoo. Man advert of man in jacket and trousers standing beside a Rolls Royce.

then we found a quiet area to sit down and look at the prompt book. Sometimes this happened on the journeys if they were long enough, or at the destination – inside the station or outside in cafes, parks, and libraries. We will analyse how these encounters lent themselves to complex unravellings of participants'

Figure 5.6 Boohoo advert of woman in tassel bodysuit and thigh high boots.

experiences. But first, we need to outline some of the salient research literature on gender and advertising to demonstrate how our intersectional feminist framing captures participant experiences in ways that have been neglected in the research to date.

Advertising as assaultive: theorizing the effects and affects of advertising through an intra-active, intersectional lens

Feminist deconstructions of advertising use a representational lens to think about how specific tropes or discourses construct women, femininity, and masculinity, creating unequal gendered power relations through these depictions of gender and sexuality norms, ideals, and fantasies (Gill, 2012; Lazar, 2006). Incredibly useful, these approaches help us to code the gendered and sexualised configurations, poses, and messages in the images using feminist discourse analysis to think about how words and images construct gendered representations through technologies like cropping to emphasise body parts, and adopting particular types of angles, stances, and gazes to emphasise shape, size, colour, and many more (Zacharis, 2016; Khors and Gill, 2021). Sexism in advertising is a long-established tool for creating a deficit dynamic by idealising women's bodies and offering products and services to fill the gap between consumer and advertising image (Amy-Chinn, 2006). What we do not know, however, is how a range of diverse women experience these types of advertising tropes: how do they relate to them? Our question then is, by showing the lack of relatability to such advertising material in a city like London, could we shift the parameters of sell-ability for advertising producers and sellers?

Using a Baradian notion of intra-action (2007), our aim is to think about how the advertising content intra-acts (rather than interact, as intra-act denotes a relation of agentic forces that shape the encounter) with participants in our empirical research through our travelling interviews in specific place time 'matterings', as Barad calls them. To conceptualise the agentic force of advertisements, we incorporate a Baradian understanding with Rosewarne's Australian research on the proposed effects of public sexualising advertising as a form of sexual harassment (2007). She has argued that advertisements in the public sphere that sexualise and objectify women have a direct impact on the relational space surrounding the advertising. Within social environments that are already charged with a "hostile male sexuality", Rosewarne argues (2009: 69) that female sexual objectification in advertisements enforces male dominance and potential male aggression. Sexualised public advertisements are therefore a form of sexual harassment due to a wider social context of sexism, and in public space these images are inescapable.

Our approach was informed by Rosewarne's groundbreaking work describing how sexist advertising "charges the atmosphere" in outdoor spaces; how audiences of outdoor media are "held captive", and specifically she discusses the presumed effect that the adverts "excite the male passersby", reinforcing ideals of "masculinity" (2007: 321). What is significant is the gendered power dynamics, so in a social context already defined through sexism, the effects will create relays and reinforce dominant norms of masculinity and femininity. However, the limitation of Rosewarne's work is that it is speculative and theoretical; she doesn't explore her ideas through empirical research. We believe these spatial relations must be felt affectively through a range of feelings and responses in real time space. We aim to think anew about how the agentic force of advertisements shape the environment and intra-acting with those in space and place in contextually specific but also patterned ways in a sexist society. Not only do the advertisements have effects, but the spatial *relations of looking* and being looked upon in time and space (Ringrose and Coleman, 2013) generate affects – that is, a range of unknown relations in encounters with advertisements that have not yet been mapped.

Conceptually, Rosewarne's theories are also limited by a gender binary: heteronormative framing. Her analysis of sexism in space and time only draws out points about an assumed heterosexual 'male gaze' in a position of dominance and the effects upon an assumed heterosexual woman who is positioned as having to experience such advertisements as sexual harassment. Ros Gill and others have discussed new disciplinary postfeminist 'girlfriend gazes' (Winch, 2012), where women gaze upon and regulate one another's bodies via the sexist sexualisation of advertising; women may also enjoy objectification and experience it as 'empowering' in some ways (Banet-Weiser, 2018). Therefore, we set out to ask: How do women experience these disciplinary gazes in a range of ways?

Another critical omission is that Rosewarne's theorisation of effects of sexualised advertising in public space does not pay attention to race and racialisation as intersecting with sexualisation of bodies (Collins, 2005); therefore, it does not encompass an intersectional frame that is cognizant of a range of structural and discursive power relations that intersect with experiences of sexism like race and class (Yuvall-Davis, 2006). Gill and Kanai (2019) have explored how diversity is inserted into sexist and sexualising advertising, exploring instances of what they call the latest trend of "affirmative advertising", or advertising that appears to "respond to social justice activism based on unequal identities by promising visibility and the inclusion in the consumer marketplace". They argue that the way that affirmative advertising includes diversity tends to be hollow and superficial, and differences of race, body shape, age, and ability tend to be "homogenized through a combination of aesthetic means (makeup, clothes, stylization) and affective means (an upbeat emphasis upon self-worth and confidence) that renders everyone the same". Their argument is that through inclusion of one element of 'difference', such as skin colour or age, onto other normative traits such as thin and perfectly groomed, the model of normative deficit logic continues.

We will show how a new set of advertisements on TFL attempt to signify difference around women's body shape and size and colour, whilst also homogenising difference. We will argue the mode through homogeneity is exacted through a repeated and compulsory sexualisation of women's bodies; although this takes new forms, it still creates a deficit logic through a specific form of gaze experienced as harassing in ways that have not been empirically documented. Our research captures how participants experience postfeminist consumer sexualised address as always implicitly or explicitly racialised, and how these raced addresses around whiteness and Blackness are felt and navigated. We complicate a single axis focus on heterosexist objectification that predominates earlier accounts, to think about how images also objectify and interpolate through axes of race, class, ability, and age.

Methodologically, we will document the affective terrain of such intra-active experiences with advertising drawing on an affective-discursive psychosocial approach (Wetherell, 2012) to understanding intersectional complexities of participants' experiences (Lykke, 2010). Through our transcripts and images, we capture salient affective processes of looking and being looked upon (Ringrose and Coleman, 2013) and relational experiences of encountering a range of advertisements in public spaces as intersectionally located participants. For instance, we consider how responses such as repetition, pauses, silence, and laughter are all affective dynamics that can help us understand how participants are navigating difficult and unpleasant feelings and responses to racism and sexism in advertisements in our research encounters (Hollway and Jefferson, 2001; Walkerdine et al., 2001). We also show how we as a research team negotiate these relational and affective intra-actions (see Ringrose et al., 2018) with the participants in ways that cultivate practices of meaning-making that help us to dwell in some of the difficult and painful experiences of advertising.

Sierra: encountering white racialised sexualisation

April 26, 2018 marked the very first research encounter for our project. Our team met Sierra at Kennington tube station with the plan of taking the bus to the local library, where Sierra spends time each week. Sierra is a single mother of two who identifies as black British, and she uses two sticks to support her walking due to limited mobility. As we moved from the station, we were immediately faced with a large advertisement for American Apparel on a bus stop. The ad showcased a large-scale image of a woman in Caucasian flesh-coloured underwear and black over-the-thigh socks, with the caption: "We're Back. To basics."

American Apparel 'Back to Basics' advert

The advertisement conscribes to a typology outlined by Khors and Gill (2021) as a sexualised confident gaze of the slim, white, young model addressing an audience. It is significant to us as researchers that this was the very first advertisement that we encountered in our entire project, given the history of criticism of American Apparel for child sexualisation and irresponsible advertising largely through a sock and underwear trope evocative of childhood and sexualisation at once – a schizoid motif (Renold and Ringrose, 2011) that capitalises on the contradiction between age and desire, virginity and taboo to create a cocktail of risqué attention economy. What has not perhaps been considered in enough depth in these accounts is how differently embodied and racialised subjects encounter these advertisements. This was exactly the remit of our project, which set out

Figure 5.7 American Apparel Advert of woman in flesh coloured underwear and thigh high socks.

explicitly to understand how diverse women and girls experienced mainstream advertising content, which excludes them at the most basic level through skin colour, valuing whiteness as idealised sexual property in the dominant advertising scape. Our project sought to also see, but what gaze would be invoked back? To understand this, we needed to employ an intersectional lens that considers the multiple axes of identity constituting an audience of a product; recall that Sierra is black, disabled, and her body shape and size do not conform to normative white standards of 'girlish, slim' femininity (reference).

In approaching the bus stop, Jessica noticed the American Apparel advert first. When she asked Sierra about it, the question was met with nervous laughter. Jessica then encouraged Sierra, stating, "Seriously, we'd really love to have your input". Sierra then continued cautiously, "It is a good advert, it's very bold and entertaining for men". After a further pause, Sierra continued to express that even though it was "a good advert", it could be unpleasant for women. When questioned further about this, Sierra explained that the model looked "nude" and was revealing "too much flesh".

It is salient that Sierra, not knowing us and not wanting to speak out of turn, at first finds the 'positives' of the advert for the industry and 'for men', noting it is 'good' and 'bold' by those standards. Jessica tries to immediately intervene to enable a critical commentary with the injection "seriously, we'd love to have your input". Sierra offers the carefully crafted statement that it could have been made "more discreet or more pleasant" for women, and we press on this, asking what is unpleasant, and she says it is revealing so much flesh. We try to engage with this direction, discussing the way the advert draws the eye and is meant to look nude from afar, but Sierra is hesitant to go further, and she resumes an evaluation of the advertisement as successful from the perspective of what advertisers are attempting to do, which is attracting attention. The conversation lagged at this point, and we boarded the bus.

Further, it is noteworthy that we often encountered a hesitation in women to express critique of either sexualisation or sexism, particularly from the older participants. On multiple occasions, they tried to counterbalance any criticism by saying they were not 'prudes' and they were not against nudity or sex, whilst some of our younger participants went further to position themselves as 'sex positive' to counter association with a 'prudish' response to sexualised content.

Once on the bus, there were no ads visible, so we continued to discuss advertising she had seen that was remarkable on previous journeys, and Sierra mentioned liking a specific advert that included diverse representations that had "so many different people on it, and it was colourful, everybody could relate to it in some way or form". The interviewer picks up on this concept of 'being able to relate', which offers a critical space to open up discussion again:

Kaitlyn: Is that important to you, being able to relate to things that you see around you?
Sierra: I think everybody relates to different things, and something I might find interesting somebody else might not, so advertising can be quite good, but sometimes it can be a bit overwhelming also.
Kaitlyn: What do you mean by overwhelming?
Sierra: It can be in your face too much, like for example the one at the bus stop, it was very bold, it looked like she was wearing no clothing at

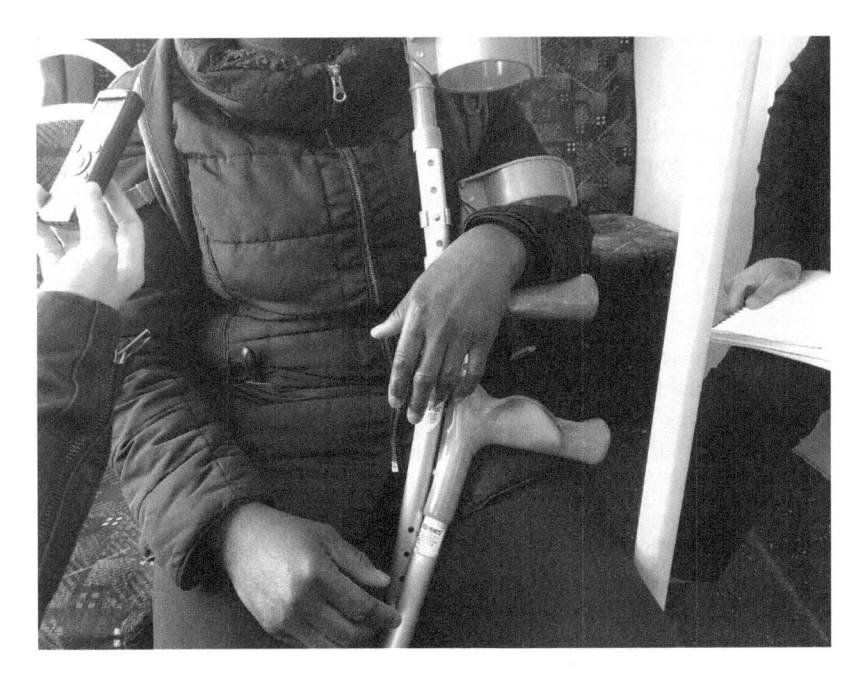

Figure 5.8 Sierra on the bus with her walking supports and recording device.

	all, and not until you get closer do you realise she's actually wearing something.
Jessica:	Can you just describe to us, because we're really interested in your story and how you put it, what it felt like when you saw the ad?
Sierra:	When I saw the advert I was quite shocked, I thought it was a half-naked woman, then I thought they really couldn't be so bold to put something like that on an advert for children to see, for adults to see, and I find sometimes that adverts can be quite sexual and it seems like they seem to be advertising more for sex than actually for the actual product, but it seems like people seem to pick on that a lot more than, you know, I think there is a way to do it, but I don't know what the right way is and what the wrong way is, but . . .

By affirming Sierra's perspective and picking up on her own positive feelings about being able to relate to advertising content, she is able to formulate her response to the American Apparel advertisement and explains what she has hidden prior to that. Her feelings of being 'shocked' emerge and take shape in relation to children, which became a significant direction of the conversation. The bus was getting more crowded and we discussed Sierra's dependency on it for her children getting to and from school, after which she returned to the adverts on public transport:

> Yeah. Because these adverts can also have um . . . adverse effects on the children as well, because at the end of the day you don't know what they're seeing, and sometimes I think for even my daughter, she'll say mum, what does that mean, or what does that mean, or I like that advert because it's got so many toys in it, or you know, different, different, things, but sometimes the things on the bus are not really appropriate for children, I think they need to make them a bit more children-friendly.

We continued discussing issues like overcrowding on the bus and the types of supports that could be helpful for Sierra and slowly, through this more personal discussion, she began to open up further about her experience with the American Apparel advert. Turning to Kaitlyn, who had conducted a short telephone interview to determine a journey to take with Sierra, she explained:

Sierra: I thought about the advert and you were talking to me; I thought I wonder if it's still going to be there, or if it's changed, you know, because you just don't know when it's changed.
Jessica: So you had seen it previously?
Sierra: I had seen bit previously, yes . . . and my daughter was like mum, that woman's naked. I said I don't think she is, but . . . if she is, don't look. She was like how can I stop looking?

We see that a form of shame or embarrassment is experienced around the American Apparel advert, but not because Sierra sees a lack between her own physicality and the markers of ideal embodiment in the advert, which was the basis of critique of Beach Body Ready; rather, it is because the advert sexualises the space and endorses a form of sexualised embodiment as a site of feminine value, which Sierra does not agree with and does not want to shape her daughters experience of gender, sexuality, and femininity:

Here we can see more complex layers emerging: that Sierra has seen the advert and intra-acted with it previously with her daughter, but she wasn't confident about telling us that, likely as she may have thought we were representatives from the advertising company itself. This was a common thread throughout the project, where we found some participants initially sceptical or cautious in their dealings with us, assuming that we were a part of a market research company. However, often after explaining that we were, in fact, feminist researchers and that we really did want their honest experiences of the advertisements, conversations tended to flow more freely. Our discussion continued into the public library, Sierra's destination for her journey that day, and we found a table to sit at to look at the 'prompt book'.

Sierra's critique of sexualisation continued as she explored the prompt book advertisements:

> I think they need to be more conscious about sexualising everything, everything seems to be about sex nowadays, and it's not fair on the young people, they need to be able to grow and identify who they are, and what they want in life, without being forced to see certain images and think they have to comply to them. I really think it's hard on young girls growing up, but also on young men who are developing and think it's . . . OK for a woman to look like the Boohoo advert, and that's what they expect of them, you know.

In the case of Sierra, once we were able to situate ourselves in relationship to the project, the dynamic of perspective based and intersectional looking, gazing and objectifying came through. We began to get to the gritty affective crux of what advertisements are doing and supposed to do and how they are experienced as 'forced' and something to 'comply' with, and how this lack of 'fairness' is something that is negotiated by Sierra and her daughter and her son in a range of highly complex ways on a daily basis in relation to advertisements in public spaces:

> Advertising like that doesn't really help [young people] identify who they are. . . . My son, I tell him to respect women, it's very important that he respects women. I said to him, you know, if somebody was looking at your sister in a particular way, how would you feel? It's very hard with young girls to show them the right way, because there's so much advertising that shows them different things on how to be a woman, but not in the correct way, it's more sexualised. For me, it doesn't have to be about our sexuality, we are not sexualised objects, we are women, we need to be seen in a positive light, not a negative light.

Sexualisation or the defining construction of women as 'sexual objects' is experienced by Sierra as an 'unpleasant' reality for her as an adult woman, but becomes a live protective concern for her children, although the concern is articulated differently between her daughter and her son. Whereas the concern for her daughter is being constructed as a sexualised object, she is worried about how to teach her son to 'respect women' and the challenge that the normalised sexualisation and modalities of looking that it enforces creates for heterosexualised masculinity.

Towards the end of the interview our discussion also turned to targeted advertisement, and here the contrast between strategies of looking and turning off became apparent. Sierra explained:

> Sometimes when ads come up on my daughter's tablet I tend to turn it down, turn it over, and we count for five seconds and we turn it over and look again. . . . If you're that type of parent, or that type of parent who doesn't

Figure 5.9 Sierra engaging with the prompt book.

want to see them, then there is the obvious strategy of turning it, the device, the other way, but there really isn't [when you are in public] because it's always around you, always around you, you can't get away from it.

If it's something I can walk away from then I will, but if like for example when I was walking towards the bus stop, there is no way that I'm walking towards a bus stop to see the bus but it is there in front of me, that I cannot avoid it really. I can't flip it over, it's just there, and it's permanent, it's a permanent fixture, so it's not something that can disappear. But I have noticed that they've started to use the electronic advertising as well, so it's rotational.

While flipping over the tablet and counting to five to see if the ad has passed is a viable strategy on personal media devices, the same tactic is obviously not available in public space, and Sierra stated frankly about the bus stop: "I cannot avoid it really". Even if the advert rotates, offending material will pop back up.

Sierra's experience with the American Apparel advertisement exemplifies Craig's comments about how advertising in the TFL cannot be 'switched off', and Rosewarne's positioning of unwanted sexist advertisements as sexualising the public space around it in ways that are experienced as harassing. The example illustrates in vivid detail just how public space is dissimilar to advertising in private space, given that switching the page isn't an option. Conceptually, we need to understand that public advertising holds a great deal of agentic force and is experienced therefore as non-consensual and something that is imposed on people as they travel around the city in a range of complex intersectional and intra-actional ways, and race, age, and other factors are critical in how this advertising content is experienced.

Naomi: racist hyper sexualisation of black femininity

Sierra's encounter was not the only instance of negotiating hostile racialised and sexualised advertising content. We met Naomi, who has identified herself to the recruiter as black, British, and 34 years old, at Wood Green station in North London close to a music venue we will be walking to. Naomi operates a music booking company and wore a red felt cloak, a black tam, black overalls, and a white t-shirt with "Book a Beat" – her company's name – printed across the front. We began to walk to the venue via the street and a local mall to explore advertising in context and immediately encounter a rolling JC Decaux billboard that interspersed ads for Burger King, McDonalds, New Look, and a chocolate bar.

Naomi expressed concern about the pressure to buy for young people and the problem of incessant advertising for cheap junk food in poorer areas like this one:

> You know, you've got a huge percentage of our city which are on the breadline or below, and every advertisement you look at it's about spending money . . . and if you're a single parent with three children, I mean there's just no way, and then you've also got the young generation that are constantly look[ing] at, you know, materialistic, things to buy, which adds more pressure to their whole social circle, then it adds more pressure to their parents in terms of having to purchase. . . . But you think it's cheap, right? It's that false economy, like buying the cheap roll of toilet paper, but you don't actually save money. Everything's disposable, everything can be re-bought, everything can be thrown away, no one likes to reuse or stitch up or recycle, which is really unfortunate.

When I was living also in Chelsea, they don't have hardly any fast-food takeaways open until late. [Here in Wood Green] we've got twenty-four-hour off-licence advertised everywhere . . . junk food, cheap junk food advertised everywhere and all the kids as walking around with their one pound or ninety-nine pence chicken and chip box. And it's like – what? It's not nice, it's not nice, and a bad way to spend your money when you don't have money.

From the outset, we recognized that Naomi has a particularly critical take on advertising and expressed sophisticated arguments about why marketers target poorer areas for consumption of junk food, liquor, and cheap clothing, contrasting this with her experience of living in Chelsea for a period of time. After the street advertisements, we had a quick round of the mall, but Naomi said she didn't spend time in it as "it's all of the same, cheap shops, fast food, so henceforth I don't really need to hang around here". We headed back to the music venue Naomi booked gigs for, called Green Rooms. Once inside, Naomi ordered a green tea from a hipsterified bartender. She then sat down at a wooden counter by a window, where she settled into looking at our prompt book, flipping through the initial images of a Black woman's afro in an advertisement for Swoon furniture company and a woman draped over patio furniture for made.com; she responds to an advertisements for Pretty Little Things as paradoxical because the models were not 'little':

I feel funny looking at that, I don't know. . . . Because I'm reading Pretty Little Things and I'm looking at the picture and I don't know if they match. But something doesn't feel right. They are supposed to be, yeah, larger-bodied women. So it's, some people have embraced it, some people haven't. Super-size models, it's not their size; it's, I don't know, I don't know what it is.

. . . Maybe it's because it says they're little and there's nothing little about them, and that's absolutely fine, so I don't know why you called it little.

With this statement, Naomi is commenting upon the use of 'plus-size' models for the Pretty Little Things brand, and the word little jars her; set against the women's bodies highlighting that they are not little perhaps undermines the move towards 'embracing' larger-bodied women. However, it was when we came to Boohoo's advertisement featuring a plus-size black model that Naomi reacted the most strongly. She sees the advert and first bursts into laughter. She then repeats "It's a lot" a few times before settling into a more nuanced analysis:

Right, so I mean one, you are stereotyping how all black people speak, and this is all of our lingo. Get down with the kids. I don't like, this is clearly black talk, would you have that shethedon underneath a white chick? I don't think so. Also, you've got a black chick and she is oversized in the areas which used to be, you know, if you go back to colonisation what the white men were fascinated, what European people were fascinated about the Africans, the large bust, the large buttocks, large butts. You know, on overly contoured face, in terms of the makeup. Yeah, it's a lot. She The Don. Yeah.

Difficult research effects/affects 83

Figure 5.10 Boohoo She.The.Don advert.

Whereas before Naomi had expressed her thinking in clear rational tones through her critiques of fast-food style consumption and 'over-sexualised' advertising, when confronted with this advertisement she became less composed and more overcome, bursting out laughing at first and repeating over and over "it's a lot". Indeed, Naomi struggles here with her words, saying its 'a lot' four times before stating, "look at that makeup". She then goes on to analyse the image alongside the hashtag #shethedon, saying it was stereotyping how "all black people speak"; she also comments that the "black chick" is "oversized" in the areas that fascinated white men, like the large buttocks, and comments upon the "overly contoured" face. Naomi appears to feel the white male gaze so strongly in this encounter and feel uncomfortable about what we might say is a hypersexualised and exoticised image of black women. Naomi was also particularly concerned about the advertisements about waxing and what this meant for black women's bodies and hair:

> Like, come on. Why? Why? I don't get it. Like when you're in African cultures, a lot of African women tend to still keep a lot of their body hair, and some of them even have it on their chest or their chin, and they have husbands and children, but even still their advertisements don't represent that, don't show that, so it's really a global thing.

Her concern about racialised and sexualised looks and representations continued to the final part of the interview, where Naomi presented us with an image she had taken on her phone from the tube, which was from a series of advertisements for 'orphans in need':

Naomi: It's racist. It makes me feel uncomfortable, and I'm just like, seriously, I would like there to be a lot more thought process behind how they . . . how they use their advertisement space. . . . Side by side. And it's almost like he's looking at the little girl. I'm just like. . . . There's a lot of money that goes behind advertisement and I'd like to think this was a happy accident.
Kaitlyn: It's already so voyeuristic around like poverty porn and then . . . to have him actually, his male gaze on her . . .
Naomi: Yeah.

Naomi's discomfort is around this type of advertising, which Kaitlyn calls 'poverty porn', and the image of the small black girl, which is also noted to have probably been taken without her consent. Further, the advertisement's placement beside an image of a white man looking across heightens the voyeurism Naomi feels about the image. Naomi's strong reaction to imagery that objectifies and dehumanises black women and children in stereotypes and tropes for easy consumption was something that marked her as unique in our study and offered one of the strongest set of findings that we could use to position advertisements like #shethedon as stereotyping and racist, rather than evidence of diversity and inclusion because they contained a 'black' and 'female' body. What we think is significant in the discussion is us and Naomi grappling together in intra-action, to make sense of this discomfort and to show her relationality to representations of black women's and girls' bodies; her ill-ease and upset at how such representations reduce these bodies for white middle-class consumption. This comes out of our engagement and the research encounter as a complex affective process through

Figure 5.11 Pretty Little Things advert next to Orphan's in Need.

which experiences of racism, normally silenced or whitewashed in normative British society, are confirmed and valued. Intersectional, black, and speculative feminist methodologies understand these moments as integral for creating new situated knowledges (Collins, 2005; Haraway, 2016), rather than bias or lacking objectivity or neutrality. This attention to affective complexities and nuance is what constitutes methodological rigour in this perspective (Ringrose et al., 2018).

Towards the end of this research encounter, we thanked Naomi for her intelligence and insights, and as we were getting ready to leave Naomi told us about her girlfriend, revealing her queer identity – something she had not disclosed to the recruitment firm, but which was also an important intersectional dimension around her discomfort with the heterosexual white male gaze in relation to her own positionality and material knowledge as a black queer feminist identified woman (Ahmed, 2017). Naomi's accounts confirm and extend Rosewarne's (2007) suggestions that sexist public advertising enforces male dominance and potential male aggression as "an environment charged with a hostile male sexuality" (p. 31), but this is complicated and complexified by racism, exoticisation, and stereotyping of black femininity into colonial tropes of the Hottentot and/or the third-world girl (Ringrose et al., 2018), which are critical to consider as we explore and intervene into exclusionary and harmful normalised tropes of everyday public advertising.

Conclusion

In this chapter, we have developed an intersectional framing to think about the effects and affects of encounters with sexualised and racialised advertisements. The methodology of travelling interviews was pivotal in showing how advertisements are affectively experienced in space time encounters and how racialised sexualisation were experienced as difficult and problematic and navigated in a range of ways by our participants. Overall, we argue our approach of sitting with difficult effects and enabling successive moments of reflection and discussion is critical for going beyond a media effects argument (Ringrose and Coleman, 2013) and/or hypodermic needle idea that sexualisation discourses are simply internalised by viewers in universalising and therefore reductive ways (see Egan, 2013 for a critique). Rather, our participants' accounts show the reflexive and thoughtful ways they are interrogating the complexities of axes of inequality, such as sexualisation of different women's bodies in ways that uncover historical patterns of constructing patriarchal, racist value, and with differential impacts based on elements like the age and gender/sexual identifications of the viewer (Sierra's boy and girl children; Naomi as a queer woman).

Returning to the opening of the chapter, while the idea of advertising causing people to "ashamed of their bodies" as suggested by the mayor of London, who lambasted "body-shaming" advertising is really important, we argue we need an intersectional and affective frame which can help us see that shame is not *universally* experienced by all woman in the same ways; it is qualified by a range of relational and diversity factors. Sierra's experience of the London advertising scape became central to our understandings of how the normative white sexualised ideal of femininity is experienced as problematic for diverse women and young people. This is not necessarily because these subjects are excluded from the mode of address as a desirable subject, which was the basis and logic of a body-shaming critique – everyone should be included and 'celebrated' in a sexualising gaze. Rather, sexualisation is seen as a negative form of power being exerted in space and time, a force which endorses a mode of valuation of particular forms of idealised femininity. (See Ringrose et al., 2018.) This hierarchical mode of looking is understood to disempower girls and potentially toxify boys (Sierra explaining the impact on her children). This puts girls at risk in a social context that is already characterised by lack of "respect" for women and girls, as was carefully discussed by Sierra. This is important, as the advertising is co-constitutive of intra-active power relations in real time and space encounters as our methodology made clear; it is not an advertisement on a screen or billboard in a vacuum.

Indeed, Sierra's account also showed us powerfully how such public media cannot be turned off or flipped over if it is looming large in public spaces. By thinking about advertising with her in a range of mobile locations, such as the bus stop, on the bus, and in the library, our approach demonstrates and proves Rosewarne's theory that sexualised advertisements in particular public spaces are experienced as harassing and assaultive, but we showed the specific harms of hypersexualised white, hierarchical, femininity experienced by a single black mother with her son and daughter on their journeys to and from school.

As we've noted, the Beach Body Ready controversy seemed to imply that the deficit logic of body-shaming could be fixed by opening up the bounds of representation to include a more diverse range of bodies in adverts. This is the representational logic behind campaigns like Dove Real Beauty (Murray, 2013), but these have been critiqued as still orienting self-worth as dependent upon an external gaze upon women in their 'knickers'. This also seems to be the logic of Boohoo's #SheTheDon campaign, which commodifies the hypersexualised body parts of a black woman through a silhouette of her breasts, waist, and presumably digitally enhanced buttocks. Gill and Kanai (2019) argue that 'diversity advertising' that includes more colours and shapes widens the representational scope only fractionally, keeping the dominant tropes of visual *idealisations* of particular modes of femininity (sexualised body parts) intact.

Our encounter with Naomi showed us how this issue of representational inclusion of new differently shaded and sized bodies into advertisements remains highly problematic if the mode of address is *hypersexualised objectification* of women's body parts. Naomi's interview indicated she experienced the #shethedon advertisement as unsettling and disturbing to the point she was unable to respond at first. She then articulated that she finds it racist and stereotyping and therefore harmful and positions the advertisement as part of a colonising gaze (Sastre, 2014), alongside other racialised representational tropes of otherness, such as the depiction of the third-world girl as poverty victim, that appeals to a white middle-class philanthropic audience to contribute to save others and become (s)heroes (Koffman and Gill, 2013; Switzer, 2013; Ringrose and Epstein, 2017).

From here we can argue that a hypersexualised black woman in the London advertising scape is not, therefore, part of a positive embrace of diversity. Simply including more and different types of bodies and parts into who and what is permissible as sexually objectified simply expands this circuit of sexualised commodified exchange (Skeggs, 2004). And it was this type of key finding, made possible through our intersectional framing and methodological process, that we fed back into our recommendations for TFL, with the hope of opening up the window of criticality around gendered (and other axes of inequity) advertising effects and affects more widely than was previously possible. For in a city such as London, where public transit is subsidised by advertising, it is critical we take seriously Sierra and her children's inability to "walk away" from American Apparel adverts at their daily bus stop that promote a lack of "respect" for women and girls, and listen to Naomi's conviction that Boohoo advertisements like #shethedon are "stereotyping" and "racist".

Bibliograhy

Ahmed, S (2017) *Living a Feminist Life*. Durham & London: Duke University Press.

Amy-Chinn, D (2006) This is Just for Me(n): How the regulation of post-feminist lingerie advertising perpetuates woman as object. *Journal of Consumer Culture* 6(2): 155–175, 1469–5405.

Banet-Weiser, S (2018) *Empowered: Popular Feminism and Popular Misogyny*. Duke University Press, USA. https://doi.org/10.2307/j.ctv11316rx

Barad, K (2007) *Meeting the Universe Halfway*. Durham: Duke University Press.
Boland, S (2015) The inspiring young feminists who took back the beach from Protein World. *New Statesman*. 5 May 2015.
Collins, P.H (2005) *Black Sexual Politics: African Americans, Gender, And the New Racism*. New York: Routledge.
Cooper, C.S.M (2012) Fat activist community: A conversation piece. *Somatechnics* 2(1): 127–138. doi:10.3366/soma.2012.0045.
Egan, R.D (2013) *Becoming Sexual: A Critical Appraisal of the Sexualization of Girls*. New York: Polity Press.
Gill, R. 2012. Media, Empowerment and the 'Sexualization of culture' debates." *Sex Roles* 66 (11–12): 736–745. doi:10.1007/s11199-011-0107-1.
Gill, R. and Kanai, A (2019) Affirmative advertising and the mediated feeling rules of neoliberalism In M. Meyers (ed.) *Neoliberalism and the Media*. New York: Routledge (pp. 131–146).
Gill, R. and Orgad, S (2015) The confidence cult(ure). *Australian Feminist Studies* 30: 324–344. doi: 10.1080/08164649.2016.1148001.
Haraway, D (2016) *Staying with the Trouble: Making Kin with Chthulecene*. Durham: Duke University
Hollway, W. and Jefferson, T (2001) Free association, narrative analysis and the defended subject: The case of Ivy. *Narrative Inquiry* 11(1): 103–122.
Khors, K. and Gill, R (2021) *Confident Appearing: Revisiting 'Gender Advertisements' Contemporary Culture*. Hoboken: Wiley, Handbook of Language Gender and Sexuality.
Koffman, O. and Gill, R (2013) The revolution will be led by a 12-year-old girl: Girl power and the global biopolitics of girlhood. *Feminist Review* 105: 83–102.
Lazar, M (2006) Discover the power of femininity! Analyzing the global "power femininity" local advertising". *Feminist Media Studies* 6(4): 505–517.
Lykke, N (2010) *Feminist studies: A Guide to Intersectional Theory, Methodology and Writing*. New York: Routledge.
Mcphie, J. and Clarke, D (2018) Nature matters: Diffracting a keystone concept of environmental education research – Just for kicks. *Environmental Education Research* 26(9–10): 1509–1526.
Mintchev, N. and Moore, H.L (2017) Super-diversity and the prosperous society. *European Journal of Social Theory* 21(1): 117–134.
Mohanty, S.P (1989) Kipling's children and the colour line. *Race & Class* 31(1): 21–40. https://doi.org/10.1177/030639688903100103
Murray, D.P (2013) Branding "Real" social change in dove's campaign for real beauty. *Feminist Media Studies* 13(1): 83–101. DOI: 10.1080/14680777.2011.647963
Pinnegar, S. and Daynes J.G (2007) Locating narrative inquiry historically: Thematics in the turn to narrative. In D. J. Clandinin (ed.) Handbook of *N*arrative *I*nquiry: Mapping a *M*ethodology. Thousand Oaks: Sage Publications (pp. 3–34).
Renold, E. and Ringrose, J (2011) Schizoid subjectivities?: Re-theorizing teen girls' sexual cultures in an era of 'sexualization. *Journal of Sociology* 47(4): 389–409.https://doi.org/10.1177/1440783311420792
Ringrose, J (2007) Troubling agency and 'choice': A psycho-social analysis of students negotiations of black feminist 'intersectionality discourses in women's studies, *Women's Studies International Forum* 30(3): 264–278.
Ringrose, J. and Coleman, B (2013) Looking and desiring machines: A feminist Deleuzian mapping of affect and bodies. In B. Coleman and J. Ringrose (eds.) *Deleuze and Research Methodologies* Edinburgh: Edinburgh University Press (pp. 123–144).

Ringrose, J. and Epstein, D (2017) Postfeminist educational media panics: Girl power and the problem/promise of successful girls. In M. Peters B, Cowie and I Menter (eds.) *A Companion to Research in Teacher Education.* Singapore: Springer

Ringrose, J. and Regehr, K (2018) The women we see: Experiences of gender and diversity. *Advertising in London's Public Spaces Greater London Area.* Available from: https://www.london.gov.uk/who-we-are/what-mayor-does/behindeverygreatcity/women-we-see

Ringrose, J. and Regehr, K (2020) Feminist counterpublics and public feminisms: Advancing a critique of racialized sexualization in London's public advertising. *Signs* 46(1): 259–227.

Ringrose, J., Tolman, D. and Ragonese, M (2018) Hot right now: Diverse girls navigating technologies of racialized sexy femininity. *Feminism & Psychology* 29(1): 76–95

Rodgers, C. Charlotte rogers: Protein world has decided to grow up, but will consumers buy it? *Marketing Week*. 4 January 2018.

Rosewarne, L (2007) Pin-ups in public space: Sexist outdoor advertising as sexual harassment. *Women's Studies International Forum* 30(4): 313–325.

Rosewarne, L (2009) *Sex in Public: Women, Outdoor Advertising and Public Policy.* Cambridge: Cambridge Scholars Publishing.

Sastre, A (2014) Hottentot in the age of reality TV: sexuality, race, and Kim Kardashian's visible body. *Celebrity Studies* 5: 1–2, 123–137. DOI: 10.1080/19392397.2013.810838

Skeggs, B (2004) *Class, Self, Culture* (1st ed.). Routledge, UK. https://doi.org/10.4324/9781315016177

Switzer, H (2013) (Post) Feminist development fables: The Girl Effect and the production of sexual subjects, *Feminist Theory* 14(3). DOI: 10.1177/1464700113499855

The Guardian (2016) *Sadiq Khan moves to ban body-shaming ads from London transport.* Guardian.com www.theguardian.com/media/2016/jun/13/sadiq-khan-moves-to-ban-body-shaming-ads-from-london-transport

Walkerdine, V., Lucey, H. and Melody, J (2001) *Growing Up Girl: Psycho-Social Explorations of Gender and Class.* London: Red Globe Press.

Wetherell, M (2012) *Affect and Emotion: A New Social Science Understanding.* London: Sage.

Winch, A (2012) The girlfriend gaze. *Soundings* 2012(52): 21–32.

Yuvall-Davis, N (2006) Intersectionality and feminist politics. *European Journal of Women's Studies* 13(3): 193–209. https://doi.org/10.1177/1350506806065752

Zacharis, M.S (2016) The need of a new theory of visual rhetoric in sexist advertisements. *Bharata Mata Journal of Multidisciplinary Studies* 3(1), 62–71.

6 Calling out and piling on

Deliberation and difficult conversations in feminist digital social spaces

Akane Kanai

In recent years, social media has become an increasingly central site for the circulation of feminist ideas, as well as providing spaces through which to encounter, discuss, and debate them. Digital culture has been credited with the spread of feminist activism, and scholars have explored possibilities of feminist connection and collective witnessing through activist hashtag campaigns such #beenrapedneverreported, #metoo, and #timesup (Mendes et al., 2019). Yet at a time when access to feminism is significantly mediated through digital culture, we still do not know enough about *how* such ideas are deliberated by feminists themselves. While digital culture has facilitated the open flow of ideas to some extent, structures of information customisation and the commercial underpinning of social media more generally have raised questions about the extent to which such ideas are open to question and meaningful conversation. This chapter explores the possibilities and constraints on deliberation, and collective discussion in feminist digital social spaces, through its highly affective, everyday dimensions.

Circulating via texts, media, and cultural practices, feminism has been characterised as a broad 'headless movement' (McRobbie, 2015: 16) that is often subject to considerable tensions within itself. Here, I focus on the vexed questions of differentiated identities, knowledge, and authority that have constituted a continuing debate within feminism for some time. I discuss some findings from a pilot project conducted in 2017–2018 on learning and participation in feminism through digital culture, focusing on how conversations about difference take place in a context where intersectional feminism (Crenshaw, 1989) has, to an extent, been notionally accepted as an aspiration in the feminist blogosphere. From this project, I explore two difficult conversations about how feminism deals with difference and how they play out in mixed online spaces of feminist sociality. The first illustrates dynamics of disagreement in affectively charged online conversations about the intra-action of gender, sexuality, race, and colonial histories. The second difficult conversation takes place in the context of protests against the criminalisation of abortion, regarding the place of cisgender female embodiment in formulating feminist claims. I follow with some comparison to a current project on online feminism, showing these continue to be live issues. In these examples, I seek to highlight the challenges of not only undertaking but staying *with* difficult conversations in digital culture.

DOI: 10.4324/9781003088417-9

Identity, difference, and feminist disagreement

This chapter positions feminist digital culture as a set of contemporary everyday spaces in which feminist theorisation and deliberation takes place. It is important to situate such deliberation by first acknowledging that feminism has long been reflexively interested in how power and identity shapes knowledge claims, understandings of justice and deliberation. Feminist theory recognises inequalities in the valorisation of knowledge on the basis of identity and power (Collins, 1990), and thus operates from the perspective that identity cannot be neatly truncated from 'ideas' or political position, as in Habermasian or Rawlsian notions of deliberation (Bickford, 1996). While arguably presenting a more sophisticated understanding of the stakes of politics, such an understanding can pose conundrums in terms of settling, however provisionally, on feminist 'truths' in the face of conflict and difference, particularly when adjudicating between claims by those with notionally 'less' or 'more' power.

Such tensions are captured by Sylvia Walby (2000) in her discussion of the politics of location. For Walby, contemporary Western notions of difference may hinder rather than help collective forms of theorisation. Drawing on the example of the Western interpretation of the work of Chandra Talpade Mohanty and other Two-Thirds world feminist theorists, Walby argues that the Western foregrounding of specific 'difference' misreads their advocacy for a more expanded and rigorous set of shared presumptions and values based on argument. The power of argument and the appeal to shared concepts and modes of argumentation are in fact the primary tools of less powerful groups, who cannot impose their knowledges on the more powerful ones: 'to leave the matter as merely that of difference would be to acquiesce to the knowledge of the powerful group' (Walby: 200). Western feminist preoccupation with difference has been similarly argued to be misdirected into theorisation that domesticates notions of difference, leaving intact Western epistemic hegemony. Mohanty (2013) argues that her own germinal work on difference in 'Under Western Eyes' has been misread as primarily against 'all forms of generalisation' in the making of knowledge claims. According to Mohanty, this reading of her work as a call for ever greater 'specificity' constitutes a depoliticisation of her theoretical contributions that aim to contribute to a better understanding of common struggle that fundamentally *reshapes* white Western feminism. In a context where neoliberal circuits of culture transform theory into a transnational commodity that flows primarily through academic centres in the Global North, such a perspective shores up rather than challenges the epistemological authority of privileged feminist circles (Mohanty, 2013).

Simply *recognising* difference, then, does not necessarily translate into a more equal knowledge exchange or meaningful deliberation over conflicting perspectives (see Nagar, 2000). 'Race-liberalism' (Crenshaw, 2017), or the appropriation of intersectionality by 'the white-dominated mainstream of feminist thought' (Carastathis, 2016: 2) may reproduce hegemonic understandings that continue to sideline the marginalised. In the Australian context of white academics researching Indigenous issues, Cowlishaw (2004) notes that the declaration or recognition of inequalities may in a circular fashion reinforce the moral authority of whiteness. However, Cowlishaw also notes that to move beyond the limitations of declarative difference politics, identities need to not only be recognised as 'dominant', 'privileged', or 'limited' but necessarily and practically, as points from which substantive engagement may begin. As such, it is important to note that productive antiracist and feminist exchange and knowledge can be built despite a context of unequal power, and without direct experience of the same forms of oppression.

In practical terms, these debates raise continuing questions of how to listen (Dreher, 2009) and how to speak across difference. These debates are now carried over and further complicated in the digital arena. Digital culture is credited with the facilitation of feminist networks, consciousness-raising, and feminist witnessing (Mendes et al., 2019), and with leading the promotion of antiracist, feminist, and queer theory in everyday spaces. Indeed, the hashtag #intersectionalfeminism has been listed on Instagram over 300,000 times (Villesèche et al., 2018), and the exploration of gender identity is a frequent topic of discussion on platforms like Tumblr (Byron et al., 2019). Yet, there are pressing questions over how deliberation takes place in digital culture, in which the architectures of the attention economy (Marwick, 2015), and the 'social media agon' (Elerding, 2018) of competition often structure visibility and debate. The culture of 'infoglut' (Andrejevic, 2013) or excess of information that social media culture exemplifies is intimately tied to a market model for sorting through knowledge claims; that is, as a competition deciding 'winners' and losers based on interactivity and popularity. Further, as a highly affective and intimate genre of communication (see, e.g. Dobson et al., 2018), social media can intensify and personalise the felt stakes of discussion.

These architectures raise concerns in terms of the implications for continuing complex feminist discussions that require nuance, care, and a commitment to duration in the face of disagreement or conflict. Many analyses of the limitation of debate and conversation online focus on the effects of digital customisation in the examples of filter bubbles (Pariser, 2011) and the polarisation of social media (Sunstein, 2007), analysed through the increased opposition of left- and right-wing political perspectives. However, such issues are not limited to politics that neatly fall into such binary 'progressive' or 'conservative' categories. What I attempt to provisionally explore here are potential implications for everyday feminist practices in view of these broader concerns over conflict, deliberation, and discussion in digital culture.

Methods

The data I discuss is drawn from a 2018 pilot project mapping contemporary digital feminisms, which I also briefly compare with emerging themes in a similar larger-scale project commenced in 2021. In the 2018 pilot project, semi-structured interviews were conducted with 15 participants in one regional and one metropolitan area in Australia. Participants acted both as informants of the digital feminist cultures they participated in, as well as providing accounts of their own feminist beliefs and practices. These feminist cultures often blurred the boundaries of online and offline, as participants who volunteered to give their time to the project often participated in groups that had an 'offline' feminist presence as well as an online group. I did not specify gender in my recruitment, but all those who volunteered to participate identified as women, and most participants were younger, with twelve participants in the age category of 18–35, and half of those 30 or younger. Twelve participants were white Anglo-Celtic Australians, with three of Indigenous Australian and non-European ethnic backgrounds (Lebanese, Brazilian, and Pakistani), one of whom who did not grow up in Australia. Four out of the fifteen self-identified as queer. In the data collection process, participants were asked to share examples of feminist resources they consulted, or if they published any work, any blog posts, or relevant feminist social media content with me prior to conducting interviews.

During interviews, to explain their practices and experiences, participants would show me examples of digital resources they used, and sometimes, the discussions that would take place in private feminist groups on Facebook of which they were members. Observing the interactional dynamics of these groups *in situ* was beyond the scope of the project and requires further research. However, participants' accounts of deliberation within these groups, I suggest, provides a rich starting point for reflection. I have not used the real names of participants of these groups in order to protect their anonymity.

Group	Members	Online or offline presence
Feminist group 1	2000	Online only
Feminist group 2	200	Online only
Feminist group 3	100	Online and offline
Feminist group 4	300	Online and offline

Call-out culture, knowledge, and authority

What struck me in the accounts of participants who discussed these private feminist groups was a common thread of burnout and disaffection regarding the way that conflictual discussion was managed in the groups. The groups of which participants were members often insisted upon a level of regulation of interaction that participants at times found frustrating and patronising. Natalie, an activist and community organiser in her 40s, explained:

> each space has different rules, like [in Feminist Group 2], you're not allowed to say hey ladies, or hey women, or hey girls, or hey females or anything like that – you have to use these ridiculous non-gendered terms that are 50 times more patronising and exclusive than, say, the word woman is . . . like 'Petal' or 'Buttercup', or like these fucking ridiculous . . . cutesy nature things.

Natalie saw as a disproportionate (and youth-based) preoccupation with niceness that she felt did not in reality effect greater inclusion. A similar ambivalence was also expressed in relation to common rules regarding the use of trigger warnings. Comparing three private feminist Facebook groups to which she belonged, Olivia, a university student in her late 20s, told me that one of her primary groups [Feminist Group 3] didn't have any requirement to put a content warning before posts that members contributed in the group. However, in contrast, in Feminist Groups 1 and 2:

> there's a content warning for everything. Even if it's not of a sensitive nature, there's a content warning for everything [to avoid traumatising readers]. I'm on the fence with thinking that's borderline ridiculous, but also respecting that . . . I kind of prefer [Feminist Group 3] in a way, where you don't have to have a content warning for everything, and you don't have to worry about hurting everyone's feelings.

This requirement of 'niceness' can be situated within the highly intimate context of social media, perhaps facilitating communication in a context where social cues may be more difficult to read. However, this niceness and care to not offend also appeared to be highly precarious. As Arlie Hochschild writes on the precariousness of public civility (2003: 9) that the social regulation of feeling, or 'feeling rules', aims to preserve, participants reported that the girlfriendly culture (Winch, 2013) of these groups could quickly turn severe based on the offending post.

The first instance of what an offending post might be was recounted to me by Chloe, a 30-year-old white queer woman devoted to research on feminist popular culture, who had been the object of corrective action in Feminist Group 1. Feminist Group 1 operated primarily as a social supportive space rather than pursuing specific activist projects, with frequent topics of discussion including exercise, dating, and selfie-sharing. The group also had relatively high barriers to entry, requiring new members to be vouched for as intersectional feminists. In hearing this from Chloe, I was intrigued. For me, in a context where intersectionality has become 'the happy point' of diversity in Ahmed's (2012, 14) words, how could one with confidence 'vouch' for the intersectional politics of another, particularly with a concept that has been so debated, adapted, and been mobilised in such varying contexts (Cho et al., 2013)?

In this group, Chloe recounted, she had attempted to start a conversation about the US Netflix TV series, *The Unbreakable Kimmy Schmidt*, a comedy about a young white woman who is incessantly upbeat in the face of gruelling life circumstances. In response to Chloe's post 'Who's enjoying *The Unbreakable Kimmy Schmidt*?', the backlash 'went on for days':

> I got yelled at, basically, like, that show's not intersectional . . . they just go, oh, I see a stereotype, that means this, and there's no nuance, I think, in the younger girls sometimes. I tried to talk to my sister about it, because she was one of the people who was like no, I can't even watch that show, it's really offensive.

The discussion centred on a number of key points: the argument over what was understood as a 'stereotypical' depiction of a Native American character on the show and of the Black gay male best friend of Kimmy Schmidt. Chloe felt that the stereotypes were 'heightened' to subvert and send up the stereotype. Chloe attempted to draw on the perspectives of Native American writers, audiences, and interviews with the actor playing the gay best friend that she had researched to make her argument. However, the responses she received were to the effect that this show, described as 'cotton candy humor' by *The Atlantic* (Gilbert, 2018), was 'too offensive to watch' and that any reference to the stereotype itself 'reinforced it'. These points evidently parallel ongoing questions in scholarly feminist media debates about feminist representation in media. However, for Chloe, her attempts at conversation were, in her words, essentially 'shouted down'.

As another participant, Mel, put it, once you are the subject of a 'pile-on', 'you cannot defend yourself' if you want the pile-on to stop happening. Speaking from the perspective of both having been on the top as well as on the bottom of pile-ons, Mel explained the rules: one must unreservedly apologise rather than defend, situate, or discuss. A 'pile-on' is an event, often in a social media space or forum, where one participant's assertion or statement is negated, criticised, or sometimes attacked by multiple people with little opportunity for the original participant to respond to the criticisms. The pile-on can be analysed in terms of Cass Sunstein's (2007) identification of social media's informational and reputational 'cascades': a point in a debate where individuals cease to rely on their own private information and instead rely on the signals conveyed by others as to the credibility of the information and the reputability of the person conveying it. Indeed, reputation may be a significant consideration in these surveillant feminist spaces where desire to be a good feminist is often intensely felt (Kanai, 2020).

Reflecting on the experience, Chloe said she had moved away from argument in such contexts, because it was too hard:

> I . . . feel like I can never really respond to people because I just feel like there's going to be an issue, and you can't properly talk to people about it, so I end up not saying anything, which is terrible, but you know.

Mel, an Indigenous feminist organiser and part-time teacher in her late 20s, similarly gave the example of these dynamics in one pile-on where she was representing a larger feminist group. In a forum where the group was critiqued for its language, Mel explained:

> It was just to do with the fact that we had used language that could have been interpreted as colonialist . . . and cisgendered, but, in actuality, I didn't feel that it was. There's an inability to defend yourself in that setting, because the second you try and stand up for yourself, you'll just be accused of not fully accepting and apologising and that kind of stuff, which is what we did.

What is striking in Mel's anecdote is how being called out implies that one has been *caught* in wrongdoing. Attempts to complicate the space between a clear 'right' and 'wrong' position is met with further energy in the pile-on. While this might suggest a debate between positions, I propose it paradoxically demonstrates real challenges in allowing for ambiguity or difference; the pile-on demonstrates that the *one* position must be reached. These dynamics of piling on also demonstrate some resonances with the social media 'agon' of Elerding's discussion, which refers to 'extremist combativeness as well as its Internet economy, grounded like all capitalist contexts in competition' (2018: 163). In this situation, clear 'winners' and 'losers' are demarcated.

Beyond the clear classification of right and wrong, what was also notable in Mel's example was the presumed whiteness of this space. According to Mel, as an Indigenous woman:

> my identity was completely erased during this . . . I was actually offered, by a white person, to educate me on colonialism, because they said they'd been learning about it for two or three weeks, and if I ever wanted to learn more, then I could speak to them about it . . . without them actually realising that I didn't need that education.
>
> I never clarified that or stood up for myself in that setting, because I didn't – you can't. It's very difficult to have those nuanced conversations online, particularly when it's bigger than you, when you're representing something bigger than you, which, in this case, I was . . . It's just difficult.

In this particular situation, as an Indigenous woman, making credible claims depended on her position being declared in advance. Mel perhaps did not want to add further energy to the conflict. She was also uncomfortable doing this as she had only in recent years learned of her Indigenous heritage and often did not feel 'Black enough' to speak, both in terms of her immediate family history and in her fair-skinned appearance. Learning of one's Aboriginality later in life is not an uncommon experience in Australia, given the national settler-colonial context of cultural, legal, and social practices in killing and displacing Aboriginal peoples, and claims to be recognised as Indigenous are highly contested in the politics of sociality, not to mention under formal government regulation (Carlson, 2016). Notably, the dominant whiteness of the space with its narrow expectations of pre-stated declarative identity further produced a contradictory and invisibilising position for Mel.

What ties together Chloe's and Mel's experiences was the tactical adoption of silence in the face of the perceived contravention of rules in relation to speech, representation, and identity. In the face of well-intentioned (and not unfounded) critiques of particular practices, the surveillant digital environments in which they were operating made it virtually impossible to offer a different line of reasoning. In the highly intimate nature of these social media spaces, holding on to one's position was framed as personal recalcitrance for which it was necessary to apologise. What also links these encounters is the centring of fixed notions of

Calling out and piling on 97

difference; the question of representation, marginalised identity, and coalitional politics affectively magnetising these discussions into what were understood to be opposing positions.

The body, gender, and essentialisation

I now turn to another highly charged and difficult, if not impossible, conversation that a number of my participants recounted to me in the context of proposed reform of abortion law. The existing legislation criminalised abortion in all circumstances apart from danger to the 'life of the mother', giving doctors a wide power of discretion. Feminist Group 3 members, who also used an offline space for workshops, meetups, and activist work, organised a protest by knitting uteruses to send to politicians. This particular campaign was critiqued by a cisgender woman acting as representative of another group, Feminist Group 4. Posting on the Feminist Group 3 public-facing Facebook page, the representative stated she wouldn't be recommending Feminist Group 3 as a 'trans-safe space', because:

> you guys aren't inclusive of trans people. You wanted to have breasts in your logo, and you were knitting uteri, and that's really insensitive to people who don't have female body parts.

This statement was met with anger. One participant stated frankly: 'we didn't want our speech to be censored'. Natalie was frustrated by what she saw as a quickness to mete out judgment by other cisgender women. In Natalie's words:

> you think that you can come into this [online] space and tell all these women not to talk about uteruses or vaginas or boobs. . . . I'll be like, well, why don't you come here and [see] instead of just deciding from afar that we're exclusionary. . . . Some of the women in the [online] space that had never been here [to the physical space] were like, 'I don't think I can come there because it's exclusionary', *even though they were straight, cisgender women.*

The fact that this disagreement took place among cisgender 'allies' of trans people rather than those with direct lived experience arguably intensified rather than placated the affective tenor of these arguments. Olivia observed to me that fellow members of Feminist Group 3 'really attacked' the representative of the outside group. Knowing the representative was also a student at her university, she tried to reach out to her through a private message to continue the conversation, to no avail. Alexandra, another member, remembered the incident slightly differently, saying that:

> numerous women did reach out to her, from memory, on the post saying, oh look, we'd like to get together and meet with you or you know can we come there or can we meet somewhere, so there was an effort made to try and resolve the problem.

While stating that the knitting of these 'little, tiny uteruses' with faces on them and sending them to politicians was both 'hilarious' as well as 'directly relevant' to the protest, Alexandra also reflected on the broader parameters of this debate:

> I sort of tried to look at it from that external viewpoint and go, oh well, I can see how some things could have been taken as being offensive. It also seemed to spark off a bit of debate about whether we should be allowed to be body positive . . . or whether doing that was being disrespectful for transwomen. So I think that's a broader issue. That's not just something specific to this space.

Lana, another participant who very much sympathised with the representative of Feminist Group 4, tried to reconcile their positions:

> I know that the majority of the women in that group are very conscious of not using gender exclusive language, so obviously to have an abortion you need to have a uterus. You don't necessarily need to have the female identity. So, I don't think it was gender exclusive to do the uterus. . . . Obviously, I'm a cis woman as well, so what I'm saying is very narrow view . . . I could be wrong . . . [But] it was to do with a specific cause, and the reason we were doing a uterus was just to make people talk about, have these conversations. It wasn't to do with women. It was to do with abortion.

In her desire to reconcile the oppositional perspectives in this complex issue, Lana explained the protest as 'not to do with women' but 'to do with abortion'. Evidently, not all women have uteruses, and uteruses are not exclusive to women. Yet, I wondered while abortion is evidently not *only* to do with women, in activism, how might feminists reference it as a historically gendered practice linked to the control of cisgender women's bodies and sexuality?

This question is a recurring one in my 2021 project investigating similar themes, discussed by participants in relation to the hardline Texas abortion ban in August 2021. Loni, one of my non-binary participants, showed me through their social media feed that it was still all too necessary to remind activists that abortions do not only concern cisgender women. Another participant, Leah, a young cisgender queer woman, proudly noted that in her feminist collective, they had stopped depicting genitalia and reproductive organs in any signmaking or activism. However, practically 'knowing the line' was tricky. When Leah showed me an image of a woman protestor holding a placard that she had screenshotted from her social media feed: 'if I wanted a politician in my vagina, I'd fuck a Senator', I asked her how she felt about this, given her political stance on reproductive organs she had mentioned.

Leah was shamefaced. She ruefully said that 'she hadn't realised' and 'wouldn't share it with the collective'. With a working-class, rural upbringing, coming to a larger metropolitan town and becoming part of this feminist collective was central to Leah's life in discovering and learning about gender politics and sexuality. She had taken on a leadership role in it and was continually organising inclusive events to create a welcoming space on her campus, liaising with the queer and abilities collectives. I felt bad for inadvertently embarrassing her, and hastily suggested perhaps that the protestor was 'just speaking from her own experience'. But the question loomed of how, if at all, these kinds of questions were to be discussed.

Returning to my earlier project, Alexandra explained that she recognised difference had to arise in circumstances when bodies became a central site of politics not simply in terms of regulation by cisgender men, but in terms of transgender and cisgender difference:

> I don't have a problem with there being confusion or with there being problems. I think that part of being a feminist is working through issues, it is talking about [them]. I don't want to still have one uniform voice.

As such, Alexandra explicitly emphasised the importance of continuing conversations about uncomfortable differences.

As Halberstam (2018) observes, in many Western social contexts, questions concerning trans people have become the 'litmus' test of progressive politics; thus here, questions of continuing discussion were perhaps deferred in the need to clearly draw a line. The representative of Feminist Group 4 did not take up the invitation of those who reached out to her – perhaps aggrieved by the defensiveness she saw. The conversation was, if not ended, paused indefinitely.

Conclusion

There are some broader questions that these difficult conversations raise. Despite the ostensibly blurred boundary of the online and offline in many ways, the members of Feminist Group 3 seemed to feel that there was an important distinction between online discussion and offline discussion in terms of continuing difficult conversations and directions within feminism. Perhaps this distinction relates to the degradation of notions of the 'commons'; it is all too easy to 'exit', as Sarah Sharma (2017) puts it, in these technologies that seemingly provide ubiquitous connectivity but on terms that do not necessarily allow tricky, sensitive, and complex discussions to endure. Further, there are questions raised about the easy and immediate categorisations and implicit rules relating to authority, knowledge, and discussion fostered within these spaces of feminist deliberation. While enabling the quick denunciation of the 'offensive' nature of Netflix sitcoms, such digital cultures may also constrain difficult conversations; indeed, they may make them so difficult that the most viable option, as Chloe noted, is to 'not say anything', or to leave.

Such debates are not new. Feminism has long been subject to many tensions and ongoing disagreements, and such conflicts may be productive and generative. However, what the experiences of my participants indicates is that while conflict is a continuing feature of digital culture, it may be expressed through a competitive model of winning and losing and that its stakes are highly affective and personally significant. While digital culture has been able to translate and circulate important feminist ideas to new audiences, it may be necessary to also have regard to the constraints and the costs of particular digital architectures and arrangements in allowing for meaningful and continuing feminist deliberation.

References

Ahmed, S (2012) *On Being Included: Racism and Diversity in Institutional Life*. Durham: Duke University Press.

Andrejevic, M (2013) *Infoglut: How too Much Information is Changing the Way We Think and Know*. New York: Routledge.

Bickford, S (1996) *Listening, Conflict and Citizenship: The Dissonance of Democracy*. Ithaca and London: Cornell University Press.

Byron, P., Robards, B., Hanckel, B., Vivienne, S. and Churchill, B (2019) Hey, I'm having these experiences: Tumblr use and young people's Queer (Dis)connections. *International Journal of Communication* 13: 2239–2259.

Carastathis, A (2016) *Intersectionality: Origins, Contestations, Horizons*. Lincoln and London: University of Nebraska Press.

Carlson, B (2016) *The Politics of Identity: Who Counts as Aboriginal Today?* Canberra: AIATSIS.

Cho, S., Crenshaw, K. and Williams, L (2013) Toward a field of intersectionality studies: Theory, Applications, and praxis. *Signs* 38(4) 785–810.

Collins, P.H (1990) *Black Feminist Thought: Knowledge, Consciousness, and the Politics of Empowerment*. New York: Routledge.

Cowlishaw, G (2004) Racial positioning, privilege and public debate. In A. Moreton-Robinson (ed.) *Whitening Race: Essays in Social and Cultural Criticism*. Canberra: Aboriginal Studies Press.

Crenshaw, K (1989) Demarginalizing the intersection of race and sex: A black feminist critique of antidiscrimination doctrine, feminist theory and antiracist politics. *University of Chicago Legal Forum* 140: 139–167.

Crenshaw, K (2017) Race liberalism and the deradicalisation of racial reform. *Harvard Law Review* 130(9): 2298.

Dobson, A., Carah, N. and Robards, B (Eds) (2018) *Digital Intimate Publics and Social Media*. London: Palgrave Macmillan.

Dreher, T (2009) Listening across difference: Media and multiculturalism beyond the politics of voice. *Continuum* 23(4): 445–458.

Elerding, C (2018) The social media agon as differencing machine: A materialist feminist perspective. *Communication, Culture and Critique* 11: 162–178.

Gilbert, S (2018) The bleak truths of unbreakable kimmy schmidt. *The Atlantic*. May 31. www.theatlantic.com/entertainment/archive/2018/05/the-bleak-truths-of-unbreakable-kimmy-schmidt/561506/

Halberstam, J (2018) *A Quick and Quirky Account of Gender Variability*. Berkeley: University of California Press.

Hochschild, A (2003) *The Managed Heart: The Commercialisation of Human Feeling*. Berkeley: University of California Press.

Kanai, A (2020) Between the perfect and the problematic: Everyday femininities, popular feminism, and the negotiation of intersectionality. *Cultural Studies* 34(1): 25–48.

Marwick, A (2015) Instafame: Luxury selfies in the attention economy. *Public Culture* 27: 137–160.

McRobbie, A (2015) Notes on the perfect: Competitive femininity in neoliberal times. *Australian Feminist Studies* 30(83): 3–20.

Mendes, K., Ringrose, J. and Keller, J (2019) *Digital Feminist Activism: Girls and Women Fight Back against Rape Culture*. Oxford: Oxford University Press.

Mohanty, C.T (2013) Transnational feminist crossings: On neoliberalism and radical critique. *Signs* 38(4): 967–991.

Nagar, R (2000) Footloose researchers Traveling' theories, and the politics of transnational Feminist Praxis. *Gender, Place and Culture* 9(2):179–86.

Pariser, E 2011 *The Filter Bubble: What the Internet is Hiding from you*. New York: Penguin Press.

Sharma, S (2017) Exit and the extensions of man. *Transmediale*. Available from: https://transmediale.de/content/exit-and-the-extensions-of-man (Accessed 11 August 2019)

Sunstein, C (2007) *Republic.com 2.0*. Princeton: Princeton University Press.

Villesèche, F., Muhr, S.L. and Śliwa, M (2018) From radical black feminism to postfeminist hashtags: Re-claiming intersectionality. *Ephemera: Theory & Politics in Organization* 18(1): 1–16.

Walby, S (2000) Beyond the politics of location: The power of argument. *Feminist Theory* 1(2): 189–207.

Winch, A (2013) *Girlfriends and Postfeminist Sisterhood*. Basingstoke: Palgrave Macmillan.

7 Interviewing with intimacy

Negotiating vulnerability and trust in difficult conversations

Rikke Amundsen

> "... once you open the door to what is personal, intimate, you never know what you are going to find"
>
> – Jacqueline Rose (2014, p. x).

In her preface to *Women in Dark Times*, Jacqueline Rose (2014, pp. ix–x) makes a rallying call for a new kind of "scandalous feminism", one that is grounded in women's ability to share their deepest, darkest, and most painful stories. These stories, she claims, should be placed "at the very core of the world that feminism wants to create", thus "allowing – obliging – us to look full on what they, in their dreams and nightmares, have had to face" (Rose, 2014, pp. ix–x, x). In this chapter, I explore the implications inherent in my taking this understanding of feminism on-board, as I set out to conduct semi-structured interviews with adult self-defining women for a project on digitally mediated intimacy and 'sexting'. Broadly speaking, this chapter is hence concerned with the method of feminist interviewing and with how it informed my process of data collection.

Whilst the feminist interviews conducted for this project often involved light-hearted, funny, and happy conversations, the emphasis of this chapter is on the instances where these conversations became difficult, particularly as they turned to potentially painful accounts and experiences. Drawing on my approach to feminist interviewing, I discuss how the feminist epistemology or "theory of knowledge" with which I operate informed this process of data collection (Harding, 1987, p. 3). More specifically, I examine how a concern with gender and power influenced this approach to interviewing and how it drove my desire to establish rapport between the interviewees and myself. This longing to establish a sense of affinity between interviewer and interviewee rendered intimacy a key element in this approach to interviewing, meaning that intimacy was a concept that I was interviewing *with* and not just *about*. Here, I refer to this practice of interviewing as the 'interviewing with intimacy'.

I commence the chapter by laying out how this particular feminist approach to interviewing is based on an understanding of intimacy as a communicative practice, constituted by a constant negotiation of trust and vulnerability (Giddens,

DOI: 10.4324/9781003088417-10

1992). Next, I discuss the ethical concerns and considerations conjured by my interviewing with such an understanding of intimacy, especially as it involved a particular emphasis on, first, trust, and, second, vulnerability. I conclude the chapter by discussing the ethical concerns and considerations conjured by this practice of feminist interviewing. Before doing so, however, I provide a brief introduction to the project from which these insights are derived.

Interviewing women about digitally mediated intimacy and sexting

The 44 interviews on which this chapter is based were conducted between June 2016 and February 2017 with self-defining adult women aged 18 to 38 and based in Cambridgeshire, UK. The interviews centered on these women's experiences of creating, sending, and receiving private sexual images – a digitally mediated activity that is also known as 'sexting' (Bond, 2016). In analyzing these interviews, my key aim was to see what these women's accounts of sexting could tell us about the influence of digital mediation on experiences of intimacy. The interviews formed part of a broader research project on the increasing incorporation of digital technology into the intimate domain. The focus of this study was limited to an exploration of sexting as it occurs in heterosexual relationships, because my interviewees mainly discussed sexting as an activity that takes place between women and men. This was the case, even though a significant proportion of them were or had been involved in romantic and/or sexual relationships with another woman, and despite the fact that 14 of the 44 women identified as 'bisexual', 'queer', 'lesbian' or as 'not sure' about their sexualities (the remaining 30 interviewees identified as 'heterosexual').[1] This chapter is, consequentially, restricted to an examination of intimate interviewing on the topic of sexting as it occurs in heterosexual relationships between women and men (as these gender groups are socially defined).

The decision to apply adult women's accounts of sexting as a case study for the examination of digitally mediated intimacy was grounded in the fact that adult women are amongst the gender and age groups most affected by the non-consensual distribution of private sexual images in the UK (see, for example: Ward, 2021, p. 12), which is where this research was based. This finding does therefore also indicate that, in the UK, adult women are among the gender and age groups most affected by and involved in the (usually) consensual sexting practices that often precede this kind of privacy violation (Citron and Franks, 2014, p. 2; McGlynn, Rackley and Houghton, 2017, p. 27). My focus on adult women's accounts and experiences of sexting was hence informed by my desire to contribute to the existing literature on sexting by bringing in new insights about the sexting practices of a gender and age group that deserves further attention. This decision was also informed by my wish to generate novel knowledge about the underlying dynamics through which private sexual images acquire their intimate and/or harmful meanings, and that can be used in the academic and non-academic work to prevent the abuse of such imagery from the outset.

In planning this study, I sought to find a method of data collection that enabled me to gain an in-depth insight into women's individual perceptions and experiences of sexting as explained in their own words (Kvale, 2007, p. 11). Furthermore, I was eager to find a method of data collection that made it possible for my participants to convey the richness and complexity of their experiences, whilst feeling as little discomfort and pressure (for example to say certain things) as possible. With these prerequisites in mind, I decided to conduct individual, semi-structured interviews. Because of my feminist convictions, and because of my desire to contribute to the development of a "scandalous feminism" (Rose, 2014) grounded in women's deep and sometimes difficult stories and experiences, I turned to literature on the practice of feminist interviewing as I prepared for the interviews.

Whilst there is no fixed meaning determining exactly what a feminist approach to interviewing should involve, I follow Kathryn Roulston (2010, p. 23) in understanding feminist interviewing to be a practice of data gathering grounded in the researcher's attempts at developing "particular kinds of relationships [. . .] with interviewees – [namely] those that are ethical, non-exploitative, sincere, and genuinely interested in free and open dialogue". My approach to interviewing was thus also marked by another common trait of feminist research, namely by its challenging of the notion that the research should or even can be conducted in a neutral and objective manner (Oakley, 1981). Rather, I operated with the assumption that any interview encounter inevitably will be affected by the relations between interviewer and interviewee, and by the context in which the interview is constituted (Bernard, 2001, p. 19). This emphasis on interviewee and interviewer rapport also highlights how, in the case of my research, intimacy was an important element in the process of interviewing, as well as a key theme detected in the actual interview material. Thus, in what follows, I discuss how my process of feminist interviewing came to be both grounded in and promoting a sense of emotional closeness between interviewer and interviewee, hence leading to my referring to it as the interviewing with intimacy.

Interviewing as emotional communication

Following Rose's (2014) conviction about the need for a new, "scandalous feminism", I aimed to generate interview material that could shed light on women's own accounts and experiences. During the interviews, I thus asked the women to share with me their personal experiences of sexting. As they set out to answer my questions – often in much detail – I came to realise that my interviewees' accounts of sexting were grounded in a perception of women's heterosexual sexting practices as a means for them to establish and/or enhance a level of intimacy in their relationships with men (see also: Amundsen, 2022). The non-consensual further distribution of women's sexting material was thus not simply cast as a significant risk to their emotional and material well-being – women subjected to this kind of abuse often experience that it affects, for example, their mental health and professional relations (Citron, 2014; Bates, 2017) – but also as a significant violation of the trust placed in their sexting partner that he would not act on their sexting-generated vulnerability by sharing their private sexual images further without their consent. Sexting-induced intimacy was hence cast as "a matter of emotional communication" through which notions of vulnerability and trust are brought to the fore by their constant negotiation in relation to a sexting partner (Giddens, 1992, p. 94). This understanding of intimacy was not only useful for making sense of the intimacy established between my interviewees and their sexting partners. As I set out to establish relationships with my interviewees that were "ethical, non-exploitative, sincere, and genuinely interested in free and open dialogue" (Roulston, 2010, p. 23), I found that the understanding of intimacy as "emotional communication" (Giddens, 1992, p. 94) that I was interviewing *about* applied as a frame through which to make sense of the kind of approach that I was interviewing *with* too. Following Mónica G. Moreno Figueroa (2008, p. 76), I also found that the *doing* of intimacy drove my research approach.

The notion that intimacy is something that you can achieve through the sharing of emotions – whether expressed through private sexual images or through interview encounters – is inherently associated with a particular conception of language and its uses for the private exchange of the kind of information that is usually considered too personal to share in public (Attwood, Hakim and Winch, 2017, p. 249). Here, I follow Lynn Jamieson (1998, pp. 1–2) in referring to this as a form of 'disclosing intimacy' and use the term 'intimacy' so as to describe a state of emotional closeness between persons (Illouz, 2012, p. 221). Understood as such, intimacy is something that can be achieved through the application of a number of "linguistic strategies", used as a means to decrease the emotional distance between persons by revealing or disclosing one's emotions (Illouz, 2012, p. 221). Disclosing intimacy is thus a form of intimacy more associated with notions of the self in its abstract form than it is with physical experiences of proximity (Jamieson, 1998, pp. 1–2; Illouz, 2012, p. 221).

One of the main ways that I sought to develop a notion of disclosure intimacy between the interviewee and myself, was by dedicating time prior to the actual commencement of each interview to getting to know the interviewee and to enable her getting to know me too. For instance, when possible, I suggested that we should walk together to buy take-away coffees to bring to the interview, thus giving us some time to familiarize ourselves with each other outside of the interview context. Doing so was also a useful means to downplay the professional context of our relation, hence making our interaction less formal (Reinharz, 1992, p. 29).

I started our conversation on the topic of my research by asking a broad and general question. This was done to give the interviewee some time to get comfortable with the interview setting, before commencing on the more specific and inherently private and personal questions related to their romantic and/or sexual lives. For example, I often asked if we could begin with them telling me about the ways that they use digital technology in their daily lives. As the women responded to this question, I attempted to pick up on the elements in their answers that appeared to be the most relevant in relation to my interests (for example if they used dating apps, or whether they used digital technology to communicate with romantic and/or sexual partners). Then, I probed for further clarification and detail in relation to these more relevant aspects of their answers (Roulston, 2010, pp. 12–13), thus narrowing down the focus of our conversation and their emotional disclosure, until we reached the topic of the digitally mediated creating, sending, and receiving of private sexual images, consensually and/or non-consensually.

Each interview was based on my careful listening to what was being told to me, for so to draw on what was said in formulating my next question. Owing to this, I did not conduct a pilot interview, but rather operated with the assumption that my interviewing with intimacy was an on-going and constantly evolving process, consisting of a set of sequential and distinct, yet related intimate interview situations. Moreover, how I formulated myself during interviews was informed by the ways that the women responded to my questions, both through spoken words and through body language (Ayres, 2008, p. 811; Roulston, 2010, p. 13). In doing so, my aim was to ensure that as little emotional distance as possible was created between the two of us. For instance, because I found that several of my interviewees discussed digital image abuse in highly gendered terms – generally presenting it as an act primarily harming women and mainly conducted by men – I wanted to learn more about their perceptions of such acts in relation to their understandings of the male and female gender. In some of the interviews, I (clumsily) initiated conversation on this topic by explicitly asking whether they thought men were more likely to non-consensually distribute private sexual images of women than vice versa. When doing so, some of my interviewees reacted by becoming flustered or defensive, for instance stating that such gendered views of the non-consensual distribution of private sexual images constituted "an argument that gets into all kinds of dangerous things" (Paige, late twenties) or, relatedly, that such perceptions could be understood as "gender essentialist" (Gail, early twenties).[2] Noting their unease when I framed the question as such, I changed the way I phrased it, asking instead whether they thought gender might play a role in the practice of non-consensual sharing of private sexual images. When I framed the question in this way, none of my interviewees responded by expressing any unease or defensiveness. Moreover, they continued to stress the differences between women and men in relation to the non-consensual sharing of private sexual images. Consequentially, I also managed to not disrupt the sense of intimacy established between us, rather operating to protect and enhance it through our sharing of the same linguistic codes for describing their experiences of a particular phenomenon.

The way that I constantly re-evaluated my forms of expression in response to the interviewees' answers and body language is also illustrative of how my experience from conducting the one intimate interview came to inform my conducting of the next. After each interview, I wrote down my reflections regarding how the interview had played out and the main themes on which it had centered. Then, as I prepared for the next one, I consulted these notes to improve my interviewing skills by reminding myself of what worked well and what I should do differently this time. That is to say, I took note of the different ways that I had both succeeded and failed in my attempts at creating an interview environment marked by a level of trust conducive to emotional disclosure and openness to intimacy. I also noted the instances that I failed to convey trust and build rapport – like in the instances with Paige and Gina quoted above – thus creating an emotional obstacle to my interviewing with intimacy, something that also prevented my interviewees from opening up about their sexting experiences.

Interviewing with trust

In line with my understanding of disclosure intimacy, the establishment of intimacy between the interviewee and myself also worked to amplify the significance of trust in our encounters. 'Trust', as I use the term here, is understood as an emotional safeguard and as an inherently relational concept: trust is something that is bestowed by someone in something or someone else to protect them from the materialisation of risk (Hardin, 2002; McPherson, 2010, p. 8). My interviewees' reliance on trust in me as an interviewer became especially clear as we engaged in difficult conversations about past and potentially traumatising experiences, as illustrated by the following excerpt from my interview with Tia (late teens):

Rikke: So do you remember the first time you tried doing that, having that kind of [online sexual] conversation?
Tia: Um uh yeah, well I do [short laugh], but it's kind of not really, it's quite [. . .] like, dark – I guess [it's] uncomfortable to talk about. Um, but I don't, I don't mind talking about it if that's something that you'd [like]?

In the excerpt above, Tia specifically addresses how the recounting of her past experience does not simply constitute a difficult conversation for her; in describing this experience as 'dark', she also points out how this topic of conversation makes her feel uncomfortable and, indeed, vulnerable. In nevertheless choosing to share this experience with me – "I don't mind talking about it if that's something that you'd [like]?" – she also shows how her opening up for this kind of vulnerability through emotional disclosure is enabled by her trust in me as an interviewer. In this interaction, Tia actively engages in a negotiation of her own sense of vulnerability with my perceived level of trustworthiness before, eventually, deciding to share with me her 'dark' memories and experiences. This interview excerpt hence also highlights a key ethical concern inherent in my adopting of this kind of research practice too, namely my reliance on a level of interviewee vulnerability, conjured through her emotional disclosure.

Because it primarily was the interviewee who conducted emotional self-disclosure during the interviews, this rendered them more exposed to risk and more dependent on my being trustworthy than vice versa. The unequal distribution of vulnerability and risk between the interviewees and myself therefore also highlight the significance of my acting in a trustworthy manner both before and after, but especially during, the interviews.

As the interviews were centered on topics that were inherently personal and potentially sensitive, the participants' acts of self-disclosure had the potential of making them feel some level of emotional discomfort (Ringrose et al., 2012, p. 23). I also recognized the potential of possible re-traumatization in cases where the interviewee reflected on experiences that might have been traumatizing to her, like an event involving the non-consensual distribution of a private sexual image. In other cases, there was the possibility that my very interviewing might bring into being an increased sense of unease and concern, precisely because the questions asked prompted the interviewee to reflect on negative possibilities that they would not otherwise consider. This was the case, for instance, during my interview with Claire (early thirties), where my questions about her past and current experiences of sexting prompted her reflection on the fact that she was no longer the sole person in control of the potential further distribution of her private sexual imagery, thus leading to her exclaiming: "You're making me think about these things now: about how many people have got pictures of me naked".

I took the potential of the interviewee experiencing interview-related emotional discomfort or re-traumatization, and the associated responsibility that came with it for me, very seriously. As such, I prepared for this potentiality prior to commencing on my interviewing with intimacy by way of attending classes on interviewing and research ethics and by consulting relevant literature on interviewing about sensitive topics. I also prepared a leaflet that I handed out to each of the interviewees when the interview was over, regardless of how she seemed to be feeling during and after the interview. This leaflet included information on and the contact details of two free services providing help and support about the non-consensual creation and distribution of private sexual images: the Revenge Porn Helpline and the Queen Mary Free Legal Advice Service called SPITE (Sharing and Publishing Images to Embarrass). Nevertheless, while I did my best to protect the safety and wellbeing of my interviewees, and to communicate my own trustworthiness as they engaged in acts of emotional disclosure, it is worth reflecting further on the fact that – despite these interview situations being marked by the successful establishment of intimacy and rapport – this kind of intimacy was never grounded in the negotiation of trust and vulnerability as equally distributed between the two parties. Rather, our intimate interview encounters were primarily grounded in the interviewees' emotional disclosure and increased vulnerability, followed by their enhanced dependence on my trustworthiness. In the next section, I will engage in a more thorough discussion about the practical implications of my interviewing with vulnerability, especially as it worked to generate a sense of vulnerability through emotional disclosure that was unequally distributed between the interviewees and myself.

Interviewing with vulnerability

In situations where the interviewees are more likely to engage in emotional disclosure than the interviewer, thus making a key contribution to the intimate interview encounter, they are also more likely to render themselves vulnerable than their interviewer, and hence more reliant on the interviewer's level of trustworthiness. Understood as such, intimate interviewing does not necessarily contribute to the development of an equal interviewer-interviewee relationship. The understanding of feminist and intimate interviewing as an approach marked by its being inherently "ethical [and] non-exploitative" (Roulston, 2010, p. 23) due to the fact that it is grounded in the successful establishment of rapport between interviewer and interviewee, is thus infinitely more complex than first assumed.

As the burden of communicating intimacy through the disclosure of emotions is placed more on interviewees than it is on the interviewer, the interviewing with intimacy essentially also works to render the interviewee more vulnerable than the interviewer – hence creating an unequal power relation between the two. This is not to say that vulnerability in research is always 'bad', hence making feminist interviewing with intimacy necessarily unethical or exploitative. Here, I am simply suggesting that, in relying to such an extent on unequal levels of emotional disclosure – thus seeking to generate interview material that reflects women's own stories and experiences – feminist interviewers informed by the desire for a "scandalous feminism" (Rose, 2014) grounded in women's own stories, both enable and encourage a form of interviewee vulnerability that opens up for higher levels of exploitation and hurt, something that makes their need to act trustworthy increasingly important. That being said, whilst enhanced interviewee vulnerability in feminist research increases the need for the interviewee to act in a sincere and ethical manner, this does not imply that interviewee vulnerability through emotional disclosure is something that feminist interviewers ought to avoid. The interviewee vulnerability generated by the interviewing with intimacy can also work to open new spaces for feminist resistance.

In generating women's own accounts of their deep, difficult and/or potentially traumatising experiences, the conversations involved in the interviewing with intimacy can turn these accounts into something tangible, something that we can reflect on and discuss (Ahmed, 2015). Women's decision to render themselves vulnerable through emotional disclosure as they share their own insights can therefore be understood as an avenue of resistance too: in bringing their knowledge and experiences to light, they also work to create new pathways of reflexivity regarding the various particularities and dynamics that constitute women's lived experiences. This point was recognised by several of my interviewees as well. Many of these women explicitly voiced their appreciation over the opportunity that our interview provided for them to share their sexting stories, thus making possible the spotlighting of the kind of women's issues that they felt were often ignored or swept under the carpet – like female expressions of sexuality. This view is clearly reflected in the following quote from my interview with Holly (late teens):

> I get really into this sort of thing because [women's sexting practices is] such a big issue I think, um and something that just does happen around you, even if it's not talked about, um because there is that stigma attached to it. Like enjoying your sexuality and enjoying um like sexual aspects of your life is just like a taboo subject. And I don't know whether it's my age, whether it's my gender or whether it's like the people I'm around or the type of people

that I'm around, but it just does still seem like an issue to actually [say] like 'yeah, I really do enjoy sending like flirty photos of myself, I really do enjoy sexual acts, I really do enjoy talking about this to my friends, because it's important to me.' Um but that stigma I think just makes people very hesitant to actually address the problems which can underlie all of these things.

In the quote above, we can see how, in addressing implicit associations between expressions of female sexuality and stigma, Holly also sets out to address the underlying forces that prevent women from discussing the joys and pains of sexting and sex in the first place. In doing so, she also highlights the vicious circle of stigma and humiliation that allows for the dark and difficult to stifle women, binding such experiences to that which is shameful and problematic in their very attempts at avoiding it. In other words, in staying silent to avoid further stigma and humiliation, we allow for these stigmatising forces to take hold and get set too. Thus, Holly also points to the significance in 'talking about it', hence turning it into a "tangible thing" and, in doing so, opening up for the possible re-signification of certain acts and experiences (Ahmed, 2015, pp. 8–9).

Conclusion

Drawing on the understanding that feminist interviewing should be "ethical, non-exploitative, sincere, and genuinely interested in free and open dialogue", my approach to feminist interviewing as I conducted interviews on digitally mediated intimacy and women's sexting practices was inherently informed by the understanding that the establishment of intimacy between interviewee and interviewer is conducive to the creation of a fruitful interview environment (Roulston, 2010, p. 23). Operating with a perception of intimacy as a practice grounded in emotional disclosure and constituted by a constant negotiation of trust and vulnerability, this chapter has demonstrated how these different facets of my approach to interviewing played out as I engaged with interviewees. Throughout the chapter, I have also explained how a desire to create an intimate interview situation inevitably generates situations of vulnerability and a related reliance on the trustworthiness of the one with whom one shares difficult stories. Pointing out how this notion of vulnerability is unequally distributed between interviewer and interviewee – with the interviewee sharing more and, consequentially, rendering herself more vulnerable than vice versa – I have shed light on some of the more ethically problematic elements inherent in this approach to interviewing too. This reflection on the vulnerability of the interviewees has also encouraged my engagement in a further contemplation on the ways that the interviewing process informed my interpretation of the interview material. Owing to this, and by way of conclusion, I would like to include some reflections on the ways that the interviewing with intimacy affected me as a researcher.

The interviewing with intimacy is not just about the emotional disclosure of the interviewees and their resulting reliance on the trustworthiness of the interviewer: it is also about how a notion of intimacy informs what the interviewer sees and hears, and how they understand it. In my case, the sense of intimacy shared with my interviewees led to my not only struggling with the emotional processing of their difficult accounts and experiences. What is more, it informed how I understood my interviewees and operated to enhance my notion of responsibility in relation to them. Even though I believe that the interview-induced vulnerability of my interviewees was greater than my own, I often felt vulnerable too, as I was emotionally moved and sometimes deeply upset by the stories that they shared with me. This feeling of empathy and emotional closeness to the interviewees also shaped how I understood them and their stories, and what my study eventually ended up being about. As such, this feeling also worked as a perfect illustration of the radical potential inherent in my reliance on a "scandalous feminism" grounded in insights generated through the interviewing with intimacy as it placed women's knowledge and stories right "at the very core of the world that feminism wants to create" (Rose, 2014, pp. ix – x).

Notes

1 Here it is worth mentioning that this finding regarding the gendered nature of sexting practices clearly demonstrates the need for further research that explores sexting practices as they occur outside the context of heterosexual relationships. When I asked the interviewees why it was that they mainly discussed sexting as something that occurs between women and men, they usually answered my question simply by stating that sexting is an activity that primarily occurs in their relations with men and that, because of this, it is not usually something that they were particularly interested in, likely, or able to pursue when involved in relationships with someone identifying with another gender identity.
2 Each interviewee has been randomly allocated a standard British name as pseudonym. In order to protect the anonymity of the interviewees, I have also removed all identifying characteristics from the interview material.

References

Ahmed, S., 2015. Introduction: Sexism – A Problem With A Name. *new formations: a journal of culture/theory/politics*, 86, pp. 5–13. https://doi.org/10.3898/NEWF.86.

Amundsen, R., 2022. Hetero-sexting as mediated intimacy work: 'Putting something on the line'. *New Media & Society*, 24(1), pp. 122–137. https://doi.org/10.1177/1461444820962452.

Attwood, F., Hakim, J. and Winch, A., 2017. Mediated intimacies: bodies, technologies and relationships. *Journal of Gender Studies*, 26(3), pp. 249–253. https://doi.org/10.1080/09589236.2017.1297888.

Ayres, L., 2008. Semi-Structured Interview. In: L.M. Given, ed. *The SAGE Encyclopedia of Qualitative Research Methods*. [online] Thousand Oaks, CA: SAGE. p. 811. Available at: <http://methods.sagepub.com/reference/sage-encyc-qualitative-research-methods/n420.xml> [Accessed 13 June 2018].

Bates, S., 2017. Revenge Porn and Mental Health: A Qualitative Analysis of the Mental Health Effects of Revenge Porn on Female Survivors. *Feminist Criminology*, 12(1), pp. 22–42.

Bernard, C., 2001. *Constructing Lived Experiences: Representations of Black Mothers in Child Sexual Abuse Discourses*. Aldershot: Ashgate.

Bond, E., 2016. Sexting. *Oxford Research Encyclopedia of Criminology and Criminal Justice*. [online] https://doi.org/10.1093/acrefore/9780190264079.013.142.

Citron, D.K., 2014. *Hate crimes in cyberspace*. Cambridge, MA and London: Harvard University Press.

Citron, D.K. and Franks, M.A., 2014. Criminalizing revenge porn. *Wake Forest Law Review*, 49, pp. 345–392.

Giddens, A., 1992. *The Transformation of Intimacy: Love, Sexuality and Eroticism in Modern Societies*. Cambridge and Oxford: Polity Press in association with Blackwell.

Hardin, R., 2002. *Trust and trustworthiness*. New York, NY: Russell Sage Foundation.

Harding, S., 1987. Introduction: Is There a Feminist Method? In: S. Harding, ed. *Feminism and Methodology: Social Science Issues*. Bloomington, IN and Milton Keynes: Indiana University Press and Open University Press. pp. 1–14.

Illouz, E., 2012. *Why Love Hurts: A Sociological Explanation*. Cambridge and Malden, MA: Polity Press.

Jamieson, L., 1998. *Intimacy: Personal Relationships in Modern Societies*. Cambridge and Malden, MA: Polity Press in association with Blackwell.

Kvale, S., 2007. *Doing Interviews*. [online] London: SAGE. https://doi.org/10.4135/9781849208963.

McGlynn, C., Rackley, E. and Houghton, R., 2017. Beyond 'Revenge Porn': The Continuum of Image-Based Sexual Abuse. *Feminist Legal Studies*, 25(1), pp. 25–46. https://doi.org/10.1007/s10691-017-9343-2.

McPherson, E., 2010. *Human Rights Reporting in Mexico*. Unpublished PhD thesis. University of Cambridge.

Moreno Figueroa, M.G., 2008. Looking emotionally: photography, racism and intimacy in research. *History of the Human Sciences*, 21(4), pp. 68–85. https://doi.org/10.1177/0952695108095512.

Oakley, A., 1981. Interviewing women: a contradiction in terms. In: H. Roberts, ed. *Doing Feminist Research*. London and New York, NY: Routledge & Kegan Paul. pp. 30–61.

Reinharz, S., 1992. *Feminist methods in social research*. Oxford and New York, NY: Oxford University Press.

Ringrose, J., Gill, R., Livingstone, S. and Harvey, L., 2012. *Qualitative study of children, young people and 'sexting'*. [online] London: NSPCC. Available at: <https://www.nspcc.org.uk/services-and-resources/research-and-resources/pre-2013/qualitative-study-sexting/> [Accessed 31 March 2017].

Rose, J., 2014. *Women in Dark Times*. London: Bloomsbury.

Roulston, K., 2010. *Reflective interviewing: a guide to theory and practice*. London: SAGE.

Ward, Z., 2021. *Intimate image abuse, an evolving landscape*. [online] Revenge Porn Helpline, SWGfL, Home Office. Available at: <https://revengepornhelpline.org.uk/assets/documents/intimate-image-abuse-an-evolving-landscape.pdf?_=1639471939>.

8 Co-existing with uncomfortable reflexivity

Feminist fieldwork abroad during the pandemic

Xintong Jia

Introduction

During the global Covid-19 pandemic, fieldwork abroad involved inevitable uncertainty, tension, contradictions, and dilemmas, which made the issue of difficult conversations noteworthy. This chapter provides a retrospective and reflexive account of ethical challenges and considerations as experienced during the fieldwork in Xi'an, China between 2020 and 2021 for a project on audience reception studies of a reality dating show. The fieldwork involved a group of young and highly educated women as research participants, who participated in texts-in-action viewing sessions[1] and qualitative interviews.

The "difficult" in difficult conversations indicates the uneasy, knotty, and troubling elements which evoke confused, vulnerable, hopeless, and despairing feelings in challenging and arduous situations. The concept of difficult conversations is innovative in how it invites the researcher to critically engage in considering and reflecting on dimensions that influence the quality and feeling of communication in fieldwork. What are the implications of difficult conversations for research ethics and feminist research praxis? How do we transfer moments of dilemmas and conflicts into productive and inspirational resources informing current feminist research methods and fostering future research? In order to address the questions outlined here, the chapter will consider the research dilemmas I encountered when conducting feminist fieldwork abroad during the pandemic. The chapter will also explore the factors that affected the relationship between the researcher and participants and how to make sense of and deal with the tensions and discomfort that arose in fieldwork.

The chapter starts by referring to the notion of reflexivity that has been practised throughout the whole research process. The research dilemmas that inevitably present difficulties in ethical, practical, and methodological dimensions are explicated. Factors affecting the level of trust between the researcher and participants are considered, given the political/feminist sensitivity of the topic. Referring to the asymmetrical relationship between the researcher and researched, I propose ways of building on a reciprocal and non-exploitative relationship, particularly through conversations that are interactive, communicative, and dialogic. I also reflect on how different meeting places shape participants' behaviours and

DOI: 10.4324/9781003088417-11

interpretations of reality dating shows, highlighting the importance of contextualism in media consumption for analysis.

The Covid-19 pandemic has generated unpredictable challenges for fieldwork traversing borders, which makes the discussion about uncomfortable reflexivity more significant than in pre-pandemic times. This chapter represents an account of how to practise reflexivity within constantly changing and precarious contexts and how to engage in research with a sense of self-care from the perspective of a feminist researcher. By highlighting the notion of uncomfortable reflexivity, I aim to navigate new ways of understanding and addressing difficulties in the research process in order to transfer the feelings of confusion and despair into self-reconciliation, healing, and solidarity. With a specific focus on fieldwork across borders and the field of audience reception studies, this chapter seeks to contribute to literature on research ethics, feminist research praxis, and inspire further discussion about difficult conversations.

Uncomfortable reflexivity

From the 1970s onwards, the interpretive turn raised debates about the place of objectivity in social science research.[2] It gave space to discussion about reflexivity, centring on critiques of classical and colonial practices of ethnographic research and calling for critically self-conscious forms of conduct. In social science research, reflexivity is used to articulate how the researcher's autobiography informs the research and the power relations involved in different scenarios. As Callaway succinctly puts it, reflexivity is "a continuing mode of self-analysis and political awareness".[3] The notion of reflexivity is based on the awareness that researchers are informed by their positions and are inevitably entangled in social networks, which influence who they are and the way they interpret society and discuss research findings. Practising reflexivity with sensibility provides "nuanced, rich and meaningful interpretations of the social world and our place in it".[4] Reflexivity centres on the researcher's agency and positionality, as all observations and interpretations inextricably entangle with the self-aware statements of the researcher. Instead of regarding reflexivity as "an objective, cognitive reflection on structure", Adkins suggests that the notion of reflexivity emphasises both "reflection on the unthought and unconscious categories of thought" and "shared meanings".[5]

It might be argued that reflexivity encompasses reflection, and the distinction between the two lies in whether involved in the existence of an "other".[6] Reflection demands looking back and carefully thinking about a particular subject, while reflexivity requires both self-referential awareness and an "other". Reflexivity goes beyond reflection, as it is about how researchers experience their relationships with people and contexts, such as participants and sites. The distinction between reflexivity and reflection highlights structured power relations – something inconspicuous or unspeakable – which saturate the whole research process. While research is not bias-free or value-neutral, practising reflexivity is to ensure authenticity and trustworthiness – ensuring the awareness of personal biases and paying attention to how those biases interact with data and provide another layer of understanding of research processes and findings.

Reflexivity in feminism means "doing research differently".[7] Reflexivity has been informed by constructionism, feminism, positionality, and intersectionality. Reflexivity is commonly used as a methodological tool to deconstruct the researcher's authority. It demands researchers to take into account their self-locations, positions, and interests throughout the research process, in order to pursue a reciprocal and non-exploitative relationship between the researcher and research participants. More significantly, reflexivity practice involves being engaged and learning through a reflexive process. It is a dialogical and evolving approach rather than a linear one.[8] It involves understanding the social world and social research itself on a broader scale and across a wider timeframe. The social world and social science develop and proceed through human agents' continuing interpretation and reinterpretation of them.

Does self-reflexivity produce better research? Pillow traces and identifies the present-day uses of reflexivity in terms of "a form of self-reflexivity as confession that often yields a catharsis of self-awareness for the researcher, which provides a cure for the problem of doing representation".[9] In a broader sense, reflexivity is commonly used in a comfortable way – as comfortable reflexivity. Comfortable reflexivity refers to strategies that are reflexing towards the familiar and have been taken for granted as common practices and methodological techniques in qualitative research. In response to the inherent complexities and messiness of reality and embodied nature of research, Pillow proposes a notion of "uncomfortable reflexivity", which requires the researcher to be reflexive to the point of discomfort.[10] The uncomfortable feeling is attributed to both an attempt to know and a reflexive awareness that the knowing is tenuous. Co-existing with uncomfortable reflexivity means accepting the complexities of reality and the limitations of present-day research methods, language systems, and practices. It challenges the pursuit of objective knowledge and dismisses "a comfortable and transcendent end-point".[11] Practising uncomfortable reflexivity transcends the goal of producing better research whilst considering the difficulties and struggles involved in the research process: as Pillow insightfully puts it, "leaving what is unfamiliar, unfamiliar."[12] I echo Pillow's "uncomfortable reflexivity" by highlighting some of the epistemological, theoretical, ethical, and practical dimensions of striving for it during project fieldwork across borders and during global pandemic times. In the next section, I will analyse and critically reflect on three layers of research dilemmas that emerge on ethical, practical, and methodological levels, which have placed both solvable and insoluble difficulties in my fieldwork.

Reflections on three research dilemmas

During the global pandemic, fieldwork abroad has been expensive, time-consuming, and labour-intensive. Many research projects that would ordinarily constitute face-to-face fieldwork have been switched to online due to unpredictable difficulties such as international travel bans, inflated prices of flights, lockdown, and quarantine restrictions. Reflexivity on the part of the researcher – developing an explicit awareness that requires them to be introspective about contexts, their positions, and power relations – is arguably even more necessary during such challenging times. Apart from the constraints derived from international travel/ visa bans and continuously shifting epidemic prevention policies across frontiers, which can be partly dealt with with personal resilience and strength, and a bit of luck to secure a plane ticket, this section concentrates on research dilemmas in my fieldwork that emerged on ethical, practical, and methodological levels.

One ethical dilemma I encountered was associated with my research being carried out in mainland China and simultaneously being assessed by a UK university. Ethics requirements and measurements in social science research are not universal in different social contexts. There was a section in the ethics form asking about whether I have identified and complied with all local requirements concerning ethical approval, research governance, and data protection. However, by the time my fieldwork was conducted (i.e., between 2020 and 2021), there was no local ethics committee taking responsibility for research like mine in mainland China. In this situation, the ethics form required by my institution appeared to present an irresolvable paradox for fieldwork conducted in mainland China. If I replied "no" to the inquiry about local agencies and research ethics committees, I could not pass the ethics procedure, so I replied "yes" as a pragmatic solution.

The practical dilemma centres on the utility of the consent form. One potential participant refused to participate when she found out the requirement to sign the consent form, which made her concerned about participation. Bryman argues that obtaining participants' signatures "may prompt rather than alleviate concerns on the part of prospective participants, so that they end up declining to be involved".[13] Meanwhile, participants regarded signing consent forms as a redundant and bureaucratic formality, illustrating that the ethics procedure did not fully achieve its utility in the field. Some participants asked me, "Is this your institution's requirement? Will they check this?" while signing the consent form. Furthermore, a complaint procedure was also provided with the consent form, including the contact information of my supervisor and institution. Due to the absence of a local ethics committee, the complaint procedure I provided was the only approach for participants to express dissatisfaction with their participation. However, in order to effectively resort to the complaint procedure, a participant is supposed to be proficient in the English language and have the ability to send emails as prerequisites. Otherwise, it might be argued that some local participants were left open to potential harm and exploitation, since the protection of their well-being mainly depended on the researcher's responsibility and integrity, rather than institutional checks.

Doing fieldwork in a Chinese context and writing up in English bring difficulties into language expression and the work of translation. Language is an "impediment to the transnational flow of feminist ideas".[14] The methodological challenges confronting me are the absence or limited or ambiguous use of wording in feminism-related terms in Chinese, from basic terms of "gender" and "feminism" to more complicated and theoretical ones such as "misogyny", "sexism", and "gender relations". These expressions are less likely to be aligned with the language adopted by the Chinese state, as well as less likely to resonate with those without a higher educational background and/or access to the metropolitan hubs of China. In other words, these feminism-related expressions may be viewed as alienating or "culturally delicate" and thus unacceptable by the public.[15] Reflections on the three research dilemmas suggest limitations of the current design of ethical evaluation, research methods, and language systems, with a particular focus on feminist fieldwork across borders. These dilemmas are associated with the complex and hard-to-change reality within which we are living. Apart from the objective constraints, in the next two sections, I will articulate elements that affect interpersonal relationship in fieldwork and reflect on the practice of uncomfortable reflexivity.

The issue of trust

A research process cannot be regarded as emancipatory or consciousness-raising for both researcher and participants unless a relationship of trust between the parties has been established and developed. From a participant's perspective, taking part in a research project can be more of "an intrusion/imposition/irritation/responsibility than a benefit".[16] Suspicion and repulsion were not uncommon among potential participants. Issues making prospective respondents reluctant to participate include awareness of the unequal relationship between the researcher and the researched, matters of exploitation and control, disclosure of personal information, especially when respondents reveal, possibly for the first time to a person outside of their friendship circle, previous trauma that they have not yet overcome, and sensitive topics, such as politics, sexuality, and intimate relationships. This section reflects critically on fieldwork processes, exploring factors that affected the level of trust between the researcher and research participants, given the political/feminist sensitivity of the topic.

My project centres on exploring shifting dynamics of feminism in post-Socialist China – a topic experiencing growing conflict and tension that "reflects its precariousness as a school of thought, an activist practice, and a topic of study" in politically sensitive contexts.[17] Luo, a PhD candidate working on Chinese women's attitudes towards online feminist activism through ethnography on social media, has experienced verbal attacks and unmerited humiliation by anti-feminist groups while recruiting participants online.[18] Anti-feminist groups express anger, aggression, and hostility and spark controversy by means of tracing feminism-related hashtags. Luo's case reflects the "deeply entwined" relationship between popular feminism and popular misogyny.[19] Both popular feminism and popular misogyny are expressed and circulated on media platforms – battling it out on the contemporary cultural landscape.[20]

In Finch's research study involving interviewing clergymen's wives in the UK, she highlights "strongly and consistently" the ease with which getting women's assurances hinges on the female identity and similar life circumstances shared by her self-revelation (i.e., in Finch's case, she obtained interviewees' trust by claiming that she was also a clergyman's wife), rather than one's expertise as a researcher or a sound ethics process.[21] Finch points out that woman-to-woman interviews develop "a particular kind of identification" as both parties share a "subordinate structural position by virtue of their gender".[22] I echo Finch in the way that she identifies the basis of trust in interviews, where personal identity and similar experiences play an essential role in building a trusting relationship.

In order to navigate potential suspicion from prospective participants and verbal attacks from online anti-feminist groups, I used the snowball technique to target participants. Snowball sampling is particularly applicable when research depends on establishing trust and covers relatively sensitive issues.[23] Participants can "check out" the research and the researcher through interrelated social networks where the researcher is embedded.[24] In my fieldwork, all of the research participants either knew me in person before the research, or we had an intermediary person who had introduced us to each other. Some participants were friends, schoolmates, or even others' siblings. Every participant knew at least one participant within the research network circle. The recruitment method design of my research helped me to instil in participants a sense of security and sustain rapport with them. However, they were unaware of the sense of trust embedded in the ethics and ethical evaluation system that was firmly established within my institution. As Browne suggests, in practice, "word of mouth assurances" are essential when participants are concerned with the topic and are vigilant about leaking personal information.[25] In my fieldwork, participants' consent to participate took effect when they replied "yes" and "okay" to my invitation, rather than when they signed the consent form. They regarded their participation as a personal affair – they wanted to do me a favour, which was based on the trust rooted within my personal social network. The trusting relationship is structured in an interviewing format. In the next section, I show how I interrogate a non-hierarchical relationship and how I managed to build a non-exploitative relationship in fieldwork.

Interviewing relationship: from a non-hierarchical to a non-exploitative relationship

Interviewing, like any other method, is not bias-free. The interviewer-interviewee relationship is seen as a form of an "intrinsically socially unequal", hierarchical, and asymmetrical relationship within which the interviewer sets the agenda and structure and retains the right and initiative to raise questions.[26] Conducting interviews is viewed as "a search-and-discovery mission" aiming to elicit and extract information from interviewees, and is a complex activity.[27] According to Oakley, a good interview depends on both a non-hierarchical relationship between the interviewer and interviewee and the interviewer's subjective initiative to invest their personal identity in the relationship.[28]

Nevertheless, whether a non-hierarchical relationship exists in interviews remains a question. Feminist researchers have recognised a power differential in favour of the researcher, who also holds epistemic privilege.[29] Feminists encourage "a non-exploitative relationship" within which interviewees are not seen merely as data sources providing raw materials for research.[30] In addition, feminist researchers refuse to engage in acting as "emotionally detached and calculating" interviewers who regard participants as "passive givers of information".[31] In *The Active Interview*, Holstein and Gubrium suggest that both the interviewee and the interviewer are active and involved in meaning-making work.[32] Interviewees are not "repositories of knowledge – treasures of information awaiting excavation – so much as they are constructors of knowledge in collaboration with interviewers".[33] It was important for me to practise reflexivity that extended to research participants, rather than being entrenched in a researcher-centre perspective. I would like to highlight that the purpose of doing feminist research is not to interrogate participants for data, but to understand women's experiences in a form of dialogue. Given the asymmetrical relationship between the researcher and the researched, my aim and overriding principle is to build a reciprocal and non-exploitative relationship, particularly through interviews that are interactive, communicative, and dialogic.

In practice, a young woman in my research shared her regret about revealing personal and discomforting experiences to a researcher which in turn made her feel insecure and anxious, worrying that the information would "fall into the wrong hands".[34] From respondents' perspectives, they tended not to allow interviewing to "penetrate beyond a certain level of generality".[35] This relates to the issue of the extent to which respondents are willing to reveal private affairs and personal identity. In some cases, interviewing is the only opportunity for participants and the researcher to have a deep conversation and dive into specific topics. They meet each other for the first time in interviews. To mitigate concerns around "invasion of privacy" and alienation during interviews, I guaranteed confidentiality and anonymity for personal information.[36] In the formulation of interview questions, I used open-ended questions to prompt more reflective and narrative responses. I avoided applying leading, judging, and ambiguous phrasings such as, "Do you think candidates are signed actresses/actors performing on dating shows? Are they sincere about their participation?" I also avoided terminology and jargon that could confuse or alienate respondents, such as "How do you understand female subjectivity represented on dating shows?" I offered participants the option to choose meeting places, raise questions with me, and suggest additional topics to discuss. This approach to interviews was good for eliciting specific information, while being open to possibilities of new information. I realised participants were eager to know how other participants and I replied to the interview questions about female subjectivity, feminism in China, and social norms about relationship and marriage. They wanted to see their experience compared with other women and to get to know the general arguments of my project from a researcher's perspective. Participants' reactions demonstrated Oakley's argument that when the interviewer was prepared to invest their own identity in interviews, they would be able to find out about participants through interviewing.[37] Examples of participants' questions included, "What is your opinion about the match-door marriage norm?", "Why is there already misogyny prior to misandry?", and "Do you agree with the idea that men know about what feminism is fighting for, but they are pretending they do not?" It created an interactive dialogue and allowed them to know me as both a social science researcher and a real person. Letting participants raise questions also helped me to conduct in-depth interviews with them candidly and honestly.

How can a less hierarchical relationship be built and the power differential between interviewee and interviewer be alleviated? In practice, I found that respondents' perceptions of the interviewing relationship played a key role in the resulting interview quality. When respondents thought the interviewer and interviewee relationship was non-hierarchical or relatively equal, they tended to be more willing to talk and invest their personal identities in interviews. Respondents' perception of the interviewing relationship was related to the recruitment method, their goal or motive in agreeing to participate, and circumstances within which interviews were conducted. Whilst carrying out participant recruitment procedures for my research, I appealed to my elder relatives for help. They initially identified eligible women who were their subordinates in the workplace, and then shared those women's WeChat accounts with me to further negotiate with personally. One woman directly declined the invitation once she learnt that participation would be face-to-face and last for over one hour. Another two women agreed to participate and arranged to meet during working hours or during work breaks. They were relatively impatient and perfunctory during meetings. One woman was reluctant to give details or drill down to deep conversations. She described interview questions around identifying the main features of dating shows as "too broad" and "have no idea how to respond". What made these conversations difficult was the manner of introduction – the fact that I was associated with their line managers. Meanwhile, the two women were rather curious about the relationship between their line managers and me. For them, participating in my research was viewed as an allocated task related or not directly related to their work, which made them feel compelled to engage. The two women's resistance on being questioned reflected their defensive attitude to the unequal meeting situation as well as the hierarchical power relation in their workplaces. Fortunately, one woman was delighted after the meeting – she told me the interview questions helped her to consider many important issues in life carefully. This woman's changed attitude reflected the dynamics of interpersonal communication affected by the emotional labour I put in during interviews.

The meeting experience with the two participants demonstrated a hierarchical and tangled web of interpersonal relationships in the society within which people are living. Conducting interviews is labour-intensive and is mentally taxing on the interviewer to guide conversations and respond appropriately to interviewees. In particular, the involved complexity of emotions, unavoidable pressure, and instrumental rationality is significant for understanding the interviewee-and-interviewer relationship. Emotional labour expects one to manage feelings and expressions to "sustain the outward countenance that produces the proper state of mind in others".[38] Reflections on emotional labour in qualitative fieldwork are valuable data which dive into the invisible emotional interaction which can be easily overlooked during interview processes.[39] In my fieldwork, there were many moments where I was deeply touched and inspired by the trust, sincerity, and encouragement from my research respondents. What intensive emotional labour gave back was irreplaceable emotional value, providing me with greater strength to confront difficult situations or have difficult conversations in fieldwork. In most cases, the meeting places also have an impact on participants' behaviours and reaction to the research project, which will be explored in the next section.

How do meeting places make a difference?

In audience studies, the focus on audience interpretation not only has roots in the encoding/decoding model, but also relates to the discussion of "contextualism", exploring questions about where, when, and how media texts are encountered and integrated into the everyday lives of audiences.[40] Contextualism offers different ways to analyse media consumption moments – television consumption in particular – in domestic and non-domestic spheres.[41] In this section, drawing on the project fieldwork, I show how different contexts of the meeting place and practices of everyday life shape female viewers' behaviour and interpretation of reality dating shows. I also analyse how different meeting places affect the quality of texts-in-action viewing sessions and interviews, further advancing discussions of contextualism in media consumption and audience studies.

How did meeting places make a difference in fieldwork? I found meetings conducted in undisturbed private spaces went better than those held in the public sphere. Participants were more comfortable and more willing to engage with my research when meetings were held in their homes, offices, and classrooms, rather than in cafes or restaurants. When conducting texts-in-action viewing sessions in cafes, participants expressed concern about how other people would look at them when noticing them watching dating shows. In the public sphere, women became more introspective and were disturbed by an imagined external gaze, fearing being judged and derided by others. Hua asked me apprehensively, "Will they assume that we are in a hurry to find a partner?" while we were watching the reality dating show and several customers took their seats next to us. Jing suggested turning down the volume several times during the viewing session. In addition, if meetings were held during rush hour, the sound quality of meeting audio records was sometimes poorer with the hustle and bustle of background noise in cafes and restaurants, which was found to be a distraction to respondents' participation.

More importantly, participants' reaction to reality dating shows demonstrated that watching dating shows openly was often seen as uncivil, demeaning, and dumbed-down, and thus discouraged by well-educated young women. This is a gendered issue, related also to the distinction between private and public. According to Kramer's study of stereotyped characteristics of sex-related speech differences, female speech was featured in "gossip, trivial topics, self-revealing speech, and gibberish".[42] In my fieldwork, young women's attitude towards reality dating shows reflected their rejection of the gendered stereotypes as "empty vessels" or gossip girls.[43] Some women expressed the view that reality dating shows focusing on family gossip and small household affairs appealed to older and retired viewers[44] while young viewers were more interested in programmes with detective themes.

I prioritised participants' preferences when fixing locations. Six of the women invited me to their homes or agreed to meetings arranged in my home office. Participants felt relatively relaxed about the meeting arranged in their space. Meetings in the interviewee's own homes were more like "an intimate conversation", and the researcher acted as both "a friendly guest" and "a sympathetic listener", not "an official inquisitor".[45] Likewise, Ahmed mentioned the advantages of conducting interviews when participants were at home, as it allowed them to "leave the conversation quickly and easily", which proved to be good for their well-being.[46]

In my fieldwork, I found myself switching between the roles of a guest and a researcher when doing home interviews, which raised questions about the positioning and visibility of the fieldworker self in the field.[47] Prior to the texts-in-action viewing sessions, participants tended to offer me food and drink – unlike meetings in public spaces, where I prepared refreshments for participants. My experience in Xiao Mei's home was quite remarkable. Xiao Mei lived with her parents, and we arranged a meeting at her home after she had returned from work.

> "You become thinner and taller again! Have you ever eaten food?" Xiao Mei's mother said to me when I was coming through the door.
> "Our family doesn't normally have dinner because we all need to lose weight. But since you're here and it's dinner time, I'm gonna cook something for you," Xiao Mei's mother said to me hospitably.

I was shocked that the whole family – including Xiao Mei and her parents – did not have dinner, or at least the mother told me so. I initially refused the dinner invitation by highlighting my identity as a researcher. Ethnographers have long debated issues of familiarity, strangeness, and distance in fieldwork accounts, reflecting complexities concerning the researcher self as an essential and inherent part of fieldwork.[48] They highlight the need to cultivate and maintain a sense of strangeness in the field to gain insight into how cultural settings reframe the self. Here, the notion of strangeness was seen as "a methodological tool" and "an unambiguous and developmental position for the self".[49] When I did the fieldwork, I managed to balance the researcher role, whose activities strictly conformed to the meeting topic guide, with the moderator role, adjusting the meeting atmosphere to be neither overly casual nor excessively alien. I also tried to create an empathetic ambience in the interaction process with my research participants and people around them. However, in this case the mother ignored my unwillingness to have dinner and insisted on preparing food.

The dinner included a vegetable, stir-fried potato chips, steamed buns, and corn congee. The dinner was only made for me. During the dinner, Xiao Mei just picked at several pieces of greens to eat without touching anything else on the table. She was doing this only to keep me company. When I was conducting my fieldwork, she was preparing for her wedding. She said to me, "Wedding dress photos don't bother me because there's Photoshop. But at the ceremony, guests will see me in person. I have to try really hard to lose weight – a month to go."

Her mother was sitting with us but also not eating. She kept praising me for being slim and asked me about how to keep fit. The mother compared me with Xiao Mei and encouraged Xiao Mei to lose weight and become as slim as me.

> "Slimness is the top topic forever." I sighed with frustration.
> "You are right. Slimness is the top topic forever," the mother repeated, without recognising my implication.

It was not the first time that my research participants commented on my figure. Another interviewee, Tian, was asking about my height and weight in the first two minutes when we met. I assume that in women's interpersonal social contact, this type of body-related questioning can be an icebreaker conversation, a friendly greeting, or a mode of compliment, since slimness is regarded as the current ideal of feminine appearance in China.[50] The body, its weight, size, and shape, along with the related aesthetic work to transform the body, are all initial topics to begin a conversation with a stranger in women's conversations. The complexity of human interaction leads to difficult situations for the researcher, who decides the discussion topics and how to respond to knotty inquiries while caring about participants' well-being. In response to body-related questions, I prepared an answer which I thought was scientific and honest. I replied to them, "I didn't manage to be slim. Being slim is because of genes and the digestive system." There was usually short silence after I said this. This answer did not meet their expectations, perhaps because it did not convince them that a slim body did not require consistent aesthetic labour. My response positioned me as a "marginal native" of the body-related conversations.[51]

The ethnographic turn in media reception studies has been valuable in positioning media use and consumption as an activity in the context of the domestic sphere and daily life. Conducting audience reception studies in participants' homes provided rich, complex, and detailed accounts of viewers' use of time and space during media consumption, as well as of their different family and personal relationships. Furthermore, the ethnographic turn in audience reception studies relates to an ethnographic sensibility signposting a broader and richer conception of what constitutes data. Data includes the spoken, unspoken expressions from the side of participants, as well as observations and reflections that the researcher makes. All of these cues open a window onto the worlds of participants, allowing the researcher to make sense of the information gathered, including how participants interpret the research topic.

Conclusion

This chapter provides a retrospective, descriptive, and reflexive account of my fieldwork journey, ethical dilemmas of conducting qualitative research during the pandemic, how I managed to build a trusting and non-exploitative relationship with participants, and how the meeting places shaped participants' behaviour and interpretation of my project and further had an impact on the quality of fieldwork. The fieldwork was informed by a complicated reality – with obstacles consisting of international travel bans, the limitations of present-day research methods and language system, all of which have made conversations in fieldwork difficult and knotty. During these challenging times, Pillow's "uncomfortable reflexivity" provides an inspirational perspective to perceive insoluble and unspeakable difficulties along with tensions and discomfort in qualitative fieldwork across borders, which has helped me to move beyond difficult conversations.

Given the paradox lying in the utility of the ethics form, the situation experienced in my fieldwork reflected how the design of ethics form overlooked the specific local circumstances that varied in different countries. Namely, how can the interests of disadvantaged or less privileged groups be protected in research being carried out outside of the UK? This question perhaps cannot be solved by means of imposing training courses offered by university institutions on social science researchers. Instead, I call on more practice of "uncomfortable reflexivity" on the side of researcher so as to ensure authenticity and trustworthiness of fieldwork and illuminate future research across borders.

Furthermore, there were many dimensions from the side of participants affecting conversations in qualitative fieldwork, which included concern about "invasion of privacy"[52], discomforting feelings arose when revealing certain experience or information, and unavoidable pressure entangled in hierarchical social networks, etc. In response to the issue as outlined here, my attitude was to take a step back and remain silent when my questioning was deemed as disturbing, instead of trying to dig out "the hidden truth" by probing participants deeply, which would make participants worry about the potential risks of being exploited by opening themselves up to "interrogation". In her research on women's magazines, Gill articulates an orientation of critical respect which involves "attentive, respectful listening" and at the same time not to "abdicate the right to question or interrogate".[53] While providing essential support to research participants, Gill stresses the right to engage critically, rather than act as "a mute supporter".[54] I agree with the idea that showing respect is an ethical principle. Meanwhile, the success of fieldwork also depends on a demonstration of trustworthiness by respecting respondents' boundaries and actively leaving some stones unturned.[55] When carrying out fieldwork, I avoided ferreting out participants' privacy where I was not wanted. I did not force anyone to respond to anything that they did not want to share by means of interviewing techniques. I equally valued the importance of raising questions to participants and listening to them carefully.

My stance on taking a step back from confronting difficult conversations in fieldwork is also related to the constructionist stance of qualitative research. Qualitative research implies an ontological position indicating that knowing the social world relies on people's interpretation and reflection-oriented understandings of the world, rather than through an examination of "out there" phenomena.[56] As Edley and Litosseliti put it, constructivist researchers treat conversations in fieldwork as indicative or illustrative data that offers insights about what participants say they think or believe.[57] In this sense, it is not helpful to think of research participants as having open or heart-to-heart conversations with the researcher; it is also important to think of silence, or what is left unsaid, as an integral part of a conversation. What matters for a constructivist researcher is to consider why participants express certain opinions in certain ways within certain contexts.

Notes

1 Texts-in-action is a method developed by Helen Wood. It refers to observing and capturing the dynamic interaction between television texts and viewers' immediate reaction. Texts-in-action allows the researcher to conceive live moments of television reception. Helen Wood, "Television Is Happening: Methodological Considerations for Capturing Digital Television Reception," *European Journal of Cultural Studies* 10, no. 4 (2007): 485–506.
2 Ulrich Beck, Anthony Giddens and Scott Lash, *Reflective Modernisation: Politics, Tradition and Aesthetics in the Modern Social Order* (Cambridge: Polity, 1994).
3 Helen Callaway, "Ethnography and Experience: Gender Implications in Fieldwork and Texts," in *Anthropology and Autobiography*, ed. Judith Okely and Helen Callaway (New York: Routledge, 1992): 90.
4 Michaela Benson and Karen O'Reilly, "Reflexive Practice in Live Sociology: Lessons from Researching Brexit in the Lives of British Citizens Living in the EU-27", *Qualitative Research* 22, no. 2 (2020): 3.
5 Lisa Adkins, "Reflexivity: Freedom or Habit of Gender?", *Theory, Culture & Society* 20, no. 6 (2003): 24–25.
6 Elizabeth Chiseri-Strater, "Turning in upon Ourselves: Positionality, Subjectivity, and Reflexivity in Case Study and Ethnographic Research," in *Ethics and Responsibility in Qualitative Studies of Literacy*, ed. Peter Mortensen and Gesa E. Kirsch (Urbana: NCTE, 1996): 130.
7 Wanda Pillow, "Confession, Catharsis, or Cure? Rethinking the Uses of Reflexivity as Methodological Power in Qualitative Research", *International Journal of Qualitative Studies in Education* 16 no.2 (2003): 178.
8 Benson and O'Reilly, "Reflexive Practice in Live Sociology".
9 Ibid. 181.
10 Ibid. 188.
11 Ibid. 193.
12 Ibid. 177.
13 Alan Bryman, *Social Research Methods* 5th edition (Oxford: Oxford University Press, 2016), 131.
14 Shan Huang and Wanning Sun, "#Metoo in China: Transnational Feminist Politics in the Chinese Context", *Feminist Media Studies* 21, no.4 (2021): 680.
15 Ibid.
16 Liz Kelly, Sheila Burton and Linda Regan, "Researching Women's Lives or Studying Women's Oppression? Reflections on What Constitutes Feminist Research," in *Researching Women's Lives from a Feminist Perspective*, ed. Mary Maynard and June Purvis (Abingdon: Taylor & Francis, 1994), 36.
17 Sara Liao, "Feminism without Guarantees: Reflections on Teaching and Researching Feminist Activism in China," *Asian Journal of Women's Studies* 26, no. 2 (2020): 259.
18 Taoyuan Luo, "Young Chinese Women's Attitudes towards Feminism" (PhD dissertation, University of Leeds, forthcoming).
19 Sarah Banet-Weiser, *Empowered: Popular Feminism and Popular Misogyny* (Durham and London: Duke University Press, 2018), 2.
20 Ibid.

21 Janet Finch, "'It's Great to Have Someone to Talk to': The Ethics and Politics of Interviewing Women," in *Social Researching: Politics, Problems, Practice*, ed. Colin Bell and Helen Roberts (London: Routledge and Kegan Paul, 1984), 78.
22 Ibid. 76.
23 See Patrick Biernacki and Dan Waldorf, "Snowball Sampling: Problems and Techniques of Chain Referral Sampling," *Sociological Methods and Research* 10, no. 2 (1981): 141–163. Kath Browne, "Snowball Sampling: Using Social Networks to Research Non-heterosexual Women," *Social Research Methodology* 8, no. 1 (2005): 47–60.
24 Ibid. 50.
25 Browne, "Snowball Sampling," 50.
26 Jaber Gubrium and James Holstein, *Handbook of Interview Research: Context & Methods* (Thousand Oaks: Sage, 2022).
    Sandra Harding, "Feminist Standpoints," in *Handbook of Feminist Research: Theory and Praxis*, ed. Sharlene Nagy Hesse-Biber (California: Sage, 2012), 52.
27 Nigal Edley and Lia Litosseliti, "Critical Perspective on Using Interviews and Focus Groups," in *Research Methods in Linguistics*, ed. Lia Litosseliti (London: Bloomsbury, 2018).
    James Holstein and Jaber Gubrium, *The Active Interview* (London: Sage, 1995), 2.
28 Ann Oakley, "Interviewing Women: A Contradiction in Terms," in *Doing Feminist Research*, ed. Helen Roberts (London: Routledge and Kegan Paul, 1981), 41.
29 Joan Acker, Kate Barry and Joke Esseveld, "Objectivity and Truth: Problems in Doing Feminist Research," *Women's Studies International Forum* 6, no. 4 (1983): 423–435.
    Bat-Ami Bar On, "Marginality and Epistemic Privilege," in Feminist Epistemologies, ed. Linda Alcoff and Elizabeth Potter (New York: Routledge, 1993).
30 Mary Maynard, "Methods, Practice and Epistemology: The Debate about Feminism and Research," in *Researching Women's Lives from a Feminist Perspective*, ed. Mary Maynard and June Purvis. (Abingdon: Taylor & Francis, 1994), 16.
31 Mary Maynard and June Purvis, "Introduction: Doing Feminist Research," in *Researching Women's Lives from a Feminist Perspective*, ed. Mary Maynard and June Purvis. (Abingdon: Taylor & Francis, 1994), 15.
32 Holstein and Gubrium, *The Active Interview*.
33 Ibid. 4.
34 Maynard and Purvis, "Introduction," 5.
35 Patrick Peritore, "Reflections on Dangerous Fieldwork", *American Sociologist* 21, no. 4 (1990): 360.
36 Bryman, *Social Research Methods*, 131.
37 Oakley, "Interviewing women".
38 Arlie Russell Hochschild, *The Managed Heart: Commercialisation of Human Feeling* (Berkeley and Los Angeles: University of California Press, 2012), 7.
39 Kathleen Blee, "White-Knuckle Research: Emotional Dynamics in Fieldwork with Racist Activists," *Qualitative Sociology* 21, no. 4 (1998): 381–399.
40 Matt Hills, "Audiences," in *The Craft of Criticism: Critical Media Studies in Practice*, ed. Michael Kackman and Mary Celeste Kearney (New York and London: Routledge, 2018).
41 Anna McCarthy, *Ambient Television* (Durham: Duke University Press, 2001).
    Lynn Spigel, *Make Room for TV* (Chicago: University of Chicago Press, 1992).
42 Cheris Kramer, "Perceptions of Female and Male Speech," *Language and Speech* 20, no. 2 (1977): 159.
43 Helen Wood, *Talking with Television: Women, Talk Shows, and Modern Self-Reflexivity* (Urbana and Chicago: University of Illinois Press, 2009), 15.
44 Several participants used the expression *jiachangliduan* to describe the feature of dating shows, which meant small household affairs.

45 Finch, "'It's Great to Have Someone to Talk to'," 74–75.
46 Sara Ahmed, *Complaint*! (Durham and London: Duke University Press, 2021), 12.
47 Amanda Coffey, *The Ethnographic Self* (London: Sage, 1999).
48 Coffey, *The Ethnographic Self*.
   John Lofland, David Snow, Leon Anderson, and Lyn Lofland, *Analysing Social Settings: A Guide to Qualitative Observation and Analysis*, 4th edition (CA: Wadsworth, 2006).
49 Coffey, *The Ethnographic Self*, 22.
50 Freedom Leung, Sharon Lam and Sherrien Sze, "Cultural Expectations of Thinness in Chinese Women," *Eating Disorders* 9, no. 4 (2010): 339–350.
   Meng Zhang, "A Chinese Beauty Story: How College Women in China Negotiate Beauty, Body Image and Mass Media," *Chinese Journal of Communication* 5, no. 4 (2012): 437–454.
51 Morris Freilich, *Marginal Natives: Anthropologists at Work* (New York: Harper and Row, 1970).
52 Bryman, *Social Research Methods*, 131.
53 Rosalind Gill, "Critical Respect: The Difficulties and Dilemmas of Agency and 'Choice' for Feminism," *European Journal of Women's Studies* 14, no. 1 (2007): 78.
54 Ibid.
55 Liisa Malkki, *Purity and Exile* (IL: University of Chicago Press, 1995).
56 Bryman, *Social Research Methods*, 375.
57 Edley and Litosseliti, "Critical Perspective on Using Interviews and Focus Groups".

Bibliography

Acker, J., Barry, K. and Esseveld, J (1983) Objectivity and truth: Problems in doing feminist research. *Women's Studies International Forum* 6(4): 423–435.

Adkins, L (2003) Reflexivity: Freedom or habit of gender?. *Theory, Culture & Society* 20(6): 24–25.

Ahmed, S (2021) *Complaint*! Durham and London: Duke University Press, 2021.

Banet-Weiser, S (2018) *Empowered: Popular Feminism and Popular Misogyny*. Durham and London: Duke University Press.

Beck, U., Giddens, A. and Lash, S (1994) *Reflective Modernisation: Politics, Tradition and Aesthetics in the Modern Social Order*. Cambridge: Polity.

Benson, M. and O'Reilly, K (2020) Reflexive practice in live sociology: Lessons from researching brexit in the lives of British citizens living in the EU-27. *Qualitative Research* 22(2): 1–17.

Blee, K (1998) White-Knuckle research: Emotional dynamics in fieldwork with racist activists. *Qualitative Sociology* 21(4): 381–399.

Biernacki, P. and Waldorf, D (1981) Snowball sampling: Problems and techniques of chain referral sampling. *Sociological Methods and Research* 10(2): 141–163.

Browne, K (2005) Snowball sampling: Using social networks to research non-heterosexual women. *Social Research Methodology* 8(1): 47–60.

Bryman, A (2016) *Social Research Methods* (5th edn). Oxford: Oxford University Press.

Callaway, H (1992) Ethnography and experience: Gender implications in fieldwork and texts. In J. Okely and H. Callaway (eds.) *Anthropology and Autobiography*. New York: Routledge.

Chiseri-Strater, E (1996) Turning in upon ourselves: Positionality, subjectivity, and reflexivity in case study and ethnographic research. In P. Mortensen and G. E. Kirsch (eds.) *Ethics and Responsibility in Qualitative Studies of Literacy*. Urbana: NCTE.

Coffey, A (1999) *The Ethnographic Self*. London: Sage.

Edley, N. and Litosseliti, L (2018) Critical perspective on using interviews and focus groups. In L. Litosseliti (ed.) *Research Methods in Linguistics*. London: Bloomsbury.

Finch, J (1984) 'It's great to have someone to talk to': The ethics and politics of interviewing women. In C. Bell and H. Roberts (eds.) *Social Researching: Politics, Problems, Practice*. London: Routledge and Kegan Paul.

Freilich, M (1970) *Marginal Natives: Anthropologists at Work*. New York: Harper and Row.

Gill, R (2007) Critical respect: The difficulties and dilemmas of agency and 'choice' for feminism. *European Journal of Women's Studies* 14(1): 69–80.

Gubrium, J. and Holstein, J (2022) *Handbook of Interview Research: Context & Methods*. Thousand Oaks: Sage.

Harding, S (2012) Feminist standpoints. In S. Nagy Hesse-Biber (ed.) *Handbook of Feminist Research: Theory and Praxis*. Thousand Oaks: Sage.

Hills, M (2018) Audiences. In M. Kackman and M. Celeste Kearney (eds.) *The Craft of Criticism: Critical Media Studies in Practice*. New York and London: Routledge.

Hochschild, A. R (2012) *The Managed Heart: Commercialisation of Human Feeling*. Berkeley and Los Angeles: University of California Press.

Holstein, J. and Gubrium, J (1995) *The Active Interview*. London: Sage.

Huang, S. and Sun, W (2021) #Metoo in China: Transnational feminist politics in the Chinese context. *Feminist Media Studies* 21(4): 677–681.

Kelly, L., Burton, S. and Regan, L (1994) Researching women's lives or studying women's oppression? Reflections on what constitutes feminist research. In M. Maynard and J. Purvis (eds.) *Researching Women's Lives from a Feminist Perspective*. Abingdon: Taylor & Francis.

Kramer, C (1977) Perceptions of female and male speech. *Language and Speech* 20(2): 151–161.

Leung, F., Lam, S. and Sze, S (2010) Cultural expectations of thinness in Chinese women. *Eating Disorders* 9(4): 339–350.

Liao, S (2020) Feminism without guarantees: Reflections on teaching and researching feminist activism in China. *Asian Journal of Women's Studies* 26(2): 1–23.

Lofland, J., Snow, D., Anderson, L. and Lofland, L (2006) *Analysing Social Settings: A Guide to Qualitative Observation and Analysis* (4th edn). Thousand Oaks: Wadsworth.

Luo, T (forthcoming) *Young Chinese women's attitudes towards feminism*. (PhD dissertation). Leeds: University of Leeds.

Malkki, L (1995) *Purity and Exile*. Chicago: University of Chicago Press.

Maynard, M (1994) Methods, practice and epistemology: The debate about feminism and research. In M. Maynard and J. Purvis (eds.), *Researching women's lives from a feminist perspective*. Abingdon: Taylor & Francis.

Maynard, M. and Purvis, J (1994) Introduction: Doing feminist research. In M. Maynard and J. Purvis (eds.), *Researching Women's Lives from a Feminist Perspective*. Abingdon: Taylor & Francis.

McCarthy, A (2001) *Ambient Television*. Durham: Duke University Press.

Oakley, A (1981) Interviewing women: A contradiction in terms. In H. Roberts (ed.), *Doing Feminist Research*. London: Routledge and Kegan Paul.

On, B-A. B (1993) Marginality and epistemic privilege. In L. Alcoff and E. Potter (eds.), *Feminist Epistemologies*. New York: Routledge.

Pillow, W (2003) Confession, catharsis, or cure? Rethinking the uses of reflexivity as methodological power in qualitative research. *International Journal of Qualitative Studies in Education* 16(2): 175–196.

Peritore, P (1990) Reflections on dangerous fieldwork. *American Sociologist* 21(4): 359–372.
Spigel, L (1992) *Make Room for TV*. Chicago: University of Chicago Press.
Wood, H (2007) Television is happening: Methodological considerations for capturing digital television reception. *European Journal of Cultural Studies* 10, no. 4 (2007): 485-506.
Wood, H (2009) *Talking with Television: Women, Talk Shows, and Modern Self-Reflexivity*. Urbana and Chicago: University of Illinois Press.
Zhang, M (2012) A Chinese beauty story: How college women in China negotiate beauty, body image and mass media. *Chinese Journal of Communication* 5(4): 437–454.

Section 3
Gender, sexuality and embodiment

9 Sexing in the cities

Sex, desire, and sexual health of black township women who love women

Phoebe Kisubi Mbasalaki

Every time [I] am around women, [I] am really happy. [I] am like, [I] am in a world of my own. When [I] am here, I feel at home, I feel at home.
(Limakatso research participant, Johannesburg[1])

Introduction

Since I have been immersed in the study of gender and sexuality, I have been uncomfortable with the unidimensional discourse of sex and sexuality being read through HIV prisms – the strong coupling of sex with sexual reproductive health and public health. This alludes to how HIV/AIDS and its implications have redefined sexuality in Sub-Saharan Africa, prompting the question: Has desire permanently been contaminated with the connotations of AIDS? This highlights the difficult conversation and tension between sex, desire, and disease. As Susan Sontag proclaims: 'AIDS obliges people to think of sex as having, possibly, the direst consequences: Suicide or Murder? How does a society idealize love, community, family, and procreation in and environment in which all these acts and relationships become dangerous?' (Sontag, 1988 quoted in Attree, 2010: 67). The strong association of sex with the discourse of disease in gender and sexuality studies not only silences but also erases pleasure, eroticism, and other positive aspects – seemingly only equating sex with death. This foregrounds the difficulty in conversations of pleasure and desire in knowledge production on African sexuality – especially as it relates to same-sex desire.

Indeed, HIV and disease more generally have played a substantial role, not only in knowledge production on African sexuality in Africa south of the Sahara, but also – if we go by Marc Epprecht's (2008) argument – in the way that knowledge is framed. Epprecht (2008) reminds us of how dominant discourse on African sexuality – read through the dominant HIV discourse – does not simply ignore, but rather works firmly under the assumption that there is no homosexuality in Africa.[2] Development discourse is the main machinery of knowledge production as it relates to African sexuality and has greatly contributed to the normalisation of the coupling of African sexuality and disease (Tamale, 2011). It is vital to highlight the paucity of research on any form of African sexuality that falls outside of dominant discourse, as well as the misrepresentation of African sexualities that has followed the development of discourse – a dynamic that post- and decolonial scholars equate to epistemic violence (Fanon, 1961; Ndlovu-Gatsheni, 2016; wa Thiongo'o, 1998). Therefore, in this chapter I will try to navigate this tense terrain, drawing out the invisibilities of desire, pleasure, and lust as a decolonial intervention that opens up possibilities to engage in this difficult conversation. I work within the framework of decolonial feminism, noting Lugones (2007) emphasises that 'colonization of gender is still with us; it is what lies at the intersection of gender/class/race as central constructs of the capitalist world system of power' (746). Decolonial feminism therefore usefully offers us 'a lens to understand the hidden-from-view interconnections between race and gender and the relation of each to normative heterosexuality' (Tamale, 2020: 7). The conversation here is framed in knowledge production on African sexuality, especially as it relates to same-sex desires. I will take time to analyse the lived experiences of African same-sex intimacies[3] by making full use of the tool I call decolonialised sexual scripts. I will focus on early experiences, centring participants' first same-sex encounter in its broader understanding and meaning. This way, this difficult conversation will contribute to making intelligible local knowledge concerning sex, desire, and pleasure of black township womxn who desire womxn[4].

Why decoloniality matters when talking about African (same-sex) sex, desire, and pleasure

Decolonial prisms become not only necessary, but crucial given the ways in which knowledge production on African sexualities has largely followed colonising and medicalised paths. Indeed, decolonial prisms shed some light on the genealogies that have made it difficult to have conversations and knowledge production on lust, desire, and sexual pleasure in relation to African sexuality – and in this case, same-sex desire and pleasure. Silvia Tamale (2011), Desire Lewis (2011), and Anne McClintock (1995) all posit that sexuality was central to the colonising project. In addition, the colonial imagination and misrepresentation of African sexuality constructed it through the essentialised that located it as 'closer to nature', which led to the perception of Africans as purely heterosexual (Lewis, 2011). This misrepresentation persisted in postcolonial South Africa through sexual, reproductive, and public health rubrics in which the main focus was disease and pregnancy prevention – something both Tamale (2011) and Lewis (2011) read as the curbing of sexual excesses and perversion. Tamale suggests that this narrow approach meant (as it often still does) that the 'research of biomedical experts, epidemiologists, and demographers ignored sexual wellness and issues of eroticism and desire, leading to limited theoretical framings of African sexualities' (Tamale, 2011: 25).[5] This frames the coloniality of gender and sexuality in Africa as one of the main contributors to silencing of sexual desire and pleasure, making it the subject of a difficult conversation.

In line with Tamale's argument, Signe Arnfred's *Re-thinking Sexualities in Africa* (2004a) takes a groundbreaking look at African sexuality, noting that:

> even if sexuality and (white, male) sexual desire have been active factors in establishing the very notion of Africa and Africans, sexual pleasure and desire have rarely been objects of study for scholars studying Africa – female sexual pleasure and desire even less.
>
> (Arnfred, 2004a: 20)

This, I add, is even less for black womxn in same-sex relationships. This falls broadly within what Epprecht (2008) has eloquently argued as same-sex practices being understood as largely non-existent in Africa. Epprecht clinically dissects how the notion that homosexuality did not exist in Africa was not only endorsed, but was in fact cemented by HIV discourse – as a major player in the defining and researching of African sexuality, albeit one seen purely through heterosexual prisms. This in essence affirms a form of colonial continuity that positioned Africans 'closer to nature', as mentioned earlier, and thus by construction and definition heterosexual. As such, homosexuality can thus be seen as an imposition on the African continent, deeming homosexuals as inherently 'un-African.' Epprecht (2008) notes how this has been endorsed through the political homophobia of leaders such as Robert Mugabe and Yoweri Museveni – albeit a decade or so later, when the heterosexual HIV in Africa discourse had already been set and established. Such rhetoric only adds to colonial continuities on the imagination of African sexuality as exclusively heterosexual.

By their very existence, African same-sex intimacies negate this remnant of the colonial imagination – the exclusively heterosexual narrative. I would like to read these same-sex desires through a decolonial lens in order to magnify how they destabilise heterosexual privilege. Indeed, decolonisation takes on many forms, one of them being the decolonisation of sexuality. In their book *Decolonizing Sexualities: Transnational Perspectives Critical Interventions*, Sandeep Bakshi et al. (2016) articulate that 'an ongoing critical reflection on decolonial readings of queerness is necessary since heteronormativity is sustained upon epistemic categories, among others, of race, gender and sexuality' (1). Walter Mignolo (who writes the foreword of the aforementioned book) explains that 'decolonial healing requires building to re-exist rather than energy to only resist' (Mignolo, 2016: viii). He adds that 're-existence means that you de-link from the rules imposed on you, you create your own rules communally, and therefore you re-exist affirming yourself as a human being' (ibid.). I read this in line with the sexual arrangements and codes that black township womxn in same-sex relationships have made intelligible within their communities. To add to this, Jeff Corntassel (2012) explains that decolonisation is made up of 'everyday acts of resurgence' that regenerate indigenous or local knowledges, epistemologies, and ways of life which are always adapting, creating, and moving forward. Indeed, what this chapter brings to light is precisely those local knowledges through the rubric of sex, desire, pleasure, and love, as well as their associated meanings as a difficult conversation that opens up possibilities for democratised knowledge production on African sexuality.

I read the same-sex desires, lusts, and loves of black lesbian womxn who reside in townships through these decolonial prisms, as a way of de-linking them from the dominant heterosexual paradigm – from heterosexual scripts. A decolonial rubric therefore does not only foreground roots of the difficult conversations but also opens up possibilities for positive change in knowledge production on desire and pleasure among African same-sex intimacies. Indeed, there was a celebratory air of openness in the way the womxn expressed themselves, talking about sex with ease, even in big focus group discussions and with a complete absence of coyness. The scenarios presented in this chapter therefore contradict former colonial discourse that posits female sexuality as passive and docile, instead foregrounding womxn as active agents with a claim over their own bodies: drivers of their own sexual desires, sexual encounters, and sexual pleasures with fellow women. In doing so, these womxn dispel the colonial and traditional tropes that have dominated African female sexuality. This takes place within a discourse of sexual freedom – from pregnancy, HIV, and other STIs – a case of sexual enjoyment, desire, pleasure, and eroticism that is untouched by reproductive and/or HIV (specifically the zero-risk myth) discourse that has previously dominated sexuality and sexual knowledge production in Africa. This discourse thus relies on the participants' experiences, perceptions, and verbalisations of their own scripts, rather than any generic cultural (heteronormative) script on how sexuality in South Africa is perceived.

'Every time [I] am around women, [I] am really happy' – sex, desire, and pleasure: first same-sex desire and encounter

Here, I dive more into aspects of desire. Indeed, not much has been written about adolescent same-sex desires in South Africa. Exceptions include the work of Tanya Chan-Sam (1994), who puts forth the personal narratives of same-sex sweethearts at boarding high schools, who refer to each other as *amachicken*, as well as that of Judith Gay (1986), who brought to the fore the narrative of 'mummies and babies' in Lesotho. Using this as a starting point, I trace early experiences, such as a first crush on a woman or a first kiss, in early adolescence. Foregrounding the participants' experiences, perceptions, and verbalisations of their own pleasure and desire via their own scripts, rather than through a generic cultural (heteronormative) script, illuminates how sexuality is enacted, whilst always acknowledging the agency of the individual.

The early teenage years and adolescence are periods of great change, identity being central to one's self-discovery. Sexual self-discovery for womxn in same-sex relations takes place against an overtly heteronormative backdrop – one that penetrates all aspects of society, from formal sexual education to implicit scripts of sexual activity that are regulated by norms of heterosexual courtship and marriage. For most teenagers, the process of sexual discovery is one of exploration, uncertainty, and questions precipitated by other physical, mental, and social developments, all aggravated by social interactions – both platonic and of a sexual nature. These emotions are mirrored and come across as a dominant narrative for most of the womxn I interviewed. Additionally, many were confused by and questioning their attraction to womxn, not least because this was not in line with societal heteronormative expectations and practices as currency or capital. The investment is in a sexuality that is a conglomeration of colonialism, capitalism, neoliberalism, African culture, and patriarchy, all of which coalesce in their privileging of heteronormativity. Here, capital manifests in the form of an 'ideal' trajectory – 'girl meets boy; girl dates boy; girl marries boy.' These are the undertones (or sometimes even overtones) of the experiences of womxn in same-sex relationships in South African townships. I will focus on three narratives which I will unpack together. Take Letsego, a 22-year-old lesbian from Daveyton Township in Gauteng, whose early teenage experience embodies some of the aforementioned capital and heterosexual under-/overtones. During the in-depth interview, her voice is full of excitement as she recalls her early teenage years and early sexual attractions and encounters, especially when she gets to the point of narrating the discovery of her same-sex attraction.

Phoebe: How long ago did you realise you were attracted to womxn?
Letsego: Oooh, that thing, yhoo. It made me go around, searching for myself. It started in grade 8 when I got to high school. I used to stay, I used to sleep with this guy, this boy. And he would always be like yhoo, your eyes are so beautiful. And [I] am like, ok thanks. But when a girl says your eyes are beautiful, [I] am like yhoo [she says it with such passion in her voice] thanks. I have this special, yhoo!! So I was like man; this thing confuses me. . . . So, hau, this one day, this other friend of my mum's, he is a gay, he came with his sister and he was, his sister was about my age. . . . When I sat with that girl, I was staring at her. She was soooo cute. Speaking, I was like damn, if I could kiss you, yhoo, you wouldn't imagine that right now. So it came about then that maybe I might be lesbian. I don't know. So I started asking my half-brother from my father's side. If . . . you are a person who is like this, how do you go about controlling such things? He told me that if you are like [this], don't try to judge yourself.

Similarly, Zandi (a 20-year-old femme lesbian) and Limakatso (a 21-year-old femme lesbian) from eTwatwa township in Johannesburg, whose interviews were conducted together, describe their development and discovery process as follows:[6]

Zandi: Yah, mina [I] did date a boy. And I found out when I was in grade 11, that I was different, apart from my friends. Because . . .
Phoebe: Grade 11, how old is grade 11?
Zandi: I think I was 16, yah, 16, 16 or 15. So like that time, you know girl talk, they always talk ukuthi [so] last night, me and my boyfriend, we did this and that. So it's so nice. And mina [I], I [was] like, I didn't know anything about sex at that time. So, they would say, you have to try it. Like it's nice. Since it was me, I was like,

	I had two boyfriends, like boy boyfriends. The first one, when I slept with him, it was not nice. Like, it was horrible. My experience of copulating with my first boyfriend was really terrible. Then like, I told my friend, no, mina [I], am not feeling the guy, it's not like . . . the sex is not good. . . . Then in my matric dance [high school prom], at the party of my matric dance, then I, yah, that's when I do it with another boy. It was so painful, like, it was also horrible. I didn't like see a nice thing about it. Everything that they were telling me, I didn't see it or I didn't feel it. So, I just like let it go. I didn't tell them, when they ask[ed] me, how was it? I would just say, it was great. And I enjoyed it blah blah blah . . . Then, in my first year in college, then I met this girl, she was butch. So, I didn't know what was really going on with her. So she would say like, yhoo, mina, me and my girlfriend, yhoo mina I do my girlfriend like so [and] so and I was so interested in that thing she was talking about. And I become friends with her. Like I was so interested in her life, how do you do? Yabona [you see], then she was my first girlfriend and then it was a blast. Since then, I have never looked back.
Limakatso:	I would say I had my first boyfriend when I was in grade 9, standard 8, I was 15 or 14, 14, yah, I was 14. That's when I had my first boyfriend. Actually, it was because of the influence of friends. I had lots of friends, all of them who had been in grade 9 [and] repeated a class, and I was more interested in their lives, more than I was in mine. So we became friends and then they were like 'Ohhh Limakatso, you don't know things.' I grew up in a very traditional family, whereby a girl every year would be taken to, you know the old days, and be checked and see if you are still a virgin. Yes, I used to be checked.
Phoebe:	Oh really, how do they check?
Limakatso:	You just open your legs, they put a finger [inside of you], a small finger. And then they take it out and look at you and say that you are a virgin.
Zandi:	You know, they say your behind is like a tissue, a cloth.
Limakatso:	There's a tissue, a cloth. So if something got in, they will see, it will have a hole. . . . So I had to be checked all the time when I grew up. I had to every term, I used to go home and get checked if I was still a virgin, so I was afraid of sleeping with anyone. Thinking that the minute they find out [that I] am not a virgin, [I] am going to die, my mum is going to kill me. That's the first thing that came to my mind. So that was the influence, but they didn't know, so they got me a boyfriend, like quick. Like 'ha wenna [you] Limakatso you don't know things, let us get you a boyfriend.' Then I was like, I broke up with the guy because he wanted to sleep with me. . . . My friends were like every day 'Yho, yhooo you don't know what you are missing.' You know that, I had to lie, and say that I did it. Like I would

lie, like 'oh it was so great,' not knowing what it was like. Because my first experience I had with a guy was in 2011 . . . which wasn't great at all. Which had me ended up being chased out of school, and me regretting doing that. Why did I do it? Because of [a] friend or me wanting to know what it's like. So like when my mum found out, she took me back to KZN [KwaZulu Natal], I had to go live in KZN, and I stayed there for five months maybe, and then I came back. I had another boyfriend, I did it again, [but] it just wasn't good. The problem is, I didn't have feelings for the guy. . . . Then a few years later, a friend of mine introduced me to this friend of hers, who was femme but lesbian. Then like, [we] talked, like we talked every night, every day, like something about her would just turn me on. It was like she would turn me on. The first time I kissed her, I approached her and kissed her, and that's when I had sex with her and it was like greater than anything I . . . ever did previously. And then I was like, something is wrong, something is definitely wrong. Then I came with her and she took me like to events with lesbians, and that's when I realised that I am attracted to women. Every time [I] am around women, [I] am really happy. [I] am like, [I] am in a world of my own. When [I] am here, I feel at home, I feel at home.

Stevi Jackson (1996) notes that sexuality is ' "socially scripted" in that it is a "part" that is learned and acted out within a social context, and different social contexts have different scripts' (62). The conversations are illustrative of this, with the early to late teens being expressed as a time of self-discovery, uncertainty, and exploration, conducted against a backdrop of sexual policing traditions – religion, culture, family, friends, and peer pressure. Dominant heteronormative sexual scripts – i.e. sexuality-based cultural capital – are clear where opposite-sex attraction and exploration are all-pervasive in this context. A blend of African culture, religion, capitalism, neoliberalism, and colonialism has informed and assigned meaning, importance, and privilege to these heteronormative sexual scripts. Thus, following this heteronormative social convention, all three participants – Letsego, Zandi, and Limakatso – experienced their first sexual encounter with a boy. In a way, this concurs with the notion of cultural labour, in the sense that through slippages, womxn in same-sex relations are able to articulate deficits, claim resources, and seek inclusion in national narratives – in this case, sexuality and sexual identity (Maxwell and Miller, 2006). These slippages manifest themselves through dating or pretending to date boys and thus appearing to conform to the demands of heterosexuality whilst still finding ways to engage in same-sex attraction. However, this tension brings out feelings of initial confusion and often fear of verbalising same-sex attraction. In this context, exploration and understanding of sexual development takes place in a heavily policed environment of family, friends, the wider community, and inherently patriarchal institutions. Take Limakatso, where policing is realised via virginity testing and being repeatedly asked by her peers what her heterosexual encounters were like.

However, Limakatso undertakes cultural labour to conform to this virginity testing by undergoing the test without failing as well as her falsification of having had sex with boys to peers.

However, through counter-discourse, these three womxn managed to develop what I will refer to as their own 'counter-sexual scripts.' Because of the heavy social policing, I do note here that there is a tension between appearing to conform to heteronormative expectations as discussed earlier, and these women finding their own subversive ways to express same-sex desire – sometimes occurring simultaneously. The latter is what I am referring to as counter-sexual scripts. As these scripts occur in their everyday lives, they speak directly to what Jeff Corntassel (2012) refers to as 'every day acts of resurgence.' Through these counter-sexual scripts, I read the narratives articulated by these womxn as a 'de-linking' (Mignolo, 2016) from prevailing heteronormative discourses and sexual capital. For Limakatso, Zandi, and Litseho, early teenage experiences articulate these counter-sexual scripts. For instance, all felt no attraction to boys (despite dating them), feeling instead a stronger attraction to girls and taking the initiative with the first kiss, thus affirming their real feelings. On this point, Walter Mignolo (2016) posits that 'the decolonial struggle at hand: [is] to de-link from the fictional categories and classifications installed and instilled in the narratives of modernity' (xii). Mignolo sees modernity as the hidden part of coloniality and with it, has invented categories of gender and sexuality. Hence, this fictitious heteronormative imagination and categorisation is exposed here by the interlocutors, which is why I read this through decolonial frames. De-linking from dominant discourses and engaging with their own same-sex doxa during their first sexual encounters, these womxn find ways to enable re-existence. For instance, the womxn fondly recall how enjoyable their first same-sex kiss was, even though social convention dictated their initial heterosexual interaction, which did not match their feelings and desires.

In one way or another, the womxn all managed to identify someone with whom they could identify and could have conversations with about their same-sex attraction. These relationships may exist only in the practical state, in material and/or emotional exchanges which help to maintain them. Through identifying and networking with other womxn (or men) in same-sex relations – lesbians feel affirmed in who they are, which they then celebrate through their own relationships.

In conclusion, the coloniality of gender and sexuality has made the conversation on sexual desire and pleasure as well as homosexuality difficult in South Africa. We see this imprinted in the singular narrative of heterosexuality as well as the development machinery that has endorsed the coupling of sex/sexuality with disease and death. The invisibility of same-sex relationships as well as pleasure and desire are evident, both in the public domain as well as in knowledge production. In its most literal sense, a difficult conversation is often characterised by emotions such as fear, anger, frustration, conflict, and other strong dividing emotions. A difficult conversation at times means sitting with discomfort or conflict or confusion – we see this brought in by the dominant narrative of heterosexuality, which causes interlocutors' first desire to be framed within that, which brought on cognitive dissonance with their same-sex desires. In other words, the invisibility or lack of conversation that engages with the topic of pleasure and desire then calls for talking about experiences of navigating this dense terrain of normativity, which brings out the tension between normative heterosexual desire and same-sex desire. However, it becomes clear that in pursuing their same-sex desires, the cognitive dissonance, discomfort, and confusion brought on by the tension between normative heterosexuality and same-sex desire eventually eases and instead brings with it joyful moments of same-sex pleasure and eroticism. Moreover, it is important to point out that there was no difficulty in talking about same-sex desire and pleasure, as shown by the earlier conversations. And so, in the navigation of sexual pleasure brought on by tension between normative heterosexuality and same-sex desires, this difficult conversation in fact contributes to knowledge production on diverse experiences of African sexuality, pleasure, and desire, de-linking from the colonial misrepresentation that homogenised African sexuality.

Notes

1 Limakatso – research assigned name, given name of the participant not used here for anonymity and confidentiality purposes.
2 I would argue that the amount of research and work done on African sexuality within the framework of HIV discourse is vast: it is possibly one of the most researched areas in relation to sex and sexuality in Sub-Saharan Africa. This is glaringly visible at AIDS conferences, which are attended by tens of thousands of participants and include thousands of presentations – what is presented at these conferences being only a fraction of exciting efforts related to this topic.
3 In this chapter, I mostly work with the terms 'womxn in same-sex relationships' interchangeably with 'African same-sex intimacies' due to their all-encompassing nature. This is especially so because same-sex practices are understood differently across different historical and cultural contexts and are thus not necessarily labelled and contextualised as 'homosexual' or 'gay' or 'lesbian.' Therefore, to focus upon intimacies brings the historical (dis)continuities of same-sex sexual cultures to the fore. Moreover, the term 'intimacy' opens up horizons for intimate sexual encounters beyond relationships, which taps into same-sex sexual desire and pleasure. I locate people of colour who self-identify as lesbian, queer, trans*, gender binary, gender non-conforming, intersex, asexual, and pansexual within this framing.
4 I work with womxn – an alternative spelling of the English word 'woman/women.' Like fellow intersectional feminists I work with the term 'womxn' to avoid perceived sexism in the standard spelling – which contains and derives from the word 'man' – and to explicitly include or foreground trans and non-binary interlocutors in this research.
5 It seems the turning point was at the United Nations International Conference on Population and Development held in Cairo in 1994, a point at which studies on African sexualities steered away from colonial epistemologies. Studies such as those of Baylies and Bujra (2000), McFadden (2003), Arnfred (2004b), Khamasi and Maina-Chinkuyu (2005), Bennett (2005), Morgan and Wieringa (2005), Amadiume (2006), Maticka-Tyndale et al. (2007), Tamale (2011), and Goud and Fick (2008) analyse African sexualities in an inclusive manner, including its pleasurable and empowering aspects.
6 Both Zandi and Limakatso were happy to be interviewed together. They are friends and both coordinators for Uthingo – a community-based organisation under the umbrella of the Forum for the Empowerment of Women (FEW), an NGO that works with lesbian, bisexual, and transgender women in Johannesburg and the greater Gauteng townships (info4africa 2014).

References

Amadiume, I (2006) Sexuality, African religio-cultural traditions and modernity: Expanding the lens. *CODESRIA Bulletin* 1: 26–28.

Arnfred, S (2004a) Re-thinking sexualities in Africa: Introduction In S Arnfred (ed.), *Re-Thinking Sexualities in Africa*. Stockolm: Almqvist & Wiksell Tryckeri (pp. 7–29).

Arnfred, S (2004b) African sexuality/sexuality in Africa: Tales and silences. In S. Arnfred, *Re-thinking Sexualities in Africa*. Stockholm: Almqvist & Wiksell Tryckeri (pp. 59–76).

Attree, L (2010) Women writing aids in South Africa and Zimbabwe. In P. Dodgson-Katiyo and G. E. Wisker (eds.) *Rites of Passage in Postcolonial Women's Writing*. Amsterdam and New York: Rodopi (pp. 65–92).

Bakshi, S., Jivraj, S. and Posocco, S (2016) Introduction In S. Bakshi, S. Jivraj, and S. Posocco (eds.) *Decolonizing Sexualities: Transnational Perspectives Critical Interventions*. Oxford: Counterpress (pp. 1–16).

Baylies, C. and Bujira, J (eds) (2000) *AIDS, Sexuality and Gender in Africa*. London: Routledge.

Bennett, L.R (2005) *Women, Islam and Modernity: Single Women, Sexuality and Reproductive Health in Contemporary Indonesia*. London: Routledge.

Chan-Sam, T (1994) Five women: Profiles of black lesbian life on the reef In M. Gevisser, and E. Cameron (eds.) *DEFIANT Desire: Gay and Lesbian Lives in Southf Africa*. Johannesburg: Ravan Press (pp. 186–192).

Corntassel, J (2012) Re-envisioning resurgance: Indigenous pathways to decolonization and sustainable self-determination. *Decolonization: Indigeneity, Education & Society* 86–101.

Epprecht, M (2008) *Heterosexual Africa? The History of an Idea from the Age of Exploration to the Age of AIDS*. Athens: Ohio University Press.

Fanon, F (1961) *The Wretched of the Earth*. New York: Grove Press.

Gay, J (1986) Mummies and babies and friends and lovers in lesotho. *Journal of Homosexuality* 97–116.

Goud, C. and Fick, N (2008) *Selling Sex in Cape Town: Sex Work and Human Trafficking in a South African City*. Pretoria: Institute for Security Studies.

Jackson, S (1996) The social construction of female sexuality In S. Jackson and S. Scott (eds.) *Feminism and Sexuality: A Reader*. New York: Columbia University Press (pp. 62–73).

Khamasi, J.W. and Maina-Chinkuyu, S.N (2005) *Sexuality an African Perspective: The Politics of Self and Cultural Beliefs*. Eldoret: Moi University Press.

Lewis, D (2011) Representing african sexualities In S. Tamale (ed.) *African Sexualities: A Readear*. Cape Town, Nairobi, Dakar and London: Pambazuka Press (pp. 199–216).

Lugones, M (2007) Heterosexualism and te colonial/modern gender system. *Hypatia* 186–209.

Maticka-Tyndale, E., Wildish, J. and Gichuru, M (2007) Quasi-experimental evaluation of a national primary school HIV intervention in Kenya. *Evaluation and Program Planning*, Vol. 30, 172–186.

Maxwell, R. and Miller, T (2006) The cultural labour issue. *Social Semiotics* 1–6.

McClintock, A (1995) *Imperial Leather: Race, Gender and Sexuality in the Colonial Context*. New York, London: Routledge.

McFadden, P (2003) Sexual pleasure as a feminist choice. *Feminist Africa* 50–60.

Mignolo, W.D (2016) Foreword: Decolonial body-geo-politics at large In S. Bakshi, S. Jivraj, and S. Posocco (eds.) *Decolonizing Sexualities: Transnational Perspectives Critical Interventions*. Oxford: Counterpress (pp. vii–xxii).

Morgan, R. and Wieringa, S (2005) *Tommy Boys, Lesbian Men and Ancestral Wives*. Johannesburg: Jacana Media.

Ndlovu-Gatsheni, S (2016) Why are South African universities sites of struggle today? *The Thinker: A Pan-African Quarterly for thought Leaders* 52–61.

Sontag, S (1988) *Illness as Metaphor and AIDS and its Metaphors*. New York: Picador.

Tamale, S (2011) Researching and thoerizing sexualities in Africa In S. Tamale (ed.) *African Sexualities: A Reader*. Cape Town, Dakar, Nairobi, Oxford: Pambazuka Press (pp. 11–36).

Tamale, S (2020) *Decolonization and Afro-feminism*. Cantley: Daraja Press.

Wa Thiong'o, N (1998) Decolonising the mind. *Diogenes* 101–104.

10 Researching sex

Gender, taboos and revealing the intimate

Laurie James-Hawkins

Introduction

This chapter discusses how gender and social norms regarding sex and sexuality work to make this type of research a delicate process where the researcher is caught between their own political and moral stance and allowing one's participants to describe their own stories in ways that make sense to them – to create their own narratives and describe their experiences in a way that helps them to make sense of their own world. This is more difficult than one might think. Although I have studied issues of sexual behaviour, gender and power for years, I feel that I am constantly caught in an ethical dilemma. It is my role as researcher to elicit information, to synthesize it, to identify patterns and to describe the dynamics that are happening when it comes to men and women having sex. However, this intellectual approach and view of myself as an outsider who is simply recording other's stories is not always consistent with my need to comfort another human being who is obviously in distress, or my desire to correct misinformation or to provide them with critical information that I know will help them to protect themselves in the future. I will address these issues by first briefly reviewing the literature on researching sensitive topics and on sex, gender and power. Next, I present examples from my own research on gender, hookup culture, contraceptive use and sexual violence to demonstrate that while conversations on these topics can be difficult for the researcher and the participants, they also are necessary conversations that must be had if we are to understand the issues facing men and women today in the sexual landscape of Western society.

Researching sex means confronting difficult conversations all the time. In fact, as a sexuality researcher I consider difficult conversations to the be bread and butter of my profession. I have had a myriad of incredibly difficult conversations in the 15-plus years I have researched gendered power and sexuality, and more recently, how young adults define sexual consent. So, what does it mean to research sex and sexual consent? It means navigating a minefield of taboos, power and trauma, while asking people to tell you the most intimate details of their sexual lives. It means having a series of difficult conversations in which both the researcher and the participants must engage in emotion management just to make it possible to have the conversation. In my research, based in the United States

DOI: 10.4324/9781003088417-14

and the United Kingdom, I have found that young adult women see sex as a taboo topic (Montemurro et al., 2015). As the gender with less power, women often have internalised the idea that women should defer to men, particularly in sexual situations (Tolman et al., 2016), and intimate inequalities are very much present in today's world (Dalessandro, 2017). Women are not supposed to talk about sexuality at all, and men are taught to talk about sex couching it in terms of 'locker room' talk, where men are primarily engaging in a demonstration of their masculinity to other men, rather than engaging emotionally with their sexual partners (Montemurro et al., 2015). While social norms regarding sex and sexuality have changed over time, the normative cultural messages both men and women are exposed to leave everyone simultaneously surrounded by sex and cut off from it.

As researchers, we reconcile the desire to investigate sexual behaviour, to understand it, to dig deep for those details that we hope will provide us with the key to that understanding with the need to protect and respect our participants and the intimate details of their lives they share. Because there are large degrees of social desirability biases around the topic of sex, it is on us as researchers to lead the conversation with our participants in such a way that we are validating their lived experiences and their narrative descriptions of their experiences, while at the same time questioning and investigating the underlying motivations of those narratives. For example, we might ask why and how participants have constructed a particular narrative for us, and how that narrative may reflect – or not reflect – their actual experiences. We may also question if it is our goal to reflect our participants' feelings and interpretations, or their actual experiences.

The ethics of researching sensitive topics

Sensitive topics have been defined as those which are taboo or intimate (Dempsey et al., 2016; McGarry, 2010), or those topics with the potential to cause emotional harm or negative emotional reactions such as anger, fear or anxiety (Elmir et al., 2011). Certainly, then, researchers who address the topic of sexual behaviour are researching a sensitive topic (O'Brien, 2010). However, we should also consider that what is thought to be a sensitive topic is highly dependent on prevailing cultural norms and values (O'Brien, 2010).

Feminist research methods call for approaches to research that are 'nonexploitive, subjective, compassionate, and inclusive' (Jaggar, 2015: 36), which dovetails nicely with the issues at hand in researching sensitive topics. As researchers, we must advocate for this type of research, as avoiding sensitive topics may actually result in our evading our responsibility as social science researchers to represent the lived experiences of those whom we interview (Dempsey et al., 2016). As researchers, we should investigate problems with an acute awareness that those whom we most often want to research are often vulnerable and may be suffering, thus we must also be careful to assess when it makes more sense not to conduct the research (O'Brien, 2010).

Our goal as qualitative researchers is to understand and to some extent experience others' stories through their eyes, which makes us a tool of the research and requires both emotional and intellectual engagement on the part of the researcher (Dickson-Swift et al., 2009). Hearing about emotional experiences from the point of view of the person who experienced it means that emotions are a central part of research into sensitive topics, as is strong engagement in emotion work (Dickson-Swift et al., 2009). What can be the most difficult is that even when we have a strong emotional reaction, we often have to be careful not to outwardly react to or display our emotions (Hochschild, 2012). Thus, researchers investigating sexuality must exert effort, sometimes tremendous effort, to maintain their emotional equilibrium (Dickson-Swift et al., 2009). Scientists in general are trained that suppression of their emotions is necessary in order to conduct 'good' research, and thus often modify their own behaviour in an attempt to manage their emotions. However, this effort can also lead a researcher to question what the 'correct' way to conduct research really is (Dickson-Swift et al., 2009). Thus, research on sensitive topics can be difficult for both the researcher and for the participants (Elmir et al., 2011). Given this context, how we conduct research is critically important, and we must always ask ourselves how we can protect our participants while also protecting ourselves.

I have often been surprised at how willing participants are to talk about their most private and intimate experiences (Ashton, 2014) and in research into sexual behaviour, this can result in both wonderful insight into what it means to be a sexual being in today's world, while simultaneously making it very difficult to appropriately establish rapport while maintaining our boundaries as researchers (Ashton, 2014; McGarry, 2010). When we develop a rapport with our participants, it results in rich data with a wealth of meaning that can contribute real insight into the participants' world and experiences, but it may also feel embarrassing, awkward or invasive for both you as researcher, and for those whom you are researching (Elmir et al., 2011). Maintaining the balance between rapport and boundaries can also be challenging because it requires managing not only your own emotions, but often those of your participants as well (Dickson-Swift et al., 2009). In this context of emotion management as a central part of the sex researchers mandate, we often struggle with how much of our own experiences and feelings to reveal as we listen to stories that are clearly painful for a participant to talk about (Elmir et al., 2011; Newton, 2017). Revealing parts of ourselves to our participants, then, is often a both necessary and anxiety-inducing process, and is also a process which can be confusing and can blur the line between being a researcher and a friend (Elmir et al., 2011). Researchers also can struggle with not being overly sympathetic or too comforting to their participants, despite the powerful reactions we may have to hearing the intimate stories of others (Ashton, 2014). This struggle also reveals a tension between our very human personal desire to help those in need and our need to remain objective as a researcher (McGarry, 2010). Researchers can feel that they are not doing enough when they interview someone in pain or telling a traumatic story when all they can offer are referrals to outside sources of help (Ashton, 2014), which can produce guilt on our part when we feel we have left the participant alone in their struggle with their sometimes traumatic experiences (McGarry, 2010).

There is often a mismatch between the intentions on the part of the researcher and the researched (Newton, 2017). While we as researchers take the very private and intimate moments of people's lives and make them into a public affair to be analysed and reported to a broader community (Newton, 2017), often measuring our success by the degree of disclosure we feel we have achieved, participants are far more likely to view the experience as either a therapeutic or cathartic one (Ashton, 2014; Dempsey et al., 2016; Newton, 2017). However, researchers are not trained therapists and generally cannot provide any follow-up or resolution to a participant who discloses trauma – sometimes for the first time – in the research setting (Newton, 2017). We may be asked for advice (Newton, 2017), as I have been on many occasions, but we must remember that while we should be empathetic, we are researchers and not therapists (Ashton, 2014).

The often difficult conversations we have as researchers, in which we manage not only our own emotions, but often those of our participants as well, can lead to emotional stress and burnout (McGarry, 2010). We as researchers are negotiating personal interactions about often intensely personal subjects in highly charged emotional environments (McGarry, 2010). While we know these interactions have an impact on the participants, less often examined is the influence on the researcher when they undertake these sorts of conversations (Newton, 2017). It is crucial that researchers are aware of the impact this sort of emotion work may have on their own emotional health and mental well-being (Ashton, 2014; Dickson-Swift et al., 2009; Newton, 2017). Researchers may empathise with the experiences of participants, or they may hear stories that bring up their own emotional trauma or reactions (Dickson-Swift et al., 2009). As a result, researchers can be traumatised by engaging in their own research, which can lead to researcher burnout (Elmir et al., 2011). It is especially important that researchers consider what steps they can undertake to recover from the emotional trauma they may experience when they engage in the difficult conversations that surround researching sensitive topics (Ashton, 2014). We must also consider how our own emotional reactions may bias our analysis of the data and to be especially aware of our own emotional biases as we report our data in an ideally unbiased way free from the impact of our own emotional responses (Ashton, 2014).

When it comes to sexual behaviour, respondents are often being asked to describe and define non-normative and private behaviours which may make them feel vulnerable (O'Brien, 2010). Researchers must acknowledge that we hold power in the dyadic relationship between us and those we research, and we are essentially wielding that power to get what we need according to our own research agenda, but trying to do so without violating the rights and damaging the well-being of the participants (Newton, 2017).

Unacknowledged sexual assault among young adults

About one in five women and one in 25 men in the United Kingdom report being a victim of sexual assault (Statistics, 2018). Young adults between the ages of 18 and 24 experience the highest risk of sexual violence, sexually transmitted infections and unintended pregnancies compared to other age groups (Fantasia et al., 2014; Leiting and Yeater, 2017). Young adult women are more likely to be victimised than are young adult men (Coy et al., 2013; Firmin, 2010; Maxwell, 2006), with around 83% of victims who report to the police being women (Humphrey, 2016). Reported assault numbers potentially underestimate the true prevalence of sexual victimisation for both women and men due to disagreements over what qualifies as assault. For example, the use of sexual coercion and date rape – sexual assault committed by a romantic partner – are often not acknowledged by perpetrators or victims as constituting a sexual assault (Emmers-Sommer, 2015; Leiting and Yeater, 2017), and instead are framed as 'miscommunication' (Dardis et al., 2017) or as 'bad sex' (Wilson et al., 2018), despite meeting legal definitions for assault (Leiting and Yeater, 2017; Wilson and Miller, 2016). A meta-analysis of unacknowledged sexual assault among women found that 60% of acknowledged sexual assault survivors may also fit the criteria for unacknowledged sexual assault (Wilson and Miller, 2016), but they often fail to seek support to help them better cope with their experiences because they have not identified their experiences as assault. While some victims may view a lack of acknowledgement as a coping strategy, victims of unacknowledged sexual assault still exhibit serious and lasting health consequences (Littleton et al., 2018; Wilson and Miller, 2016; Wilson et al., 2018). Further, acknowledging their experiences can help victims because labels and interpretations are associated with long-term mental and physical health and well-being (Conoscenti and McNally, 2006; Littleton et al., 2018).

Sexual consent, alcohol and hookup culture

Consent is a multi-layered and complex concept (Halley, 2016). It is generally assumed that there is a shared understanding of the concept of consent (Beres, 2007; Beres, 2014; Gotell, 2007), but research shows that working definitions of consent to sexual activity can vary widely (Beres, 2014; Halley, 2016). Some definitions of consent focus on enthusiastic, explicitly verbal definitions of consent – often called active consent – while other definitions include a variety of verbal and non-verbal behaviours that may (or may not) indicate that consent has been given (Beres, 2014; Humphrey, 2016; Jozkowski and Peterson, 2013). For some, the 'gold standard' of consent is when there is explicit verbal agreement by both partners that they consent to sex (Beres, 2007; Beres, 2014), while others feel that even an explicit verbal agreement is insufficient because such a definition does not take into account cases where there is pressure or coercion to have sex (Lamarche and Seery, 2019), which may nullify any agreement obtained (Beres, 2007; Beres, 2014; Humphrey, 2016) even when someone verbally says 'yes'. Laws have specified that consent given while under the influence of any alcohol, explicit or otherwise, is not freely given consent (Eileraas, 2011; Marciniak, 2015; Muehlenhard et al., 2016).

The rise of hookup cultures has led to social norms suggesting that casual sexual encounters under the influence of alcohol and drugs are normal and appropriate during young adulthood, especially among young adults attending university

(Armstrong and Hamilton, 2013; James-Hawkins, 2019; James-Hawkins et al., 2019; Wade, 2017). These norms persist among young adults, despite ambiguity regarding consent in cases of sexual encounters while intoxicated. Furthermore, despite steadfast societal definitions of rape as occurring when one is attacked by a stranger, the majority of sexual assaults are perpetrated by people known to the victim, including romantic partners (Cowling and Reynolds, 2004; Statistics, 2018). Thus, lived experiences of sexual assault often do not match the circumstances presented in the typical rape myth (i.e. stranger assault at night; Peterson and Muehlenhard, 2011). Stranger-based rape myths have contributed to many victims of sexual assault not labelling their experiences as such, even when those experiences meet legal definitions of rape (Deming et al., 2013; Peterson and Muehlenhard, 2004). Until recently, laws in the UK have defined rape as penile penetration, making rape of a male by a female impossible (Lowe and Rogers, 2017). Similarly, definitions of sexual assault have only recently been changed to include non-penetrative sexual acts which women can perform on men (Lowe and Rogers, 2017). Despite these recent changes, laws still do not adequately address the reality that most young adults are engaging in high levels of sexual activity under the influence of drugs and alcohol (Armstrong and Hamilton, 2013; Marciniak, 2015; Wade, 2017) where consent is, at best, ambiguous.

The struggle to figure out how to research sexual behaviour while monitoring my own emotions and those of my participants has been an ongoing issue throughout my research career. Here, I draw on examples from my research on hookup culture, presenting narratives of women's experiences which I as a researcher would identify as unacknowledged sexual assault. I use these examples to delve into the feelings that these difficult conversations brought up for me as a researcher.

Difficult conversations about unacknowledged sexual assault

In 2013, I was conducting research on hookup culture and contraceptive use at a western United States university. Women interviewed were paid $30.00 for their participation. To participate, women had to be between the ages of 18 and 24, able to become pregnant (to their knowledge), and had to have reported taking a contraceptive risk at some time in the past. Because the purpose of the research was to explore risk of pregnancy, only heterosexual women were included.

Several times whilst conducting these interviews, I found that women described instances that to me sounded very much like sexual assault, usually whilst under the influence of alcohol, but which the women themselves did not necessarily frame as problematic encounters. Naively, when I began the research, I did not anticipate the stories of questionable sexual experiences while under the influence of alcohol and was somewhat unprepared to deal with them.

In the interviews, more than one participant described a situation in which she was unsure if she'd had sex at all because she was black-out drunk. To my mind, these experiences clearly constituted a sexual assault. At the time, I was torn as to whether I should discuss the possibility that an assault had occurred. On the one hand, I felt that was the right thing to do as a human being, especially as I was aware that there are known physical and mental consequences that affect women even if they do not acknowledge their experiences as assault. However, as a researcher, I didn't feel it was my place to offer advice, to counsel or to tell women how to define their own experiences. In the end, I fell back on the researcher as observer and recorder of narrative role with which I was trained and probed the experience without telling women how I saw the situation. The pull between our inner self and the human reactions we experience and the trained researcher can be confusing. As a human being, my instinct is to comfort, to help and to offer support. As a researcher, my training tells me that I am not there to help or comfort, but to listen, record and analyse. In my situation, discussing very private and often distressing experiences with women, I wanted to engage as a person, not as a researcher, but also had to be aware of the ways in which that type of non-research-led interaction may influence the data I was collecting. I still struggle with the degree to which we as researchers have an obligation to our participants to provide knowledge, and the need to do the research 'correctly' and according to the principles in which I was trained. This is not a dilemma that I have resolved, but instead is something with which I constantly struggle, and which makes most of my interactions with participants into difficult conversations, albeit ones that are important to have. Here, I use examples from multiple studies over the last two decades to demonstrate the ways in which our position as human beings can sometimes be in conflict with our training as researchers.

Maria, an undergraduate who agreed to participate in my research study on sex, contraceptive use and hookup culture, told me about the sexual experiences she had as a teen and at university. At this point in my research career, I was focused on investigating reasons that women do not use contraceptives when they don't want to become pregnant. I was entirely unprepared to hear stories like the one Maria presented, and was taken aback when she brought up an instance in which she was unsure whether she had engaged in sex. Here is how my conversation with her went:

Maria: I just remembered another time when I was really, really drunk and – it's just come back to me – and I'm pretty sure I slept with him. And that was unprotected as well.
Laurie: [pause] Did you worry about [pregnancy] after?
Maria: No, because I didn't really know [I'd had sex] until later and by that time, I had already had my period. He was like, 'oh yeah, we had sex'. I was like, 'okay'.
Laurie: So, you were drunk enough that you didn't know you had sex?
Maria: Well, I kind of remembered it. But it was one of those things where you don't remember until someone brings it up to you. And you're like, 'oh yeah, oh that. I remember that' . . . I remember him saying, 'are you on the pill', and that's the last, I think I remember saying 'yeah'. So, I'm pretty sure that's what happened. Because I didn't hear what he actually said. Then the conversation came back to me, so he

was under that belief [that a condom was not necessary] because we talked about it later. I was like, 'oh sorry. I didn't mean to say yes. So that was probably my fault.'

One of the hardest issues for me as a feminist researcher was hearing a young woman tell me a story which to me constituted sexual assault. Although she did remember discussing contraceptive use, she did not remember the sexual encounter, while her partner did. Further, despite her condition and clear inability to give consent to sexual activity, Maria blamed herself for not insisting on the use of a condom. This was an extremely difficult interview for me, and it highlights some of the issues that arise for people who are researching sexual behaviour. I was uncertain what to do in this instance, and simply continued on with the interview. A similar instance occurred when I interviewed Jenn, a young woman who described her first sexual encounter to me:

> That was my first time having sex, and I remember that night . . . I wasn't even planning on going out . . . But I still got dressed and went out. Kind of a peer pressure kind of thing. So I did, and I ended up drinking a lot more than I planned on . . . We went to one of our friends' house . . . That night, even the whole point leading up to it kind of, I don't remember very much at all. But the guy that I slept with I met before once or twice. And it was like really weird why I even did it in the first place. Just because I hated him and did not like him at all . . . And then we ended up having sex and then I kind of remember just bits and pieces. And then that next morning, because he lives in the same dorm that I did, I went back downstairs [to my room]. Like, the walk of shame. How I felt afterwards, I was kind of, like, somewhat embarrassed too. And then also kind of mad at myself that I had sex while I was drunk. My one criteria was to be sober. And I broke that. So, I was kind of mad at myself for that.

Like my interview with Maria, the interview with Jenn has stayed with me over many subsequent years of additional research on this topic. Not only was Jenn's first sexual experience something that in my judgement describes a sexual assault, but she also disclosed to me that she'd had sex two more times – only three times in her life at the time of the interview – and that her other two experiences were essentially under the same circumstances. After this interview, it took some time to reconcile what I had heard with my decision to not probe more deeply into the event. I spent much time thinking about it, and in retrospect I am struck by her response to my asking if the man she was with was also drunk:

Laurie: Was he also drunk?
Jenn: I think so. Hopefully.

Jenn's response of 'hopefully' to this question highlights that she was experiencing a certain amount of concern and doubt about what had happened herself. Yet her initial inclination was to describe the situation in terms of being mad at herself for drinking, rather than upset that her partner had engaged in sex with her when she was clearly drunk and unable to consent. Some of her motivations for this way of describing her encounter were revealed later in her interview, when Jenn expressed the idea that once women start interacting sexually with a man it is not appropriate for them to change their mind and stop the encounter. Jenn said:

> I remember one of the nights I was going out and not really planning on it but then I met someone that I kind of liked and then we were both kind of drinking so that impaired more of not really thinking about it. But then once the action was already set in motion and things were already going, it's kind of hard to be like, 'well, just kidding. I change my mind completely'.

In this circumstance, I was again in a position of feeling that the right thing to do was to tell her that she absolutely had the right to change her mind no matter what point she was at in a sexual encounter. However, I remained hesitant to define a participant's experiences for them, and I held back and did not discuss this experience with her further or ask her to tell me more about why she felt it was not okay to stop sex once started. In retrospect, I wish that I had discussed this with her after the interview and presented my perspective that she absolutely had a right to change her mind at any point during a sexual encounter.

Another participant, Amber, also described a sexual experience where she made the assumption, like Jenn did, that the man she had sex with was also too drunk to remember the encounter. Amber, along with many other women who have told me similar stories, felt that her male partner also being drunk explained or excused the situation and made it okay. She told me this story:

Laurie: You didn't ever ask him [if he used a condom]?
Amber: No.
Laurie: Why didn't you? Why did that feel so strange to ask him?
Amber: Because [I'd have] to text him that and have to scroll through my log and it would be like 'eww' . . . And also, I'm pretty sure that if I was too drunk to remember he's also almost too drunk to remember. Even if he was like, 'yeah', I'm pretty sure I would doubt him.

Like Jenn, Amber was also somewhat hesitant in her choice of language to describe her partner's alcohol intake, saying 'I'm pretty sure' and 'he's also *almost* too drunk to remember' [emphasis mine]. I had the feeling afterwards, as I read both Jenn's and Amber's stories, that it served an important function for them to view their partners as also being too drunk to remember the encounter. By framing their partner as also drunk, these women framed their sexual experience as perhaps a bad sexual encounter, but it allowed them to avoid labelling the encounter as a sexual assault or rape. Women supported this interpretation of their experiences by refraining from verifying that their male sexual partner was also too drunk to remember the encounter by asking him. From my perspective,

Researching sex 153

knowing that sexual assault has an impact on health and well-being, even if one does not acknowledge the experience as a sexual assault, I now wish that I had provided both young women with resources and encouraged them to talk to someone about their experiences. The difficulty of engaging in the conversation at the time led me to remain mute.

Other women interviewed also discussed engaging in sex and not being able to remember whether contraceptives were used because they were drunk at the time. One participant, Kim, described having 'black-out drunk' sex, as she did not remember the encounter at all. Like Jenn, her inclination was to blame herself for the encounter rather than defining black-out sex as problematic in and of itself.

> I didn't know if I had sex with him and if we used a condom or anything . . . And I had a lot of personal, 'what's wrong with me, what did I do?' . . . I woke up . . . naked and I was like, 'Fuck, again?' . . . I was like, 'That's not okay'.

Kim experienced shame over her behaviour although, again in this instance, I would classify the experience she described as a sexual assault. Another participant, Erin, also told a story in which she was so drunk she could barely speak. However, Erin was insistent that she knew what she was doing and stressed that her partner was also drunk as a way of explaining the event to me and framing it as a consensual encounter. She said:

> I remember being very drunk and I had sex with him . . . I literally could barely even talk . . . [but] I knew exactly what I was doing, and I was okay with it. And I remember, even when I was sober and I first met him I was like, 'oh my God'. I was talking about how I wanted to hook up with him and he was so cute. So, it was definitely consensual because I was aware that I wanted to the entire night and then it actually happened, but at that point I was so drunk because I had been drinking with him and I was, like, not paying attention to how much I was drinking. And he was pretty drunk too.

Erin insisted that the experience was consensual. Yet I question if someone can consent to sex if they can 'barely even talk'. However, again in this instance, I did not question her interpretation of her own experiences. Another participant, Jasmine, also described an experience that I would classify as sexual coercion at the very least, and perhaps assault because she was drunk at the time. Jasmine said:

> We had a condom, and it broke or came off or something and then we didn't have any more. But he still wanted to like keep going. And I was like, 'no, I don't think so' . . . So, he went to go find another one and couldn't so he came back and was just like, 'can't find it, but I still want to have sex'. And I was just kind of like, 'I don't know, I think I'm kind of over it'. [I was] just done. And he didn't want to stop. So, it's just like, 'no, [I don't want to]'. [It happened when] I was super drunk . . . and so I was just like, 'oh, okay'. Just did it because he wanted to . . . it was pretty much like, 'Oh God, why am

I doing this? Like, this is so stupid' . . . I didn't tell him to stop, didn't tell him to get off.

Like Erin, Jasmine did not classify this experience as a sexual coercion or assault, primarily because she did not 'tell him to stop'. This story, and many others I have experienced, illustrates the complex ways in which young women interpret issues of consent and sexual assault. Although Jasmine clearly told her male partner no before they had sex since they did not have a condom, she was drunk, and he persisted and had sex with her anyway. Yet, Jasmine viewed this as a 'stupid' action on her part rather than an instance of coercive sex or as a sexual assault.

Two women who took part in this study did identify similar experiences to those described by Erin, Jasmine and others, as date rape, though at the time the date rape occurred, neither woman saw it that way. Hannah described her encounter but was somewhat hesitant in the language she used when describing it as a sexual assault:

> There was a time when I had a random sexual encounter, and I don't know if we used condoms. I would almost say it was date rape because I was so drunk that I could not consent, I guess . . . He was less drunk, probably. We drank like a whole bottle of Capt. Morgan's between three of us. It was horrible. And once everything was over, because nobody – the males were like, I mean they were gay, they were both gay and so it was weird because then I was there – I have flashes of memory of that . . . I found three condoms under my bed after that night. So, I knew that they were attempted, I just don't know if they were employed. And I was so ashamed of the whole thing because I was dating [someone] . . . I hated myself. Mostly because I had hurt [my boyfriend] so badly and at the time I couldn't see it. With the hindsight that I have now it's like, it was basically date rape. I mean everybody was date raping each other, kind of. Just because we were all so drunk there was no – like I just remember laying there. Didn't actively do anything. I didn't say yes, I didn't say no, I can't remember most of it.

During this conversation, I probed her a bit on her classification of the experience as date rape, as I had heard similar experiences from other women who did not classify their experiences that way and wanted to understand the impetus behind her reclassification of her experience from bad sex, as was her initial inclination, to date rape.

Laurie: That's something I've actually heard repeatedly talking to women on this campus. 'I was black-out drunk; I don't know if we used a condom'. You're the first person I've heard categorise it as date rape.

Hannah: It took me forever to come to that conclusion. At first, I [told my boyfriend at the time], 'I cheated on you, I'm so sorry, I'm a horrible person, I hate myself'. And then later with my new boyfriend . . . he's like, 'that sounds like date rape'. I was like, 'Oh my God, you're right!' And [my boyfriend at the time of the incident] actually said something similar like a year later. He was like, 'you were practically raped, just stop'. Well, it didn't occur to me . . . I felt responsible. Partially because my alcohol intake is my responsibility. In some ways it was kind of my problem. I shouldn't have been drinking that much alcohol around people that I didn't know very well or thought I knew. I shouldn't have been that drunk.

Even though Hannah hesitantly describes her experience as 'almost' a date rape, she, like the other women who described similar sexual encounters while blackout drunk, still took on blame for the experience and cited her alcohol intake as the reason why she felt responsible for the encounter. Hannah's reaction supports the idea that women internalise cultural norms of blaming the victim of a sexual assault when an assault occurs (Hackman et al., 2017). The young women cited here shared very intimate and sometimes distressing stories with me, and their willingness to engage in difficult conversations will always be something that I value as I strive to do justice to their stories in my research.

Conclusion

Overall, the conversations had in this research and subsequent research have propelled my research agenda and moved it forward from an investigation of the gendered power dynamics involved in negotiating contraceptive use, to an examination of how we, as a society, as researchers and as individuals, define what it means to consent to sex. While I have some regrets about not providing resources to the women I interviewed, I have also reconciled my role as a researcher and my desire to counsel the young women that I interview, reaching a compromise by providing all my research participants with information on sexual assault and local sexual assault services available. While that helps me resolve the original dilemma I faced, it does not make these conversations any less difficult. I have come to value these types of difficult conversations as ways in which I can identify the nuances of women's narratives, and work towards a definition of sexual consent that is dynamic and meaningful in the real-life circumstances young women face in their lives. My research has also made me more conscious of the many ways in which victim-blaming operates, including women's own constructions of themselves as personally responsible due to, for example, alcohol consumption. This hopefully helps to move forward the conversation about consent to identify these myths so that we can challenge gendered power dynamics around consent.

So, what does it mean to research sex? It means that I regularly engage in, think about and dream about the many difficult conversations I have had in the last decade and a half spent researching sexual behaviour. It means I spend a lot of my time critically reflecting on the ways that I do my research in order to ensure that I respect participants' dignity, that I don't unwittingly reinforce sexual myths or damaging assumptions and that I also protect myself emotionally. Both my willingness to initiate these conversations, and women's willingness to engage with me in this way, demonstrate how difficult conversations can work to move a field forward by highlighting the issues that people face, and allowing a peek into how they themselves define those issues and deal with them in their everyday lives. I encourage us all to continue having these conversations, closely listening to the experiences of the women who are willing to share the most personal and intimate details of their private lives.

References

Armstrong, E.A. and Hamilton, L.T (2013) *Paying for the Party*. Cambridge: Harvard University Press.

Ashton, S (2014) Researcher or nurse? Difficulties of undertaking semi-structured interviews on sensitive topics. *Nurse Researcher* 22(1).

Beres, M.A (2007) Spontaneous sexual consent: An analysis of sexual consent literature. *Feminism & Psychology* 17(1): 93–108.

Beres, M.A (2014) Rethinking the concept of consent for anti-sexual violence activism and education. *Feminism & Psychology* 24(3): 373–389.

Conoscenti, L.M. and McNally, R.J (2006) Health complaints in acknowledged and unacknowledged rape victims. *Journal of Anxiety Disorders* 20(3): 372–379.

Coy, M., Kelly, L., Elvines, F., Garner, M. and Kanyeredzi, A (2013) Sex without consent, I suppose that is rape: How young people in England understand sexual consent. *Office of the Children's Commissioner*. Available from: chrome-extension://efaidnbm nnnibpcajpcglclefindmkaj/https://cwasu.org/wp-content/uploads/2016/07/CONSENT-REPORT-EXEC-SUM.pdf

Cowling, M. and Reynolds, P (2004) *Making Sense of Sexual Consent*. New York: Routledge.

Dalessandro, C (2017) Manifesting maturity: Gendered sexual intimacy and becoming an adult. *Sexualities* 1363460717699779.

Dardis, C.M., Kraft, K.M. and Gidycz, C.A (2017) "Miscommunication" and undergraduate of sexual women's conceptualizations assault: A qualitative analysis. *Journal of Interpersonal Violence* 0886260517726412.

Deming, M.E., Covan, E.K., Swan, S.C. and Billings, D.L (2013) Exploring rape myths, gendered norms, group processing, and the social context of rape among college women: A qualitative analysis. *Violence against women* 19(4): 465–485.

Dempsey, L., Dowling, M., Larkin, P. and Murphy, K (2016) Sensitive interviewing in qualitative research. *Research in Nursing & Health* 39(6): 480–490.

Dickson-Swift, V., James, E.L., Kippen, S. and Liamputtong, P (2009) Researching sensitive topics: Qualitative research as emotion work. *Qualitative Research* 9(1): 61–79.

Eileraas, K (2011) Legal definitions of rape. In *Encyclopedia of Women in Today's World* 1205–1209. Sage.

Elmir, R., Schmied, V., Jackson, D. and Wilkes, L (2011) Interviewing people about potentially sensitive topics. *Nurse Researcher* 19(1).

Emmers-Sommer, T.M (2015) An examination of gender of aggressor and target (un) wanted sex and nonconsent on perceptions of sexual (un) wantedness, justifiability and consent. *Sexuality Research and Social Policy* 12(4): 280–289.

Fantasia, H.C., Sutherland, M.A., Fontenot, H. and Ierardi, J.A (2014) Knowledge, attitudes and beliefs about contraceptive and sexual consent negotiation among college women. *Journal of Forensic Nursing* 10(4): 199–207.

Firmin, C (2010) *Female Voice in Violence Project: A Study into the Impact of Serious Youth and Gang Violence on Women and Girls*. London: Race on the Agenda.

Gotell, L (2007) The discursive disappearance of sexualized violence: Feminist law reform, judicial resistance and neo-liberal sexual citizenship. *Feminism, Law and Social Change: (Re) Action and Resistance* 127–163.

Hackman, C.L., Pember, S.E., Wilkerson, A.H., Burton, W. and Usdan, S.L (2017) Slut-shaming and victim-blaming: A qualitative investigation of undergraduate students' perceptions of sexual violence. *Sex Education* 17(6): 697–711.

Halley, J (2016) Currents: Feminist key concepts and controversies. *Signs: Journal of Women in Culture and Society* 42(1): 357–379.

Hochschild, A.R (2012) *The Managed Heart*. California: University of California press.

Humphrey, W.A (2016) Let's talk about sex: Legislating and educating on the affirmative consent standard. *USFL Review* 50(35).

Jaggar, A.M (2015) *Just Methods: An Interdisciplinary Feminist Reader*. New York: Routledge.

James-Hawkins, L (2019) Adolescent sexual norms and college sexual experiences: Do high school norms influence college behavior? *Advances in Life Course Research* 39: 61–76.

James-Hawkins, L., Dalessandro, C. and Sennott, C (2019) Conflicting contraceptive norms for men: Equal responsibility vs. women's bodily autonomy. *Culture, Health & Sexuality* 21(3): 263–277.

Jozkowski, K.N. and Peterson, Z.D (2013) College students and sexual consent: Unique insights. *Journal of Sex Research* 50(6): 517–523.

Lamarche, V.M. and Seery, M.D (2019) Come on, give it to me baby: Self-esteem, narcissism, and endorsing sexual coercion following social rejection. *Personality and Individual Differences* 149: 315–325.

Leiting, K.A. and Yeater E.A (2017) A Qualitative analysis of the effects of victimization history and sexual attitudes on women's hypothetical sexual assault scripts. *Violence against women* 23(1): 46–66.

Littleton, H., Layh, M. and Rudolph, K (2018) Unacknowledged rape in the community: Rape characteristics and adjustment. *Violence and Victims* 33(1): 142–156.

Lowe, M. and Rogers, P (2017) The scope of male rape: A selective review of research, policy and practice. *Aggression and Violent Behavior* 35: 38–43.

Marciniak, A.L (2015) The case against affirmative consent: Why the well-intentioned legislation dangerously misses the mark. *University of Pittsburgh Law Review* 77(51).

Maxwell, C (2006) Understanding young women's sexual relationship experiences: The nature and role of vulnerability. *Journal of Youth Studies* 9(2): 141–158.

McGarry, J (2010) Exploring the effect of conducting sensitive research. *Nurse Researcher* 18(1).

Montemurro, B., Bartasavich, J. and Wintermute, L (2015) Let's (not) talk about sex: The gender of sexual discourse. *Sexuality & Culture* 19(1): 139–156.

Muehlenhard, C.L., Humphreys, T.P., Jozkowski, K.N. and Peterson, Z.D (2016) The complexities of sexual consent among college students: A conceptual and empirical review. *The Journal of Sex Research* 53(4–5): 457–487.

Newton, V.L (2017) It's good to be able to talk: An exploration of the complexities of participant and researcher relationships when conducting sensitive research. *Women's Studies International Forum* 61: 93–99.

O'Brien, J (2010) Building understanding: Sensitive issues and putting the researcher in the research. *Anthropology Matters* 12(1).

Peterson, Z.D., and Muehlenhard, C.L (2004) Was it rape? The function of women's rape myth acceptance and definitions of sex in labeling their own experiences. *Sex Roles* 51(3–4): 129–144.

Peterson, Z.D. and Muehlenhard, C.L (2011) A match-and-motivation model of how women label their nonconsensual sexual experiences. *Psychology of Women Quarterly* 35(4): 558–570.

Statistics, O.F.N (2018) *Sexual offences in England and Wales: Year ending March 2017.* www.ons.gov.uk/peoplepopulationandcommunity/crimeandjustice/articles/sexualoffencesinenglandandwales/yearendingmarch2017

Tolman, D.L., Davis, B.R. and Bowman, C.P (2016) That's just how it is. A gendered analysis of masculinity and femininity ideologies in adolescent girls and boys heterosexual relationships. *Journal of Adolescent Research* 31(1): 3–31.

Wade, L (2017) *American Hookup: The New Culture of Sex on Campus.* New York: WW Norton & Company.

Wilson, L.C. and Miller, K.E (2016) Meta-analysis of the prevalence of unacknowledged rape. *Trauma, Violence, & Abuse* 17(2): 149–159.

Wilson, L.C., Newins, A.R. and White, S.W (2018) The impact of rape acknowledgment on survivor outcomes: The moderating effects of rape myth acceptance. *Journal of Clinical Psychology* 74(6): 926–939.

11 Building a community of trust

Participatory applied theatre workshop techniques for difficult conversations on consent

Natasha Richards-Crisp

Building a community of trust: participatory applied theatre workshop techniques for difficult conversations on consent

Introduction

Police recorded over 83,000 child sexual abuse offences in the year ending March 2020,[1],[2] an increase of approximately 267% since 2013. Research estimates indicate that about one-quarter of all child sexual abuse cases involve a perpetrator under 18.[3] Despite the prevalence of the issue, the recent UK Ofsted review of sexual abuse in schools and colleges highlights the difficulty of conversations around consent, sexual harassment and sexual violence. Young people emphasised they did not want to discuss these topics for many reasons, including:

> the risk of being ostracised by peers or getting peers into trouble is not considered to be worth it for something perceived by children and young people to be commonplace. They worry about how adults will react, because they think they will not be believed, or that they will be blamed. They also think that once they talk to an adult, the process will be out of their control[4]

In this chapter, I discuss how building a community of trust can provide the potential for difficult conversations with young people around consent, sexual harassment and sexual violence. I suggest that a community of trust can be built through participatory applied theatre workshop techniques.

I employ a Practice-as-Research methodology, facilitating participatory applied theatre workshops in an LGBTQ+ youth group and an independent school in the east of England. Over ten weeks, the workshops explored different weekly topics based on the UK Relationships and Sex Education (RSE) statutory guidance: this chapter focuses on workshop three, which explored consent, sexual harassment and sexual violence, and the difficult conversations around these topics. The term "young people" used in this chapter refers to 14- to 18-year-olds, based on the participants' ages in the workshop. The chapter incorporates data collected in the video recordings of the workshop, participants' reflective journals and participants' final feedback surveys. I map the journey and the development of the

DOI: 10.4324/9781003088417-15

pedagogical approaches employed in the workshop described, thereby mirroring the scaffolding of the workshop in the structure of the chapter.

Theoretical framework

It is often argued that applied theatre can create "safe spaces" for participatory work.[5] However, tensions exist in the notion of a safe space, as risk can be necessary for positive change.[6] Applied theatre educator and researcher Alice O'Grady highlights the inherent risk in participatory work, as "participatory performance invites spectators into its frame of play".[7] Through participation, young people risk standing out amongst their peers. Yet, risk can be an impetus for positive change as it poses a challenge to the status quo. For the prominent feminist scholar bell hooks, it is desirable to be part of a community of resistance to undertake that challenge.[8] In my workshops, the community of resistance is built through a community of trust; a shared space where participants are encouraged to take risks within a boundaried framework. Building a community of trust that values different voices can create a participatory workshop space that mitigates harm from risk in difficult conversations, while making positive change possible.

This chapter brings feminist perspectives on consent into conversation with applied theatre scholarship. Although there is extensive research on participatory theatre workshops as an educational tool, little attention has been paid to the tensions in using this method to educate on consent utilising a feminist approach. Prominent feminist activist Kitty Stryker combines a variety of voices in her anthology *Ask: Building a Consent Culture*, referred to from this point as *Ask*. The anthology advocates for building a consent culture sensitive to a wide range of lived experiences. I build upon the contributions of *Ask*, suggesting a community of trust can enable difficult conversations around consent, sexual harassment and sexual violence by valuing the lived experiences of young people through participatory applied theatre workshop techniques. In 'Risky Aesthetics, Critical Vulnerabilities, and Edgeplay: Tactical Performance of the Unknown',[9] O'Grady introduces the theory of "edgeplay", whereby participatory play can be a vehicle for young peoples' development of knowledge and skills.[10] O'Grady proposes that "edgeplay" can be a new category of voluntary risk-taking, building on theories of edgework. She considers how "edgeplay" offers a way of thinking imaginatively through risk in other areas. Utilising O'Grady's theories, I argue that developing participants' knowledge and skills around negotiations of consent can help to build Stryker's desired consent culture and increase young people's confidence and ability to engage in difficult conversations of consent.

Setting the boundaries: content warning

At the start of the workshops, I remind the participants they do not need to share anything personal during the session, and if they do disclose anything that involves risk to themselves or to someone else then it cannot remain confidential. Thereby, I set the boundaries of trust between educator and participant through clarity and transparency. I give a content warning, informing participants the session will address consent, sexual harassment and sexual violence and they can leave, and re-join, at any time. I also stated in the participant information sheet, which was provided prior to the overall project, that participants did not have to participate if they did not want to and were assured that not participating would have no impact on their school records.[11] Introducing content warnings at the start of participatory workshops, as well as in information provided before commencing projects, can allow students the understanding and the language to control their involvement in the project. Content warnings can also provide agency and allow participants to set and maintain their own boundaries. In these steps, I aim to address the issues young people detailed of feeling like the process is outside of their control, to build a community of trust that can encourage difficult conversations around consent, sexual harassment and sexual violence.

Though increasing in prevalence, content warnings may be something participants have not been exposed to before. There is the potential for young people to feel uncomfortable in the unknown, which poses a risk to them taking content warnings seriously. There is also a risk that the content warning might stop the young person from wanting to be involved in the workshop or the difficult conversations, without fully understanding what the content warning means, especially if they have not received one before. Content warnings may potentially increase generalised feelings of anxiety, prejudicing material based on assumptions rather than the content itself. However, these potential issues should not negate the use of content warnings. In *Ask*, contributor Kate Fractal discusses live-action role-playing and suggests "players who trust that their boundaries will be respected are more willing to take a risk and play a more intense game".[12] Therefore, I argue that building a community of trust can mitigate the potential issues of content warnings. In this project, participants were exposed to content warnings each week and experienced their boundaries being respected. I introduced topics that are more likely to be triggering, such as consent, in later weeks of the project, in order to establish a community of trust in less potentially risky topics with the aim of increasing the opportunity for positive change through difficult conversations.

I also gave the content warnings after playing a game. Playing simple competitive games at the start of a participatory applied theatre workshop can start to build the community of trust by participants respecting the rules and boundaries of the game. In the workshop described in this chapter, I played a game called Heads Up, Heads Down.[13] The game involves a circle of participants looking down, and then when they hear "Heads Up", they look directly at someone else in the circle. The rule is they must look up immediately, make it clear who they are looking at and not change who they pick. Participants are "out" if they lock eyes with another participant, but they remain in the game if the participant they are looking at is looking at another person. Applied theatre is known for including such games to improve participants' communication and confidence.[14] I argue that communication and confidence are key to difficult conversations, as they enhance the ability to set, maintain, communicate and respect boundaries. A community of trust starts to be built through participants respecting the rules and boundaries of the game and the other participants.

There is a risk the content warning cannot give all the information because the nature of participatory workshops means informed consent is not fully possible. The educator and the participants can never fully know what is going to happen due to the live nature of participatory work. However, that does not mean the educator should not try to provide information or opportunities for participants to leave. Fractal asserts the "safer an environment feels the greater the ability to enjoy the surprises of how the story unfolds".[15] I attempted to provide this desired environment by giving unlimited opportunities to step out of the exercises or even the room. The participants' assent forms completed prior to the project highlighted this option, asking participants to confirm they "understand that [they] can participate in the workshops, but [they] do not have to do any of the exercises or join in any of the discussions that [they] do not want to, and that this will have no wider consequence".[16] Having multiple points of exit and (re)entry builds a community of trust that encourages participation in difficult conversations. In a way, tension exists with the community of trust here, as it is not until someone uses the exit point, and potentially re-enters, that trust is witnessed or experienced.

Valuing voices: check-in discussion

The next stage of the workshop is the check-in: a discussion activity involving participants being seated in a circle with each being asked to respond to a prompt. Participatory workshops can platform a multitude of voices, including habitually silenced ones. The check-in asks the participants to take a risk and be vulnerable in not only having their voices heard, but on a topic that they may not have discussed before, thereby practising for more difficult conversations. O'Grady argues that "the journey towards agency begins with an experience of vulnerability and an awareness of its productivity as a generative tool".[17] By potentially being vulnerable in the check-in, the participants generate new understandings based on their own thoughts. They are also exposed to the productivity of being vulnerable, as they learn from the vulnerability of others in the circle. Allowing space for every voice to be heard within the circle acknowledges the individual, whilst also sharing the space with others. The check-in can help to build value in the community trusting each other to speak as well as, importantly, to listen: essential elements of difficult conversations.

However, participants do not have to speak if they do not want to. A community of trust is built as they can say "pass" when it comes to their turn: they can set their own boundary. Still, tension exists as to whether they would say "pass" due to the power dynamics of educator and participant. O'Grady emphasises that in "participatory performance in particular, where individuals are asked to risk something of themselves through the act of involvement, situated or contextual power relations take on added significance".[18] As an educator, I must constantly reflect on the power I hold in the participatory space to ensure it does not exacerbate harm. These thoughts are echoed in *Ask* when feminist teacher Cherry

Zonkowski reflects on the power dynamics present when asking students a question in the classroom: "This all makes me wonder, as a teacher, whether consent can ever really be taught in a mandatory class . . . I can teach consent, but the practice is elusive".[19] The workshops explored in this research were not mandatory. The students did not have to participate, and therefore the power dynamics are slightly different to those Zonkowski is discussing. There is political difficulty in non-mandatory education, as some young people, particularly at-risk young people, may not receive education around topics relevant to their lives. However, due to the participatory element, the power dynamics may hold greater significance, as O'Grady suggests. Therefore, consent needs to become the focus of the format, not just the content. Even in mandatory education, participation in particular exercises or discussions should not be mandatory. A community of trust, as well as difficult conversations, can only exist if participants feel they can say "no".

The check-in not only allows voices to be heard, but it also values what the participants have to say. It shifts the power dynamics as it values the input of the participants, rather than solely valuing the educator's input. A tension exists, though, when participants say something potentially problematic. For example, at the LGBTQ+ youth group, one participant stated that asking, "do you want to come in for a nightcap?",[20] was the universal saying for, "want to bang?".[21] They also said that if you go to a gay club and "a bottom flirted with a top"[22] it is "implied consent".[23] Rather than simply tell the participant the potential issues with their response, I asked them "why might that potentially be problematic?". The participant's answer, "because some people might see that literally",[24] demonstrated that they knew that asking someone to come in for a nightcap might mean only what they literally say: the participant just needed encouragement to critically reflect, which I was able to provide by not shying away from the difficult conversation. A colleague of mine observing this session commented afterwards they felt I was "really great at asking the right questions and sensitively challenging problematic views, getting them to reconsider what they have said without enforcing ideas upon them".[25] To build a community of trust, the educator should question the ideas, not chastise the speaker, so the participant feels respected while the problematic point is still challenged. Here, the educator provides the potential to increase young people's confidence and ability to engage in the difficult conversation of consent.

Enjoyment and challenge: sharing opinions

After the check-in, I asked the young people for their opinions on statements concerning consent. The RSE guidance recognises there may be a range of opinions with regards to relationships and sex.[26] In the framework I advocate, these opinions need to be acknowledged and discussed through critical reflection for positive change to be possible. I employ a different approach in each workshop to gather participants' opinions, to differentiate for different learners' needs and to ensure that within the routine of the workshops an element of variation remains. This particular week, the participants discussed their opinions on statements concerning consent, sexual harassment and sexual violence in smaller groups, without me facilitating. One participant at the independent school wrote in their reflective journal they "thought [small] group discussions were so much better – we got to have proper discussions which was great".[27] Positive change through difficult conversations is made more possible through enjoyment in the participatory workshop. However, there is tension between the educator wanting to value the enjoyment of the participants whilst also enabling critical reflection. When observing and listening in this exercise, I thought the discussions were less critical and in-depth than in previous weeks. I may have felt this way because I was previously able to hear all points made by participants as I was facilitating the whole group discussion, whereas in the smaller group discussions I lost that ability. The knowledge and understanding were only based on their peers, rather than an educator challenging and guiding them towards new discoveries. One participant acknowledged they had differences with other people's opinions,[28] demonstrating critical reflection. Yet, I do not know if the smaller group discussions or the full group discussions with the educator had the most positive impact, so there is tension in not knowing which approach is better for difficult conversations.

The educator aims to avoid being hierarchical but also cannot disregard the knowledge they hold. Intersubjective consensus in the applied theatre community tends to value the voices and expertise of the participants, which I aimed to do in my workshops, but at times there were tensions when the opinions shared conflicted with my own values and knowledge. As an experienced educator and academic, I have knowledge concerning RSE and theatre which participants may not hold. My role is to elevate their voices, but also to share my knowledge. I may need to challenge an individual's opinions in the process of challenging harmful rhetoric or misinformation within difficult conversations. However, I also need to appreciate my opinions might not be "right" despite the knowledge I hold. Stryker states: "There is no 'right answer' – we are all products of our environment".[29] When building a community of trust, the educator needs to also trust the participants and appreciate the knowledge they hold, particularly with regards to the context of their own lives. To do so, educators need to let go of assumptions that their way is the "right" way within difficult conversations.

In the quote at the start of this chapter, the Ofsted report highlighted that young people avoided difficult conversations around consent, sexual harassment and sexual violence because of "the risk of being ostracised by peers"[30]. When provided with the statement, "it is easy to resist pressure to have sex", one participant strongly agreed with the statement, but another pointed out that if they are older, or if you are scared, it is not easy, as the other person might not take it well. In challenging their peers, they risked the ostracisation mentioned in the report. In *Talking Back: Thinking Feminist, Thinking Black*, hooks articulates the ways speaking can be a radical act:

> When we dare to speak in a liberatory voice, we threaten even those who may initially claim to want our words. In the act of overcoming our fear of speech,

of being seen as threatening, in the process of learning to speak as subjects, we participate in the global struggle to end domination[31]

By risking speaking, this participant provided the opportunity for other participants to reconsider their own positions. By participating in the difficult conversation, they offered the opportunity to challenge others and themselves, opening the possibility for positive change.

Knowledge is power: defining terms

After discussing their opinions on consent, sexual harassment and sexual violence, I provided definitions for these terms. The RSE guidance states that young people should learn the definitions of sexual harassment and sexual violence.[32] Knowing the definitions can help young people to participate in difficult conversations by providing them with the required knowledge. In their reflective journal, one participant at the independent school detailed: "I was shocked when learning the definitions of sexual harassment and violence as I previously viewed them as 'big' and 'extreme' 'newsworthy' events whereas many acts I thought were just part of everyday life".[33] The student's shock when realising that consent is not only an issue in extreme circumstances emphasises the absence of comprehensive education on this topic. The response also highlights the prevalence of sexual harassment and how embedded it is in everyday life. In a reflective journal from the LGBTQ+ youth group, a participant noted that they had "learnt about definitions of sexual harassment and sexual violence" and that they are "now aware of them for [their] future".[34] Both quotations highlight that the participants did not previously know the definitions, and that they thought the definitions would be useful in their own lives. Arming participants with the knowledge to navigate their lived experiences can increase confidence and ability to partake in difficult conversations as well as navigate situations of consent.

One of the reasons children do not report sexual abuse until adulthood is that they do not have the language.[35] Defining sexual harassment and sexual violence provided participants with the language to describe and understand their experiences to participate in difficult conversations. Once young people have the language and the understanding, participants might recognise an experience, either their own or someone else's, as sexual harassment or sexual violence, and be able to discuss and even report them accordingly. During the discussion on the definitions of sexual harassment and sexual violence, an independent school participant realised that one of their past experiences equated to sexual harassment. Difficult conversations on consent can unlock different understandings of past experiences. "We experience things in our past differently as we gain more information and grow as people".[36] Here, Stryker is focused on those realising they perpetrated non-consent, whereas the moment in the independent school was a realisation for the individual that they were a victim. Safeguarding procedures can mitigate harm from disclosures during difficult conversations. Alongside myself, a teacher was present when this situation occurred, so they could hear the conversation and follow the institution's safeguarding procedures. Positive change from disclosures in difficult conversations may occur as participants can receive appropriate support.

Avoiding fixed understandings: law on consent

As well as discussing the definitions of sexual harassment and sexual violence, I discuss the law on consent. The RSE guidance states the starting point for RSE should be the law and "should be taught in a factual way so that pupils are clear on their rights and responsibilities as citizens".[37] I would argue consent is one of the most difficult conversations to have with young people with regards to relationships and sex since there is a lack of understanding regarding the law, from educators as well as participants. If educators do not know the law, they cannot teach it. If young people do not know the law or their rights within it, actions and behaviours can unquestionably be passed off as 'banter' or 'just a laugh'.[38] Sexual harassment and sexual violence then become normalised. The Ofsted report, referenced at the start of this chapter, noted young people do not see difficult conversations as "worth it for something perceived by children and young people to be commonplace".[39] By shining a light on the law, difficult conversations on consent can challenge normalisation of harmful behaviours.

However, the law is not a static instrument, and therefore tension exists in the interpretation and application of the law. The Sexual Offences Act 2003 defines consent as: "if he agrees by choice, and has the freedom and capacity to make that choice".[40] The terms "freedom" and "capacity" can be nuanced and potentially interpreted differently. Injustices based on intersecting identities ensure the interpretation and application of the law is not the same for every individual. There are also a lot of problems with the way current laws are heteronormative and do not always take non-penetrative and non-heterosexual experiences into account. Therefore, educators should encourage questioning the law, and how it works for different groups and individuals, to ensure difficult conversations can aid participants in challenging myths and injustices concerning consent. Participatory workshops can help young people to develop into critical reflectors so they can make decisions, armed with developed knowledge and skills, in the multitude of situations they will face in the context of their own lives.

Part of the reason for misinterpretation of the law comes from representations in the media, as well as mediatised rape trials,[41] which highlight a lack of consequences for perpetrators and a prevalence of victim-blaming. At the independent school, the participants questioned whether Donald Trump saying "grab her by the pussy"[42] was sexual harassment. They decided Trump's remark could be considered sexual harassment, as it was "unwanted" behaviour of a "sexual" nature.[43] They were concerned the rhetoric came from someone in a position of power, with no tangible consequences. Educators need to highlight the limitations of a focus on the law and encourage participants to question power dynamics and their implications for consent culture. To achieve Stryker's desired "freedom to" rather than "freedom from", the law should not be the only yardstick by which we base all understandings of consent. However, young people do need to know the law in the first place to critically reflect upon it during difficult conversations.

An educator may not have all of the answers during difficult conversations. Discussions of the law in the workshop prompted participants to ask for answers on specific examples. While emphasising outcomes would be on a case-by-case basis or on a legal precedent basis, I also highlighted that I am not a lawyer. Additionally, I admitted when I did not know the answer to a question, then offered to help find the answer. A participant at the independent school thanked me for this approach, expressing gratitude for my honesty. I know a lot of educators would not feel confident in admitting they do not know an answer, as they may be scared it would show weakness. But I argue vulnerability can be a strength, especially when encouraging participants to take risks and be vulnerable. Furthermore, in RSE it is important to acknowledge that the world and the law evolves and therefore educators need to be willing to continually learn and adapt. Consent can be a difficult conversation because of a fear of a lack of knowledge. The educator needs to be willing to risk getting it wrong to create and maintain the community of trust that is needed for difficult conversations to potentially have positive outcomes.

What comes next: theatre

From this point in the workshop, the participants meet Stacey, my 15-year-old alter ego, and listen to her describe an issue she is dealing with in her life concerning consent. A boy at school kissed her even though she did not want him to, but she did not say "no". The story poses problems, providing the platform for the participants to seek solutions. The participants ask Stacey questions before giving her advice on the situation. They then create their own theatre pieces using Stacey and her story as a creative stimulus. The approach I have described in this chapter aims to increase the positive impact of the theatre work. In the afterword to *Ask*, Carol Queen states that she knows when "readers set this book down, they'll have the skills and perspectives they need to make change, in their lives and in society".[44] I agree they will have more perspectives, but why would they have more skills? I argue that it is in the act of *doing* that the skills are acquired. Of course, it can be argued that all learning is *doing*, as even thinking silently can be participating; but I utilise performance techniques to open up the difficult conversation, to facilitate the grey spaces by using a proxy in a way that presenting and lecturing in traditional formats cannot. The naming of experiences is complemented by the intimacy of the performance, where participants are then asked to do something more with the difficulty of the conversation. With a community of trust created and maintained, the participants witness and create theatre. Theatre allows participants to gain the confidence and ability to navigate difficult conversations of consent through the act of *doing*.

Acknowledge the tensions: creating safe space

At the end of the project, participants completed a feedback sheet. One of the questions asked: "Do you feel a 'safe space' was created and why?" All the participants that responded to the question agreed, to an extent, that a safe space had been created. One participant answered:

> 100%. We were in a small group – who were put into a situation where maturity and trust was needed to talk about certain things and were capable of doing that- creating a sense of a safe place as sharing (when comfortable) was key. Alongside that, we also had very accepting adults with us, there wasn't any feeling of judging or intruding on the student info[45]

The participant suggests a small group was important to cultivating a safe environment. Other participants also mentioned "trust" to describe the relationships between participants, reasoning this was "because everyone was so open" and "brutally honest which encouraged us all to share things and deal with those problems".[46] Even though the participants were never asked to disclose personal information, there was still a willingness to share. A community of trust can be seen as a practice where people feel safe to stretch outside of their comfort zone and to be open, without fear of judgement, allowing participants the ability and confidence to participate in difficult conversations.

However, the community of trust is not guaranteed, and not everyone in the community may feel the same. The word choice of being "brutally" honest is not necessarily compatible with a community of trust, as it implies the participant felt there was the potential for violence in these transactions. A different participant stated:

> While I think the group definitely grew closer and I felt more comfortable as the sessions progressed, I don't think I could ever completely let my 'guard' down. This was because I don't feel that I have a positive relationship with a few of the girls when we're outside of the group and I always felt that I was moments away from animosity, and I could never be completely sure if what I said would stay inside the group[47]

These workshops do not exist in a vacuum and therefore interactions outside of the community of trust impact the feelings within the workshops. O'Grady argues context is significant when working with a risky aesthetic.[48] To build upon O'Grady, I argue context is even more significant when also working with a typically taboo topic which has ramifications in everyday interactions. Educators need to consider the context of the participatory workshops, as well as the limitations of a community of trust, if positive outcomes are to be achieved within difficult conversations.

Conclusion

This chapter evaluated the tensions present in the potentially difficult conversation of consent; what measures can mitigate these tensions; and how these tensions may lead to positive change. I argued that a community of trust can help to mitigate these tensions, and positive change can occur through young people's increased confidence and ability to participate in difficult conversations around consent. The research is based on limited sample size, so more research is needed to determine the efficacy of the approach detailed with other groups of young people, particularly those in marginalised communities. Future work will also explore theories from Katherine Angel's (2021) recent book, *Tomorrow Sex Will Be Good Again*, which was published after this workshop and raises further questions regarding the balance between risk and desire.[49] As stated before, the law is not static, and neither is this approach to education. I hope the pedagogical approach detailed can provide a useful blueprint, but one that is malleable and invites educators to shift and change it to their context. Mostly, I hope my vulnerability in sharing my practice can encourage others to risk the same: because in that risk is where positive change lies.

Notes

1 "Tackling child sexual abuse strategy", Home Office, accessed March 30, 2022, www.gov.uk/government/publications/tackling-child-sexual-abuse-strategy.
2 Due to the way this data is collected and different sexual offences are defined, these figures do not capture certain sexual offences committed against 16- and 17-year-olds, such as rape.
3 "Protecting children from harm", Children's Commissioner, published November 2015, www.childrenscommissioner.gov.uk/report/protecting-children-from-harm/.
4 "Review of sexual abuse in schools and colleges", Ofsted, published June 10, 2021, www.gov.uk/government/publications/review-of-sexual-abuse-in-schools-and-colleges/review-of-sexual-abuse-in-schools-and-colleges.
5 Paul Dwyer, Mary Ann Hunter, and Justine Shih Pearson, "High Stakes: Risk and Performance", in *About Performance* (Sydney: University of Sydney, 2014), 1.
6 Alice O'Grady, "Risky Aesthetics, Critical Vulnerabilities, and Edgeplay: Tactical Performance of the Unknown" in *Risk, Participation, and Performance Practice Critical Vulnerabilities in a Precarious World* (London: Palgrave Macmillan, 2017).
7 O'Grady, *Risk, Participation, and Performance Practice*, 2.
8 bell hooks, *Yearning: Race, Gender and Cultural Politics* (New York: Routledge, 2015), 42.
9 O'Grady, *Risk, Participation, and Performance Practice*, 21.
10 O'Grady, *Risk, Participation, and Performance Practice*, 21.
11 Participant Information Sheet.
12 Kate Fractal, "Games, Role-Playing, and Consent", in *Ask: Building a Consent Culture* (Portland: Thorntree Press, 2017), 152.
13 I cannot find the original reference for this game. It is a marker of Applied Theatre that practitioners have a wealth of games/activities in their toolkit, acquired over time, but cannot always remember where they were first exposed to them.
14 Chris Johnson, *Drama Games for Those Who Like to Say No* (London: Nick Hern Books Limited, 2010), xvii.
15 Fractal, *Ask*, 147.
16 Participant Assent Form.
17 O'Grady, *Risk, Participation, and Performance Practice*, 15.
18 O'Grady, *Risk, Participation, and Performance Practice*, 5–6.
19 Cherry Zonkowski, "The Green Eggs and Ham Scam", in *Ask: Building a Consent Culture* (Portland: Thorntree Press, 2017), 50.

20 Workshop Participant, *Applied Theatre Workshop*, January 1, 2020.
21 Workshop Participant, *Applied Theatre Workshop*, January 1, 2020.
22 Urban Dictionary describes "bottom" and "top" as terms used for sex between two women or two men. The top is the giver and the one on bottom is receiving.
23 Workshop Participant, *Applied Theatre Workshop*, January 1, 2020.
24 Workshop Participant, *Applied Theatre Workshop*, January 1, 2020.
25 Colleague, *Applied Theatre Workshop*, January 1, 2020.
26 "Relationships Education, Relationships and Sex Education (RSE) and Health Education Statutory guidance for governing bodies, proprietors, head teachers, principals, senior leadership teams, teachers", Department for Education, accessed March 30, 2022, https://assets.publishing.service.gov.uk/government/uploads/system/uploads/attachment_data/file/908013/Relationships_Education__Relationships_and_Sex_Education__RSE__and_Health_Education.pdf.
27 Participant Reflective Journals.
28 Participant Reflective Journals.
29 Kitty Stryker, *Ask: Building a Consent Culture* (Portland: Thorntree Press, 2017), 3.
30 Ofsted, "Review of sexual abuse in schools and colleges".
31 bell hooks, *Talking Back: Thinking Feminist, Thinking Black* (New York: Routledge, 2015), 18.
32 Department for Education, 'Relationships Education, Relationships and Sex Education (RSE) and Health Education Statutory guidance for governing bodies, proprietors, head teachers, principals, senior leadership teams, teachers', https://assets.publishing.service.gov.uk/government/uploads/system/uploads/attachment_data/file/908013/Relationships_Education__Relationships_and_Sex_Education__RSE__and_Health_Education.pdf (accessed 22.03.21).
33 Participant Reflective Journals.
34 Participant Reflective Journals.
35 "Bodily Autonomy for Kids", Akilah S. Richards, in *Ask: Building a Consent Culture* (Portland: Thorntree Press, 2017) 109.
36 Stryker, *Ask*, 21.
37 Department for Education, "Relationships Education, Relationships and Sex Education (RSE) and Health Education Statutory guidance for governing bodies, proprietors, head teachers, principals, senior leadership teams, teachers".
38 "Girls' Attitudes Survey 2014", Girlguiding, accessed March 22, 2021, www.girlguiding.org.uk/globalassets/docs-and-resources/research-and-campaigns/girls-attitudes-survey-2014.pdf.
39 Ofsted, "Review of sexual abuse in schools and colleges".
40 "Section 74", Sexual Offences Act 2003, accessed March 28, 2022, www.legislation.gov.uk/ukpga/2003/42/section/74.
41 "Irish outcry over teenager's underwear used in rape trial", BBC News, accessed March 22, 2021, www.bbc.co.uk/news/world-europe-46207304.
42 "Transcript: Donald Trump's Taped Comments About Women', New York Times, accessed June 11, 2021, www.nytimes.com/2016/10/08/us/donald-trump-tape-transcript.html.
43 "What is sexual harassment?", Rape Crisis England and Wales, accessed March 31, 2022, https://rapecrisis.org.uk/get-informed/types-of-sexual-violence/what-is-sexual-harassment/.
44 Carol Queen, "Afterword", in *Ask: Building a Consent Culture* (Portland: Thorntree Press, 2017), 175.
45 Participant Final Feedback.
46 Participant Final Feedback.
47 Participant Final Feedback.
48 O'Grady, *Risk, Participation, and Performance Practice*, 16.
49 Katherine Angel, *Tomorrow Sex Will Be Good Again* (London: Verso, 2021).

References

Angel, K (2021) *Tomorrow Sex Will Be Good Again*. London: Verso.

BBC News (2021) *Irish outcry over teenager's underwear used in rape trial*. Available from: www.bbc.co.uk/news/world-europe-46207304 (Accessed 22 March 2021).

Children's Commissioner (2015) *Protecting children from harm*, (published) Available from: www.childrenscommissioner.gov.uk/report/protecting-children-from-harm/ (Accessed November 2015).

Colleague (2020) *Applied Theatre Workshop*.

Department for Education. *Relationships Education, Relationships and Sex Education (RSE) and Health Education Statutory guidance for governing bodies, proprietors, head teachers, principals, senior leadership teams, teachers*. Available from: https://assets.publishing.service.gov.uk/government/uploads/system/uploads/attachment_data/file/908013/Relationships_Education__Relationships_and_Sex_Education__RSE__and_Health_Education.pdf (Accessed March 30, 2022).

Dwyer, P., Mary, A.H. and Justine, S.P (2014) *High Stakes: Risk and Performance. In about Performance*. Sydney: University of Sydney.

Fractal, K (2017) *Games, Role-Playing, and Consent. Ask: Building a Consent Culture*. Portland: Thorntree Press.

Girlguiding. *Girls* (2014) *Attitudes survey*. Available from: www.girlguiding.org.uk/globalassets/docs-and-resources/research-and-campaigns/girls-attitudes-survey-2014.pdf (Accessed 22 March 2021).

Home Office. Tackling child sexual abuse strategy. *Home Office*. Available from: www.gov.uk/government/publications/tackling-child-sexual-abuse-strategy (Accessed 30 March 2022)

hooks, b (2015) *Talking Back: Thinking Feminist, Thinking Black*. New York: Routledge.

hooks, b (2015) *Yearning: Race, Gender and Cultural Politics*. New York: Routledge.

Johnson, C (2010) *Drama Games for Those Who Like to Say No*. London: Nick Hern Books Limited.

New York Times. *Transcript: Donald Trump's Taped comments about*. Available from: *Women*.www.nytimes.com/2016/10/08/us/donald-trump-tape-transcript.html (Accessed June 11, 2021).

O'Grady, A (2017) Risky aesthetics, critical vulnerabilities, and Edgeplay: Tactical performance of the unknown In *Risk, Participation, and Performance Practice Critical Vulnerabilities in a Precarious World*. London: Palgrave Macmillan.

Ofsted. *Review of sexual abuse in schools and colleges* (published). Available from: www.gov.uk/government/publications/review-of-sexual-abuse-in-schools-and-colleges/review-of-sexual-abuse-in-schools-and-colleges (Accessed June 10, 2021).

Queen, C (2017) Afterwor. In *Ask: Building a Consent Culture*. Portland: Thorntree Press.

Rape Crisis England and Wales. *What is sexual harassment?* Available from: https://rapecrisis.org.uk/get-informed/types-of-sexual-violence/what-is-sexual-harassment/ (Accessed 31 March 2022).

Richards, A.S.B (2017) Autonomy for kids. In *Ask: Building a Consent Culture*. Portland: Thorntree Press.

Sexual Offences Act 2003. "Section 74". Available from: www.legislation.gov.uk/ukpga/2003/42/section/74. (Accessed 28 March 2022).

Stryker, K (2017) *Ask: Building a Consent Culture*. Portland: Thorntree Press.

Workshop Participant, *Applied Theatre Workshop*, 1 January, 2020.

Zonkowski, C (2017) The green eggs and ham scam. In *Ask: Building a Consent Culture*. Portland: Thorntree Press.

12 Women's experiences of marital rape in Turkey

Ethics, voice and difficult conversations

Gulcimen Karakeci

Introduction

This chapter focuses on empirical data about women's experiences of marital rape in Turkey. It draws on data from a larger qualitative study I did that analysed social and institutional responses to domestic abuse against women in Turkey (Karakeci, 2019). Beyond discussing women's experiences of marital rape, in this chapter I share my experiences of the ethical dilemmas that I encountered while researching domestic abuse against women. Throughout, I will reflect on the ways in which 'difficult conversations' became an inherent part of the research when addressing marital rape.

The existence of marital rape has only been legally and socially recognised during recent decades (Painter, 1991; Bergen and Barnhill, 2006). Although studies in this field have gained momentum recently, it is still one of the least-studied areas of domestic abuse literature. Studies in this field began to emerge in the 1980s. The findings of early research played a vital role in publicising the voice of the victims and the prevalence of marital rape (Tellis, 2010; Finkelhor and Yllo, 1983). Despite some important research and activism, it remains taboo to discuss issues related to sexuality and sexual violence in many countries, including Turkey. This prevents victims of sexual abuse from speaking about their experiences and receiving the necessary social and institutional support. At the same time, it makes it particularly difficult to conduct research on this topic in these regions.

Due to the sensitive nature of my research, it was difficult to randomly access women who experienced domestic abuse, hence I decided to interview women who were residing in domestic abuse shelters. I worked with gatekeepers to access the research population. Historically, Turkey has not developed a feminist shelter movement like its Western counterparts. Domestic abuse shelters started to open in the early 1990s and since then, most of the shelters in Turkey work in cooperation with municipalities or the central government (Korkmaz, 2012). Currently, the Ministry of Family and Social Policies in Turkey is responsible for women's shelters at the governmental level. Since they are directly responsible for most of the shelters, I had to obtain permission from the ministry to collect my data. I was given access on the condition of not collecting data on victims' experience

DOI: 10.4324/9781003088417-16

of sexual abuse. This was stipulated by the gatekeepers because they claimed that talking about sexual abuse has the risk of traumatising women.

During the interviews, my participants discussed their experiences of marital rape although I did not ask any questions related to sexual abuse. Some of my participants sought help from shelters due to experiencing sexual abuse by itself, rather than other forms of abuse. All participants had left abusive marriages and were residing in a women's shelter. Almost one-third of participants described experiencing both domestic abuse and marital rape. It was perhaps inevitable that in interviews they spoke about their experiences of sexual abuse, despite none of my questions asking about it directly. While there is a growing literature on domestic abuse against women in Turkey (Akar et al., 2010; Ozcan et al., 2016; Kocacik et al., 2007; Sen and Bolsan, 2017), there are very few studies that specifically address women's experiences of marital rape. Mostly, brief information on marital rape is included as part of research on domestic abuse against women in Turkey. When I first started my PhD, I aimed to examine the factors that make women vulnerable to staying in situations where they experience domestic abuse and what support services are available to them, rather than focusing on analysing the different forms of abuse they experienced by their husbands. Since women discussed their experiences of marital rape, I felt that it was important to write their stories to contribute to filling the gap in the literature, raise awareness and allow their voices to be heard. This slightly changed the direction of my research. I had difficulties deciding whether it would be ethical to include the stories of women in my research. The gatekeeper did not give permission to collect data on sexual abuse, but I obtained informed consent from the women, and as it was their story to tell, I felt it was important to do so. Through sharing my experiences in this chapter, I would like to discuss ethical problems related to securing meaningful informed consent in research settings controlled by gatekeepers.

Domestic abuse in Turkey

There was no grassroots women's movement in Turkey until the 1980s. Women were granted some rights as a part of the Western-style modernisation project of the state after the establishment of the Turkish republic (Acar and Altunok, 2013). Feminist activists in Turkey were highly inspired by the second-wave feminist movement in the West (Tekeli, 2010; Gulcicek, 2015). The fight against domestic abuse against women became a primary concern (Tekeli, 2010; Gulcicek, 2015). They also used the famous slogan of second-wave feminists: "The personal is political" (Tekeli, 2010: 120–121). Women's oppression was perceived as a gender issue and demanded systematic change to eliminate gender discrimination (Acikel, 2009). In the early 1980s, feminists arranged small consciousness-raising groups to bring the problem of domestic abuse to the attention of the public (Tekeli, 2010; Gulcicek, 2015; Acikel, 2009). On the 17th of May 1987, the first campaign against domestic abuse against women, the Women's Solidarity against Beating, took place in Istanbul (Dissiz and Sahin, 2008; Altinay and Arat, 2009; Berktay et al., 2004; Gündüz, 2004; Moralıoğlu, 2012). It was the first mass public demonstration after the 1980s military coup (Moralıoğlu, 2012; Şenol and Yıldız, 2013). Around 3000 women had taken to the streets to march in protest against a judge's refusal of a divorce case of a pregnant woman on the grounds of domestic abuse (Gündüz, 2004; Henneke, 2008). The women's movement gained momentum after this campaign. A women's solidarity network was created to provide medical and legal support for abused women (Mor Cati Kadin Siginma Vakfi, n.d.). On the 4th of October 1987, the second mass women's meeting on domestic abuse took place in the garden of the Chore Museum in Istanbul (Yüksel, 1993).

In the same period, feminists in Turkey also tried to create awareness of sexual abuse against women in the public sphere (Tekeli, 2010; Gulcicek, 2015; Acikel, 2009). There was no specific emphasis on the prevention of marital rape. The existence of marital rape has only been legally and socially recognised during recent decades across the globe (Painter, 1991). Historically, sexual intercourse in marriage is seen as the "husband's right and wife's duty" (Yllo, 1996: 2). This belief made it difficult to accept that rape can happen within marriage for a long time. Today, marital rape is criminalised in many countries but it can still be treated as less serious than rape by strangers in many societies and cultures (Bergen, 1996; Martin et al., 2007). In Turkey, the discussions on the criminalisation of marital rape took place mostly after the 1990s. It was the first brought to the agenda by Yüksel Yalova, a deputy of the Motherland Party, in 1996 (Özer, 2012). The criminalisation of marital rape was intensively discussed with the 2002 Turkish Penal Code reform initiative (Özer, 2012). It was criminalised with the implementation of the new Turkish Penal Code on the 1st of June 2005 (Özer, 2012).

In Turkey, the current legislation on violence against women is highly comprehensive. The most recent legislation, which is called the 6284 numbered Law on the Protection of Family and Prevention of Violence against Women, was introduced on the 8th of March 2012 (Dural, 2016). With the establishment of 6284, the role of the state in combating domestic abuse was extended and it became mainly "government's responsibility to provide shelters to the victims" of domestic abuse (Coşar and Yeğenoğlu, 2011: 562). This law includes far-reaching regulations to protect women from all forms of abuse. However, women do not benefit from this law as much as they should due to the lack of awareness of their rights and socioeconomic and cultural factors (Alkan and Tekmanli, 2021). According to Alkan and Tekmanli (2021), women in Turkey are less likely to report marital rape because of holding the traditional belief that it is women's responsibility to meet their husband's sexual needs, and some women still do not consider nonconsensual sex with their husband as rape.

As I mentioned before, not many studies can be found on marital rape in Turkish literature. Some researchers, such as Dülger (2021) and Özer (2012), focused on discussing the legal changes on marital rape in Turkey. Several studies comparatively analysed attitudes towards marital rape. For example, in their study, Gul and Schuster (2020) comparatively examined attitudes towards sexual aggression in intimate relationships in Turkey, Germany and the UK. They argue that even if the participants from these countries grew up with different cultural dynamics, they all hold victim-blaming views and are less likely to define the incident as rape, and they are less likely to interpret marital rape as a serious crime (Gul and Schuster; 2020). They claim that the rate of participants who have such views is higher among Turkish participants compared to participants from Germany and the UK (Gul and Schuster; 2020).

Some other studies quantitatively analysed individuals' views on marital rape in Turkey. In her research, Sakizcioglu and Dogan (2020) examined married individuals' views on tolerating marital rape based on their gender, educational level, income, length of the marriage, sexual satisfaction in their marriage, having a history of domestic abuse and alcohol consumption and substance misuse. Her research found that there is no strong correlation between individuals' sexual satisfaction, alcohol consumption and substance misuse and tolerating marital rape (Sakizcioglu and Dogan, 2020). She claims that people with no history of domestic abuse are more likely to oppose marital rape compared to individuals who previously experienced domestic abuse (Sakizcioglu and Dogan, 2020). People with high educational levels and income are less likely to find marital rape acceptable compared to those with low income and less educational background (Sakizcioglu and Dogan, 2020). Men are more likely to find marital rape acceptable in comparison to women and there is a direct correlation between the length of the marriage and the acceptance of marital rape (Sakizcioglu and Dogan, 2020).

Several studies focused on analysing the prevalence of domestic abuse against women, and they conducted data on different forms of abuse including sexual abuse. Nationwide research that was conducted in 2015 claims that 12% of married women in Turkey had experienced sexual abuse by their husbands at least once during their marriage (Yüksel et al., 2015). A study conducted in Ankara, Turkey, with 1,178 women found that 31.3% of participants experienced sexual abuse by their husbands at least once (Akar, et al, 2010). In their study, Alkan and Tekmanli (2021) quantitatively analysed factors related to women's experiences of sexual abuse by their husbands by using cross-sectional data from the National Research on Domestic Violence against Women in Turkey study in 2008 and 2014. The data conducted in 2008 includes 12,795 women participants, and the data conducted in 2014 has 7,462 women participants (Alkan and Tekmanli, 2021: 5). They found that women who live in rural areas are more likely to experience sexual abuse by their husbands compared to women living in urban areas (Alkan and Tekmanli, 2021). The research claims that younger women and women with low educational backgrounds were more likely to experience sexual abuse by their husbands (Alkan and Tekmanli, 2021). However, employed women are more likely to experience sexual abuse by their husbands compared to unemployed women (Alkan and Tekmanli, 2021). Additionally, the researchers claim that unemployed men with no educational background are more likely to sexually abuse their wives/partners compared to employed men and men with some educational degrees (Alkan and Tekmanli, 2021: 9). These studies suggest that sexual abuse within marriage is a relatively widespread issue.

Researching domestic abuse support services in Turkey

The data presented in this chapter was collected from 7 women's shelters and 5 domestic abuse women's organisations in 2 cities in Turkey in 2015. Turkey has undergone serious institutional, political and social changes after the failed military coup attempt on the 15th of July 2016. The Turkish government declared a state of emergency on the 21st of July 2016 and many women's organisations, including some women's organisations that I collected data from, were shut down due to political reasons during the state of emergency. I chose to collect data from 2 cities where there were well-established women's shelters and organisations, as this made my target populations more accessible.

Research involving victims of domestic abuse usually requires working with gatekeepers due to difficulties related to accessing the research participants. Working with gatekeepers is one of the hardest parts of conducting research and it can be even more complicated for sensitive research. Many researchers face substantial difficulties in attempting to gain access to "organisations where they would like to carry out their research" (Johl and Renganathan, 2010: 42). As mentioned in the introduction, in Turkey, domestic abuse organisations and shelters are highly institutionalised. They are either run by the central government or cooperate with municipalities and/or the central government (Korkmaz, 2012). At the governmental level, the Ministry of Family and Social Policy is responsible for the shelters and domestic abuse support organisations. Hence, I needed to obtain the permission of the Ministry of Family and Social Policies to collect my data.

When I initially contacted the ministry to secure access, I was asked to make a formal request to collect my data and send them some documents, such as my research proposal, a letter from my supervisor(s) and a list of interview questions. I intended to conduct open-ended interviews with abused women. For this type of interview, there is no need to create a set of predetermined closed interview questions. But as I did not want to lose my opportunity to secure access, I created a list of questions and submitted it along with other documents. I received an email from the ministry quite a while after making my formal request. In their email, they requested that I remove the questions about sexual abuse in order to process my data collection application. I did not understand the purpose of asking me to remove those questions and I replied to their email to ask about the reason. I was told that the questions related to sexual abuse have a risk of traumatising women. Despite talking about their experiences of domestic abuse having a high risk of traumatising women regardless of types of the abuse they experience, it was interesting to see that specific attention was being given to sexual abuse. Their justification was not very meaningful, and it suggested that not all forms of domestic abuse are seen as equally serious. I was worried about not securing access and I removed those questions and resubmitted my updated interview question list. I was given access to collect my data a month later, on the condition of not collecting data on sexual abuse. As I previously mentioned, during the interviews my participants discussed their experiences of marital rape although I did not ask any questions related to sexual abuse. The gatekeeper did not permit me to collect data on sexual abuse, but I obtained informed consent from women to use the information. The gatekeepers hold a powerful position to give or withhold access, but they do not hold any legal rights to give or deny consent on behalf of the participants (Heath et al., 2007). Since I obtained informed consent, I included their stories on marital rape in my research.

In total, 30 in-depth interviews were conducted with women who had experienced domestic abuse and who were residing in the shelters in Diyarbakir and Ankara. Nine out of 30 participants shared their experiences of sexual abuse. I also conducted 5 interviews with women who experienced ongoing mental health difficulties. The interviews with them were not used for this research, since I did not feel that they were able to make an informed decision. I interviewed them because of respecting their time, their decision to be interviewed, and their willingness to tell their story. As a feminist scholar researching domestic abuse, I perceived listening to their stories as a way of empowering those women. The interviews were done in the places that were chosen by the staff members or in the women's shelters when I was allowed to visit the shelters. I could not directly contact women to ask them whether they would like to take place in my research due to the sensitive nature of my research and working with gatekeepers. I do not know exactly what kind of information was initially provided to the participants about my research. Hence, it was difficult for me to understand whether women freely exercised their agency to make their initial decision to participate in my research, in the case of women with ongoing complex mental health issues.

Anonymity and confidentiality of the participants were ensured. Pseudonyms are used instead of the participants' original names. Before the interviews, I provided a written statement that included all the required information about me, my research, the role of participants in the research process and the rights of the participants. Then they were verbally informed of the same in order to obtain informed consent. After receiving this information, some of the participants claimed that they initially decided to participate in my research with the expectation of financial incentives and that they were not aware that their participation is voluntary and there were no financial benefits for them. I informed them that they have no obligation to take place in my research if doing so did not meet their expectations. However, they still wanted to be interviewed.

Some of the participants who were residing in government organisation shelters were accompanied by staff members during the interviews. I was told that the staff members were required to attend the interviews with the women for the protection of the women. The staff members spent some time with us during the interviews and then they left the interview room together. The lives and decisions of women staying in these shelters were strongly monitored by these staff. I interpreted this as indicating that the women were seen as lacking the capacity to freely act or protect themselves without external control. Most of my participants were individuals who were denied the possibility of making decisions about their lives due to a patriarchal society and lack of opportunities for financial independence. Instead of empowering women, the shelters were disempowering women by practising similar forms of controlling behaviours. Their presence restricted women's opportunities to freely express themselves. Although the staff members were practising such behaviours in the name of protection, as a researcher I interpreted it as a different form of abuse.

Participants' accounts of marital rape

Nine participants discussed their experiences of marital rape during the interviews. Using the terms "sex" or "rape" was difficult for them. Either consciously or unconsciously, the participants ignored using these terms. For example, Lisa said:

> I do not know how to tell. Eee, he was forcing me to do things that I did not want to do. That is why he was beating me all the time.
>
> Lisa

The participants experienced physical abuse when they refused to have sex with their husbands. Similarly, another participant mentioned that:

> He was getting angry. He was getting angry whenever I said no to him. He was telling me you are not a woman and beat me afterwards. Once, he kicked me out of the house late at night. It was winter and I had to stay out.
>
> Nicola

Nicola mentioned that her experience of physical abuse had a direct connection with her decision to not have sex with her husband. Another participant claimed that her husband was using having sex as a form of conflict resolution after physically abusing her. For example, Jessamine mentioned that:

> He used to force me to sleep with him after he beat me. He was telling me that I am trying to be the same as before whenever I refuse him . . . I used to tell him, how come you can expect me to sleep with you after you beat me? The same thing happened again and again. He was beating me and then telling me that you are my wife. It has to happen whenever I want. You cannot refuse me.
>
> Jessamine

Jessamine's refusal to have sex with him was interpreted by her husband as failing to fulfil her role as a wife. Jessamine said that he was even complaining about this to his family:

> He was telling me you are not fulfilling your duty as a wife. He was saying to his family Jessamine does not fulfil her duty as a wife. I did not want to do it after he abused me. I did not want him to get close to me. I was feeling disgusted.
>
> Jessamine

A participant had epilepsy and she said that she was raped several times when she had an epileptic seizure around her husband:

> He used to sleep with me whenever I had an epileptic seizure around him. Many times, he did it in front of my children. They saw it. They saw it. I could not do anything. I was unconscious.
>
> Jennifer

Experiencing marital rape in front of her children was particularly painful for her and she had deep feelings of shame, which is unfortunately a common emotion among victims. She claimed that she lost her mother at an early age and her father neglected her and her siblings. This made her vulnerable to exploitation. She had a history of sexual abuse before her marriage, including being sexually harassed by her brother-in-law. As she had a problematic family background and suffered from severely adverse childhood experiences, she had chosen marriage to escape from her family problems and rebuild her life. But she ended up with an abusive partner. Posttraumatic stress disorder, anxiety, and distress are higher among women who are sexually abused (Classen et al., 2005: 117). Jennifer had serious psychological problems when I met with her, and she claimed that she was on antidepressants. She was about to leave the shelter when I interviewed her. She stated that she was asked to find a job by the staff members although her health conditions did not seem to be suitable for working. Often the shelters only offered a temporary reprieve from violence for the women there, who were frequently left with no option other than to return to the abusive relationship.

Another participant claimed that her husband was sexually abusing her, as well as demonstrating abusive behaviour towards her daughters from her previous marriage:

> It was my second marriage. I have two grown-up daughters. They were living with me when I got married, but I sent them away to protect them. My husband was forcing me to leave the door open when we were sleeping together [having sex]. He wanted my daughters to see us.
>
> Charlotte

She also claimed that:

> A couple of times he told me that your daughters are so innocent and they do not know anything about sexuality. We should ask them to come to watch us while we are having sex.
>
> Charlotte

Despite her husband sexually abusing her and posing some threat of abuse to her daughters, she did not leave him or report him to the police. She stated that she was worried about the possibility of her daughters being sexually abused by her husband, so she asked her daughters to leave the house. She said that she perceived having unwanted sex with her husband as a way of protecting her daughters:

> He was forcing me to sleep with him. A few times I kept quiet and just let him do it with the fear of him doing something to my daughters.
>
> Charlotte

Anxiety about not being able to continue her life as a single woman after certain age frightened her. Despite the problems she was experiencing, she still tried to continue her marriage due to her fears. According to Charlotte, she was also blindly in love with her husband, so she could not leave him. Charlotte had some health problems because of her husband forcing her to have anal sex:

> Eee! He always wanted it. I did not want to. I did not want to because it is "haram" prohibited. He used to get upset and stop talking to me whenever I was refusing him. I was feeling bad and guilty whenever he was refusing to talk to me. I was in love and could not stay away from him. I was crying and feeling so down whenever he was doing it [referring to anal sex]. My intestines cracked because of doing it. I could not sit for months.
>
> Charlotte

She said that she decided to leave him due to experiencing serious health problems because of sexual abuse. As she did not have enough financial resources to support herself when she left him, she sought help from women's shelters. Due to her religious beliefs, experiencing anal rape was particularly traumatic for Charlotte. Rebecca was another participant who had similar experiences due to her religious belief:

> I am so sorry to say it, but he wanted from the back. It is a sin. What could I do? I am a believer. He was always beating me because of it. He was telling me that you are not a woman whenever I refused him.

Another participant had similar experiences. Emily claimed that:

> He was forcing me [anal sex]. It happened one or two times. Then he stopped when he saw I am feeling bad about it. He was forcing me. I did not want to.
>
> Emily

Emily also stated that her husband accused her of being unfaithful because of refusing to have sex with him:

> He was telling me you have another person in your life. That is why you refuse me. Sorry, but I am going to share it with you. He was asking me, do you have any other men? Why do you not want me? He was forcing me to do it. He kept doing the same thing.
>
> Emily

These experiences of sexual violence are part of the continuum of coercive control and domestic abuse that the women also experienced. Social policy, support, activism and education must be informed by research on this topic in order to offer adequate support to survivors and prevent it from happening in the future. Although I developed a good interview rapport with participants and these women bravely shared their stories with me, it is possible that other participants had similar experiences but did not disclose them to me in the circumstances we were in – as they were accompanied by a refuge worker. Some participants mentioned that they experienced marital rape because of their mother-in-law:

> On our first night, I said to him that I am scared of having sex. He understood, and he was trying to be kind to me. Then the next morning my mother-in-law came to ask about it. My husband told her that Jessamine is scared, and I will wait until she feels ready. His mother said to him to go and finish it. Your brothers are waiting to see the blood.
>
> Jessamine

In Turkey, women's virginity is still important, although this traditional view of female sexuality is declining. Families might still request that newly married couples show proof of virginity. Failure of providing proof of virginity can have serious consequences for women, including being victims of honour killing. Jessamine claimed that her mother-in-law threatened to end their marriage if they failed to provide proof of her virginity:

> [They said] We will send her back if she is not a virgin. Then we did it although I was not ready and too scared. My husband said that his mother is waiting in front of the door. I felt bad. He showed that blood to everyone. He showed it to his brothers to prove that I was a virgin. They showed it to everyone.
>
> Jessamine

Freya was another participant who experienced sexual abuse by her husband because of her parents-in-law. She claimed that her husband was a sex worker and gay:

> There were some weird things on our nuptial night. I learned that my husband is a gay man, and he is a drug addict. He told me, he told me on our nuptial night. He said I am gay. He showed me the picture of his boyfriend. His family knew he is gay. They thought he would change if he got married.
>
> Freya

According to her, her husband's family knew about his situation. They perceived homosexuality as a health problem, and they thought that marriage would change their son's sexual identity. Classifying homosexuality as an illness that should be diagnosed and cured has a long history (Plummer, 1998). Its original placement within the international standards of healthcare such as the Diagnostic Statistical

Manual and the World Health Organisation as a mental illness has left many with the opinion that it is indeed a curable illness, despite its removal from both of these institutions of healthcare in 1973 and 1992, respectively (Plummer, 1998). Today, therefore, perceiving homosexuality as an illness has no medical basis (Plummer, 1998). However, Freya's experience indicates that these outdated beliefs on homosexuality still exist in Turkey. Freya also had similar views on homosexuality, and she claimed that:

> I was praying and crying all night. I was saying why has this happened to me. I was praying for him to heal.
>
> Freya

Freya stated that she did not want to have sex with her husband and she tried to distance herself from him, especially after she got pregnant. But this created tension in her marriage, and her husband started to physically abuse her:

> I did not want to get close to him. I completely distanced myself from him after I got pregnant. I stayed away from him. I stayed away, that is why he was beating me. He changed a lot. He became a different person.
>
> Freya

Freya tried to seek help from her family and leave her abusive husband. According to her, her family accused her of slandering her husband when she told them that he was gay and a sex worker. She could not get any support from them. Her husband's partner was also married to a woman. He forced Freya to have group sex with his partner and clients. That is why she left him. She stayed in her aunt's house for a short period, but her family accused her aunt of separating Freya from her husband. Freya stated that she did not want to return to her husband and felt guilty about putting her aunt in a difficult situation. Hence, she decided to seek help from domestic abuse support organisations. Her story poignantly illustrates the ordeal that women in these circumstances experience and the lack of options available to them, even when they are ready and willing to leave an abusive marriage.

Discussion

This chapter aimed to discuss women's experiences of marital rape in Turkey and the difficulties related to conducting this research. There are hardly any studies on women's experiences of marital rape in Turkish literature. This might be due to problems related to conducting research in this area. Domestic abuse women's shelters in Turkey are highly institutionalised and they do not operate with feminist organisational principles. Feminist organisational principles are based on offering the necessary support to empower women, increase their self-esteem, and help them "take control of their own lives" (Reinelt, 1995: 88). It is also important to create non-hierarchical and non-bureaucratic shelters to effectively empower women (Reinelt, 1995). In the highly institutionalised Turkish shelter system, women who escape from domestic abuse find themselves in another abusive environment. All aspects of women's lives are controlled by the shelters under the name of protecting them. In such institutional settings, it is particularly challenging to conduct sensitive research. As I discussed in the previous sections, I was allowed by Turkish authorities to conduct my research under the condition of not collecting data on sexual abuse. However, I obtained informed consent from the participants, some of whom chose to share their experiences of marital rape during the interview. Hence, I wrote their stories. During some interviews, staff members accompanied the women and attended the interview. It was difficult to obtain meaningful consent from the participants in this circumstance and I was not sure whether women felt comfortable and able to freely share their stories. As a feminist researcher, this was a particularly complicated. I wanted the women to feel at ease with me and to afford them and their stories dignity. Feeling conscious that they may not have been properly informed about the interview, or that their narratives were being overheard by often unsympathetic shelter staff was an ethical dilemma for which there was no easy answer.

The findings of the research indicate that women who experience marital rape also simultaneously experience different forms of abuse, such as coercive control, emotional abuse, psychological or physical abuse. Women who refused to have sex with their husbands experienced physical abuse. Although women made a connection between their experiences of marital rape and physical abuse, they did not directly emphasise that what they experienced was also a form of coercive control or emotional or psychological abuse. According to the findings of this research, the traditional view of wives as the sexual property of their husbands is still in practice in Turkey, and this is one of the main reasons for women's experiences of marital rape. Existence of such a belief can make it difficult for women to understand their victimisation, to seek help or report it.

Culture has a strong impact on shaping women's experiences of domestic abuse (Kasturirangan et al., 2004). In contrast to "the typical domestic abuse scenario in the West that usually involves a lone man battering a lone woman", women from many economically developing countries experience domestic violence by the members of their husbands' families (Fernandez, 1997: 434). In some cases, the members of the husbands' family become one of the main factors for women's experiences of domestic abuse by their husbands (Fernandez, 1997; Clark et al., 2010; Yuksel-Kaptanoglu et al., 2012). This research found that a mother's control over their son's marriage is potentially one of the trigger factors of women's experiences of marital rape. The existing literature in this area mainly discusses the role of mothers-in-law in terms of physical abuse (Fernandez, 1997; Clark et al., 2010; Yuksel-Kaptanoglu et al., 2012; Wu et al., 2010; Rew et al., 2013). The connection between the role of mothers-in-law and women's experiences of marital rape has not been discussed. In this context, the findings of this research are unique.

Conclusion

Difficult conversations were a key aspect of this research. Firstly, marital rape or any sexual abuse is a painful story to share and to listen to. The fact that these participants bravely spoke out revealed a level of trust that I wanted to honour, both in how their stories are represented and also in attempting to use this research to raise awareness and influence social policy. This means not flinching from the realities of their experiences, while also attempting to protect their stories from prurience or insensitivity. Secondly, as a feminist researcher deeply committed to ethics, empowerment, voice and respect in the research process, having to do this research within the context of shelters, where I often witnessed women being profoundly disempowered, led to many difficult conversations, both internally in my own thoughts and with those offering feedback and support on my work. Finally, this research also opens up difficult conversations about ethics and research with vulnerable populations. In feminist research tradition, obtaining informed consent from participants has been seen as a "cornerstone of research ethics" (Kadam, 2017: 108; Coomber, 2002; Miller and Boulton, 2007). The process of obtaining informed consent includes providing the required information to participants in order to allow them to autonomously and rationally decide on their participation (Wiles et al., 2007; Kadam, 2017; Nijhawan et al., 2013). Ethics committees overly emphasise the necessity of obtaining informed consent (Miller and Bell, 2012). But not enough attention is given to questioning the complexity of obtaining meaningful consent from vulnerable research populations, especially when accessing them through gatekeepers. The participants of this research were exposed to serious institutional control. Although they gave their consent to participate in this research, it should be questioned whether they had opportunities to autonomously make the decision about their participation and freely express their stories under such circumstances.

As Miller and Bell (2012: 63) claim, "the difference between gaining access and consent is not always clear". Gatekeepers' attempt to prevent me from collecting data on sexual abuse also restricted my opportunities as a researcher to freely conduct my research. Due to my concerns about strictly complying with the requirements of the gatekeepers, I tried to exclude women's experiences of marital rape while collecting my data. This research could not have been written if women had not shared their stories by themselves. It was their choice to bravely share their difficult stories with me that enabled me to write this work and honour their decision to do so.

References

Acar, F. and Altunok, G (2013) The 'politics of intimate' at the intersection of neo-liberalism and neo-conservatism in contemporary Turkey. *Women's Studies International Forum* 41: 14–23.

Acıkel, S (2009) *Kadına Yönelik Şiddetle Mücadele Kadın Sığınmaevi Önlemi: Türkiye Örneği*. Unpublised (PhD thesis) SBE: Ankara Üniversitesity.

Akar, T., Aksakal, F.N., Demirel, B., Durukan, E. and Özkan, S (2010) The prevalence of domestic violence against women among a group woman: Ankara, Turkey. *Journal of Family Violence* 25(5): 449–460.

Alkan, Ö. and Tekmanlı H.H (2021) Determination of the factors affecting sexual violence against women in Turkey: a population-based analysis. *BMC Women's Health* 21(1): 1–15.

Altınay, A.G. and Arat, Y (2009) *Violence against Women in Turkey: A Nationwide Survey*. Istanbul: Punto.

Bergen, R.K (1996) *Wife Rape: Understanding the Response of Survivors and Service Providers*. Thousand Oaks, CA: Sage.

Bergen, R.K. and Barnhill, E (2006) *Marital Rape: New Research and Directions. The National Online Resource Center on Domestic Violence, Pennsylvania Coalition against Domestic Violence*. VAWnet: The National Online Resource Center on Violence Against Women.

Berktay, F., Kerestecioğlu, İ.Ö., Çubukçu, S.U., Terzi, Ö. and Forsman, Z.K (2004) *The Position of Women in Turkey and in the European Union: Achievements, Problems, Prospects*. New York: KA-DER Press.

Clark, C.J., Silverman, J.G., Shahrouri, M., Everson-Rose, S. and Groce, N (2010) The role of the extended family in women's risk of intimate partner violence in Jordan. *Social Science & Medicine* 70(1): 144–151.

Classen, C.C., Palesh, O.G. and Aggarwal, R (2005) Sexual revictimization: A review of the empirical literature. *Trauma, Violence, & Abuse* 6(2): 103–129.

Coomber, R (2002) Signing your life away?: Why research ethics committees (REC) shouldn't always require written confirmation that participants in research have been informed of the aims of a study and their rights-the case of criminal populations. (Commentary). *Sociological Research Online* 7(1): 1–4.

Coşar, S. and Yeğenoğlu, M (2011) New grounds for patriarchy in Turkey? Gender policy in the age of AKP. *South European Society and Politics* 16(4): 555–573.

Dissiz, M. and Şahin N.H (2008) *Evrensel Bir Kadın*. Sağlığı Sorunu: Kadına Yönelik.

Dural, S (2016) *The Violence Against Women Policy of the AKP Government and the Diyanet*. Unpublised (MA thesis). Leiden University.

Dülger, P (2021) Evlilik Birliği İçinde Gerçekleşen Cinsel Saldırı (Sexual Assault Within the Marital Union). *Available at* SSRN 3790556.

Fernandez, M (1997) Domestic violence by extended family members in India: Interplay of gender and generation. *Journal of Interpersonal Violence* 12(3): 433–455.

Finkelhor, D. and Yllo, K (1983) Rape in marriage. In D. Finkelhor, R. Gelles, G.T. Hotaling and M.A. Straus (eds.) *The Dark Side of Families: Current Family Violence Research* (p. 119). Sage.

Gul, P. and Schuster, I (2020) Judgments of marital rape as a function of honor culture, masculine reputation threat, and observer gender: A cross-cultural comparison between Turkey, Germany, and the UK. *Aggressive Behavior* 46(4): 341–353.

Gulcicek, D (2015) Rethinking second wave feminism: A poststructuralist approach to the late 1980s feminist movement in Turkey in *the cases of Feminist and Kaktüs magazines* (Master's thesis, Sosyal Bilimler Enstitüsü).

Gündüz, Z.Y (2004) The women's movement in Turkey: From tanzimat towards european union membership 1. *Perceptions: Journal of International Affairs* 9(3): 115–134.

Heath, S., Charles, V., Crow, G. and Wiles, R (2007) Informed consent, gatekeepers and go-betweens: negotiating consent in child and youth-orientated institutions. *British Educational Research Journal* 33(3): 403–417.

Henneke, J (2008) *Combating Domestic Violence in Turkey*. Unpublished (thesis).
Johl, S.K. and Renganathan, S (2010) Strategies for gaining access in doing fieldwork: Reflection of two researchers. *Electronic Journal of Business Research Methods* 8(1), pp25–34.
Kadam, R.A (2017) Informed consent process: A step further towards making it meaningful!. *Perspectives in Clinical Research* 8(3): 107.
Karakeci, G (2019) *Response to Domestic Abuse in Turkey: A feminist analysis*. Unpublished (PhD thesis). Colchester: University of Essex.
Kasturirangan, A., Krishnan, S. and Riger, S (2004) The impact of culture and minority status on women's experience of domestic violence. *Trauma, Violence, & Abuse* 5(4): 318–332.
Kocacık, F., Kutlar, A. and Erselcan, F (2007) Domestic violence against women: A field study in Turkey. *The Social Science Journal* 44(4): 698–720.
Korkmaz, M (2012) *A feminist standpoint analysis of women's shelters: A case in turkey*. Unpublished (PhD thesis). Dumlupınar: Middle East Technical University.
Martin, E.K., Taft, C.T. and Resick, P.A (2007) A review of marital rape. *Aggression and Violent Behavior* 12(3): 329–347.
Miller, T. and Bell, L (2012) Consenting to what? Issues of access, gatekeeping and 'informed' consent. In T. Miller, M. Birch, M. Mauthner and J. Jessop (eds.) *Ethics in qualitative research*. SAGE Publications (pp. 61–75). https://dx.doi.org/10.4135/9781473913912
Miller, T. and Boulton, M (2007) Changing constructions of informed consent: Qualitative research and complex social worlds. *Social Science & Medicine* 65(11): 2199–2211.
Mor Cati Kadin Siginma Vakfi (n.d.) www.morcati.org.tr/tr/. Accessed: 8 August 2017.
Moralıoğlu, A (2012) 80'li yıllarda kadın hareketi ve kampanyalar. *Türkiye Barolar Birliği Dergisi* 6(99): 292–296.
Nijhawan, L.P., Janodia, M.D., Muddukrishna, B.S., Bhat, K.M., Bairy, K.L., Udupa, N. And Musmade, P.B (2013) Informed consent: Issues and challenges. *Journal of Advanced Pharmaceutical Technology & Research* 4(3): 134.
Ozcan, N.K., Gunaydın, S. and Çitil, E.T (2016) Domestic violence against women in Turkey: a systematic review and meta analysis. *Archives of Psychiatric Nursing* 30(5): 620–629.
Özer, Y (2012) Türkiye'de evlilik içi tecavüz suçu tartışmaları. *Kadın Araştırmaları Dergisi*, 2(11): 1–20.
Painter, K (1991) Wife rape in the United Kingdom. A paper presented at the American Society of Criminology 50th Anniversary Meeting, *San Francisco*. November 20th-23rd 199. Available from: https://www.semanticscholar.org/paper/WIFE-RAPE-IN-THE-UNITED-KINGDOM-Francisco-Painter/b80847f38a43abf8224ad37f116c914be-d3ad4a3
Plummer, K (1998) Homosexual categories: Some research problems in the labelling perspective of homosexuality. In *Social Perspectives in Lesbian and Gay Studies: A Reader*. London: Routledge (pp. 84–99). Available from: https://books.google.co.uk/books/about/Social_Perspectives_in_Lesbian_and_Gay_S.html?id=DhCoT2wkfFMC&source=kp_book_description&redir_esc=y
Reinelt, C (1995) Moving onto the terrain of the state: The battered women's movement. In M. Ferree and P.Y. Martin (eds.) *Feminist Organizations: Harvest of the New Women's Movement*. Philadelphia: Temple University Press (pp. 84–104).
Rew, M., Gangoli, G. and Gill, A.K (2013) Violence between female in-laws in India. *Journal of International Women's Studies* 14(1): 147–160.

Sakizcioglu, S. and Dogan, T (2020) Evli Bireylerin Evlilik Içi Tecavüz Olgusu Hakkındaki Görüşleri: Nitel Bir Çalışma. *İstanbul Üniversitesi Kadın Araştırmaları Dergisi* 20: 19–49.

Schuster, I., Tomaszewska, P., Gul, P., Ribeaud, D. and Eisner, M (2021) The role of moral neutralization of aggression and justification of violence against women in predicting physical teen dating violence perpetration and monitoring among adolescents in Switzerland. *New Directions for Child and Adolescent Development* 2021(178): 115–131.

Sen, S. and Bolsoy, N (2017) Violence against women: Prevalence and risk factors in Turkish sample. *BMC women's health* 17(1): 1–9.

Şenol, D. and Yıldız, S (2013) Kadına yönelik şiddet algısı-kadın ve erkek bakış açılarıyla. *Mutlu Çocuklar Derneği Yayınları*, Ankara, 70–111.

Tekeli, S (2010) The turkish women's movement: A brief history of success. *Quaderns de la Mediterania* 14: 119–123.

Tellis, K (2010) *Rape as a Part of Domestic Violence: A Qualitative Analysis of Case Narratives and Official Reports*. Texes: LFB Scholarly Publishing LLC.

Wiles, R., Crow, G., Charles, V. and Heath, S (2007) Informed consent and the research process: Following rules or striking balances? *Sociological Research Online* 12(2): 99–110.

Wu, T.F., Yeh, K.H., Cross, S.E., Larson, L.M., Wang, Y.C. and Tsai, Y.L (2010) Conflict with mothers-in-law and Taiwanese women's marital satisfaction: The moderating role of husband support. *The Counseling Psychologist* 38(4): 497–522.

Yllo, K (1996) *Marital rape*. Minneapolis: The Battered Women Justice Project.

Yüksel, Kaptanoğlu, İ., Çavlin, A. and Akadlı Ergöçmen, B (2015) Türkiye'de kadına yönelik aile içi şiddet araştırması.

Yüksel, Ş (1993) Eş Dayağı ve Dayağa Karşı Dayanışma Kampanyası. In Ş. Tekeli (ed.) *1980'ler Türkiye'sinde Kadın Bakış Açısından Kadınlar*. Istanbul: Iletişim Yayınları (pp. 341–350).

Yüksel-Kaptanoğlu, İ., Türkyılmaz, A.S. and Heise, L (2012) What puts women at risk of violence from their husbands? Findings from a large, nationally representative survey in Turkey. *Journal of Interpersonal Violence* 27(14): 2743–2769.

Section 4
Bounded knowledge

13 Lost for words

Difficult conversations about ethics, reflexivity and research governance

Sophie Hales, Paul Galbally and Melissa Tyler

This chapter focuses on some of the difficult conversations that arise during the academic research process. It takes the form of a dialogue between the principal researcher (Sophie), her (male) partner (Paul) and her (female) research supervisor (Melissa), reflecting on the heteronormative assumptions that appeared to underpin and play out in conversations about research governance, specifically the conditions of possibility attached to institutional ethical approval[1]. The approach that we take draws inspiration from Crowhurst and Kennedy-Macfoy (2013) in thinking about research gatekeepers, and gatekeeping as a theoretical problem rather than simply a practical one. The research, discussed here as a case study, consisted of an autoethnography of lap dancing clubs based in the South East of England. It involved undertaking observational research in lap dancing clubs, for which the University recommended that the female researcher's male partner accompany her in a chaperoning capacity, implicitly making this a condition of institutional approval. It was even suggested at the time that this might be a 'perk' for him. The conversations that took place during this period and subsequently left those involved, for different reasons, lost for words insofar as we found our discomfort difficult to articulate and act on. Here, we reflect on this experience as co-authors, individually and collaboratively, in order to share some thoughts on how these assumptions and practices might be avoided in future.

The chapter begins with a brief outline of the case study and of the governance mechanisms involved, working through the three authors' recollections and reflections of the ethical approval process that took place. We then draw from specific phases of Judith Butler's writing on gender, subjectivity and ethics to consider, respectively, three parallel 'difficult' conversations through which this process was shaped. First, we draw from Butler's (2000) early work on the heterosexual matrix in order to reflect on some of the ontological issues raised, relating particularly to who we were/are as researchers and to the gendered subjectivities that were 'hailed' into being through the research governance process we consider. Second, we reflect on epistemological issues raised by questions of whose knowledge and expertise was recognized with reference to Butler's (1997) work on the relationship between language and subject formation. Finally, we discuss methodological concerns relating to how reflexivity and ethics were negotiated,

DOI: 10.4324/9781003088417-18

drawing on insights from Butler's (2016, 2020) more recent writing on vulnerability and/as resistance.

Reflecting on these three parallel sets of conversations enables us to consider how gender inequalities were reinforced through the implicit lack of reflexivity in the governance process we discuss, and to consider how the implicit lack of reflexivity in research governance effectively rendered the ethical approval process unethical. In conclusion, we emphasize the importance and challenges associated with embodied ethics, reflexivity and 'speaking out' about the kinds of difficulties we encountered as part of a more dialogical approach to research governance, and in academic discussions more widely.

Situating research ethics and governance

We begin by reflecting (separately and then in dialogue) on the heteronormative assumptions that appeared to underpin and play out in the process of securing institutional ethical approval for an autoethnographic doctoral study. The research, discussed here as a case study, consisted of an autoethnography of lap dancing clubs based in the South East of England. Before we begin, we would like to situate these reflections in relevant dialogues and insights in academic discussions about research governance and ethics.

First, in organizational research we often encounter unreflexive assumptions about gender, particularly when researching sexualized and embodied forms of work. Tyler (2020b: 160) notes, for example, that the Soho-based sex shop workers she interviewed were often assumed by their friends and family to have the 'best job in the world' as they were surrounded by pornography all day. As academic researchers, not only do we study and write about these kinds of unreflexive gendered assumptions, but we also experience them ourselves, as we discuss here. Therefore, there is a need to consider how research, particularly embodied research, can be undertaken more reflexively.

Second, research has highlighted the different ways people embody aspects of their identity such as age, class, gender and sexuality in and through work, yet there are relatively few accounts of how researchers embody their identity in the context of research design and practice, particularly their experiences of research governance. Emphasizing the embodied nature of academic work, Harding et al. (2021: 2) note how 'we work ideas through our bodies; we write through our bodies, hoping to get into the bodies of our readers, and our academic bodies are on display while we teach'; our bodies are also the way in which we encounter one another, and embed ourselves in, the academic research process, yet this is largely 'written out' of the administration and regulation of what we research, why we do so and how, constraining what is seen as legitimate scholarship and who is regarded as a credible researcher.

Feminist writers such as Iris Marion Young (2005) have argued that the normative expectations governing recognition of gender identities and performances mean that women and girls learn to inhabit and experience their bodies in ways that accentuate bodily constraint, undermining agentic capacity. In the academic sphere, gendered expectations have been written about particularly in co-authoring relationships in which the man is expected to have done the intellectual 'heavy lifting' in support of the woman co-author. Such assumptions, Brewis (2005) argues, mean that when men and women co-author, a presumption might be made that the man makes a greater intellectual contribution than the woman.

Notably, Brewis (2005) has shared her experience of being 'signed' in particular ways because of her research on sex work, recounting her experience of assumptions being made about her working history, namely that if you research sex work you must have some experience of the type of work you write about. Brewis goes on to state how sex work research is treated differently by the academy and is 'particularly likely to be subject to signings by others' (Brewis, 2005: 496)[2]. Brewis emphasizes that people often assume that she has worked in the sex industry in the roles that she studied (namely sex work), making the presumption that her work is autoethnographic. Drawing on and developing insights from Brewis, our discussion here reflects on the assumptions shaping research on the sex industry when the study is known to be autoethnographic, considering how that institutional knowledge shaped research governance. Further, while Brewis explored her experiences at an individual level, focusing on self-reflection, we explore how heteronormative assumptions were embedded in institutional practices and procedures, and in the difficult and ongoing conversations between us.

Third, scholarship relating to research ethics in embodied research tends to focus on how research may encroach on the personal lives of participants and how the researcher/participant relationship can be negotiated as ethically as possible. While these insights are no doubt a crucial aspect of ethical practice, the researcher and participant are not the only research stakeholders, so further exploration of the positioning and experiences of broader stakeholders is important in understanding the wider ethical implications of embodied research and how gender and other hierarchies relate to processes of research governance in the wider context of the situated self. We might suggest that this is especially the case in situations in which co-researchers and other stakeholders are 'intimate others' Ellis (2007: 3), as was the case in the research we discuss here. In this sense, the chapter also responds to calls for 'continued deliberation and innovation – in particular, deliberation over the ontological relation between self (as researcher) and Other (as researched)' (Rhodes, 2009: 665, see also Rhodes, 2019), extending this call to encompass the need for reflexive dialogue about the relationship between all stakeholders in the research process, including of the power relations within which they are situated.

Finally, there is a persistent tendency for academic publications to provide 'cleaned up' accounts of research and academic writing for publication (Bell and Willmott, 2020; Pullen and Rhodes, 2008; Thanem and Knights, 2019). As Gilmore et al. (2019: 3) have emphasized, this reproduces intellectual norms that are restrictive, and which 'inhibit the development of knowledge and excise much of what it is to be human from our learning, teaching and research'. Released from these restrictions, they argue, it might be possible to 'invoke new political and ethical practices'. With this in mind, our aim here is to share an account of what we feel went wrong during our experiences of the institutional research governance process, with the intention that doing so will provide valuable, reflexive insight into gendered assumptions embedded in the research process and on the ethical implications of undertaking research unreflexively.

Our reflections led us to develop the argument that unreflexive research is unethical and that embodied reflexivity is vital to the research process. With that in mind, we make three suggestions for conducting gender reflexive research; taken together, they constitute the approach that we would adopt if we were to do the research discussed here again. First, gender reflexive research needs to identify gendered assumptions and their impact on and throughout the research process. Our experiences suggested that these assumptions should be reflected on in-situ, incrementally as a cumulative process and in dialogue, in our case, between researchers. Second, research should be anti-hierarchical to avoid positioning researchers as vulnerable or protective merely based on gender; third, and connected to this, is the importance of adopting an anti-essentialist approach to the research to avoid bifurcation of researchers into simplistic, binary categories of male and female, masculine and feminine, knowing/expert or not, that lend credence to the heterosexual matrix (Butler, 2000) rather than challenge it. The latter, we argue, has important epistemological implications for whose knowledge and expertise are recognized, and in what respect.

Case study: an autoethnography of the lap dancing industry

The lap dancing industry is situated in what can be thought of as a grey area between sex work and sexualized labour (Bott, 2006; Hales et al., 2019; Lister, 2015), where the latter may be consumed as part of a wider service experience but is not the only, or even main, object of commercial exchange. As such, it is a particularly apposite context within which to consider the gendered dynamics of the research process, as women who work in sectors or settings associated with commercial sex are typically 'ubiquitous yet also somehow out of place' (Tyler, 2020b: 166). In other words, while women are the main providers of the labour that is studied, the wider setting of the club and the industry itself are almost exclusively male-dominated, with most customers, managers and owners being men (2022). The focus of our discussion of this case study is on what this means, being somehow 'ubiquitous' yet also 'out of place' for lived, embodied experiences of the research process, in particular of research governance, within these kinds of settings but also more widely.

Lap dancing is a commission-based sales role within a nightclub environment where typically men can buy striptease dances from workers who are typically young adult women. The work itself consists of dancers interacting with customers with the purpose of trying to sell lap dances or so-called 'sit-downs' (both of which form the paid work and usually happen in private areas of the club); at other times dancers are expected to perform pole dances on stage. This is usually an unpaid aspect of the work[3] that takes place in the main club area, in view of all customers, and is intended to provide a means for dancers to promote themselves and build rapport with customers, often through the use of eye contact to build a more personal connection between dancer and (potential) customer. Because dancers don't get paid for stage performances, the interactions with customers during this time are very much focused on nurturing a relationship that will lead to a monetary transaction.

The case study itself focused on the lived, embodied experiences of women working in the lap dancing industry to understand more about how and why specific modes of sexuality become valued and how the portrayal of a specific, narrow and heightened form of sexuality is performed, embodied and negotiated as dancers age (Hales et al., 2019, 2021). The research took the form of a retrospective autoethnography because Sophie had worked as a lap dancer for four years, beginning when she was aged 18, some five years prior to the start of the project. The study incorporated three phases of data collection including a website analysis, participant observation and interviews with women working as lap dancers. It should be noted that during data collection phases, the observations were conducted in the guise of club customers. Given that Sophie had accumulated several years' experience of working as a dancer, she thought that participating in the industry with a different role would add depth and a different perspective to her insider knowledge, with her 'new' academic positioning and the passing of five years since she had worked in the industry (at the start of her PhD) providing some invaluable opportunities to reflexively occupy an 'insider/outsider' role.

The fieldwork took place over a period of 12 months, during which the website analysis, observations and interviews took place. Some 32 hours of observations were undertaken in nine lap dancing clubs situated in the South East of England, all located within easy travelling distance from home for Sophie and enabling her to make use of her existing contacts for snowball sampling purposes. The focus of the fieldwork was on gathering embodied data and a lot of time was spent considering how to tap into dancers' embodied accounts of their work and, during observations, how Sophie would focus on the ways that dancers embody the role of a lap dancer as they inhabit and negotiate the lap dancing club environment.

As is the norm in a university setting, and in accordance with funding council best practice guidelines, institutional ethical approval was required before the project could proceed. In this instance, this involved completing a written application for ethical approval that was considered initially by the relevant departmental Ethics Officer. Given the nature of the setting and the methods proposed, including covert participant observation in lap dancing clubs, the application was referred, in accordance with institutional guidelines, to a university-level Ethics Committee for consideration. Feedback from this Committee, communicated informally by the departmental Ethics Officer, forms the basis of our reflections here, and required amendments to the research design that we considered.

Negotiating ethical approval

Sophie: I was apprehensive about the ethical approval process and aware that gaining approval for researching a sexualized field was likely to be more complex than if I had been studying a more mainstream industry, and even more so because I was hoping to do covert observations in the research setting and would have to provide a robust ethical justification for doing so.

It quickly became apparent that alongside the proposed covert observations, the marginalized 'grey' area of the lap dancing industry and specifically my safety within it was at the forefront of the negotiations for ethical approval. This was understandable given the position of lap dancing in the night-time economy, in the shadows of the sex industry (Sanders, 2008) and with a presumed closeness to prostitution[4]. However, an important reason for doing this research was because I was familiar with the industry and had access to it. So, when the Ethics Officer told one of my supervisors (Melissa) that because it was 'a bit of a dodgy environment' I would need to be chaperoned during observational fieldwork, I felt while this was understandable, I had also been re-positioned in a way that minimized my knowledge and expertise of the industry, and in some way, the institution had 'cleaned me up' by distancing me from my ex-lap dancer identity. Taking this step was interesting given that my familiarity with that setting would likely be greater than any of my potential chaperones', yet at the time, it also seemed understandable as the fieldwork would involve moving around city centre settings at night.

Specifically, the conditions for doing fieldwork were as follows: for me to be accompanied by someone at all observations who was close enough to me to have my best interests at heart, preferably a family member. While this seemingly provided me with a range of options for chaperones, the choice was largely illusory once those whom I would be uncomfortable with in that setting were discounted; for example, parents and siblings. The most obvious option was my partner, Paul, so as long as I could convince him to give up his time, then I could go ahead with my fieldwork.

Paul agreed to help out; when we discussed my research in social settings, however, he encountered comments about him enjoying being able to participate in the fieldwork, seemingly underpinned by the assumption that we would be happy about being in this position. Yet the reality was quite different. While Paul had agreed quite quickly to assist me by accompanying me during the observational sessions in lap dancing clubs, little thought had seemingly been given to how he would actually feel about this, or to what the practicalities of his involvement would be. Accompanying me on a Saturday night once a month is one thing, but gathering ethnographic data across a spread of weekly night shifts in lap dancing clubs after having worked long days himself is quite another. It wasn't long before I felt very guilty about asking him to come out for a night, especially when I knew he would rather be at home (despite the perception of some of our friends).

In discussions about ethical governance with my supervisor (Melissa), with the departmental ethics officer and with relevant academics at the University, the whole focus seemed to be on protecting me as a student researcher, and in adopting this focus, assumptions were made that Paul would be both comfortable being there (even thinking it was a 'perk', in the case of the female ethics officer) and protective of me in that environment. At the time, my concern was to get the research underway, but with hindsight, the focus of these discussions was on my relative vulnerability as a researcher and on his capacity to provide paternalistic protection as my (male) chaperone. Added to this was the presumption, beyond the institutional governance process, of the pleasure he might derive from being in this particular setting. Quite quickly I could sense his discomfort as we spent time in lap dancing clubs; notably, this contrasted with my own sense of familiarity with the environment and the work involved. Unlike my male partner, I found myself feeling quite quickly 'at home' in the clubs I was studying.

Melissa: We always expected Sophie's application for ethical approval to be referred to a university-level committee, but with hindsight I'm not sure why we made this assumption. The referral, the way it was articulated and communicated (as being because the project and setting were 'a bit dodgy') and the conditions that were subsequently attached to ethical approval had important consequences for Sophie, and for the research project. First, I recall how it accentuated Sophie's anxiety about presenting the research in academic contexts, causing her (in my perception, anyway), to doubt her own academic abilities and the credibility of the project. In the months and years that followed, I felt my role was to be supportive when Sophie seemed to avoid explaining that the project was autoethnographic and played down her own 'insider' knowledge and its value to and for the project. As her supervisor, what I should have done was embraced that discussion as a 'sticky moment' (Riach, 2009) in the research process, encouraging critical reflexivity. It struck me at the time, being with Sophie during presentations and listening to her feedback from those that I hadn't attended (e.g. conferences) that there was a very embodied dimension to the institutional scrutiny of Sophie's research (and by implication, of Sophie), one that was highly gendered but also implicitly class- and age-based. Second, I also failed to critically reflect on the assumption that because the observational research would take place in clubs that were often located on the outskirts of city centres in relatively quiet areas that Sophie would be leaving in the early hours of the morning, that she would be vulnerable, and that having a (male) chaperone with her would keep her safe. At the time, we barely spoke about the implications of being positioned in this way, not just for Sophie, but also for her (male) partner, Paul.

Paul: When I was asked by Sophie to accompany her during her fieldwork, I was intrigued both personally and professionally. At the time I was working as a couple's therapist and had an interest in erotic activities within relationships, instilling an inquisitive fascination with the idea of going to these kinds of clubs.

I was interested in the covert nature of the fieldwork setting, and in how I might be perceived by the dancers in this context. And I was acutely aware that my social position was altered by the intention of my visit, mainly by creating a shift away from the archetypically male-bonding activity of going to strip clubs for pleasure and my current visit with my (female) partner, whereby I was entering the same venue in a quasi-professional, albeit undercover research capacity. Leaving me feeling somewhat on edge, this contrasted, in my mind at least, with the presumption that a man would feel comfortable inhabiting this kind of environment, perhaps anticipating it with excitement rather than the sense of dread that I experienced.

This sense of being 'on edge' was also accentuated by the extent to which I was curious to see how the dancers would perceive us as a hetero couple. My own experiences of this type of establishment previously, while minimal, had been with groups of men on homosocial and 'macho'-style male outings. This is an interesting juxtaposition because typically in this context pleasure is assumed to be gained by a man watching the sexualized female performances, but in this case, I was intrigued about being watched by the dancers and by wondering how they perceived my partner and I and our relationship.

In many ways, however, I also felt forced into the strip club environment, as this is not a night-time economy that I would usually choose to engage in. Reflecting on the discomfort I had experienced on previous occasions with friends, as well as my growing sense of edginess in anticipation of further visits as a chaperone, I feel that Sophie inadvertently placed me in a rather problematic position, where I felt obliged to accompany her. Fulfilling the conditions set out by the institutional ethical approval process led me to experience a feeling of restricted autonomy, because my refusal may have been seen as both unhelpful and unsupportive in the context of our personal relationship. On reflection, this placed me – and our relationship – in an untenable position as I could have jeopardized not only the research but also potentially the sense of trust and mutual support between us.

Yet the approval process to which Sophie had to conform seemed to position me within a hegemonically heteronormative set of assumptions that presumed that, as a heterosexual man, I would inevitably enjoy accompanying Sophie to a strip club, or at least that I would be happy to do so and would see this as within the remit of my role as her (male) partner. Perhaps it is somewhat unsurprising that I was viewed in this way by the institution, given the reaction from several of my peers. They positioned my role in the fieldwork as akin to 'winning the lottery', as one of them put it, by being offered an opportunity to visit several strip clubs.

I saw this as a 'work' commitment, however, one that I felt compelled to undertake in order to support my partner's academic research. Again, perhaps ironically, this set of assumptions made me question my own masculine identity and notice that I often hold or at least publicly express significantly different attitudes to that of several of my contemporaries. This sense of discomfort has led me to question my legitimacy within particular social groups, including all-male social groups.

Sophie, Melissa and Paul: Looking back on the different experiences and recollections described here leads us to rethink the institutional ethical approval process, bringing to the fore aspects of our own positioning and practice that, for various reasons, we retired at the time. Heavily gendered assumptions were made that a man (in this case, Paul) could and would need to protect a woman (Sophie) from her position of relative vulnerability. This had significant implications for the researcher, for the research and for wider stakeholders that we have reflected on so far. To make sense of these, we now turn to insights from Judith Butler's writing on the heterosexual matrix, subjectivity and ethics to consider, respectively, three parallel 'difficult' conversations through which the experiences discussed here were shaped.

Discussion: heteronormativity, knowledge and vulnerability in dialogue

Research governance within the heterosexual matrix

Although she has moved away from the term in her more recent thinking, Butler's (2000) early work on the heterosexual matrix persists as an important backdrop to her more recent writing, and to critical analyses of gendered governance within organizational settings. In order to reflect on some of the ontological issues raised here, relating particularly to who we were/are as researchers, and to the gendered subjectivities that were 'hailed' into being through the gendered assumptions and norms governing research we have considered here, we draw from this idea to reflect on our respective positioning according to the terms of the heterosexual matrix.

Butler writes about the heterosexual matrix as an ontological, epistemic schema through which a normative – binary, hierarchical and linear – relationship between sex, gender and sexuality is sustained.[5] The heterosexual matrix is effectively an organization of ontology – a structured, sense-making process that serves to compel and constrain particular ways of being, conferring or denying recognition and allocating access to rights, responsibilities and resources accordingly (Tyler, 2020a); it is the mechanism through which 'the *organization* of gender comes to function as a presupposition about how the world is structured' (Butler, 2004: 215, *emphasis added*). According to the terms of this matrix, intelligible and therefore recognizable and livable genders are those which cohere a continuous, even causal relationship between sex, gender and sexual desire; this relationship and its normalizing effects, Butler maintains, are not natural or pre-social but have the constitutive *effect* of being so. The matrices of cultural intelligibility that shape social (and institutional) life therefore govern gender as a 'performative accomplishment' (Butler, 2000: 179) by compelling certain subjectivities (those that conform to normative expectations), at the same time as foreclosing others.

In the experiences discussed here we each, in different but related ways, found ourselves situated within the binary, hierarchical terms of the heterosexual matrix as part of the research governance process in at least three ways. First, the protective paternalism articulated within the ethical approval process positioned Sophie and Paul as embodying, respectively, the need for protection and the capacity to provide it. Second, heteronormative assumptions were articulated explicitly by his friends/associates and implicitly/more informally, through the presumption that Paul would enjoy accompanying Sophie to lap dancing clubs, even that it would be a 'perk' for him to do so. Finally, in doing so, Sophie's embodied, experiential knowledge and expertise were disregarded, or 'written out' of the ethical approval process as part of the way in which her subjectivity as a researcher was framed.

Hailing the research subject

Our final point raises epistemological concerns about whose knowledge and expertise was recognized. We discuss these with reference to Butler's (1997) work on the relationship between language and subject formation. Amongst a wide range of intellectual influences, Butler's performative theory of gender draws heavily on the concept of interpellation as it is developed in Louis Althusser's (2001) discussion of the ideological processes through which particular subject positions are 'hailed' into being, a concept she refers to throughout much of her work (see Butler, 2016). For Althusser, it is through the process of hailing (being beckoned into a response) that individuals become 'interpellated' into subject positions that are continually re-enacted. To illustrate this process, Althusser makes reference to a police officer commanding, 'Hey! You there!' In the combined act of calling out, acknowledging and responding, the police officer and the person being hailed effect the latter as a 'suspect', someone who is required to account for him- or herself (e.g. their actions or presence). Through this process, even fleetingly, a particular subject position is taken up.

The same interpellatory process can be identified in the proclamation: 'It's a girl/boy' when a baby is born. Butler argues that the presumption of subject positions such as these serve to perpetuate the idea that the division of humanity into two sexes is somehow normal and natural; rather, she argues, it is the outcome of a social process of interpellation through which gendered subject positions are performatively, continually re-enacted. These performative re-enactments and recitations give the impression that something socially constructed is pre-social or essential. Illustrative examples of such performative enactments include the sex-based classification of competitors by sports committees, or inter-sex babies being routinely 'sexed' at birth or shortly afterwards. It is not simply this process that is of concern to Butler, but the normative conditions or governmental regimes compelling or constraining it.

To reiterate, for Butler, gender performativity is driven largely by the desire for recognition of ourselves as viable, intelligible subjects. In other words, underpinning our performance of gender and other aspects of our identities is the desire to project a coherent and compelling identity, one that is recognized and valorized by others, but one that in Butler's terms, produces its coherence at the cost of its own complexity. In *Giving an Account of Oneself*, Butler (2005) considers how this relates to the self as a narrative composition, considering the ways in which our existential vulnerability, socially and economically induced precarity and subjection to processes that 'undo' us require us to cohere a version of ourselves designed to elicit recognition, and to secure the rights and opportunities that recognition of one's social (and organizational viability) potentially brings. Here 'accounting' for oneself involves not simply telling a story about oneself but providing a convincing ethical defence of one's claim to recognition. Butler's (2005) view of narrative, developed most fully in her discussion of how and why the self is continually called to 'account', provides a performative lens through which to understand how narratives operate in the process of becoming a subject, including within and through research processes (Riach et al., 2014, 2016).

In particular, Butler's largely phenomenological understanding locates narrative, as an attempt to cohere and convey a livable life, within the context of the desire for recognition of oneself as a viable subject; as she puts it: 'I come into being as a reflexive subject only in the context of establishing a narrative account of myself' (Butler, 2005: 15). Framed in this way, narrative is not simply telling one's life story, but rather the response we are compelled to provide when being 'held to account' for ourselves (Butler, 2005: 12), or are 'hailed' in Althusser's terms.

As we reflect on our respective and collaborative complicity in the way in which we were each positioned within the research governance process discussed here, we are reminded of how, in situ, our sense of responsibility to progress the research, and of our identification with it, rendered us vulnerable to complying with the terms of recognition on offer. We did not, at the time or since, formally challenge the decision taken by the school's Ethical Officer or the University Ethics Committee, nor did we question the way in which this decision was articulated or rationalized. It is only as the research process unfolded, over a period of some four years, and as we worked independently and collaboratively on subsequent presentations and publications that we have come to position ourselves differently – to question the subject positions into which we were hailed, and on what basis. Not least, our concern is with the epistemic hierarchies that were played out in the process of securing ethical approval and with the consequences of these for relations of meaningful, knowing consent within the research process.

Vulnerability in/as resistance in research governance

With our final point in mind, we discuss our methodological concerns relating to how reflexivity and ethics were embedded into the research process, drawing on insights from Butler's (2016, 2020) more recent writing on vulnerability and/as resistance. In some of her most recent work on ethics, Butler shows us how the paternalistic forms of power to which those designated as 'vulnerable' and in need of protection are subject shores up their disenfranchisement (Butler, 2016, 2020), further paving the way for the epistemic violence enacted by those who – however well-intentioned – claim to 'know better'. But she also reminds us how those who are excluded from the locus of ontological and/or epistemic privilege haunt the borders of subjective viability, and in doing so, she offers us a way into a rich understanding of how powerful processes and practices permeate the organizational lifeworlds we inhabit, enabling us to interrogate our vulnerability to these both critically and reflexively.

In Butler's frame of reference, embodied ethics broadly refers to the idea that the basis of our ethical relationship to one another is our embodied inter-connection and the mutual, corporeal vulnerability that arises from this. Recognition of the organizational potential and implications of this ethical relationship has been a strong theme in writing about research ethics and reflexive practice as situated, embodied and relational. Recognition of mutual vulnerability as the basis of an ethical and reflexive approach to research governance strikes us as being quite distinct from the hierarchical, bifurcated process we experienced. It is one that encourages us to think about alternative ways of understanding and enacting the ethical approval process in ways premised upon a questioning of assumptions, a dismantling of hierarchies, and a recognition of all ways of knowing – including (but not limited to) those that are embodied and experiential.

Concluding thoughts: embodied ethics, reflexivity and the challenges of speaking out

Reflecting on these three parallel sets of conversations here enables us to consider how gender and other class-based inequalities were reinforced through the implicit lack of reflexivity in the governance process we discuss, and to consider how this absence effectively rendered the ethical approval process unethical. In conclusion, we would like to emphasize the importance of 'speaking out' collaboratively and reflexively about the kinds of difficulties we encountered as part of a more dialogical, situated and embodied approach to research governance, and in academic discussions more widely, one that recognizes mutual vulnerability as the basis of research ethics. As the previous reflections show, in our case it took some time to absorb and acknowledge the assumptions embedded in the research process and to become fully, reflexively aware of their implications for the subject positions into which we were (respectively) hailed. This highlights for us, and hopefully for others, that difficult conversations may be ongoing and emergent, unfolding over time and, in our case, in dialogue, in order to make sense of complex – but we also hope, contestable – experiences.

In this sense, as a moment of 'disruptive reflexivity' (Bell and Willmott, 2020: 1371), our dialogue has illustrated some of the ways in which embodied knowing is central to reflexive research practice (Johnson, 2020), yet is often written out of our accounts and experiences of it, including within and through paternalistic approaches to research governance. Perpetuating adherence to 'scientific' norms, such approaches govern what is regarded as worthy of being studied, excising much of what it is to be human and inhibiting our knowledge, understanding and learning (Gilmore et al., 2019). Hence, we would agree with other researchers' calls for 'a complete review of ethics processes . . . to empower participants and researchers to recognize the reality of the process as co-created and negotiated' (Connor et al., 2018: 400). As a starting point for this, we would point to the work of feminist writers who advocate departing from abstract ethical principles and working with an embodied, relational ethics (Gilmore et al., 2019; Mandalaki and Fotaki, 2020; Tyler, 2020a), reconsidering ethics as a process emerging through shared recognition of mutual, inter-corporeal vulnerability. Such an approach, we contend, could avoid similar experiences to those discussed here, if research governance was shaped instead by a relational ethics of reciprocity that brought embodied ways of knowing to the fore.

Notes

1. In working in this way, we found inspiration in Harding et al.'s (2021) use of Stern's (2004) 'methodology of moments', recalling experiences that were un-narrated at the time and which our recall brings to the fore for analytical scrutiny. In treating our narratives in this way, as part of a retrospective, reflexive 'difficult conversation', we use the chapter as an opportunity to speak up and out as a series of transgressive acts about experiences that might otherwise have remained hidden. Technique-wise, we draw on Harding et al.'s (2021) adoption of feminist approaches to memory work, in which a research collective (in this case, the three of us) (i) recalls instances of specific events and (ii) explores them in recursive rounds of communal interrogation. This facilitates an onto-epistemological mapping of performative moments in which something new (in this instance, a dialogue about hitherto silenced experiences) emerges, one that is attuned to all stakeholders' embodied ways of being as 'active and agentive' in the research process (Harding et al., 2021: 1).
2. See also Attwood (2010), Hammond and Kingston (2014) and Shaver (2005) for a discussion of some of the ethical and methodological challenges associated with researching sex work, and Sinha (2017) for a reflexive discussion of the concerns raised about safety protocols in research design.
3. See Hardy and Sanders (2015) and Cruz et al. (2017) for further discussion of the self/employment conditions of lap dancing work.
4. Although prostitution is stigmatized, it is a legal occupation in the UK with the exception of Northern Ireland. For more information see the Sexual Offences Act 2003, the Policing and Crime Act 2009 and the Sexual Offences (Northern Ireland) Order 2008.
5. Butler explains the origins of the heterosexual matrix as lying in Gayle Rubin's 'The Traffic in Women' (see Rubin with Butler, 1994), but as Lloyd (2007: 34) points out, it is also conceptually and theoretically indebted to Foucault's (1980) notion of a 'grid' of intelligibility in *The History of Sexuality*.

References

Althusser, L (2001) *Lenin and Philosophy and Other Essays*. London: Monthly Review Press.

Attwood, F (2010) Dirty work: Researching women and sexual representation. In R. Ryan-Flood and R. Gill (eds.) *Secrecy and Silence in the Research Process*. London: Routledge (pp. 177–187).

Bell, E. and Willmott, H (2020) Ethics, politics and embodied imagination in crafting scientific knowledge. *Human Relations* 73(10): 1366–1387.

Bott, E (2006) Pole position: Migrant British women producing 'selves' through lap dancing work. *Feminist Review* 83(1): 23–41.

Brewis, J (2005) Signing my life away? Researching sex and organization. *Organization* 12(4): 493–510.
Butler, J (1997) *Excitable Speech: A Politics of the Performative*. London: Routledge.
Butler, J (2000) First published 1990. *Gender Trouble*. London: Routledge.
Butler, J (2004) *Undoing Gender*. London: Routledge.
Butler, J (2005) *Giving an Account of Oneself*. New York: Fordham University Press.
Butler, J (2016) Rethinking vulnerability and resistance. In J. Butler, Z. Gambetti and L. Sabsay (eds.) *Vulnerability in Resistance*. London: Duke University Press (pp. 12–27).
Butler, J (2020) *The Force of Nonviolence*. London: Verso.
Colosi, R (2022) I'm just with the guys and we're having a laugh: Exploring normative masculinity in a lap-dancing club setting, as a heteronormative space. *Sexualities* 25(3): 222–241.
Connor, J., Copland, S. and Owen, J (2018) The infantilized researcher and research subject: Ethics, consent and risk. *Qualitative Research* 18(4): 400–415.
Crowhurst, I. and KENNEDY-MACFOY, M (2013) Troubling gatekeepers: Methodological considerations for social research. *International Journal of Research Methodology*. 16(6): 457–462.
Cruz, K., Hardy, K. and Sanders, T (2017) False self-employment, autonomy and regulating for decent work: Improving working conditions in the UK stripping industry. *An International Journal of Employment Relations* 55(2): 274–294.
Ellis, C (2007) Telling secrets, revealing lives: Relational ethics in research with intimate others, *Qualitative inquiry* 13(1): 3–29.
Foucault, M (1980) *The History of Sexuality*. New York: Pantheon Books.
Gilmore, S., Harding, N., Helin, J. and Pullen, A (2019) Writing differently. *Management Learning* 50(1): 3–10.
Hales, S., Riach, K. and Tyler, M (2019) Putting sexualized labour in the picture: Encoding 'reasonable entitlement' in the lap dancing industry. *Organization* 26(6): 783–801.
Hales, S., Riach, K. and Tyler, M (2021) Close encounters: Intimate service interactions in lap dancing work as a nexus of "self-others-things". *Organization Studies* 42(4): 555–574.
Hammond, N. and Kingston, S (2014) Experiencing stigma as sex work researchers in professional and personal lives. *Sexualities* 17: 329–347.
Harding, N., Gilmore, S. and Ford, J (2021) Matter that embodies: Agentive flesh and working bodies/selves. *Organization Studies* 1–20.
Hardy, K. and Sanders, T (2015) The political economy of 'lap dancing: Contested careers and women's work in the stripping industry. *Work, Employment and Society* 29(1): 119–136.
Johnson, R (2020) *Ethical Considerations in Embodied Research*. London: Routledge.
Lister, B.M (2015) Yeah, they've started to get a bit fucking cocky'. . . Culture, economic change and shifting power relations within the Scottish lap-dancing industry. *Graduate Journal of Social Science* 11(2): 38–54.
Lloyd, M (2007) *Judith Butler: From Norms to Politics*. Cambridge: Polity Press.
Mandalaki, E. and Fotaki, M (2020) The bodies of the commons: Towards a relational embodied ethics of the commons. *Journal of Business Ethics* 166: 745–760.
Pullen, A. and Rhodes, C (2008) Dirty writing. *Culture and Organization* 14(3): 241–259.
Rhodes, C (2009) After reflexivity: Ethics, freedom and the writing of organization studies. *Organization Studies* 30(6): 653–672.
Rhodes, C (2019) Sense-ational organization theory! Practices of democratic scriptology. *Management Learning* 50(1): 24–37.

Riach, K (2009) Exploring participant-centred reflexivity in the research interview. *Sociology*. 43(2): 356–370.

Riach, K., Rumens, N. and Tyler, M (2014) Un/doing chronomormativity: Negotiating ageing, gender and sexuality in organizational life. *Organization Studies* 35(11): 1677–1698.

Riach, K., Rumens, N. and Tyler, M (2016) Towards a Butlerian methodology: Undoing organizational performativity through anti-narrative research. *Human Relations* 69(11): 2016–2089.

Rubin, G. and Butler, J (1994) Sexual traffic (interview with Judith Butler). *Differences: A Journal of Feminist Cultural Studies* 6(2–3): 62–99.

Sanders, T (2008) Selling sex in the shadow economy. *International Journal of Social Economics* 35(10): 704–716.

Shaver, F (2005) Sex work research: Methodological and ethical challenges. *Journal of Interpersonal Violence* 20: 296–319.

Sinha, S (2017) Ethical and safety issues in doing sex work research: Reflections from a field-based ethnographic study in Kolkata, India. *Qualitative Health Research* 27(6): 893–908.

Stern, D (2004) *The Present Moment in Psychotherapy and Everyday Life*. New York: W.W. Norton.

Thanem, T. and Knights, D (2019) *Embodied Research Methods*. London: Sage.

Tyler, M (2020a) *Judith Butler and Organization Theory*. London: Routledge.

Tyler, M (2020b) *Soho at Work: Pleasure and Place in Contemporary London*. Cambridge: Cambridge University Press.

Young, I-M (2005) *On Female Body Experience: "Throwing Like a Girl" and Other Essays*. Oxford: Oxford University Press.

14 Gender studies, academic purity and political relevance[1]

Sabine Grenz

Introduction

Gender Studies as an institutionalised field of research is situated within manifold power relations and struggles, including struggles related to institutionalisation as well as struggles within the field itself. This chapter will focus on recent political developments concerning Women's, Gender and Feminist Studies (WGFS)[2] in Germany. I will engage with academic and public discourses on gender and WGFS, identifying how certain difficult conversations within these discourses are avoided or made impossible. First, I will look at the position of WGFS within academia, wider society and research policy. I will then move on to recapitulate feminist research, especially on historical gender constructions, the historical exclusion of women and other "Others" and gendered knowledge cultures that still echo within academic institutions. These feminist reconstructions exemplify WGFS' political relevance with critical perspectives on the university as a historical institution as well as knowledge production. Subsequently, I will have a closer look at attacks against WGFS from within academia in order to sketch possible discursive connections between conservative academic scepticism and populist right-wing campaigns against WGFS that are part of extremists' normalisation strategies aimed at connecting right-wing extremism to mainstream discourses. I will argue that we need to see the kind of scepticism in the frame of the "symbolic glue" that is formed with "gender" as an "empty signifier" (Kováts, 2015; Mayer, 2017). In Germany, this becomes particularly clear at a moment where the political realm as well as research policy are seemingly becoming more open to gender research, perhaps also as a result of populist attacks. Thus, I will not end on a pessimistic note (after all, hope dies last), and will instead describe certain positive developments in Germany. This difficult conversation involves asserting the importance and value of WGFS with those who either do not understand it or are profoundly ideologically opposed to it. At the same time, defenders of WGFS are also required to have difficult conversations among ourselves about how best to support and defend this important field of theory, research and teaching.

DOI: 10.4324/9781003088417-19

Gender studies and their institutionalisation

Researchers in Women's, Feminist and Gender Studies have been producing knowledge on a global scale for more than 50 years now. Feminist academics all over the world have done an enormous amount of disciplinary and interdisciplinary research; have critically investigated androcentrism as well as male biases in malestream research; have developed new epistemological and methodological approaches; have scrutinised their own research in terms of its own exclusionary mechanisms; and have reflected on the history of their interdisciplinary field of research (e.g. Hark, 2005; Hemmings, 2011; Liinason, 2011; Pereira, 2017; Nash, 2019). This has happened within disciplines and as an inter-/trans- and postdisciplinary endeavour (Lykke, 2010). Furthermore, WGFS have been institutionalised in many countries, often on low budgets. Today, we can find a number of undergraduate, post-graduate and PhD programmes and courses on gender. We also encounter professors of interdisciplinary Gender Studies as well as chairs for disciplinary specialisations in gender research. Numerous journals have been founded, awards have been established and other networking structures have been developed, such as national and international associations and their regular conferences. In conclusion, for Europe and the German-speaking area, one can follow Maria do Mar Pereira in stating that

> WGFS has become . . . an academic institution in itself, one which is more or less (inter)disciplinary . . . and autonomous, and has its own structures of creation and validation of knowledge and its canonical but contested narratives about what its objects, boundaries, aims and histories are, or should be.
> (Pereira, 2017, 29)

These developments signal that WGFS have become increasingly established within academia. However, despite the fact that there are, by now, structures of institutionalisation, WGFS – including overlaps with other interdisciplinary fields such as Disability, Black, Intersectionality, Postcolonial, Queer, Trans and other studies – are not only an institution in itself but instead comprise a complex inter-/post-/disciplinary structure (Lykke, 2010). Additionally, despite these developments, they are still contested outside the discipline, even though the situation differs between countries. Whereas the Hungarian government banned Gender Studies in 2018 in an illiberal political move, gender researchers in Sweden enjoy relatively widespread acceptance. Other countries have institutionalised WGFS to various extents. Overall, although well-established and respected in some places, the field is still often met with ambivalence by mainstream disciplines and has a relatively low epistemic status (Pereira, 2017), particularly in some regions. As a result, it is frequently met with scepticism. Often, this scepticism is articulated in relation to WGFS' (unavoidable) political relevance as well as their close relationship to their fields of practice: social movements and institutions (cf. Hark, 2005;

Pereira, 2017). The argument is that WGFS is *mostly political* or *too political*. The knowledge produced is, thus, not as *purely academic* as it should be and, as a consequence, not "proper knowledge" (Pereira, 2012). The political relevance of research in WGFS is turned against the field in order to devalue it. One result of this devaluation is an unstable institutionalisation: existing Gender Studies centres and courses close down as often as new ones emerge. Institutionalisation of Gender Studies is not linear but forms a continuous up and down shaped by numerous institutional paradoxes (Pereira, 2017). This in turn leads to structural failures that lower the performance of the field as measured in neoliberal metrics (Kahlert, 2018). As if this were not enough, for more than a decade now, WGFS has been attacked by right-wing populism, a point I will come back to later.

If we compare this struggle with the historical development of other areas of academic research, we can see scepticism at their beginning as well. For instance, during the 19th and up to the turn of the 20th century, mechanical and electrical engineering were struggling for acceptance in academia. Engineers were faced with the assumption that their knowledge was *too technically oriented* for it to be accepted as academic knowledge (Paulitz, 2010). Tanja Paulitz (2010) reconstructs their struggle for acceptance, which she interprets as a struggle among men for what counts as hegemonic masculinity. The result of this struggle is well known: engineering sciences today have a higher status than the humanities and social sciences – including for their economic capacities (in society and the entrepreneurial university). However, their place within academia was not self-evident but used to be questioned, though for different reasons than WGFS. Their example shows that a discipline's finding a place in academia not only depends on plausibility on purely epistemological or methodological questions, but rather on power struggles as well as struggles for resources.

The (historical) misogyny of academia and the political relevance of women's, feminist and gender studies

In parts of Europe, in early modernity, as "traditional prohibitions against marriage [for scholars; SG] were eroding" (Algazi, 2003: 9) and scholars were increasingly moving out of colleges and setting up their own households, these scholars relied heavily on women for establishing the infrastructure they used to enjoy in colleges. They needed someone – a woman – to look after and sometimes also finance them (e.g., rich widows). Nevertheless, they still exhibited (traditional) misogynist attitudes and felt disturbed in their work by their wives and the children they had with them. One of the outcomes of these developments was the emergence of the study, a private room within the household that replicated and at the same time transformed the distance between scholarly work and society established in cloisters. Gadi Algazi (2003) shows that "the scholarly habitus" (Algazi, 2003) – which later in natural philosophy became the inner attitude of the disinterested researcher and the "modest witness" (Haraway, 2005) – was not natural or self-evident. Rather, "the emotional detachment of learned men was itself a learned habit" (Algazi, 2003, 9). A number of academic norms go back to the fact

European science was derived from Christian theology. Scholarly celibacy was one of them. Another one is the concept of "purity" that is closely connected to the idea of emotional detachment (Braun and Stephan, 2005: 17). As Christina von Braun and Inge Stephan (2005) point out, in Christianity, blood was divided into good and bad, the blood of the martyr and the blood of the sexualised body. The blood of the sexualised body was impure. As a result, women who menstruated every month were constructed as impure and excluded from higher offices (a practice that continues until today in the Catholic church).

Both aspects – purity and emotional detachment – play an important role in the accusation levelled against WGFS that they are *too political*. The charge of being *too political* indicates that WGFS scholars bring something into academia that does not belong there. They contaminate knowledge with something that has no part in science and proper academic knowledge production. Pure and disinterested knowledge has become part of the ideal of objectivity and neutrality that excludes any non-academic interests. It is a view from nowhere, which Donna Haraway (1988) called the God trick. Even though understandings of what purity entails have changed, there is an obvious continuity indicating the historic situatedness of the idea of purity itself. The lofty scientific values that are linked to purity (distance, neutrality, objectivity) did not develop outside gendered and raced power relations. In Christianity, men gained dominance and women were marginalised, including for their bodily impurity. Similarly, academia became a purely masculine institution and the "scientific persona" (Daston, 2003; Braun, 2005) was established as a man. Only this scientific persona is able to demonstrate a disinterested gaze from nowhere, while persons identified as women were constructed as being caught up in their sex/gender, their nature, emotionality and hence intellectual impurity.

One example for the construction of a masculine scientific persona in the humanities is the development of history as academic discipline. As Falko Schnicke (2015) reconstructs, historians in the 18th and 19th centuries were eager to prove that only men could become historians. Their vision of the academic historian included qualities that had been culturally associated with femininity – such as emotions and imagination. Nonetheless, women were declared incapable of real historical research because they would be overwhelmed by their emotions, whereas men were able to master them (and make use of them in just the right amount). In their effort to define history as a masculine field of inquiry and to preclude the possibility of women historians, they therefore relied heavily on modern constructions of femininity and masculinity that were part of the endeavour to build a society based on establishing a (lost) natural order in place of the divine order that had come before (cf. Honegger, 1991; Daston, 1992; Schiebinger, 1993).

This supposed natural social order also included differentiations on the basis of race. Black, Indigenous and People of Color were constructed as unfit for intellectual (and hence academic) work (Schiebinger, 1993; McClintock, 1995). Thus, academia developed not only as masculine, but also as white. Research itself has been shaped by these dominant perspectives. White European men researchers collectively created knowledge about their "Others", be they non-white, feminine, from a lower-class background, from outside the European centres or all of those together. This knowledge was not neutral but depended on and formed part of the workings of boundary work intended to keep unwanted subjects outside of academia and in a lower social status. Would anyone still argue today that these exclusions were not (also) politically motivated?

The problem is not simply that such boundary work happened in the past but that these historical developments still resonate in academic institutions and, as a result, knowledge production.[3] The "leaky pipeline", indicating the "disappearance" of women (and, in turn, the increasing prevalence of men) on the path from student to professor is but one symptom of this phenomenon. In 2019, merely 26% of professors in Germany were women, whereas 74% were men.[4] The percentage of women decreases further if we include other social categories, as Christina Möller's (2015) research in North Rhine Westphalia exemplifies: women professors who were the first in their families to finish university made up only 7% of the total number of professors. If women of colour had been considered separately, the figure would certainly have been even lower. As research has shown, imaginations of who can count as a scientific persona are still shaped by masculinity and whiteness in knowledge cultures within both the humanities and the sciences (Paulitz, 2016; Beaufays, 2015; Guthoff, 2013; Wekker, 2016). Women, People of Color and all other "Others" are still treated as "space invaders" (Puwar, 2004): subjects that, while not formally excluded, are treated as not belonging in these institutional spaces. While there have been changes in the participation of academics from marginalised groups, there is also continued resistance on all levels (Ahmed, 2012). The issue, however, is not just about counting heads. It is about knowledge cultures shaped by this social situation in academic institutions.

For the last 50 years, WGFS scholars have undertaken research on gender and race and analysed historical as well as current gendered and racialised social relations in which exactly this kind of knowledge consciously or unconsciously still plays a role: knowledge that is prone to supporting positions of power that some social groups hold over others and that hence needs to be addressed in democratic societies that are based on equality.[5] WGFS scholars, among others, have made these inequalities visible. They found that knowledge about women, their bodies and their minds was built on sociopolitical intentions to exclude them and, as a consequence, questioned mainstream academic knowledge production, including mainstream epistemologies and methodologies. This is what makes them politically relevant within academia as well as wider society – it's no wonder that they are greeted with scepticism.

In this frame, WGFS scholars have produced an immense body of research on what "political" can mean in academic knowledge production. The relationship between power and knowledge is a key research area for WGFS scholars. They have analysed exclusionary measures, have challenged the androcentrism in all academic fields and have made biases visible (e.g., Paulitz et al., 2016; Richardson, 2010). They have also reflected on the lack of research on so-called women's issues and have investigated power relations in research processes. Furthermore, they have reconstructed the social marginalisation and exclusion of racialised and sexualised "Others" as well as the practice of speaking for these "Others" – including within feminist research, thus scrutinizing feminist research itself (e.g., Mohanty, 1988, Scharff, 2010). What has been gained through this research is the insight that there is no knowledge production outside this power-knowledge connection and thus no knowledge production that is entirely apolitical, unstained by politics. In other words: these researchers have dug up the ground of academia. As a result, they have challenged (not only) the assumption of a free-floating mind that is emotionally detached from its body or – in the case of a discipline in the humanities such as Philosophy – is strong enough to take on the insecurity of an academic career (Guthoff, 2013). Instead, they have developed (and continue to do so) reflexive and alternative epistemological and methodological strategies in order to make one's involvement as transparent as possible. Research on knowledge production as a social process exemplifies that epistemology is a constructive process integrated in entire "machineries of knowledge production" (Knorr-Cetina, 1999, 3), that the establishment of what counts as truth is not simply an individual but a collective endeavour (Fleck, 2012; Foucault, 1981) and that scholars actively participate in boundary work (Gieryn, 1999). Such considerations reflect the insight that politics and research are inextricably intertwined and that there is no such thing as a purely objective standard – instead, it is essential to accept different epistemologies (Knorr-Cetina, 1999) in order to guarantee the freedom of research. Against this background, saying that WGFS are *too political* may well serve as a deflection against such critiques.

Attacks against gender studies

Scholars have been observing right-wing populists' fight against "gender" for at least the last decade (e.g., Paternotte, 2015; Paternotte/Kuhar, 2017; Henninger et al., 2021). "Gender" functions as an empty signifier that includes gender equality as well as equality in terms of sexual and reproductive rights. Thus, these attacks aim to move societies in a less liberal direction. "Gender" functions as symbolic glue (Kovats, 2015) and as a connection to mainstream society by normalising anti-democratic perspectives and actions (Strube et al., 2021). This becomes evident through links to anti-immigration activism: "For Kovats . . . it is precisely the focus on *authentic womanhood* that ties anti-gender to the anti-immigration narratives of the national modern" (Hemmings, 2020) – because authenticity of womanhood is connected to the nation.

Such attacks are not only directed at activists, but also at WGFS scholars and their institutions (e.g. Petö, 2021). Over the last decade, individual gender scholars in the German-speaking area have become targets of right populists and have been threatened. This hostility against WGFS scholars has become part of a wider hostility against researchers as well as politicians (Engeli, 2019). However, populists also draw links between activism and academia (and thus the scepticism that still exists within academia) that serve normalisation.

Attacks against equality politics and WGFS as an entire field started as a reaction to the 1995 International Women's Conference in Beijing and have increased since then (Paternotte, 2015). In the early 2000s, they have become more prominent. They have been launched not only by right-wing actors (either secular or religiously motivated) or men's rights activists outside of academia, but also by academics positioned on the right as well as conservative mainstream media (Frey et al., 2014; Näser-Lather, 2019, 2021). Some of these attacks even came from academics who consider themselves left-wing or outspokenly position themselves as *not* men's rights activists, like Peter Borghossian, James A. Lindsay and Helen Pluckrose.[6] They invented the term "grievance studies" to devalue fields of research concerned with forms of discrimination and inequality (such as WGFS) and spent a year writing and publishing several hoax articles in order to show that academic fields concerned with inequality are merely following specific doctrines. Their attack was not aimed at having a conversation with the WGFS scholarly community (though difficult conversations might be the result) but addressed to a wider public that might be less able to critically analyse their claims and procedures. This way, they developed discursive power in a counter discourse to equality debates and administrative metrics. In Hungary, the effects of these counter discourses became very clear when Gender Studies were banned in 2018.

Supposedly academic knowledge as well as awkward combinations of knowledge claims have repeatedly been used by populists in order to create powerful knowledge claims as the basis for their restrictive perspectives (Valkovičová and Hardoš 2018). Furthermore, right-wing academics in various academic disciplines ranging from biology to sociology write about "gender", with texts that are intended not for their academic peers but for the wider public. Even though WGFS is not their field of expertise, they claim expertise over the field by publishing on it. And because they are academics (professors or at least people holding PhDs), they are imbued with an aura of academic knowledge and hence authority. Their common claim is that WGFS creates an ideology (rather than proper knowledge) that they reject with an authoritative stance. Thus, their texts are not written as starting points for or contributions to social debates but rather in order to close down such debates.

My own experience can serve as an example of the effectiveness of academic writings against Gender Studies. When I started my position at the University of Vienna in 2017, I was invited to an interview with the Austrian broadsheet newspaper *Der Standard*. The online version of the interview received 700 reader comments, which is an enormous number compared to the average of 35 posts per article. The interview was published in the science rubric of the paper, and the posts also made use of academic vocabulary that is part of an everyday understanding of academic practice. Several posters mentioned their own academic background and two quoted Ulrich Kutschera. Kutschera is a professor for evolutionary biology specialising in plants and one of several German academics who regularly publish about their opposition to Gender Studies.

This "anti-gender" discourse creates a discursive connection to the scepticism within academia towards WGFS as being political or too political to be properly academic. As mentioned before, the anti-equality knowledge production of modernity still resonates within academia, even though many essentialist claims on the grounds of biology that were historically used to justify inequality have been challenged. While universities are changing slowly, the effects of that knowledge are still part of academia's cultural memory. This is displayed on the level of methodologies as well as representation, such as in galleries of important scholars that display only busts and portraits of men.

Thus, academic developments parallel the ones that take place in wider society when right-wing extremists connect to mainstream gender conservative society via "gender". In wider society, discomfort and unwillingness regarding change is used as a door-opener for extremist ideas. Similarly, within academia, right-wing populists create links to mainstream academic society. The danger is that, since academia is a highly prestigious institution, right-wing perspectives enhanced with academic reputation may become normalised even further.

Hope (dies last)

In contrast to the weak infrastructure of WGFS and the scepticism that greets it from some quarters, it seems that there is currently increasing support for gender research within funding organisations and the political sphere in Germany. There are a number of reasons for this. To begin with, it is the result of proactive work: WGFS scholars have approached funding bodies, have cooperated with ministries and politicians on state and federal levels, have established a public relations day (#4genderstudies) on 18 December and so forth. Furthermore, there is the lucky circumstance that some members of the German federal parliament (the Bundestag) have studied Gender Studies, including Kai Gehring, an expert on education and research for the Green Party. However, some of these developments are probably also linked to the rise of right-wing populism and the fact that right-wing extremism is now perceived as the biggest threat by most parties as well as the Federal Office for the Protection of the Constitution. The most right-wing extremist party in German federal and state parliaments is the AfD (Alternative for Germany), and the abolition of Gender Studies is part of their party programme. Since the German Constitutional Law guarantees academic freedom, this move clearly contradicts the Constitutional Law and, hence, makes their illiberal approach to academic knowledge production transparent. It seems obvious that WGFS is just the first field of research they target. Over the last years, the AfD has managed to enter all 16 state parliaments as well as the Bundestag. Whenever they entered a state parliament, they launched parliamentary inquiries (Kleine Anfragen) to find out how much state funding goes into gender research in that state, which is relevant because the states are responsible for all education including higher education. However, research is also funded through major research institutions on the federal level, and the AfD formally launched a proposal to ban gender research in general in the Bundestag in 2020. That proposal included an "explanation" as to why WGFS is a useless research area that relied on the same strategies I already mentioned: connecting research results to each other in a strange combinative way and utilising arguments by mainly right-wing academics writing publicly against WGFS.

214 Sabine Grenz

Watching the parliamentary debate on the proposal, a feminist scholar might have rubbed her eyes in disbelief: members of all other parties, even conservative Christian Democrats, spoke out for Gender Studies. Of course, one should not be naïve. Much of what was said was rhetorical and symbolic, and due to Germany's history, taking a position against proposals by the AfD – a right-wing extremist party – is the default approach in German parliaments. The very few incidences in the past in which non-AfD members of parliament cooperated with the AfD in a state parliament were consistently treated as scandals in the public and such cooperation in the Bundestag is unimaginable (so far). Thus, applause for their proposal by other members of parliament was not to be expected anyway. Instead, the proposal served to probe the Bundestag, perhaps banking on the aforementioned un-/conscious alliances against equality. Notwithstanding these points, the debate overall communicates a very clear message in favour of gender research.[7] In fact, populist attacks against WGFS may have helped the field, which is exemplified by a move on another level. The minister of science, education and equality of the state of Hamburg, Katharina Fegebank (Greens), recommended that the German Science and Humanities Council evaluate the structural situation of WGFS in all states. The evaluation began in 2020, and the result is expected this year. Since the aim of the council is to support academic work in Germany, there is hope that the evaluation will result in recommendations that help improve and further develop the structural situation of WGFS. So, it seems that there is hope, even though the aforementioned right-wing academics are already lobbying against any such possibilities.

To sum up: In this chapter, I have sketched some of the layers that make up what can be seen as difficult conversations surrounding the academic field of WGFS. Attempts of the populist right to make use of anti-feminist discourses in order to connect to mainstream society within and outside of academia are particularly concerning here. Within academia, these discourses connect to the lower epistemic status of WGFS in the academic system. However, there is hope: while engineering sciences were perceived as being "too technically oriented", Gender Studies is sometimes seen as "too political". There is an analogy in the "too" that is perceived to contaminate academic knowledge production: might there be a parallel development for WGFS in the future, with it becoming one of the most institutionalised and respected academic fields of research? Is it possible that social and academic change might bring about change in the status of WGFS, and that global anti-gender populism is merely one of the last cries of a dying dragon? In any case, it is high time for our sceptical colleagues to realise what company they are in and to reconsider their attitude.

Notes

1 This chapter is based on the opening speech of the 10th European Feminist Research Conference published in Biele Mefebue, Astrid/En, Boka/Grenz, Sabine/Meshkova, Ksenia/Sifaki, Agge-liki/Tuider, Elisabeth (eds.), 2020, *Difference, Diversity, Diffraction. Beiträge* zur *10th European Feminist Research Conference und 7. Jahrestagung der Fachge-sell-schaft Geschlechter-studien e.V. 2018*, www.genderopen.de/handle/25595/2056, pp. 11–16.

2 I will use this acronym, coined by Maria do Mar Pereira (2017), throughout the article.
3 For a more detailed analysis of who can actually do boundary work in academia, see Pereira (2019). Her work clearly shows how subjects other than white men are regularly marginalised as researchers.
4 See: www.destatis.de/DE/Themen/Gesellschaft-Umwelt/Bildung-Forschung-Kultur/Hochschulen/Tabellen/frauenanteile-akademischelaufbahn.html (seen 21 May 2022).
5 For images of the scientific persona and how they support the exclusion of women as well as hinder the development of diversity within academia, see Paulitz, Kink, Prietl (2016).
6 See: https://en.wikipedia.org/wiki/Grievance_studies_affair (seen 21 May 2022).
7 Cf. the report: https://dserver.bundestag.de/btd/19/303/1930345.pdf or the entire sitting: www.youtube.com/watch?v=DGTyat-09JM (both seen 21 May 2022).

References

Ahmed, S (2012) *On Being Included*. Durham: Duke University Press.
Algazi, G (2003) Scholars in households: Refiguring the learned habitus, 1480–1550. *Sci Context* 16: 42.
Beaufaÿs, S (2015) *Wie werden Wissenschaftler gemacht?: Beobachtungen zur wechselseitigen Konstitution von Geschlecht und Wissenschaft* (transcript) Verlag: Bielefeld.
Braun, C.von and Stephan, I (2005) Einführung: Gender@Wissen. In C. von Braun and I. Stephan (eds) *Gender@Wissen. Ein Handbuch der Gender-Theorien*. UTB GmbH Böhlau: Stuttgart Köln.
Daston, L (1992) The naturalized female intellect. *Science in Context* 5: 209–35.
Daston, L (2003) Die wissenschaftliche Persona. Arbeit und Berufung. In T. Wobbe (ed.) *Zwischen Vorderbühne und Hinterbühne. Beiträge zum Wandel der Geschlechterbeziehungen in der Wissenschaft vom 17. Jahrhundert bis zur Gegenwart* (Transcript: Bielefeld).
do Pereira, M.M (2012) Feminist theory is proper knowledge, but . . . The status of feminist scholarship in the academy. *Feminist Theory* 13: 283–303.
do Pereira, M.M (2017) *Power, Knowledge and Feminist Scholarship: An Ethnography of Academia*. London and New York: Routledge.
do Pereira, M.M (2019) Boundary-work that does not work: Social Inequalities and the Non-Performativity of Scientific Boundary-work. *Science, Technology, & Human Values* 44(2): 365.
Engeli, I (2019) Gender and sexuality research in the age of populism: lessons for political science. *European Political Science* 2020: 226–235.
Fleck, L (2012) *Entstehung und Entwicklung einer Wissenschaftlichen Tatsache: Einführung in die Lehre vom Denkstil und Denkkollektiv*. Suhrkamp: Frankfurt am Main.
Foucault, M (1981) *Archäologie des Wissens* (Suhrkamp: Frankfurt a. Main).
Frey, R., M. Gärtner, M. Köhnen, and S. Scheele (2014) *Gender, Wissenschaftlichkeit und Ideologie: Argumente im Streit um Geschlechterverhältnisse*. Berlin: Heinrich-Böll-Stiftung.
Gieryn, T (1999) *Cultural Boundaries of Science: Credibility on the Line*. Chicago: University of Chicago Press.
Guthoff, H (2013) *Kritik des Habitus. Zur Intersektion von Kollektivität und Geschlecht in der akademischen Philosophie*. Transcript: Bielefeld.
Haraway, D. J (1988) Situated knowledge: The science question in feminism and the privilege of partial perspective. *Feminist Studies* 14: 575–99.
Haraway, D. J (2005) *Modest_Witness@Second_Millenium. FemaleMan_Meets_Onco_Mouse*. New York London: Routledge.

Hark, S (2005) *Dissidente Partizipation: eine Diskursgeschichte des Feminismus* Suhrkamp: Frankfurt am Main.
Hemmings, C (2011) *Why stories matter: the political grammar of feminist theory* Durham: Duke Univ. Press.
Hemmings, C (2020) Unnatural feelings. The affective life of anti-gender mobilisations, *Radical Philosophy* 2: 27–39.
Henninger, A., D. Bergold-Caldwell, S. Grenz, B. Grubner, H. Krügner-Kirn, S. Maurer, M. Näser-Lather, S. Beaufaÿs, and B. Verlag Barbara (2021) *Mobilisierungen gegen Feminismus und ‚Gender: Erscheinungsformen, Erklärungsversuche und Gegenstrategien* (Verlag Barbara Budrich: Opladen, Berlin, Toronto).
Honegger, C (1991) *Die Ordnung der Geschlechter: die Wissenschaften vom Menschen und das Weib 1750–1850*. Campus-Verl.
Kahlert, H (2018) 'Exzellente Wissenschaft? Das strukturelle Scheitern von Koordinierter Frauen- und Geschlechterforschung im Wettbewerb. In S. Hark and J. Hofbauer (eds) *Vermessene Räume, gespannte Beziehungen. Unternehmerische Universitäten und Geschlechterdynamiken*. Suhrkamp: Frankfurt a. Main.
Knorr-Cetina, K (1999) *Epistemic Cultures: How the Sciences Make Knowledge*. Cambridge, MA: Harvard Univ. Press.
Kováts, E. and Põim, M (Ed.) (2015) *Gender as Symbolic Glue: The Position and Role of Conservative and Far Right Parties in the Anti-gender Mobilization in Europe*. (Fondation for European Progressive Studies and Friedrich-Ebert-Stiftung Budapest: Brussels).
Kuhar, R. and Paternotte, D (2017) *Anti-gender Campaigns in Europe: Mobilizing against Equality*. London New York: Rowman & Littlefield International.
Liinason, M (2011) *Feminism and the Academy*. Lund: Lund University.
Lykke, N (2010) *Feminist Studies. A Guide to Intersectional Theory, Methodology and Writing*. New York: Routledge.
Mayer, S. and Sauer, B (2017) "Gender ideology" in Austria: Coalitions around an empty signifier. In R. Kuhar and D. Paternotte (eds) *Anti-gender Campaigns in Europe: Mobilizing against Equality*. London and New York: Rowman & Littlefield International.
McClintock, A (1995) *Imperial Leather: Race, Gender and Sexuality in the Colonial Contest*. New York: Routledge.
Mohanty, C.T (1988) *Feminist review*, 30: 88.
Möller, C (2015) *Herkunft zählt (fast) immer. Soziale Ungleichheiten unter Universitätsprofessorinnen und -professoren*. Beltz Juventa: Weinheim und Basel.
Näser-Lather, M (2019) Wider den Genderismus! Kritik und Polemiken gegen die Gender Studies in akademischen Kontexten. In: M. Näser-Larher, A. Lena Oldemeier and D. Beck (eds) *Backlash!? Antifeminismus in Wissenschaft, Politik und Gesellschaft* Rossdorf: Ulrike Helmer Verlag.
Näser-Lather, M (2021) Academics against gender studies. Science populism as part of an authoritarian anti-feminist hegemony project. *Women, Gender and Research* 2021: 77–85.
Nash, J.C (2019) *Black Feminism Reimagined: After Intersectionality*. Durham and London: Duke University Press.
Paternotte, D (2015) Blessing the crowds. Catholic mobilisations against gender in Europe. In S. Hark and P.-I. Villa (eds) *Anti-Genderismus: Sexualität und Geschlecht als Schauplätze aktueller politischer Auseinandersetzungen*. Bielefeld: Transcript.
Paulitz, T (2010) *Mann und Maschine. Eine genealogische Wissenssoziologie des Ingenieurs und der modernen Technikwissenschaften, 1850–1930*. Bielefeld: Transcript.

Paulitz, T, Susanne, K, and Bianca, P (2016) Analytical strategy for dealing with neutrality claims and implicit masculinity constructions. Methodological challenges for gender studies in science and technology. *FQS*, 17.

Pető, A (2021) Angriffe gegen die Institutionen der Wissenschaft und ihre Instrumentalisierung im illiberalen Regime Eine Anregung zum Überdenken der gesellschaftlichen Rolle der Wissenschaft und ihre Perspektiven. In S. A. Strube, R. Perintfalvi, R. Hemet, M. Metze and C. Sahbaz (eds.) *Anti-Genderismus in Europa. Allianzen von Rechtspopulismus und religiösem Fundamentalismus. Mobilisierung – Vernetzung – Transformation*. Bielefeld: Transcript.

Puwar, N (2004) *Space Invaders: Race, Gender and Bodies Out of Place*. Oxford and New York: Berg.

Richardson, S.S (2010) Feminist philosophy of science: History, contributions, and challenges. *Synthese* 337–62.

Scharff, C.M (2012) *Repudiating Feminism*. Farnham: Ashgate.

Schiebinger, L (1993) *Nature's Body: Gender in the Making of Modern Science*. Boston: Beacon Press.

Schnicke, F (2015) *Die männliche Disziplin: zur Vergeschlechtlichung der deutschen Geschichtswissenschaft 1780–1900*. Göttingen: Wallstein Verlag.

Strube, S., Perintfalvi, R., Hemet, R., Metze, M. and Sahbaz, C (2021) *Anti-Genderismus in Europa: Allianzen von Rechtspopulismus und religiösem Fundamentalismus. Mobilisierung – Vernetzung – Transformation*. Bielefeld: transcript Verlag.

Valkovičová, V. and Hardoš, P (2018) *Science Wills It!: The Use of Scientific Claims in 'Anti-Gender' Rhetoric. In Engenderings*. London: LSE.

Wekker, G (2016) *White Innocence: Paradoxes of Colonialism and Race*. Durham: Duke University Press.

15 The feminist classroom in a Neoliberal University

Awino Okech

Introduction

Over the last decade, there has been a proliferation of work in the higher-education sector that explores questions of feminist pedagogy on the one hand and those that pay attention to the racialised and gendered experiences of women in European and North American academia on the other hand (see Bhopal, 2016; Coffey and Delamont, 2000; Culley and Portuges, 2012; Mirza, 2018; Rollock, 2012; Sanchez-Casal and MacDonald, 2002). Across the literature emerging from the Euro-American context cited here, three concerns have surfaced. The first concern is the work that is required to ensure feminist intellectual contributions are taken seriously across and within disciplines. The second concern is the work feminist academics do in universities to surface intersectional gender inequalities and the invisible and visible ways these are exhibited in hierarchical university structures. The third concern focusses on feminist pedagogy, drawing attention to the classroom structure, what is taught and how it is taught as central to feminist praxes and politics. Ultimately, this literature is undergirded by understanding how feminist intellectual ideas are taken up in an increasingly marketised university system that relies more on teaching and research metrics as well as the emphasis on student experience as the main ways to determine a successful education experience.

I return to the second and third concern in this chapter by examining the ethical questions raised in the classroom as well as the racialised and gendered concerns that emerge when building feminist learning spaces. I explore these issues by engaging with the concept of safe space as it has emerged within the higher-education sector and the ethics of care as developed by feminist movements (See FRIDA, 2016; UAF-LAC, 2018) to surface the complexities of deliberately living feminist politics in a neoliberal university. Without aiming for easy answers, I draw attention to the power relations between students and that between students and teachers within the university infrastructure as key arbiters of how we make sense of safety and care in a diverse learning environment. I draw on these reflections to examine how interpretations of feminist pedagogy within neoliberal university classrooms can and do produce complex expectations for Black women academics. In my conclusion, I draw on Arao and Clemens' (2013) work on brave spaces to highlight the distinctions between the work that happens in the

DOI: 10.4324/9781003088417-20

classroom and the historical value of safe spaces within the broader university environment. In doing so, I illustrate the attendant risks of conflating the logic that informed both the language and intention of safe spaces in the North American university landscape and the demands of a feminist classroom. In developing these questions, I adopt an autoethnographic approach, as well as rely on reflections from seven Black and women of colour academics and five students from a targeted survey I administered to twenty respondents. The survey had six questions focussed on defining the feminist classroom, safe spaces, care as a feature of feminist classrooms, and the risks and opportunities inherent in this framing. This analysis is pulled together thematically in the sections that follow.

Framing notes

I moved to London in 2016 to take up a gender studies lectureship at SOAS, University of London after a decade working in the civil society sector across various parts of the African continent. SOAS is perceived to be a radical left institution. One can unpack what radical looks like or means for a university in the middle of London with a history of training colonial officers within a higher-education system where individual academic pursuits are rewarded more than collaborative community-engaged scholarship. The students who come to SOAS are not homogenous, even though many across the institution assume a sense of shared values and approach to embodying SOAS values. Some students are attracted to the "radical" brand of SOAS and end up disappointed when they discover that this is a university like any other, where pockets of critical scholarship exist while other pockets maintain "business as usual". Other students come for a traditional degree and educational experience and find the insistence on challenging hegemonic knowledge systems and ways of knowing in some classes "political" and unnecessary. Other students are challenged and engaged by the decolonial approach to teaching in some of their classrooms, thus leaving intellectually richer[1].

It is worth noting that in the broad categories of students I described, the most disappointed tend to be Black students. The specificity of the racial experience is linked to teaching staff demographics and an expectation that decolonial objectives should cut across the university. The university has no more than twenty-five tenured or permanent Black academic staff out of a teaching staff of three hundred. This distribution means that in some departments there are no or only one Black academic. I therefore walk into a gender studies classroom with an international student body with multiple expectations depending on the positionality of the students. This classroom dynamic means that I often meet students who tell me I am the first Black woman to teach them, and this is on a post-graduate degree programme. Consequently, there are explicit and implicit expectations of me from Black students, alongside other students for whom my "unicorn" status can become a site to resolve the range of crises they encounter in the institution. While there is scholarship about student-centred learning (see O'Neill and McMahon, 2005), not enough attention is paid to what it means for a feminist teacher to facilitate a classroom in the environment I have described here. I turn to these complexities in the sections that follow, beginning with an understanding of the history of safe spaces on university campuses and then exploring the meaning of a feminist classroom as a safe space through the survey responses.

Conceptualising safe spaces

"Safe spaces" as a concept on university campuses emerge from the North American context and is used to refer to programmes devoted to supporting minority students (see Harpalani, 2017). However, there are a range of attributions to the term "safe space". There are those who link it to psychologist Kurt Lewin's (Lewin and Gold, 1999) work on "sensitivity training" for corporate leaders and other marginalised groups on college campuses. Other links to safe spaces are made to feminist and queer movements in the United States of America in the 1960s and 70s (see Beemyn, 2003). However, it is also clear that the civil rights movement in the United States of America produced a wave of autonomous organising on university campuses that were focussed on anti-Black racism, thus generating safe spaces for Black students (see Arsenault, 2006; Van Dyke, 2003). Irrespective of the origin, the use of the term is the same, which is a focus on creating physical spaces that are devoted to the needs of marginalised groups. Across university campuses in the Global North, programmes, centres, and organisations that target Black and minority students only are spaces in which conversations about structural inequalities that impact marginalised students can be unpacked, and accompanying programmes and strategies to navigate the university developed. At SOAS, the Black Staff Student Forum and the Breaking Barriers programme are such initiatives that create leadership, mentoring, and support frameworks from Black students and staff who are underrepresented in the university (see Haywood and Darko, 2021).

More recent iterations of safe spaces have emerged in relation to tenuous debates on academic freedom. Debates on universities in general and classrooms specifically as "safe spaces" have been hijacked by critics as evidence of efforts to infringe on academic freedom. In these articulations, the implicit assertion is that being held accountable for hate speech or the perpetuation of racist and sexist ideas is in fact a constraint to robust academic debate that is at the heart of university life (see Zurcher, 2021; Trilling, 2020; Dickinson, 2020). Alongside the deployment of safe spaces as evidence of "political correctness" and a limit to academic freedom and plurality of views, critics of safe spaces have also challenged the importance and value of dedicated spaces for minority groups in universities where they are a minority. At the centre of this argument is the idea that such efforts foster racial division rather than build greater multicultural understanding.

If universities have become increasingly hostile environments with the rise of fascist and right-wing political parties gaining a foothold across Europe, then the demand for safety in the university takes on a different meaning (see Allen, 2019). We are no longer talking about safe spaces as special programmes and initiatives across universities that are delinked from the classroom. Consequently, framing the classroom as a site of intellectual engagement has been used to propagate violent ideas and present them as robust academic and intellectual exploration (see Brown and Mondon, 2021; Tilley, 2021). It is in this context that feminist classrooms as safe spaces take on a different meaning, largely because of the transformative ideals that feminists in their diversity are generally geared towards. I have witnessed the bold resurgence of racism, racism denialism, and sexist political ideas framed as plurality and the embodied impact of these ideas and policies in the British context (see Commission on Race and Ethnic Disparities, 2021). Consequently, it is in this context that I have held the framing of feminist classrooms as safe spaces and conversations that emanate from it as leading to a productive tension rather than a difficult conversation. The productive tension lies in allowing us to unpack what people mean when they invoke the term "safe space" alongside the sometimes-disembodied claim about how safety is cultivated and sustained. I turn to my interlocutors to unpack this productive tension by examining their understanding of feminist classrooms as safe spaces whilst paying attention to the distinctions between the ethics of feminist pedagogy whilst also paying attention to the political moment within which the claim of safety becomes more salient.

The feminist classroom and safety

Before I turn to conceptualisations of safety through my interlocutors, I will reflect on what I see as the purpose of the feminist classroom. Constructions of the feminist classroom and the work within it tend to privilege the site, which means the one or two hours when a class is held. However, the classroom is not only limited to the room where learning engagements are mediated around a syllabus. Once the class is over, the interaction with students through office hours, assignments, and email responses to concerns and anxieties remain an active part of the teaching and learning process and therefore are part of the concept of the classroom. Therefore, the teacher as chief navigator of the learning experience remains explicit in how universities are constructed, yet the feminist classroom focusses on the expansive ways in which the labour of teaching should involve co-creation. Radhika Govinda (2020) summarises student-centred and student-led learning, co-construction of knowledge, peer-to-peer learning, situated knowledges, and reflexivity are key to feminist pedagogy. The interlocutors from the surveys corroborate this view with an emphasis on collaboration, shared learning, and co-creation as central to a feminist classroom:

> It feels like a space that is attuned to multiple sensory forms of learning beyond the textual and one that creates space for vulnerability. A feminist classroom is one in which we acknowledge that power remains, while also trying to create more spaces for openness, collectivity, and vulnerability.
> – Student

> A feminist classroom to me means a learning space that is dynamic, honest, caring, and deliberate. The space is conscious that learning and teaching is

done by all those in the room and that the personal cannot be taken away from that. It feels challenging and it also transcends the time in the classroom.

– Student

It is a class centred on the need of marginalised students and where gender, race, and class are at the core of analysis.

– Student

To me, a feminist classroom is first and foremost a space of self-reflexivity. It is a space where both teachers and students attempt to set aside ego and to think critically about the subjectivity they come into this space with. It is a space where we attempt to learn from one another rather than speak at one another. And it is a space of compassion, generosity, and forgiveness.

– Academic

An inclusive, caring, diverse space where everyone feels comfortable and safe to listen, discuss, and create.

– Student

The emphasis here on destabilising power relations as a core difference between feminist classrooms and non-feminist classrooms reflects the primary goal of feminist work. However, there are three major unexplored assumptions in the descriptions of the feminist classroom laid out previously. The first is the reality that challenging power hierarchies through a classroom experience often results in a set of isolated experiences that are rarely mirrored in the university machine. The second is that collaboration and co-creation dissolves power relations. While transformation is at the core of feminist worldmaking, pedagogical choices are not designed to dismantle power relations in a university structure that is sustained by those hierarchies. The bounded conceptualisation of the classroom where the academic is still expected to curate the feminist experience ignores that the expectation of safety moves beyond teaching time. It is in this expanded space that power relations become evident. If we take power as not dissolved but simply lived in a transformative way, then sustaining an inclusive and caring space is not necessarily a collaborative task; the role of a teacher as guide in the feminist classroom remains key. While the academic can foster collaborative learning, the assumption that they should teach remains an important feature of the neoliberal university. Third, the expectation that safety cultivates room for vulnerability leads me to the next set of questions. Who has the privilege to be vulnerable? Who is required to bear responsibility for the impact of that vulnerability in the classroom? How does the construction of a classroom as a safe space create specific responsibilities for academics and not students? I turn to these questions through my interlocutors.

As a student, it means that I can speak without judgement; a place where I am there as an individual who can learn and reflect and not be judged if my reflections are not precisely on point. For example, a classroom discussing feminist topics can be quite judgemental if you did not think exactly in the same way as the others, and a safe space would be when the teacher highlights that learning is a process.

A safe space between the students and teachers, so calling out/removing those who abuse this space or make inappropriate/uncomfortable comments; a space for non-judgemental sharing and listening; a space of respect for one another; a space without hierarchy even with teachers.

– Student

I imagine a safe space being safe from hegemonic viewpoints that erase or marginalise other viewpoints, and how those get expressed in the classroom, through lecturers, students, materials, the space itself.

– Student

A safe space is a space where one can be vulnerable and expect others to not use that vulnerability against you in the future.

– Student

For me, safe spaces are particularly important to build for historically excluded and marginalised groups for whom the simple fact of being in the mainstream is an act of resistance. As such, the guidelines for how to communicate, how to exchange, and the expectations about respect and care must be written on course outlines and discussed at the very onset of the class. It must be modelled. And the space must be rebuilt and nurtured each class session. Both students and teachers go in [and] out various places during the semester where violence is meted routinely. We must account for this and allow all participants to go through a process of re-entry. If one is lucky, that re-entry process takes less and less time with each class session.

– Academic

Safety, as described by these survey respondents, focuses on the racialised, gendered, and classed ways our societies are organised and reproduced in universities. Safety in this context therefore focuses on ensuring that while a learning environment is cultivated, harmful views are not left unchallenged. This conceptualisation of safety is one that aligns with the transformative goals of feminist pedagogy. It also becomes an important objective given a political environment in which anti-racist and critical race scholarship is under attack (see Banerjee and Sawo, 2021). However, the objective of a classroom as a collaborative learning space can be hindered if the message is that majority groups come to class to bear witness or listen as suggested by two interlocutors here. There are three distinctions to make here about hegemony. The first distinction is the decolonial objective of prioritising majority world knowledge given global knowledge inequities. The second distinction is the responsibility of the teacher to manage the unlearning process for students whose well-established worldviews are unsettled. The reasonable expectation that teachers should challenge harmful views is different from creating a classroom in which only marginalised voices are privileged. How a teacher deals with what is considered a harmful or problematic view could be the transformative turning point for the speaker or the line that leads to a formal complaint from the student for a hostile classroom. The third and final distinction is the pedagogical task of ensuring an inclusive classroom, where everyone can engage.

While a feminist classroom should be a space for reflexivity which therefore enables vulnerability, policing views, however problematic they are, is both a political and an ethical responsibility that is consistently negotiated in real-time. If we read it as an ethical task of an educator, then safety is not a helpful way to describe the responsibility we hold in the classroom. Let me develop this idea through the respondents here who capture the dilemmas associated with thinking about university classrooms as safe spaces. They point to safety as ensuring marginalised groups are not further marginalised. However, there is also a recognition that safety can be construed as not being subjected to uncomfortable or challenging topics or discussions. Finally, the notion of safety may imply that feminist classrooms are not devoid of power relations and that hierarchies cease to exist.

> I am wary of a classroom being described as safe. When I think of safety I think of comfort, and I think comfort is anathema to the kind of politics we are trying to inspire through our classrooms. We often equate safety with care and assume to be made to feel safe is to be cared for. We accuse those who make us uncomfortable of threatening our safety. Therefore, I am fearful of such terms.
>
> – Academic

> As a student, I'm always a bit sceptical of the idea of a safe space – or even a safer space – because I'm just not sure it's possible. But I would expect it to be a space in which efforts are made to support voices that are usually marginalised in UK classrooms (Black and POC voices, women's and trans people's voices, disabled voices, etc.). I would hope that it would be a space in which direct or indirect actions and speech that harm people would be identified and that attempts would be made to create accountability for those speech and actions within the classroom,
>
> I also think it is important to remind others and ourselves that a classroom is not a space of friendship or kinship, but a space of learning with strangers that can allow community to emerge if we enter it in certain ways.
>
> – Academic

In the reluctance to label classrooms as safe spaces, there is an implicit assertion that safety can be read as foreclosing the space for difficult conversations that of necessity happen in gender studies classrooms. Consequently, safety is reframed as the need to set up the conditions to have complex conversations in a manner that opens rather than forecloses learning and transformation. In essence, our task is to assume in the first instance that questions are treated as an invitation to learn, rather than leap to the view that they are intended to harm. However, there is also an expectation that the facilitation role the teacher holds is to educate without preventing and/or limiting the ability of folks to come in and out of conversations. The feminist classroom is always a place for learning and unlearning deeply held views on issues that implicate us, and this will always be a source of discomfort. How we create conditions for shared reflection during difficult conversations rather than looking to the teacher as the fixer is key. How we do this whilst not placing an additional burden on students who are racially othered and who do not experience the rewards of vulnerability in the same way is equally important. If the classroom is a collaborative space, how do we share the power of managing complexity rather than deferring to the teacher as an authority when complex situations emerge for a racially othered academic?

I turn to care as a framework that has emerged in feminist movement building spaces in ways that I find comprehensive because it is seen as critical to sustaining, building, and embodying movement work and viewed as a collective process rather than an individual one (see UAF-LAC, 2018). I draw on the work of FRIDA Fund and Urgent Action Fund Latin America, which has developed how collective care underpins the ethos to their work. In their conceptualisation of care, FRIDA and UAF-LAC make distinctions between individuals taking care of themselves by centring well-being as critical to how they move in the world, from the need for movement spaces to being deliberate about care. Collective care in these instances is about time allocated to work, rest, and the financial resources given to prioritisation of mental and physical well-being. There is mutuality in this movement articulation of collective care that requires everyone to show up fully and where mutual accountability and responsibility are upheld as an important mode of engaging. In thinking about care, I am interested in who people think should provide the care that leads to safety. The racialised, classed, and gendered nature of these expectations and the absence of reciprocity in universities forms the basis of my analysis here.

Care in feminist classrooms

> Care means pay attention to the needs of students . . . by caring more about marginalised students. As symbol I can cite the fact to adapt assignment to the need of students.
> – Student

> I see care as an essential part of building safe spaces. Part of practices of care are included in my curriculum by thinking, what do students need beyond course content? It is how I assess [the] need for flexibility in class. How we talk about care for the communities we live in by relating theories and debates to our everyday life. It is taking time to check in at the beginning of class through our "re-entry" process.
> – Academic

The descriptions of care here centre the student and the role of teachers in ensuring that educational inequalities are not reproduced in the classroom. The reference to assignments and coping expands the classroom. However, it also isolates the feminist classroom from the broader environment within which the expectation to subvert rules and norms around education are not embedded. It is also evident that the framing of care here does not address care for caregivers, even when not always called that, and who—like the students—navigate the same life worlds. The expectation that teachers should provide extensive pastoral support as part of demonstrating care, and not care as a collective praxis that is reciprocal between students and staff, is a factor of the neoliberal university. Students are clients who require good service from the institution. Even where claims about decolonising the university are made, the praxes of decolonised utopias are not actively built and envisioned. Consequently, we have a university model in which the focus is primarily on management, and the work to transform universities is seen as work that is done in the cracks of the university rather than at the centre of the university. This approach positions "us" versus "them" as a way of imagining change in universities, leading to the expectation that even where care is centred as an ethos in the feminist classroom, it should come from the teacher rather than a collective praxis to which everyone is held accountable.

The reflections ahead focus on the risks associated with discourses on care in the neoliberal university. They capture the racialised, gendered expectations of care and underscore the production of Black women as not sufficiently feminist for drawing boundaries to survive institutions that are extractive. More importantly, one interlocutor surfaces the danger of isolated non-institutionalised approaches to care which, in addition to creating more labour for staff, generate insecurity for students when similar support is absent across the university.

> I think the biggest risk is that in a university classroom, much like in other areas of neoliberal society, the burden of care is placed primarily on Black women, LGBTQ folks, and people of colour who are expected to be generous with their time, knowledge, and energy despite being given little to no support or care themselves. Care is not seen as reciprocal, and therefore when black women, for example, set up boundaries they are read as unapproachable, strict, and unhelpful. This transactional framework creates a kind of entitlement where students expect a level of care that they are not willing to give to their instructors.
> – Academic

> As a Black woman, one of the biggest risks of centring care in this context is being perceived as the quintessential Mamie. Black women are too often typecast as caregivers, problem-solvers, and strong women who are pillars of community. In the classroom, these stereotypes can lead to students disproportionately seeking you out to lay down their burdens and, in the worst cases, simply not prioritising your courses because "you care" and then asking you for indulgence when they fail to meet class expectations. – Academic
> Mostly just that the university system isn't set up to care, and so trying to make it happen in isolation in one classroom can feel hollow. Issues such as funding,

mental health, or lack of institutional support, for example, can't easily be handled there. Falling back on superficial forms of care might be easy.

– Student

Care in universities is not set up as reciprocal. My isolated experiences of reciprocal collective care are few and far between. In my four years at SOAS, I can identify only two instances of reciprocal care that I highlight here. I travelled abroad for a conference and when I returned to London, I contracted a stomach infection. I ended up in the emergency room of the hospital and was hospitalised as the doctors tried to figure out what was wrong with me. When I returned to work the next week, I found a get-well card underneath my office door from four Black women students wishing me a quick recovery and thanking me for my work. I was very touched by the small but important gesture and emailed them to say as much. A few months later, some trouble was brewing in the cohort. A student received an unsatisfactory mark for a paper marked by a teaching assistant, a complaint they brought to me. I read the paper and other papers from the modules in our programme they referenced as comparators. Any teacher will tell you that checking how a student performed in a different module is not a sound basis to explain why they did poorly in a module, but I did it. I invited the student for a subsequent meeting to carefully explain that this was not an inconsistency in marking as they claimed; the quality of the papers was vastly different. The student agreed and claimed the matter was resolved. After our conversation they attempted to instigate a collective complaint across the cohort. A Black student alerted me to this pending "collective complaint". The collective complaint did not gain traction, but it did not stop the student from revisiting what they said was a concluded matter through the student support team asserting that this was a widespread complaint in the cohort: a fact I knew not to be true. The student who sent me the "heads-up" message did not need to do it. They could have assumed that I have sufficient experience to handle these matters. However, they did so because they knew how unsubstantiated student complaints on a programme and modules convened by a Black woman can easily become questions about teaching quality and convening rigour. It is also worth flagging that the teaching assistant against whom the marking inconsistency complaint was levelled against happened to be a woman of colour and the modules where teaching and marking were done by White colleagues were the comparators.

I return to these examples to illustrate how the praxis of care within the expansive classroom actively works against reciprocity and the importance of centring personhood that feminist values privilege. While arguments are made about breaking hierarchies in the classroom, those hierarchies are reinstated where teachers are concerned and when things get difficult. When feminist academics embody and practice ways of being in a classroom that are the antithesis of what exists outside it, they are doing so based on a commitment to transformational spaces. Collective care as articulated by feminist social movements centres on reciprocity. When we say care is key in a feminist classroom and care should centre on the students, who cares for the caregivers?

What next for feminist classrooms?

> One risk is the possibility of creating an image of the classroom as one devoid of power relations, as one that can be made 'safe'. I don't think this is ever fully possible; while classrooms can be made safer or more open, I don't believe they can ever be safe spaces, and using the term might misrepresent how classrooms operate.
>
> – Academic

The university classroom is an aspirational site in which a range of interconnected things can occur. For feminist academics, it is a space to trace the lineage of feminist intellectual labour. For many feminist scholars from the majority world, this means centring the worlds of those outside the Global North and to link these lifeworlds and the ever-evolving environment we occupy within and most importantly outside the university. The university is only one part of our lives and what we witness within it is a microcosm of the world we inhabit. The deliberate work to think about power and knowledge production differently is relational, which must always be rooted in an understanding of how race, gender, and class mediate our experiences of the world. For feminists, the objective is not to reproduce harmful relationships to power but rather transform them without eliding them.

However, the wave of "academic freedom" policies designed to muzzle heterodox approaches to understanding the world demand intentionality to the classroom as a site and the university as a space that unpacks but does not sustain ideologies that reproduce inequalities. The efforts to collapse the original meaning of safe space in universities with academic freedom that mobilises "diversity" of views and "debate" to sustain racist, sexist, and therefore often violent views about racially othered groups requires that we bear more responsibility in how we manage the classroom. Consequently, how we navigate complex, sometimes difficult conversations about safety in ways that yield transformative goals rather than create greater schisms is key. Given the origins of safe spaces explored earlier in this chapter and my interlocutors' assertions about the risks associated with naming a classroom as a safe space, I would like to close with Arao and Clemens (2013: 143–148) on brave spaces. I argue that a reinterpretation of a classroom as a brave space purposefully cultivates the shared responsibility for the classroom, thus engendering care as shared and leads what are often difficult conversations into a place of transformative possibilities. Arao and Clemens (2013) offer principles of brave spaces and I focus on four of them here. The first is controversy with civility, where varying opinions are accepted. The second is the importance of owning intentions and impacts by acknowledging and discussing instances where a dialogue has affected the emotional well-being of another person. It follows that if we are required to take responsibility for what and how we engage in debate, then how people choose to surface "controversy" is thought through. Third, challenge by choice is an invitation to step in and out of challenging conversations. Fourth, respect that is rooted in one another's basic personhood and an agreement not to intentionally inflict harm on one another reframes safety through responsibility for the purpose of the feminist classroom, which is to learn and unlearn complex embodied subjects. Consequently, the responsibility we collectively bear when having difficult and uncomfortable conversations centres on personhood and respect. A brave space approach to the feminist classroom allows us to separate the decolonial work, which is a focus on the politics of knowledge production through what we teach and how we think, from the praxis of inclusive teaching, who speaks, and how people learn from the purpose of a learning environment where we challenge structural inequalities without reproducing them.

Note

1 Observations drawn from an internal Africa Review exercise co-chaired by Awino Okech and Mashood Baderin in 2020 and inclusive teaching forums convened with academic colleagues in July 2021.

References

Allen, L (2019) Academic Freedom in the United Kingdom. Available from: www.aaup.org/article/academic-freedom-united-kingdom#.YSKsWJNKjvU. (Accessed 22 August 2021).

Arao, B. and Clemens, K (2013) From safe spaces to brave spaces: A new way to frame dialogue around diversity and social justice. In L. Landreman (ed.) *The Art of Effective Facilitation: Reflections from Social Justice Educators*. Sterling: Stylus (pp. 135–150).

Arsenault, R (2006) *Freedom Riders: 1961 and the Struggle for Racial Justice*. New York: Oxford University Press.

Banerjee A and Marokey Sawo (2021) The racist campaign against 'critical race theory' threatens democracy and economic transformation. *Economic Policy Institute*. Available from: www.epi.org/blog/the-racist-campaign-against-critical-race-theory-threatens-democracy-and-economic-transformation/. (Accessed 20 August 2021).

Beemyn, B (2003) The silence is broken: A history of the first lesbian, gay, and bisexual college student groups. *Journal of the History of Sexuality* 12(2): 205–223.

Bhopal, K (2016) *The Experiences of Black and Minority Ethnic Academics: A Comparative Study of the Unequal Academy*. London: Routledge.

Brown K, Mondon, A (2021) Populism, the media, and the mainstreaming of the far right: The Guardian's coverage of populism as a case study. *Politics* 41(3): 279–295. Doi:10.1177/0263395720955036

Coffey, A. and Delamont, S (2000) *Feminism and the Classroom Teacher: Research, Praxis, and Pedagogy*. New York: Routledge.

Commission on Race and Ethnic Disparities (2021) *Commission on Race and Ethnic Disparities: The Report*. www.gov.uk/government/publications/the-report-of-the-commission-on-race-and-ethnic-disparities (Accessed 30 August 2021).

Culley, M. and Portuges, C (Eds.) (2012) *Gendered Subjects: The Dynamics of Feminist Teaching*. London: Routledge.

Dickinson, J (2020) Proposals on academic freedom would achieve anything but. *Wonkhe*. https://wonkhe.com/blogs/proposals-on-academic-freedom-would-achieve-anything-but/ (Accessed 9 August 2021).

FRIDA Fund (2016) Practicing Individual and Collective Self-Care at FRIDA. https://youngfeministfund.org/practising-individual-and-collective-self-care-at-frida/

Govinda, R (2020) Fifty years of doing feminisms in the academy – Where do we stand? Reflections from Britain, In R. Govinda, F. Mackay, K. Menon and R. Sen (eds.) *Doing Feminisms in the Academy: Identity, Institutional Pedagogy and Critical Classrooms in India and the UK*. New Delhi and Chicago: Zubaan Publications and The University of Chicago Press.

Harpalani, V (2017) "Safe spaces" and the educational benefits of diversity. *Duke Journal of Constitutional Law & Public Policy* 13(1): 117–166.

Haywood, M. and Darko, A (2021) Breaking barriers: using mentoring to transform representation, identity and marginalisation in black higher education students. *The Journal of Educational Innovation, Partnership and Change* 7(1). doi: http://dx.doi.org/10.21100/jeipc.v7i1.1026.

Lewin, K. and Martin, G (Ed.) (1999) *The Complete Social Scientist: A Kurt Lewin Reader*. Washington: American Psychological Association.

Mirza, H.S (2018) Decolonizing Higher Education: Black Feminism and the Intersectionality of Race and Gender. *Journal of Feminist Scholarship* 7: 1–12.

O'Neill, G. and McMahon, T (2005) Student centred learning: What does it mean for students and lecturers. In G. O'Neill, S. Moore, and B. McMullin (Eds). *Emerging Issues in the Practice of University Learning and Teaching*. London: AISHE.

Rollock, N (2012) The Invisibility of race: Intersectional reflections on the liminal space of alterity. Special issue: Critical race theory in England, *Race Ethnicity & Education* 15 (1): 65–84.

Sánchez-Casal, S. and MacDonald, A (Eds.) (2002) *Twenty-First-Century Feminist Classrooms Pedagogies of Identity and Difference*. London: Palgrave Macmillan.

Tilley, L (2021) On Resigning from Birkbeck Politics. Available from: https://litilley.medium.com/on-resigning-from-birkbeck-politics-3681c0f65a91. Last (Accessed 25 December 2021).

Trilling, D (2020) Why is the UK government suddenly targeting 'critical race theory'? The Guardian. Available from www.theguardian.com/commentisfree/2020/oct/23/uk-critical-race-theory-trump-conservatives-structural-inequality (Accessed 9 August 2021).

Urgent Action Fund Latin America and Caribbean (2018) Care at the centre: An ethical and political commitment. Available from: https://fondoaccionurgente.org.co/site/assets/files/1433/care_at_the_center_web.pdf

Van Dyke, N (2003) Crossing movement boundaries: Factors that facilitate coalition protest by American college students, 1930–1990. *Social Problems* 50(2): 226–250.

Zurcher, A (2021) *Critical Race Theory: The Concept Dividing the US. BBC*. Available from: www.bbc.co.uk/news/world-us-canada-57908808 (Accessed 9 August 2021).

16 Focus groups and the 'insider researcher'; difficult conversations and intersectional complexities

Clare Bowen

Focus groups and social context

Focus groups, having previously become synonymous with market research (Liamputtong, 2011: 2), have become a prominent methodological feature in numerous academic fields, assuming many different forms such as that of a 'watch party' (Wood, 2009) or 'talk show panel' (Livingstone and Lunt, 1993); yet they have arguably tended to retain an analytical frame that remains tied to their commercial roots. Audience research was one of the first areas within sociology to begin using focus groups and has generally focused on how audiences construct meaning, and the 'uses and gratifications' of media texts, not too dissimilarly from advertising focus groups, though now with the primary goal of advancing knowledge rather than selling products. It has also, to some extent, idealised 'group speak', collective voices' and 'speech networks' (Morely, 1992: 16, Wood, 2009: 115), often comprising existing collectives of friends (Morely, 1992, Wood, 2009). As focus groups have come to be used more broadly in sociology and psychology, they have evolved to be considered almost as a form of therapy, and from a feminist standpoint, focus groups are considered valuable in strengthening female collectivism by women coming together to find solutions and providing a social context in which women's 'connected selves' can be observed (Wilkinson, 1998: 112). It is in this idealisation of collective understanding that researchers are encouraged to, for the most part, allow difficult and uncomfortable conversations to happen without mediation, that marginalised and/or oppositional voices may not be lost through participant discomfort or conformity.

Concerns that focus groups might result in minimising such marginalised and/or oppositional characteristics from participants is supported by the fact that conformity is an almost accepted peril of focus group research (Hollander, 2004; Acocella, 2012). Indeed, it is considered so prevalent and impactful that many insist that focus groups should only be used as part of a mixed-methods approach, and a significant number of theorists who have used focus groups in triangulation with 1:1 interviews have reported inconsistencies in responses given by participants in each setting (Hollander, 2004: 603). This has led to an analytical turn towards the social contexts of focus groups, as some researchers insist that social interaction itself is a data source (Morgan, 2012: 162), and that taking note of

DOI: 10.4324/9781003088417-21

participants' social and cultural identities, as well as the researchers', and how these inform interaction and relationships in the focus group 'seeks to minimize the intimidation and discomfort that may be experienced in traditional research methodologies and enhance the participants' ability to co-construct knowledge within the research setting' (Rodriguez et al., 2011: 404). In her influential essay *The Social Contexts of Focus Groups*, Hollander (2004) reports an encounter with a focus group participant who describes feeling 'unsettled' after the focus group experience, as she felt she had been unable to express certain opinions in a mixed-gender group (Hollander, 2004: 603). This was reflective of some of my own experience when conducting a series of focus group watch parties in which London-based single mothers met, either online or at my home, to watch an episode of a TV dramatic comedy featuring a single mother, to discuss the show and any emerging issues that hold relevance to their lived experience (or not). These focus groups were followed by 1:1 interviews in which, on a couple of occasions, participants shared feelings that they hadn't felt able to express in the focus group. Sometimes the conversation had felt uncomfortable, or it had provoked negative feelings about the participant's own life. For example, following a focus group comprising middle-class single mothers from a desirable area of North London, an older Greek mother questioned whether she was 'doing single motherhood right', as she had felt disconnected from their conversations of dating and enjoying single life.

Yet it is difficult to fathom how a process grounded in the analysis of social context can 'minimize intimidation and discomfort' (Rodriguez et al., 2011: 405) for participants, or how it would aid in the co-construction of meaning, if voices are lost and participants fear sharing alternative opinions. Whilst researcher intervention in difficult conversations has largely been encouraged for conversations which are particularly and directly discriminatory (i.e. racist, homophobic) (Sim and Waterfield, 2019: 3012), there is less about intersectional complexities. It occurred to me that the focus group discussion mentioned earlier could have been opened up by the injection of my own experience, which is varied; it could have drawn, for instance, on the more 'lonely' aspects of single motherhood, which may have prompted alternative views.

Building on feminist methodology that centres participant well-being (Rodriguez et al., 2011) and the amplification of 'lost/silenced voices' (Ryan-Food and Gill, 2010), which is becoming more encouraging of participant/researcher collaboration in research projects (Kirsch, 1999; Harvey et al., 2016; Harding, 2020), I suggest that there is a disconnection between collective focus-group thinking, researcher passivity and social contexts analysis, and that this can be bridged by greater activity, informal interaction and intervention by the researcher in the focus group. This, I suggest, can be helpful in repositioning the analysis of social contexts from what threatens to be a very researcher-focused method that merely records the social difficulties of focus groups and does not actively do anything to make focus groups a better experience for participants. In this chapter I discuss, from the perspective of 'insider research' (Myers, 2019), the possibilities of a researcher becoming a part of focus groups (Wilkinson and Kitzinger, 2013: 253) so that they might unobtrusively diffuse uncomfortable or exclusive conversations through ongoing interaction: not necessarily shutting them down, but rather by opening them up to critique and different perspectives, thus creating a snowball effect in which particularly difficult topics are discussed in an environment participants find comfortable.

Insider researchers, 'inside' the research

Critiques of insider research are often grounded in lack of researcher objectivity, deemed by many as necessary in unbiased analysis (Simmel, 1950 in Saidin and Yaacob, 2016; Brannick and Coghlan, 2007: 60; Fleming, 2018: 311/312). Insiders are often deemed too closely connected to the subject matter to conduct objective analysis, an allegation that is repudiated by feminist research that dismisses ideals of objectivity as unreasonable, instead advocating for honest, well-considered and continuous reflexivity on the part of the researcher (England, 1994; Letherby, 2002). Moreover, critics view this close connection negatively in terms of obtaining information (Fleming, 2018: 313; Rabe, 2003: 156/7), suggesting that due to cultural norms and taboos it is impossible for researchers to ask certain questions within their own community (Rabe, 2003: 156/7). Again, this speaks to whose needs are centred in the project – the researcher's or the participant's? Cultural norms and taboos *should* be respected, and researchers should be sensitive to research subjects. Just because a community may allow a researcher to ask questions that are taboo in their culture on the basis of the researcher's assumed ignorance of group customs, it doesn't mean that this is desirable. It is also likely to impact further honest disclosure from the group if the researcher has already demonstrated a lack of knowledge and empathy. Therefore, and particularly in the study of marginalised groups, I suggest that researcher sensitivity is particularly important for difficult or 'off-limit' conversations.

Fundamentally, I argue, researchers should enter focus groups by demonstrating honesty and reflexivity, with a view to leading focus group discussion in this direction and building 'trustful and open communication' (Moree, 2018: 12). Among other merits of insider research, Bonner and Tolhurst identify one of the 'key advantages' as 'not altering the flow of social interaction unnaturally', highlighting the necessity of authentic interaction from researchers (Unluer, 2012: 1). Therefore, introducing alternate views in order to draw out opinions by offering personal experience should only be done if the experience is honest and framed by the researcher's genuine reflexivity. The conversation here is taken from my third focus group in which participants viewed *SMILF*, an American dramatic comedy centred on the day-to-day life of young single mum Bridgette and her son, and was held at my London home. As Rodriguez et al. assert, conducting focus groups in settings that 'speak to the cultural context of participants' identities and ways of knowing' (Rodriguez et al., 2011: 411) aids the flow of conversation and promotes participant disclosure. I set this focus group up to mimic a 'girls' night in' with a BBQ and cocktails after the group to thank participants for their contribution and to encourage group interaction. There was, however, an experiential divide between the three mothers who had their children as teens/young adults, and the two mothers who had been older at the time of birth, and who had been respectively married and a single mother by choice. I happened to naturally fall into this focus group as a participant and found that I was able to unobtrusively open up discussion to different opinions without discounting existing voices. The conversation follows on from a long discussion of mothers opening up about body insecurities and demonstrates how reflexive researcher interaction can broaden focus group narrative:

XX: It's difficult for me to relate to her because she is so much younger and I'm going the other way. I couldn't care less about small or big vaginas, whether I shave my legs or not. These things are minor. There are women who want to look perfect, like yummy mummies. I'm on the other end of the spectrum.

CB: I'm at the point where I couldn't care less. No makeup on school run is fine. But when I was 21 and I had J, and they all looked hot because they didn't have kids, I did feel some pressure to look the same as everyone else. I still used to go out then. Now I rarely go out except to the supermarket or school. I think it might be more pressure when you are young.

DS: I think so. I went to university after I had my daughter. I had lots of one-night stands and things, I didn't have time for a boyfriend, but used to go to clubs and flirt and drink too much. But not as often because we had to organise a babysitter and have to be home by morning.

CB: In a single mum's discussion, they were saying how they fit to their kid's behaviour rather than *vice versa*. I do that now, but I didn't used to. When I had J and L, I'd still have fun with kids, but when I was at uni, I'd take them to house parties too.

DS: Same. I remember parking my daughter behind speakers in a spare bedroom because I didn't have a babysitter. As long as she was safe.

CB: And the drunk uni students enjoyed playing with my kids. They weren't harmful or anything. A couple of the mums looked at me like this (makes face). It was fine, honestly, they were happy.

DS: I think you can only understand that if you've been in that situation. I remember telling that to older mums and they were horrified as if I was abusing my children. No, I was just trying to have a life.

XX: You would go home if it's not appropriate.

CB: I'd be there and some close friends I could trust.

DS: And then loads of randoms, right?

CB: As long as you are vaguely watching your child, or someone is . . .

DS: There were a few nights where I didn't think it was the most responsible behaviour, but my kid's fine, and she's a really cool adult now and interacts with adults really well.

CB: That's what people say about J too. He interacts well with kids too but also adults.

Such interactions rely somewhat on a subversion of power on the part of the researcher, demonstrated here through the disclosure of personal information that disrupts normative parenting standards and which veers towards negative stereotypes of young parenthood. Despite academic concerns, as well as my own experience, of stigmatisation towards the researcher as a result of oversharing (Wilkinson, 1998: 114), I assert that such disclosures can be done with humility, and that great care should be taken not to skew power dynamics further in favour of the researcher. Rodriguez et al. state that:

> by recognizing the power dynamics inherent in our roles as researchers as well as our own social and cultural identities, we seek to minimize the intimidation and discomfort that may be experienced in traditional research methodologies and enhance the participants' ability to co-construct knowledge within the research setting.
> (Rodriguez et al., 2011)

When interacting in focus group discussions, researchers should be mindful of portraying themselves as more knowledgeable than participants, who should be considered experts in the topic area and their own experience. It is important also to note that researchers can be insiders in some aspects of their study, but rarely all (Rabe, 2003). Participants and researchers will rarely if ever share 'all' characteristics and amidst varying structural differences in opportunity between the two (and between participants in focus groups) lie multiple 'micro-dynamics of power' (Ayrton, 2018) that influence focus group and interview data. Researchers may share more commonalities with some participants than others, which may be an area of concern if researcher participants interact more fluidly with some participants than others, or if they appear to favour a particular viewpoint. Whether insiders wield more or less power over participants is continually debated by academics (Mercer, 2007; Tshuma, 2021), but what is certain is that they have greater understanding of the multi-faceted social contexts that instruct focus group interactions, and greater opportunity to either subvert their own power or boost that of participants by showing enthusiasm for their testimonies and reassurance of their concerns.

Marginalised communities, micro-power dynamics and classed moralities

Sensitivity to social context and potentially difficult conversations is of heightened importance when studying under-recognised communities. Single mothers cannot be described as 'marginalised' in respect to typical sociological definitions that assert these groups as 'powerless' (Barron, 1999: 38) (arguably no groups are completely 'powerless'). However, as a result of consistently aggressive government and social policy, social and institutional stigmatisation and recurrent moral panics (Jenson, 2018: 149), single mothers can be regarded as a marginalised group in terms of *stigmatisation*, whether this narrative specifically applies to them or not. This emphasises an often-overlooked aspect of social context research, which is the 'micro-dynamics of power' (Ayrton, 2018) that are particularly associated with focus groups in marginalised communities. In addition to existing structural divisions such as class, race, gender and sexuality, marginalised groups will have their own status hierarchies and markers of morality that contribute to social context and may result in the endurance of stigmatising or excluding narratives in focus groups if not picked up upon by an observant researcher.

In my focus groups, values were often established in respect of what Maud Perrier describes as 'classed maternal moralities' (Perrier, 2013), which were often connected to either stigmatising or aspirational narratives concerning single motherhood, and which were often dependent on existing class structures, as well as experiential divisions such as age of children. Status hierarchies in stigmatised groups is discussed by Mitchell et al. as being formed through 'interpersonal and individual level manifestations of structural stigma', which is often replicated in marginalised communities, that 'reflect either an acceptance of the dominant cultural norms and stereotypes of their community, or an active resistance against them and reinforcement of their own norms' (Mitchell et al., 2021: 342). Generally speaking, focus group participants, in a more favourable economic and social position who had the luxury of developing their capacities for self-actualisation, were more likely to challenge existing ethical markers; whereas those in less favourable economic positions, for whom economic survival had been an significant facet of their experience of single motherhood, were more likely to internalise and try to find ways to *distance* themselves from stigmatising narratives through the employment of traditional classed values. For example, working-class mothers were more likely to assert their morality in respect to traditional, patriarchal markers of morality – keeping a clean house, making sure their children are well-mannered and facilitating relationships between the child and their father. Middle-class mothers, on the other hand, were more likely to challenge traditional moralities, presenting themselves as socially, economically and sexually free. They appeared more confident in recounting tales of sexual liberation, possibly because they felt securely detached from other stigmatising elements of single motherhood such as claiming benefits, having 'too many' children or 'too many' fathers of these children (there were, however, intersectional and cultural differences at play here).

At times, 'in-group moralities' either directly or indirectly allowed participants to direct their 'own frustrations and uncertainties' onto others (Moree, 2018: 7). This sometimes appeared to include attempts to realign existing power structures through classed moralities and was strongly connected to existing stigmatisation in 'the outside world', which was experienced differently by participants.

The following is an excerpt from my first focus group which was held online and recorded in spring 2021. During this focus group we watched an episode of the BBC1 comedy series *Motherland*; however, prior to watching the show (but after recording had begun), I was dogged with poor Wi-Fi and had to log out and back in again whilst the participants talked amongst themselves. The conversation focused on co-parenting and was started by a mother (MG) who was attempting

Focus groups and the 'insider researcher' 237

to co-parent with her ex-partner who is a recovering addict, a situation that was weighing heavily on her mind, and for which she has been stigmatised, as was revealed in the follow-up interview. She discusses successful co-parenting as a *morality*, connected with maturity, selflessness and wanting the best for your children, bonding particularly with one mother of a similar class and ethnic position (LT). Both mothers infer that facilitating paternal relationships with children is a mother's responsibility, to the exclusion of a third participant (PS) who does not have contact with her child's father, a decision she similarly asserts she has received stigma for. At face value, it may appear that mothers are coming together to find solutions; however, the third mother (PS) did not speak during the rest of the focus group until at the end, when the mother who initiated the conversation (MG) had left early. It wasn't until reviewing the footage that I became aware that this might have happened as a result of the difficult conversation that happened in my absence.

MG: People disagreed with how much leeway I gave his dad and how much I tried to facilitate that relationship between them, like I say 85% of people wouldn't have done the same. But to me I needed to do exactly the opposite of these women and men who were using their children against the other parent and it's just . . . I couldn't live with myself I don't know how people do it.

PS: Yeah, I was very much like that in the beginning, and I did a lot to facilitate the relationship and then it started taking its toll on me and it was having a negative effect on my son as well, and I thought, you know, I've done what I can; now there's got to be some effort and then, once I kind of withdrew myself, but that was it.

MG: Exactly. You walked away, knowing that you'd done everything you could yeah, and that's the point now I've got to go now.

PS: And you get criticised for it as well.

MG: Yeah, they're like, why are you doing that?

LT: See, I have a really good relationship with my kids' dad, and it wasn't always, though it took a lot of trial and error. And he sees all three of them, and me, I'm at the door: Bye! Leave now! Typically, people have different situations, and often a lot does happen between a man and a woman . . .

MG: We've positively co-parented, I'd say, out of the three years, I'd say about two. But you will notice that we continue to put the kids first, then all of a sudden, they lift all responsibility; they're not a parent anymore, and that's it until they've got over their tantrum, and that's where the resentment comes in for me because you are going to be there for four weeks doing what you're supposed to be doing and everything's sorted and consistent and then you're going to F off for a week, turn everything upside down and expect to come back and everything's going to be the same, and that's just what it's like, I think.

LT: So, Molly, who's five, she's the youngest; she sees him twice a week; the other two are older, they are 16 and 14, they only see their dad when they want something ... but I do know parents use their kids against the other parents for whatever reason. You know when they come back, how unsettled the children are? I've had that as well, but then, if you stick with it, I think go[ing] forward children become more settled, but I could never imagine not having my kids see their dad.

MG: No, me neither.

LT: Because, no matter how I feel about him (I don't have great feelings for him), you know I try to make sure the kids have a good relationship with him.

MG: Definitely.

PS: It has to work both ways, doesn't it?

LT: Yeah, yeah, it does, I mean we've had our issues, God yeah.

PS: That's the ideal, isn't it? Having a civil relationship with your ex-partner. I'd give anything for that to be the case, but I guess, unfortunately for some of us it just doesn't work that way.

The bonding between participants happened in some respects across cultural differences, for as with the group of middle-class, North London mothers, the two European working-class mothers (MG and LT) had previously bonded over drinking to the exclusion of the third participant, a practicing Muslim. Practices of dyadic bonding have been shown to be more prevalent in women and are often a form of protection (Barrett et al., 2015); thus it is not surprising to see this bonding from group members who feel, or are used to feeling, socially vulnerable. This form of social interaction is, however, often socially exclusive, and should perhaps be given more attention in feminist work. Had I have been present in this focus group I could have subtly intervened to provide support for the mother whose views and experiences were outnumbered.

To some extent, in-group moralities were used to restructure existing classed values in a group that was equally divided between middle- and working-class, and in which we watched a class-centred TV show, *Motherland*. Ellemers et al. note 'how moral standards and moral judgements' that emerge from 'processes of social identification and self-categorization' play a role in the regulation of individual behaviour within groups and social systems, and 'may be functional as a way to improve group-level conceptions of self' (Ellemers et al., 2013: 2). In adhering to normative moral judgements pertaining to single mothers, e.g maintaining paternal contact, participants are able to gain power that they may feel has been lost due to existing structures of power such as class, race and gender.

In reflexive/participatory approaches, the researcher's experience can also be the subject of conversation, which may not be easy to do, particularly as it can make the researcher potentially vulnerable to in-group stigmatisation. Insider researchers have recounted episodes of stigma during focus groups and 1:1 interviews (Wilkinson, 1998: 114). With a view to continuous and collaborative reflexivity, I had telephone conversations with each of the participants prior to the interviews, in which I described my current situation and the path that had led me to writing my PhD. I introduced myself again at the beginning of the focus group, and in some of the most successful groups I was actively reflexive about my experience whilst watching the show, along with the other mothers. This led to some difficult conversations as in some cases, participants used my situation to navigate their own insecurities, projecting them on to me in this process:

MG: But the thing is really you find like in real life you've got the mom with four kids usually haven't got the same dad, well, two of them have and the other two have another, that's usually why it's like, I mean I finally met one person in my whole life that's got six kids with six different men.

CB: Do you think it matters, how many dads?

MG: It matters to me.

CB: Why?

MG: To me it does, like I don't judge other people, everyone's in a different situation; yeah, me, I don't. I couldn't imagine what that's like; breaking up with Mark has made me not want to have children even more. Because I mean, again no judgement to you, but you've obviously been in two different relationships, had two sets of children. And believed in both relationships and that's absolutely fine, yeah, but for me it's like, if I get into this relationship and have a child with this person and it works out, then Saul is going to be the odd one out, and he has to be my priority, and so it's me and my insecurities and worries and anxiety for him that stops me from doing it, if you get what I mean.

CB: Yeah, I mean, people have got different views on it and absolutely like when both of my relationships broke up, it's a long time to think back to now, yeah, [at] the time I was absolutely devastated.

MG: I couldn't imagine how and again, this is not a reflection on you, it's just because I haven't been through it, I can't relate, and because, and these are the things that I worry about it's like. You have one relationship, have two children like you did, break up. You have another relationship which you believe is the one, the second one, because the first one failed, yeah, and you have another two kids, and you break up. So, for me, I'm looking for like, from the outside, like – How would my mental health be? If those two relationships didn't work out, I would be, like, questioning what's wrong with me? Like not everyone can be with, like, not everyone, apart from me, can be wrong, you know, and it's like I don't understand, like I can't appreciate what you need to go through emotionally, to be able to.

CB: Well now, after two failed relationships, I do wonder if I'll ever love again (jokes) And I definitely won't while my children are still under my roof because, like, what's the point?

MG: Because it affects them because you got the first one. The first two children. And it didn't work out and then you're adding another two children.

Whilst it is evident that challenging the participant on her views did not change her perceptions of having children with more than one partner, 'making strange' the idea that something is wrong with me because of two 'failed relationships' with light-hearted humour and a quick conclusion to all that she had said did stop the conversation in its tracks. An alternative would have been to adopt a more therapeutic dialogue, as I had in other interviews when participants had shared their worries, and to uncover the reasons behind her self-doubt (which was a prominent feature of her focus group and interview interaction). I think in many ways it is unfortunate that I was emotionally unprepared for this interaction, which reflected processes of stigma I have experienced in my own life. A huge personal benefit of this project has been the ways in which it has encouraged me to reflect on my own experiences, to be reflexive and to deal with difficult conversations in a more constructive manner. Whilst, particularly in light of the harassment reported by some researchers in focus group settings (Wilkinson, 1998: 114), I would definitely endorse researchers holding firm boundaries regarding abuse and harassment, I argue that entering into difficult conversations from a reflexive, psychologically-attuned and therapeutically-oriented position can be mutually beneficial for participant and researcher in unravelling the often traumatised emotions behind the experience of stigma. Admittedly, such a position becomes more complicated, and is not *always* desirable in a group setting which cannot provide the absolute guarantees of confidentiality that an interview does (Sim and Waterfield, 2019: 3003), and in which multiple power structures may be in play. But developing an insider researcher position which draws on personal experience in a reflexive manner can help draw out previously under-recognised complexities in a focus group, and in our understanding.

Conclusion: researcher interaction and collaborative processes

The management of difficult conversations, as I have demonstrated, requires a great deal of emotion work on the part of the researcher, who must be intuitive to the intersecting social identities of the group, including their own, and how these may form social contexts and micro-power dynamics in group interactions and impact the experience of participants. In line with current feminist theory that advocates for 'minim(ising) the distance between (researchers) and participants' and 'creating research environments that (are) welcoming and supportive of participants' social identities' (Rodriguez et al., 2011: 402), I argue that researcher participation in focus groups is a natural step in achieving more collaborative projects, and is less invasive or disingenuous than forging friendships with participants, which has been critiqued as potentially exploitative or alienating by feminist theorists (Kirsch, 1999: 26). Shulamit Reinharz asserts that:

> in feminist participatory research, the distinction between the researcher(s) and those on whom the research is done disappears . . . the researcher abandons control and adopts an approach of openness, reciprocity, mutual

disclosure, and shared risk. Differences in social status and background give way as shared decision-making and self-disclosure develop.

(Reinharz, 1992: 181)

In this environment, difficult conversations become a group project that, almost therapeutically, sees both participants and researcher take part in group healing, negotiation and mediation.

References

Acocella, I (2012) The focus groups in social research: advantages and disadvantages, *Quality and Quantity* 46: 1125–1136

Ayrton, R (2018) The micro-dynamics of power and performance in focus groups: an example from discussions on national identity with the South Sudanese diaspora in the UK, *Qualitative Research* 19(3): 323–339

Barron, K (1999) Ethics in qualitative social research on marginalized groups. *Scandinavian Journal of Disability Research* 1(1): 38–49.

Brannick, T. and Coghlan, D (2007) In defense of being 'Native' the case for insider academic research. *Organizational Research Methods* 10(1): 59–74.

David-Barrett, T., Rotkirch, A., Carney, J., Izquierdo, I.B., Krems, J.A., Townley, D., McDaniell, E., Byrne-Smith, A. and Dunbar, R.I (2015) Women favour dyadic relationships, but men prefer clubs: Cross-cultural evidence from social networking. *PLOS One* 10(3): e0118329.

Ellemers, N., Pagliario, S. and Barreto, M (2013) Morality and behavioural regulation in groups: A social identity approach. *European Review of Social Psychology*, 24: 160–193.

England, (1994) Getting personal: Reflexivity, positionality, and feminist research. *The Professional Geographer* 46(1): 80–9

Fleming, J (2018) Recognizing and resolving the challenges of being an insider researcher in work-related learning. *International Journal of Work-Integrated Learning, Special Issue* 19(3): 311–320

Harding, N (2020) Co-constructing feminist research: Ensuring meaningful participation while researching the experiences of criminalized women. *Methodological Innovations, My-August 2020*: 1–14.

Harvey, R., Brown, K.S and Miller, B (2016) Theory into research practice: Reflections and recommendations on collaborative feminist research. *Journal of Feminist Family Therapy* 28: 136–158.

Hollander, J (2004) The social contexts of focus groups. *Journal of Contemporary Ethnography* 33(5): 602–637.

Jenson, T (2018) Parenting the crisis, The cultural politics of parent-blame Manchester: Policy Press.

Kirsch, G (1999) *Ethical Dilemmas in Feminist research: The Politics of Location, Interpretation, and Publication.* State University of New York Press, New York.

Letherby, G (2002) Claims and Disclaimers: Knowledge, Reflexivity and Representation in Feminist Research, Sociological Research Online 6(4)

Liamputtong, P (2011) Focus Group Methodology: Principles and Practice. London: Sage Publishing

Livingstone, S and Lunt, P. (1993) *Talk on Television, Audience Participation and Public Debate*. New York: Routledge.

Mercer, J (2007) The challenges of insider research in educational institutions: wielding a double-edged sword and resolving delicate dilemmas. *Oxford Review of Education* 33(1): 1–17.

Mitchell, Nishida and Molina (2021) The long arm of oppression: How structural stigma against marginalized communities perpetuates within group health disparities. Health. *Education and Behaviour* 48(3): 342–351.

Moree, D (2018) Qualitative approaches to studying marginalized communities. In G. Noblit (ed.) *Oxford Research Encyclopedia of Education*. New York: Oxford University Press, pp. 1–22.

Morgan, D (2012) Focus groups and social interaction. In J. Gubrium, J. Holstein, A. Marvasti, K. McKinney (eds.) *The SAGE Handbook of Interview Research* (2nd ed.). SAGE, Los Angeles, London.

Morely, D (1992) *Television Audiences and Cultural Studies*. New York: Routledge

Myers, L (2019) Insider research, Ethics, Professionalism and Positionality, Business, Accounting and Finance Association (BAFA), Conference Ghent: Belgium

Perrier, M (2013) No Right Time: the significance of reproductive timing for younger and older mothers moralities. *The Sociological Review* 61: 69–87.

Rabe, M (2003) Revisiting 'insiders' and 'outsiders' as social researchers. *African Sociological Review* 7(2).

Reinharz, S (1992) *Feminist Methods in Social Research*. Oxford: Oxford University Press

Rodriguez, K.L., Schwartz, J.L., Lahman, M.K.E. and Geist, M.R (2011) Culturally responsive focus groups: Reframing the research experience to focus on participants. *International Journal of Qualitative Methods* 13(4), 87–91.

Ryan-Food and Gill (2010) *Secrecy and Silence in the Research Process, Feminist Reflections,* New York: Routledge.

Saidin, K and Yaacob, A (2016) *Insider Researchers, Challenges and Opportunities, International Seminar on generating knowledge through research,* UUM-UMSIDA, 25-27 October 2016, Universiti Ultara Malaysia, Malaysia.

Sim, J and Waterfield, J (2019) Focus group methodology: Some ethical challenges. *Quality and Quantity* 53(6): 3003–3022.

Tshuma, N (2021) The vulnerable insider: navigating power, positionality and being in educational technology research. Learning *Media and Technology* 46(1):1–12.

Unluer, S (2012) Being an insider researcher while conducting case study research. *The Qualitative Report* 17(29): 1–14.

Wilkinson (1998) Focus groups in feminist research: Power, interaction and the co-construction of meaning. *Womens Studies International Forum* 21(1): 111–125.

Wilkinson, S and Kitzinger, C (2013) Representing our own experience: Issues in insider research. *Psychology of Women Quarterly* 37(2): 251–255.

Wood, H (2009) *Talking with Television, Women, Talk Shows and Modern Self-Reflexivity*. Champaign: University of Illinois Press.

17 Queering the academy

Róisín Ryan-Flood

Introduction

What does it mean to live a queer life? By this, I don't mean 'who is the queerest of the queer?', a rather tiresome trope that occasionally emerges in queer theory and posits an anarchic approach as the top of a hierarchy in which any perceived tendencies towards 'assimilation' are constructed as intrinsically and inherently hetero- or homonormative. Rather, I seek to ask what does it mean to inhabit the world as a queer subject? How is it different? How do you navigate outness, the closet, homophobia, or biphobia or transphobia? What micro and macro aggressions are experienced? In what myriad ways are you made aware of your difference and how does that awareness seep into your conscious and unconscious self? Again, I ask: what does it mean to live a queer life? This chapter will explore this question in relation to institutional processes of equality, diversity and inclusion within the academy. It will draw on autoethnographic reflections from my perspective as an openly lesbian academic on the lived experience of being an LGBTQ member of staff in higher education. The chapter will analyse an incident of homophobia that took place in my workspace. I will argue that queer visibility matters, solidarity may be partial and contingent rather than absolute and complaints can be constructed as part of the problem if they are not accompanied by a nuanced understanding of queering the academy. This necessitates difficult conversations about power, privilege, vulnerability and affect.

Queer progress and neoliberalism

Generational shifts may bring many positive changes. The introduction of same-sex marriage in some countries represents one of the most dramatic changes to sexual citizenship in recent decades (Richardson, 2017). Other important legislation includes protection against homophobic discrimination at work, or the upcoming conversion therapy ban, for example. These remain relatively recent, hard-won gains and we cannot take these changes for granted. As we see from the recent repeal of Roe v. Wade in the US and accompanying fears that same-sex marriage could come under attack next (McCann Ramirez, 2022), rights can be rolled back. The proposed exclusion of trans people from the conversion therapy

DOI: 10.4324/9781003088417-22

ban in the UK highlights that rights remain contested for many. At the same time that many rights have ostensibly improved, reports of homophobic hate crimes have increased dramatically in recent years, doubling since 2014, while transphobic hate crimes have trebled in the same period (Marsh et al., 2019). In a global context, progress remains uneven and there are huge inequalities for LGBTQ people around the globe. Queer critiques remind us that although an expansion of rights is welcome, inclusion into a traditionally heteronormative institution such as marriage can also be accompanied by losses, including what Butler terms 'the lost horizon of radical sexual politics' (Butler, 2004: 40). Here she is referring to the creative imaginary that exclusionary processes necessitate.

Nonetheless, important legislative changes occur alongside, and perhaps at least partly because of, a dramatic shift in visibility for LGBTQ people in popular and media cultures. Russo (1987) traces the history of absence or subtly embedded but unnamed presence of queer people in film. Young people growing up now may be accustomed to having openly gay people and characters grace the film and TV screen or appear in adverts and popular media, but this has only been mainstream since the late 1990s. Prior to that, there was an astonishing lack of queer visibility. For those of us who grew up before this transformation, it is nothing short of astonishing. As Fanon (1970) argued, visibility is a powerful way in which we learn about the world but also ourselves. It remains an important part of feeling seen and included. Yet problems remain with those representations, of course. As Walters (2014) notes, '*For many youth (rural and otherwise), the glam stories of gay life on mainstream TV just don't resonate*' (Walter, 2014: 60). In addition, there is still a relative lack of diversity, particularly of black and minority ethnic queer people, economically marginalised or genderqueer characters. Storylines often romanticise queer experience or reproduce negative tropes – such as the lesbian storyline that ends with her death. They may also treat queer characters as partial subjects constructed solely in relation to their queerness, or as a sidelined character with no significant love life who functions only in relation to heterosexual characters. As Brady et al. (2017) argue, the apparent progress inherent in more and varied queer representations is a reflection of a changing televisual marketplace where niche audiences create demand for 'progressive content'. Thus, it is not necessarily the case that society overall is becoming more open to all sexual citizens.

Alongside these changes and continuities, a neoliberal narrative has emerged in which queer rights are seen as 'won'. This follows a linear model of progress in which equality is viewed primarily through legislative equality. It argues that it is now possible to be openly queer with few problems (Weeks, 2007). While I welcome positive change, I take issue with this narrative, which increasingly appears in popular culture storylines where queerness is depicted as both accepted and acceptable and accompanied by an absence of institutional and structural discrimination. Firstly, because in reality inequalities remain and secondly, because 'inclusion' often rests on assimilation into a heteronormative model based on monogamy, whiteness and class privilege. Walters (2014) highlights problems with what she terms 'the tolerance trap'. She argues that the low bar of tolerance does not mean inclusion, even when accompanied by legislative equality. In fact, full equality requires *transformation* of wider society through integration of queer populations.

In other words, equality does not only rest on inclusion into institutions. Queer Otherness is often experienced as affect. As Munt (2019) points out, shame continues to remain a key component of queer lives. She argues that neoliberal narratives create a new expectation of outness, in which queer lives are to be lived openly and proudly. Yet it remains the case that many LGBTQIA+ people experience profound shame in relation to their sexual identity. The neoliberal imperative to be out and proud assumes the absence of homophobia. This creates a situation in which homophobia is then located within the queer subject who therefore becomes the locus of the problem, rather than the social and interpersonal inequalities and exclusions that create this experience of Otherness in the first place.

Decolonising the academy

Efforts in contemporary higher education to decolonise the curriculum represent a long-overdue engagement with questions of white privilege and epistemic violence. These issues are often addressed through equality accreditation schemes. They are part of a wider effort to consider inequalities at universities and calls to be more inclusive that also address gender – for example, through Athena SWAN, or sexuality (previously through Stonewall accreditation). On the one hand, these endeavours represent a long-overdue engagement with inequalities in HE and as such offer positive potential for social change. However, Ahmed (2012) considers the contradictions of equality accreditation:

> Commitments to diversity are understood as "non-performatives" that do not bring about what they name. . . . racism can be obscured by the institutionalization of diversity. Diversity is used as evidence that institutions do not have a problem with racism.

Her point highlights how equality accreditation schemes are open to being exploited as mere performance of equality and inclusion, unaccompanied by any meaningful change. Rather than contribute to a transformation of university environments, the focus on the achievement of accreditation may become more significant than accomplishing social change, resulting in useless 'tickbox' exercises. This is the challenge of equality accreditation – how to bring about recognition of inequality and redress it.

'Queering the academy' requires understanding the working life experiences of marginalised groups. This necessitates analysing the tension in HE between the longing for HE as an important space for critical thinking versus the experience of HE being insecure/unsafe for queer subjects. I have written elsewhere about the lived experiences of LGBTQ staff in HE, which include: managing the closet/being out; vigilance in assessing safety; transphobic and homophobic experiences; extensive emotional labour in dealing with diversity issues; lack of visible role models; and difficulties connecting with colleagues who may not understand queer experiences, to name a few (Boyce et al., 2021; Boyce et al., 2022). Puwar (2004) refers to 'space invaders', or those who are seen as out of place within institutions because they do not inhabit the expected position of privilege in terms of whiteness, maleness and so on. The neoliberal myth of equality further serves to marginalise queer subjects who do not inhabit mainstream spaces easily, yet whose experiences of Otherness, exclusion and marginalisation are simultaneously dismissed.

'The incident'

On the 26th of April 2019, a date I remember easily because it was also International Lesbian Day of Visibility, I travelled to campus for a meeting. When I arrived at my office, I noticed that a Stonewall poster on my door had been defaced with homophobic graffiti. The poster was part of a Stonewall visibility and equality campaign. On the rare occasions when I had seen them on other office doors around campus, it had given me a thrill, a sense of solidarity, and brought a smile to my face. I liked the fact that people felt confident enough to have them on their door. As Athena SWAN lead in my department at the time, I was responsible for the Equality, Diversity and Inclusion noticeboard in the department. I cheerfully put some of the Stonewall posters up on this noticeboard, along with other EDI posters and information. As I had some Stonewall ones leftover, I put them on my own office door. The posters were not self-effacing. They made a clear statement – 'Some people are gay/lesbian/bisexual/trans. Get over it!'. But the memory of how pleased I was to see this queer visibility on a few other office doors around campus inspired me to join in and put some posters up myself.

Finding homophobic graffiti on one of these posters came as a huge shock. It might sound like a trivial thing – it was 'just' a poster, not a personal physical attack after all, a voice in my head tells me. Indeed, when I shared the incident with some gay friends a few days later, I was regaled with stories along the lines of 'that time when I had police escort me to work for weeks because of death threats', which simultaneously both expressed solidarity and minimised my own experience. I recognise this as a coping mechanism. In the face of overwhelming experiences of discrimination, a 'toughen up' attitude may become necessary to manage trauma. Yet as Valentine (1998) has pointed out, such incidents encroach upon our sense of safety in our workspaces. Drawing on her own harrowing experiences as a victim of a campaign of homophobic harassment, which included many abusive letters, she argues that they highlighted the ways in which the various spaces where they appeared were important to her sense of personal safety and well-being. In fact, she notes that we each have a 'personal geography' that shapes our sense of self:

> the letters have violated most of the important spaces of my existence: from my body, home, parents' home, and neighbourhood, to my workplace and sense of academic community. In doing so, they have highlighted to me how

much my sense of security, my well-being, and my multiple subjectivities are anchored to these locations – and consequently both how much I have a personal geography and how much I had taken it for granted until it was transgressed.

(Valentine, 1998: 323)

In a similar way, finding the poster defaced profoundly undermined my sense of safety and security in my workspace. For example, for many months afterwards, whenever I turned the corner to where my office is situated, I felt a sense of anxiety as I tensed up, wondering if there would be more graffiti, or worse, someone lying in wait. Writing about it now and looking up the emails that I sent in the aftermath for the research for this chapter has once again generated a sense of distress. Although part of me is determinedly detached and looking at the experience through the lens of academic analysis, I also feel physically shaken yet again as I confront the memory through writing about it now. Memories are also embodied experiences. Revisiting them can be experienced on a corporeal level.

One of the ways in which existence in an unsupportive world is made possible is through the act of forgetting. Women routinely forget the many instances of sexual harassment that are part and parcel of living in the world. I would argue that this is necessary in order to continue to go about your daily life. The #MeToo movement has offered an opportunity to remember and reflect on those experiences. It led to an outpouring of women sharing their experiences that were not always at the forefront of their consciousness as they lived their day-to-day routines. To survive often necessitates putting to one side the many instances of difficult moments that are entirely normative for many women and minority groups. Similarly, being queer in the world means being exposed to harassment in myriad ways. The posters incident brought many memories back to mind vividly. So many. From the series of harassing phone calls to my office when I was a post-doctoral fellow, to the homophobic written feedback on teaching evaluations, to the openly homophobic student comments in class, the looks of horror and disbelief when I came out to academics or students in lecture halls and conferences, the homophobic bank manager who didn't want to discuss a joint mortgage application between two women, or the street harassment I have experienced when out in the world holding hands with a partner plus many more. So many moments, big and small, but also cumulative: that felt overwhelming as I was flooded with these memories while navigating the aftermath of the posters being defaced.

The aftermath

Shortly after finding the poster, which I immediately took down, I have a meeting with a PhD student, which I cut short, explaining that I am too distressed by the incident to continue. I apologise and reschedule. I have a brief period of time alone in my office, during which I compose an email to Human Resources (HR) and my Head of Department (HoD), explaining what has happened. Then I attempt to attend a meeting with my HoD on another matter. I feel overwrought.

The distress is experienced viscerally, on a physical level. My legs feel weak and I wonder if I may faint, although I try to remain outwardly calm. I get through other meetings, then compose an email to all colleagues, attaching a photograph of the poster and explain what has happened:

Hi everyone,

Hope this message finds you well. I had a very unpleasant surprise this morning when I found a gay rights poster on my office door defaced with a homophobic comment.

The poster is a printout from the Stonewall (LGBT organisation) website. I also placed a trans ally poster from Stonewall on my door but that was left alone (surprisingly).

The poster with the comment is in the photo attached.

As you can imagine, I am very distressed by this.

I thought I should let everyone know that this has happened, as I think it's important to share instances of discrimination of all kinds, including homophobia. If you happen to see anyone defacing posters in future, I would be grateful if you could make a note and report them! Thanks.

Today happens to be Lesbian Day of Visibility and this is not exactly what I was hoping for. I have however reprinted the poster and put it on my door afresh.:)

Best,
Róisín

The response is swift. Alone in my office, two colleagues knock on the door at separate times, shocked by the incident. One asks for copies of the poster to put on his door, which makes me smile. They ask how I am. I cannot help being tearful. I remember the article by Gill Valentine (1998) that I read many years previously and wonder how on earth she got through such a terrible campaign of sustained harassment taking place over many months. Other colleagues send emails of solidarity. Finally, I opt to leave my office early. It is clear to me that I am simply too upset to get much more work done and I want to be at home, in my own safe space, away from this incident and with time to reflect. To my surprise, while I am travelling home, colleagues discuss the email and incident and collectively decide to put the posters on all their doors, in solidarity. I am astonished and deeply touched. This experience brings to mind Ahmed's point that '*When making a complaint changes your sense of self, it also changes your sense of the world*' (2021: 19). For many, this is a disappointing moment, when they are forced to confront inequality and further marginalisation through institutional processes. But for me in this moment, it was a rare and welcome experience of inclusion and support that opened up positive connections with colleagues.

It is interesting to me that my decision to share my experience with the wider department was directly informed by my work at the time on Athena SWAN, the gender equality accreditation scheme. Although this gender equality initiative is often dismissed as being too assimilationist, institutionalised and lacking intersectionality (e.g. Tzanakou and Pearce, 2019; Bhopal and Henderson, 2019) – all valid claims – for me it nonetheless offered a constructive opportunity to reflect on gender and other equality issues within our department. During the data collection phase for Athena SWAN, which consisted of surveys, focus groups and one-on-one meetings, as well as document analysis, I noticed a pattern that emerged when listening to colleagues' tales. Often, they internalised a problem as something they needed to manage themselves, rather than take collective action. For example, a colleague dealing with a graduate student who made her feel deeply uncomfortable asked a senior female colleague to sit in on their meetings. But the student in question was not reported to the HoD or anyone else. It is not my intention to find fault with my colleague, who was bravely asserting herself in a difficult situation. Rather, it highlights the endemic toxic nature of academia, where too often we confront difficult situations in relative isolation rather than naming the problem more publicly or feeling that there is an option to seek support or redress within the institution. Gill (2010) refers to the internalisation of neoliberal working norms in HE as 'toxic academia'. I would add that the experience of dealing with these sorts of instances of harassment in an individualised way is another manifestation of toxic academia. Many academics are filled with a sense of failure: we don't publish enough or in the right places; we aren't getting high enough ratings on our student satisfaction surveys; we aren't attracting enough funding; our social media accounts don't have enough followers; our work doesn't have the right impact factor; and so on and so on and so on and so on. These feelings of shame are a reflection of individualising problems when the real problem is structural, such as the overwhelming workload problem that is endemic throughout academia. Prior to doing this type of EDI work, I am certain that I would have taken down the poster, confided in one or two colleagues at most and at best reported it to HR. I would not have been so public about it. Perhaps I would also have felt shame or unconsciously blamed myself for having such a 'confrontational' poster on my door in the first place. But doing EDI work of this kind made me reflect on the issue of individualising problems, the importance of openness and collective solidarity. I did not expect any particular response. Simply speaking out that this had happened felt meaningful to me because I hoped that it would create awareness and potentially help to identify those responsible or facilitate intervention in future.

The next time I went to campus, I was greeted by a welcome sight. Throughout the corridors of my department, every door had a Stonewall poster on it. Writing that and remembering it brings a smile to my face. Up yours, homophobia! For a period of time, the physical space of the department was queered. It was a space that asserted and supported queer identities. I wonder if it is possible to convey what it is like, as an out LGBTQIA+ person in the world, to walk down corridors that are queered in this way. It filled me with awe and laughter. I was not the only person who felt cheered by this. Queer students spoke of their happiness at feeling supported by this show of solidarity. I heard of a queer academic going for a job interview in another department, walking down our corridors with all these posters and thinking 'I hope I get hired!' I was and remain very touched by this display of solidarity from colleagues.

And yet . . . displaying posters in this way, while a welcome retaliation, does not remove the problem. This becomes apparent when more posters are defaced. On one occasion, someone crosses out 'gay' and replaces it with 'heterosexual', so it becomes 'some people are heterosexual, get over it.' On another occasion, I arrive at work to find that all the posters have been taken down. This happens more than once. So this wonderful solidarity also makes visible that homophobia remains and visual expressions of queerness in this way become a target. The posters simply bring homophobia to the surface, in the same way that being an out academic inevitably means confronting prejudice.

A student comes forward and informs me that she knows who did the original graffiti to the poster on my office door because she witnessed it happening. We discuss it at some length. She identifies the culprits: two students. I suggest she use the 'report and support' system, an online portal for making complaints about harassment and bullying. She does so, providing her name and contact details and giving identifying information about one of the culprits who could easily be identified as a result. Although HR invites her to interview, she does not attend. As a student who suffers from anxiety and depression, she is unable to pursue the matter further. HR does not act on the information. They inform me that without speaking to the witness, their hands are tied. There are no consequences for the culprits.

A video of the office doors covered in the Stonewall posters is shared by the department on social media. It gets lots of likes. I recognise this as a further expression of the department as a queer-friendly space. Yet I am also ambivalent about my experience being commodified in this way as an expression of EDI practice. It is presented as an EDI success. But as I have already indicated, the problems with the posters continued.

Tense realisations and difficult conversations

It is never possible to draw a line under inequality in diversity work. In this sense, EDI is doomed to failure, because inequality will always reassert itself, at least in the world we currently inhabit. This does not mean that EDI work is itself without value – quite the opposite. It can still be used productively to create meaningful change, for example to policy changes that support working parents, or conscious efforts to recruit more diverse staff that involve looking at the processes of exclusion or improvements to processes supporting victims of harassment. Yet just as naming a problem makes it more possible to challenge, challenging a problem generates greater visibility of the problem in itself. Thus, putting up more posters led to more graffiti, highlighting the ongoing existence of homophobia. The danger is that the posters could be named as the problem, instead of homophobia. Indeed, this occurred in one department discussion, where a colleague referred to the posters as 'a provocation'. While staff were happy to support me and put posters on their doors, there was also an expectation that a time would come when that would no longer be necessary. Also, the fact that there continued to be problems with the posters created an uncomfortable awareness that the problem wasn't going away. The posters merely made it more visible, which was not their purpose. They were supposed to be a solution to the problem. But that was never going to be the case because homophobia remains entrenched, despite important changes and no matter what neoliberal narratives of linear progress attempt to assert. Over time, the vast majority of posters disappeared. I have no problem with this – I did not expect my colleagues to keep them up indefinitely. But they remain on my own office door and will continue to do so.

Conclusion – living a queer life

I am acutely aware that my own experience outlined in this chapter, while one example across a lifetime of many more, is far less serious than that of many others. This is not to minimise its impact on me personally, but rather to recognise that I got off very lightly compared to others who experience physical violence, sexual harassment and assault or get passed over for promotion due to sexism and racism. I am privileged as a white, able-bodied woman in academia. My cis gender and conventionally feminine appearance also provide me with privilege. This embodiment makes my transgressions – as an out lesbian, as a feminist – more palatable. I recognise that even as my politics remain undiluted.

Despite the fact that my experience was relatively minor in a bigger picture, I have chosen to reflect on it in order to explore diversity work within HE institutions. At the same time, there is a voice in my ear that asks why anyone should care about a poster being defaced because there are far more serious inequalities and violence – both epistemic and physical – taking place in the world. My response to that is simply, why was someone so incensed by a poster that they felt it necessary to deface or remove it, not just once but multiple times? By exploring this incident, I have attempted to look at the limits of diversity talk and explore how homophobia reasserts itself in response to apparent inclusivity.

Writing this chapter has in some ways taken some of the sting out of the experience, at least momentarily. Perhaps it is because revisiting a painful memory and analysing it can dull its freshness and make it familiar in a way that sometimes lessens the pain. In addition, I realise through writing that the poster incident simply made apparent what I already knew. I have been an openly gay academic for many years. Each time I out myself in a lecture, I think of the queer students who will feel affirmed and reassured by this. Indeed, statements on our Athena SWAN students' surveys picked up on this. In the survey, one student commented:

> Whilst it is absolutely every individual's right to choose to be open regarding their sexuality at their place of work, I cannot over emphasise how amazing it is to be studying in a department with lecturers who are open about who they are. There are a number of amazing role models in this department and this has undoubtedly improved the quality of my experience at the University of Essex.

Yet the poster incidents also highlight what I know in those moments: that there are also those who do not want me to speak out or to be out and to be confident in myself in that moment. The poster incidents confirmed my sensitivity to that animosity. It is not paranoia on my part.

It seems to me that inhabiting a space of visibility is therefore meaningful in and of itself. The experience with the posters has reinforced my belief in the importance of visible role models – for all minority groups – while I also recognise the structural exclusions that make some feel compelled to remain closeted. I also still believe that EDI work is valuable because it allows us to consider the practices of inequality and exclusion that are otherwise taken for granted. It creates an opportunity for rendering those inequalities visible and for challenging them. Yet the capacity for challenge and change within the institution is also limited. It can only ever be a partial aspect of the wider struggle for liberation. It may also be commandeered in ways that undo or undermine EDI goals. Ahmed (2021) points to Lorde's (1984) famous point that 'the master's tools can never dismantle the master's house'. She further exhorts us 'do not be the master's tools'.

References

Ahmed, S (2012) *On Being Included: Racism and Diversity in Institutional Life*. Durham: Duke University Press.

Ahmed, S (2021) *Complaint!*. Durham: Duke University Press.

Bhopal, K. and Henderson, H (2019) Advancing equality in higher education: An exploratory study of the Athena SWAN and Race equality charters. *Birmingham: University of Birmingham*. www. birmingham. ac. uk/research/crre/research/advancing-equalityin-higher-education.aspx.

Boyce, P., Sundberg, T. and Ryan-Flood, R (2021) *LGBTQ experiences of working in Higher Education: A Pilot Study*. Research Report (UCU).

Boyce, P., Sundberg, T. and Ryan-Flood, R (2022) *LGBTQ Experiences of Working in Higher Education: A Mixed Methods Study*. London: Routledge.

Brady, A., Burns, K. and Davies, C (2017) *Mediating Sexual Citizenship: Neoliberal Subjectivities in Television Culture*. London: Routledge.

Butler, J (2004) *Undoing gender*. London: Routledge.

Fanon, F (1970) *Black Skin, White Masks* (13–30). London: Paladin.

Gill, R (2010) Breaking the silence: The hidden injuries of the neoliberal university. In R. Ryan-Flood and R. Gill (eds.) *Secrecy and Silence in the Research Process: Feminist Reflections*. Abingdon: Routledge (pp. 228–244).

Marsh, S., Mohdin, A. and McIntyre, N (2019) Homophobic and transphobic hate crimes surge in England and Wales. *The Guardian* 14(6): 2019.

McCann Ramirez, N (2022) Same sex marriage and contraception should be next on chopping block: Clarence Thomas. *Rolling Stone Magazine*, 11. Available from: https://www.rollingstone.com/politics/politics-news/same-sex-marriage-contraception-roe-v-wade-decision-1373759/ accessed 20/07/22.

Munt, S.R (2019) Gay shame in a geopolitical context. *Cultural Studies* 33(2): 223–248.

Puwar, N (2004) Thinking about making a difference. *The British Journal of Politics and International Relations* 6(1): 65–80.

Richardson, D (2017) Sexual citizenship. *The Wiley-Blackwell Encyclopedia of Social Theory*, 1–3.

Russo, V (1987) *The celluloid closet: Homosexuality in the movies*. New York: Harper Collins.

Tzanakou, C. and Pearce, R (2019) Moderate feminism within or against the neoliberal university? The example of Athena SWAN. *Gender, Work & Organization* 26(8): 1191–1211.

Valentine, G (1998) "Sticks and stones may break my bones": A personal geography of harassment. *Antipode* 30(4): 305–332.

Walters, S.D (2014) *The Tolerance Trap: How God, Genes, and Good Intentions Are Sabotaging Gay Equality*. New York: NYU Press.

Weeks, J (2007) *The World We Have Won: The Remaking of Erotic and Intimate Life*. New York: Routledge.

Index

Note: Page numbers in *italic* indicate an illustration on the corresponding page.

abortion 97–99
academia 243, 246–251; decolonising the academy 245–246; and gender wars 22–23; interview with Sandya Hewamanne 39–49; living a queer life 251–252; misogyny of 208–211; queer progress and neoliberalism 243–245; *see also* academic purity; gender studies
academic purity 206; and attacks against gender studies 211–213; gender studies and their institutionalisation 207–208; and hope 213–214; and misogyny of academia 208–211
advertising *see* public advertising
affective elements of research encounters 63–65, 86–87; designing travelling research encounters 65–71; intra-active, intersectional lens 72–74; racist hyper sexualisation of black femininity 81–85; white racialised sexualisation 74–81
African, Sub-Saharan 133–134; and decoloniality 134–136; first same-sex desire and encounter 136–141
alcohol 148–149
American Apparel: 'Back to Basics' advert 75–81
assaultive, advertising as 72–74
authority 93–97
autoethnography 194–195

bad food 51–52; *see also* sugar
balancing acts, feminist 34–36
Barker, Meg-John (interview): academic institutions and communities 22–23; binaries 19–21; changing the conversation about trans 23; difficult conversations 23–24; feelings 11–14;
femininity 21–22; gender trauma 15–17; inclusive understanding of gender 14–15; mental health 17–19
binaries 19–21
black femininity: racist hyper sexualisation of 81–85
black township women who love women 133–134; and decoloniality 134–136; first same-sex desire and encounter 136–141
body, the 97–99
Boohoo's advertisement 82–86
boundaries 160–162
bounded knowledge: feminist classroom 218–229; gender studies 206–214; the insider researcher 231–241; queering the academy 243–252; research governance 191–203

calling out 90, 99–100; the body, gender, and essentialisation 97–99; call-out culture, knowledge, and authority 93–97; identity, difference, and feminist disagreement 91–92; methods 92–93
care 218–219, 223–228
case study 103, 191–192, 194–195
challenge: sharing opinions 163–165
check-in discussion 162–163
classed moralities 235–240
classroom *see* feminist classroom
collaborative processes 240–241
communication, emotional: interviewing as 104–107
complexities: focus groups and social context 231–240; researcher interaction and collaborative processes 240–241

Index 255

consent 148–149; law on 166–167; participatory applied theatre workshop techniques 159–168
content warning 160–162
context *see* social context
contradictory practices 34–36
Covid-19 pandemic 113–114, 123–125; and interviewing relationship 118–121; and meeting places 121–123; research dilemmas 115–117; and trust 117–118; and uncomfortable reflexivity 114–115

debate, feminist 27–29
decoloniality 134–136; decolonising the academy 245–246
defining terms 165–166
deliberation 90, 99–100; the body, gender, and essentialisation 97–99; call-out culture, knowledge, and authority 93–97; identity, difference, and feminist disagreement 91–92; methods 92–93
designing research encounters 65–70
desire 133–134; and decoloniality 134–136; first same-sex desire and encounter 136–141
difference 91–92
difficult conversations 2–3; ethics and voice in 172–184; in feminist digital social spaces 90–100; and intersectional complexities 231–241; participatory applied theatre workshop techniques for 159–168; practice 3–4; about research governance 191–203; and tense realisations 250–251; about trans 11–26; about unacknowledged sexual assault 149–155; vulnerability and trust in 102–111
difficult knowledge: female genital cutting 27–37; feminism and race in academia 39–49; gender wars 11–26; sugar 50–57
difficult research effects/affects 63–65, 86–87; designing travelling research encounters 65–71; intra-active, intersectional lens 72–74; racist hyper sexualisation of black femininity 81–85; white racialised sexualisation 74–81
digitally mediated intimacy 103–104
digital social spaces *see* feminist digital social spaces
disagreement, feminist 91–92
discursive elements of research encounters 63–65, 86–87; designing travelling research encounters 65–71; intra-active, intersectional lens 72–74; racist hyper sexualisation of black femininity 81–85; white racialised sexualisation 74–81
domestic abuse 173–175; researching support services 176–178

embodiment: black township women who love women 133–141; embodied ethics 202–203; LGBTQA+ identities 159–169; researching sex 144–156; women's experiences of marital rape 172–184
emotional communication: interviewing as 104–107
enjoyment 163–165
essentialisation 97–99
ethics 145–147, 172–173, 182–184, 191–192; autoethnography of the lap dancing industry 194–195; domestic abuse in Turkey 173–175; embodied 202–203; and the heterosexual matrix 199–200; negotiating ethical approval 195–199; participants' accounts of marital rape 178–182; researching domestic abuse support services in Turkey 176–178; and the research subject 200–201; situating research ethics and governance 192–194; and vulnerability 201–202
'Ew! Factor' 29–30
exploitation 118–121

feelings: and gender wars 11–14; and politics 30–31; 'ugly feelings' 33–34
female genital cutting: analyzing gut-level responses 31–33; changing 'ugly feelings' 33–34; contradictory practices and feminist balancing acts 34–36; and the 'Ew! Factor' 29–30; a feminist debate 27–29; politics and feelings 30–31; and uneasiness in feminist research 36–37
femininity: and gender wars 21–22; racist hyper sexualisation of 81–85
feminism: and empowerment for women in the Global South 46; and gender 43–44; and impact of feminist academics 48–49; and intersectionality 40; interview with Sandya Hewamanne 39–49; and race 40–44; and research ethics 47–48; and research on and with vulnerable populations 44–45
feminist balancing acts 34–36
feminist classroom 218–219, 228–229; and care 225–227; conceptualising safe spaces 220–221; framing notes 219–220; and safety 221–225

feminist debate 27–29
feminist digital social spaces 90, 99–100; the body, gender, and essentialisation 97–99; call-out culture, knowledge, and authority 93–97; identity, difference, and feminist disagreement 91–92; methods 92–93
feminist disagreement 91–92
feminist fieldwork 113–114, 123–125; and interviewing relationship 118–121; and meeting places 121–123; research dilemmas 115–117; and trust 117–118; and uncomfortable reflexivity 114–115
feminist practice 2–3
feminist research: analyzing gut-level responses 31–33; changing 'ugly feelings' 33–34; contradictory practices and feminist balancing acts 34–36; and the 'Ew! Factor' 29–30; feminist debate 27–29; politics and feelings 30–31; uneasiness in 36–37
feminist studies: political relevance of 208–211
feminist theory 2–3
fieldwork *see* feminist fieldwork
fixed understandings 166–167
focus groups: researcher interaction and collaborative processes 240–241; and social context 231–240
food: good/bad 51–52; *see also* sugar

gender 144–145, 155–156; and abortion 97–99; black township women who love women 133–141; calling out and piling on 90–100; and the ethics of researching sensitive topic 145–147; feminist fieldwork during the pandemic 113–125; inclusive understanding of 14–15; LGBTQA+ identities 159–169; public advertising 63–88; researching sex 144–156; sexual consent, alcohol and hookup culture 148–149; and unacknowledged sexual assault among young adults 147–155; vulnerability and trust 102–111; women's experiences of marital rape 172–184
gender studies 206; attacks against 211–213; and hope 213–214; and their institutionalisation 207–208; and misogyny of academia 208–211
gender trauma 15–17
gender wars: and academic institutions and communities 22–23; and binaries 19–21; and changing the conversation about trans 23; and difficult conversations 23–24; and feelings 11–14; and femininity 21–22; and gender trauma 15–17; inclusive understanding of gender 14–15; and mental health 17–19
good food 51–52; *see also* sugar
governance *see* research governance
gut-level responses 31–33

health *see* sexual health
heteronormativity 135–140, 199–202
heterosexual matrix 194, 199–200, 203n5
Hewamanne, Sandya (interview) 39–49; empowerment for women in the Global South 46; gender 43–44; impact of feminist academics 48–49; intersectionality 40; race 40–44; research ethics 47–48; research on and with vulnerable populations 44–45
hierarchy 118–121
hookup culture 148–149
hope 213–214

identity 91–92
inclusive understanding of gender 14–15
inequality 54–57
insider researcher: focus groups and social context 231–240; researcher interaction and collaborative processes 240–241
institutionalisation of gender studies 207–208
intersectional elements of research encounters 63–65, 86–87; designing travelling research encounters 65–71; focus groups and social context 231–240; intra-active, intersectional lens 72–74; racist hyper sexualisation of black femininity 81–85; researcher interaction and collaborative processes 240–241; white racialised sexualisation 74–81
interviews/interviewing 102–103, 110 111; Barker, Meg-John 11–26; as emotional communication 104–107; Hewamanne, Sandya 39–49; hierarchy and exploitation 118–121; interviewing women about digitally mediated intimacy and sexting 103–104; with trust 107–108; with vulnerability 108–110
intimacy: calling out and piling on 90–100; and feminist fieldwork during the

pandemic 113–125; interviewing with 102–111; and public advertising 63–88
intimate, the 144–145, 155–156; and the ethics of researching sensitive topic 145–147; sexual consent, alcohol and hookup culture 148–149; and unacknowledged sexual assault among young adults 147–155
intra-active lens 72–74

knowledge 93–97, 199–202; and power 165–166; *see also* bounded knowledge; difficult knowledge

lap dancing industry 194–195
law on consent 166–167
LGBTQA+/LGBTQIA+ identities 168–169, 245, 249; and participatory applied theatre workshop techniques 159–168; *see also* black township women who love women; queering the academy

marginalised communities 235–240
marital rape 172–173, 182–184; domestic abuse in Turkey 173–175; participants' accounts of 178–182; researching domestic abuse support services in Turkey 176–178
material elements of research encounters 63–65, 86–87; designing travelling research encounters 65–71; intra-active, intersectional lens 72–74; racist hyper sexualisation of black femininity 81–85; white racialised sexualisation 74–81
meeting places 121–123
mental health 17–19
methods 92–93
micro-power dynamics 235–240
misogyny 116–119; of academia 208–211
moralities, classed 235–240

neoliberalism: and queer progress 243–245
neoliberal university 218–219, 228–229; and care 225–227; conceptualising safe spaces 220–221; framing notes 219–220; and safety 221–225

opinions 163–165

pandemic *see* Covid-19 pandemic
participatory applied theatre workshop techniques 159–168

piling on 90, 99–100; the body, gender, and essentialisation 97–99; call-out culture, knowledge, and authority 93–97; identity, difference, and feminist disagreement 91–92; methods 92–93
pleasure 134–141
plus-size model 82–86
politics 206; and attacks against gender studies 211–213; and feelings 30–31; gender studies and their institutionalisation 207–208; and hope 213–214; and misogyny of academia 208–211
power: calling out and piling on 90–100; feminist fieldwork during the pandemic 113–125; and knowledge 165–166; micro-power dynamics 235–240; public advertising 63–88; vulnerability and trust 102–111
practice/practices: contradictory 34–36; of difficult conversations 3–4; *see also* feminist practice
public advertising 63–65, *64, 67–68,* 86–87; designing travelling research encounters 65–71; intra-active, intersectional lens 72–74; racist hyper sexualisation of black femininity 81–85; white racialised sexualisation 74–81

queering the academy 243, 246–251; decolonising the academy 245–246; living a queer life 251–252; queer progress and neoliberalism 243–245

race: and empowerment for women in the Global South 46; and feminist academics 48–49; and gender 43–44; and intersectionality 40; interview with Sandya Hewamanne 39–49; and research ethics 47–48; and research on and with vulnerable populations 44–45
racialised sexualisation 63–65, 86–87; designing travelling research encounters 65–71; intra-active, intersectional lens 72–74; racist hyper sexualisation of black femininity 81–85; white racialised sexualisation 74–81
racism: hyper sexualisation of black femininity 81–85
rape *see* marital rape
reflexivity 113–115, 123–125, 191–192, 202–203; autoethnography of the lap dancing industry 194–195; and the

heterosexual matrix 199–200; and interviewing relationship 118–121; and meeting places 121–123; and negotiating ethical approval 195–199; research dilemmas 115–117; and the research subject 200–201; situating research ethics and governance 192–194; and trust 117–118; and vulnerability 201–202

Relationships and Sex Education (RSE) 168–169; and participatory applied theatre workshop techniques 159–168

relevance *see* political relevance

research: research dilemmas 115–117; researcher interaction 240–241; researching domestic abuse support services in Turkey 176–178; research subject 200–201; *see also* difficult research effects/affects; feminist research; insider researcher; research governance; researching sex

research governance 191–192; autoethnography of the lap dancing industry 194–195; embodied 202–203; and the heterosexual matrix 199–200; negotiating ethical approval 195–199; and the research subject 200–201; situating research ethics and governance 192–194; and vulnerability 201–202

researching sex 144–145, 155–156; the ethics of researching sensitive topic 145–147; sexual consent, alcohol and hookup culture 148–149; and unacknowledged sexual assault among young adults 147–155

resistance: to research governance 201–202

safe space 167–168; conceptualising 220–221

safety: and the feminist classroom 221–225

same-sex sex 134–136; *see also* black township women who love women

sensitive topics 145–147

sex 133–134; and decoloniality 134–136; first same-sex desire and encounter 136–141

sexting 103–104

sexual assault, unacknowledged 147–155

sexual consent 148–149

sexual health 133–134; and decoloniality 134–136; first same-sex desire and encounter 136–141

sexualisation, racialised 63–65, 86–87; designing travelling research encounters 65–71; intra-active, intersectional lens 72–74; racist hyper sexualisation of black femininity 81–85; white racialised sexualisation 74–81

sexuality: black township women who love women 133–141; LGBTQA+ identities 159–169; researching sex 144–156; women's experiences of marital rape 172–184

social context: and focus groups 231–240

speaking out 202–203

sugar 50–57

taboos 144–145, 155–156; and the ethics of researching sensitive topic 145–147; sexual consent, alcohol and hookup culture 148–149; and unacknowledged sexual assault among young adults 147–155

tensions 167–168, 250–251

theatre *see* participatory applied theatre workshop techniques

theory *see* feminist theory

township women *see* black township women who love women

trans: and academic institutions and communities 22–23; and binaries 19–21; changing the conversation about 23; and difficult conversations 23–24; and feelings 11–14; and femininity 21–22; and gender trauma 15–17; inclusive understanding of gender 14–15; and mental health 17–19

trauma, gender 15–17

travelling research encounters 65–70

trust 117–118; building a community of 159–168; negotiating trust in difficult conversations 102–111

Turkey 172–173, 182–184; domestic abuse in 173–175; participants' accounts of marital rape 178–182; researching domestic abuse support services in 176–178

'ugly feelings' 33–34

UK 168–169; and participatory applied theatre workshop techniques 159–168

uncomfortable reflexivity 113–115, 123–125; and interviewing relationship 118–121; and meeting places 121–123; research dilemmas 115–117; and trust 117–118

understandings, fixed 166–167
uneasiness: analyzing gut-level responses 31–33; changing 'ugly feelings' 33–34; contradictory practices and feminist balancing acts 34–36; the 'Ew! Factor' 29–30; and feminist debate 27–29; in feminist research 36–37; politics and feelings 30–31
university *see* academia; neoliberal university

voice 172–173, 182–184; and domestic abuse in Turkey 173–175; participants' accounts of marital rape 178–182; and researching domestic abuse support services in Turkey 176–178; valuing 162–163
vulnerability 199–202; negotiating vulnerability in difficult conversations 102–111

white racialised sexualisation 74–81
women's studies: political relevance of 208–211
women who love women *see* black township women who love women

young adults 144, 149, 234; unacknowledged sexual assault among 147–148

Taylor & Francis eBooks

www.taylorfrancis.com

A single destination for eBooks from Taylor & Francis with increased functionality and an improved user experience to meet the needs of our customers.

90,000+ eBooks of award-winning academic content in Humanities, Social Science, Science, Technology, Engineering, and Medical written by a global network of editors and authors.

TAYLOR & FRANCIS EBOOKS OFFERS:

- A streamlined experience for our library customers
- A single point of discovery for all of our eBook content
- Improved search and discovery of content at both book and chapter level

REQUEST A FREE TRIAL

support@taylorfrancis.com

Routledge
Taylor & Francis Group

CRC Press
Taylor & Francis Group